［新西兰］霍建强 (Raymond Huo) 著

法之力

英美法系经典案例详解

The Power of the Rule of Law

Navigating established common law cases

中国政法大学出版社

2019 · 北京

图书在版编目（ＣＩＰ）数据

法之力：英美法系经典案例详解/霍建强著.—北京：中国政法大学出版社，2019.4
（2021.7重印）
ISBN 978-7-5620-8935-3

Ⅰ.①法… Ⅱ.①霍…②赖… Ⅲ.①英美法系－案例 Ⅳ.①D904.6

中国版本图书馆CIP数据核字(2019)第056581号

	法之力
书　名	英美法系经典案例详解
	FAZHILI YINGMEIFAXI JINGDIAN ANLI XIANGJIE
出版者	中国政法大学出版社
地　址	北京市海淀区西土城路 25 号
邮　箱	fadapress@163.com
网　址	http://www.cuplpress.com (网络实名：中国政法大学出版社)
电　话	010-58908466(第七编辑部) 010-58908334(邮购部)
承　印	北京中科印刷有限公司
开　本	720mm×960mm　1/16
印　张	23.25
字　数	350 千字
版　次	2019 年 4 月第 1 版
印　次	2021 年 7 月第 2 次印刷
定　价	68.00 元

作者简介

霍建强（**Raymond Huo**）是中国政法大学优秀校友、荣誉法学教授。20 世纪 90 年代初移民新西兰，第一份工作是在此间最大的英文日报《新西兰先驱报》（New Zealand Herald）任记者。随后回归法律专业，获新西兰高等法院律师资格，曾任谢富安伦律师事务所（Shieff Angland Lawyers）合伙人。2008 年当选为新西兰国会议员，现任新西兰国会法制委员会主席。

霍建强先生于 2011 年着手创立"新西兰中文周"，确定每年 9 月的第二个星期为全国性的中文周。新华社称，在英语国家全国范围以语言周的方式推广中华语言和文化，在西方国家尚属第一次。中国驻新西兰大使和新西兰驻中国大使为新西兰中文周的联席顾问。

霍建强先生出版著作七种，包括《新编英汉多用词典》（合译，经济日报出版社 1991 年版），《通俗美国习语集萃》（北京师范大学出版社 1994 年版），《海外创出四重天——在新西兰做国会议员、律师、记者和诗人》（北京师范大学出版社 2011 年版），《蓝天白云——诗、散文和法学笔记》（朝华出版社 2015 年版）和《飞翔的奇异鸟——新西兰中文周中英对照文选》（合编，高等教育出版社 2017 年版），等。

Raymond Huo（霍建强）

Member of Parliament

LLB（Auckland）, MLitt（1st Class Hon, Auckland）; LLB（CUPL）, BA（Anhui）; MIinstD（NZ）

Since arriving in New Zealand from Beijing in 1990s, Raymond has traversed successful careers in journalism, as Asian affairs reporter for the New Zealand Herald and law, as a Partner at Shieff Angland Lawyers.

Before returning to Parliament in March 2017, Raymond had served two terms as a list MP（2008-2014）, sitting on various select committees including Finance & Expenditure, Environment and Commerce. He now chairs the Justice Committee.

In April 2013 Raymond was appointed an Honorary Professor of Law at his alma mater, China University of Political Science and Law in Beijing. This appointment was matched by Victoria University in Wellington's Faculty of Law, where he once served as an Honorary Senior Associate.

In 2012 Raymond was presented with the "Green Angel Clean Tech Award" in Beijing recognising his contribution in promoting Auckland-based LanzaTech's renewable energy technologies and in general, NZ Inc. He is a founding trustee and co-chair of the New Zealand Chinese Language Week Charitable Trust, a cross-party initiative promoting New Zealand's understanding of China, its people and culture.

Raymond has published 7 books and is a regular Chinese media commentator on current affairs and legal issues.

序

安德鲁·利特尔（Hon Andrew Little MP）
2011 年起当选新西兰国会议员。曾任新西兰工
党主席及新西兰工党领袖。[1]2017 年起在总
理婕森达·阿德恩（RT Hon Jacinda Ardern）
领导的政府中，担任内阁司法部长和法院事
务部长。

　　我们生活在一个日益相通的世界，像中国和新西兰这样不同的国家，亦
在贸易和人文之间寻求更加密切的交流。对 21 世纪的决策者、司法专家、
商人、学者而言，要了解不同的司法体系如何运作，无疑是个挑战。

　　霍建强先生的新作《法之力——英美法系经典案例详解》为中国读者
量体裁衣，对西方法律体系进行实用解读式的分析，目的就是促进更好的
交流。

　　霍本身的学识不可低估。奥克兰律师事务所合伙人，英文日报《新西
兰先驱报》记者，中国政法大学名誉教授。2008～2014 年当选新西兰国会

---

　　[1]　新西兰工党有三套领导班子：领袖（Leader）、主席（President）、总书记（Secretary General）。
领袖领导全党以及国会团队，如果大选成功，领袖则为总理（Prime Minister）。另一大党国家党与其领导
班子相仿：领袖、主席和总经理。——译者注

议员〔1〕，2017年起又获连任。

《法之力——英美法系经典案例详解》通过对普通法系〔2〕不同司法管辖体系经典案例的分析，极富逻辑地描述了普通法的司法体系，也使我重新审示了具有里程碑意义的英国经典案例之一："唐纳秋梅诉斯蒂文森案"。我鼓励所有学习普通法系的人都好好研究一下这个案例，这则判例除了为"过失责任归责原则"和"法律谨慎责任"奠定了基础外，也为"法官造法"的实际效果提供了一个具体例证。尊崇先例与判例原则的连贯性，是判例法的基本准则。

法治是宪法框架下法律制度的核心，一方面保护商业契约的神圣性，一方面防止律法过度，而"法官造法"则为这一法律制度作出巨大贡献。它在中央政府的权威、民众的日常生活及各地方文化习俗之间架起一座桥梁。在林林而群的社区中，大家都是公民，都有一种"山高皇帝远"的心态。

普通法系不是西方国家法律体系的唯一特征，但领会普通法系是理解西方法律的关键起点。在新西兰，关于国会是否应受更多的制衡这个话题，我们有过一些争辩，其中包括成文宪法的益处以及新西兰是否需要一部成文宪法典。〔3〕

霍这本书，总览西方国家不同司法管辖体系中历史经典与现代最新的一

---

〔1〕 新西兰国会采用英国威斯敏斯特制，立法、行政、司法三权分立。在国会，行政与立法两权制衡但相互重叠，例如政府部长均由国会议员担任。新西兰又采用mmp选举制度，国会共120席，通过与其他党合作而获得61席位的政党获组阁权，成为政府。政府外其他政党则为反对党。国会议员为全职工作，任期3年，可连选连任。——译者注

〔2〕 普通法系，"普遍通行"的意思，又译作"英美法系""共同法系"，主要代表国家是英、美、澳、新、加等国。与"大陆法系"并称当今世界最有影响力的两大法系。——译者注

〔3〕 新西兰最早的两部宪法是1846年宪法和1852年宪法。1852年《新西兰宪法》是英国国会的宪法，赋予新西兰自治。之后这部宪法被1986年宪法取缔。1986年《新西兰宪法》对立法、行政、司法三权分立进行了详细定义，同时取消了英国国会（在新西兰国会同意前提下）为新西兰制定法律的权力。1986年《新西兰宪法》起源于新西兰政治历史上的1984年"宪法危机"。1984年新西兰大选之后，工党当选执政党，国家党政府下野。但国家党看守内阁拒绝循惯例在过渡期间履行看守内阁职责——主要是由于其强硬领袖Sir Robert Muldoon，直到他遭内部反弹，国家党也放狠话，如果他继续违制，国家党将更换领导人。1986年《新西兰宪法》与英国宪法相仿，属典型的不成文宪法。其制定与修改相对容易，属柔性宪法。——译者注

些标志性判例，包括美国的代表性案例，而美国成文宪法对司法和立法决定起到核心作用——这也有力地反映了新西兰对这一问题的思考。

中国因儒家文化之悠久文明以及近几十年的改革开放而举世瞩目。中国的历史和现代成就，凸显出斯国斯民对自身文明的坚守与创新，也体现了中国在全球商贸中起到的领军作用。《法之力——英美法系经典案例详解》这本著作正好出现在这一重要历史时期：中国的法学建设与时俱进，而国际上的法学发展趋向普世标准，在商贸领域也趋向确定。书中所精选的案例为我们提供了一个很好的范例，说明普通法系是如何在不同文化背景中高扬这种法理原则，而不同文化的差异可以像新西兰和中国香港特别行政区那样的显著。

我要为我的朋友霍先生点赞！这本书的贡献在于加深了我们对不同司法体系如何运作的理解，也促进了中国与新西兰以及更广泛的西方国家对法理理念的共同认知和正向交流。

Hon Andrew Little MP

2019 年 3 月

Andrew Little–foreword to The Power of the Rule of Law

The Honourable Andrew Little MP has served as an elected Member of the New Zealand Parliament since 2011. He was previously President of the New Zealand Labour Party and Parliamentary Leader of the New Zealand Labour Party. In the government of PrimeMinister the Right Honourable Jacinda Ardern, Little has served as New Zealand's Minister of Justice and Minister for Courts since 2017.

We live in an increasingly interconnected world, where countries as diverse as China and New Zealand seek ever–closer trade, cultural and interpersonal linkages. It is the challenge of the twenty first century for businesspeople, scholars, policymakers and jurists alike to gain better understandings of how different legal systems function.

*Power of the Rule of Law*by Huo "Raymond" Jianqiang 霍建强 does precisely that, by providing accessible and practical analysis of Western law systems for Chinese scholars.

Huo's expertise cannot be underestimated. A former Partner of an Auckland–based law firm, former journalist for *The New Zealand Herald*, Honorary Professor of Law at China University of Political Science and Law 中国政法大学, Huo has been an elected Member of the New Zealand Parliament between 2008–2014 and again since 2017.

*Power of the Rule of Law*logically describes the common law by analysing key cases from multiple jurisdictions. It turned my mind to the landmark decision of *Donoghue v Stevenson*, being one of the central British cases which I would encourage any student of the common law to investigate. In addition to that case's precedent–setting role in the law of negligence and the principle of duty of care, it is a good demonstration of the practical effect of 'judge–made law' where precedent and consistency are the fundamental tenets.

Judge–made law can offer a valuable contribution to a constitutional framework which places the rule of law at its centre, safeguarding against excesses and over–reaching while protecting the sanctity of commercial contracts. It is a bridge between the authority of central government and the reality of people's daily lives and local cultures—all are citizens, but the mountains are high and the emperor is far away.

The common law is not the only measure which characterises Western countries' justice systems, although appreciating the common law is a critical starting point for understanding. In New Zealand there is some debate about whether stronger checks and balances on Parliamentary power are needed, including the merits or otherwise of having a written constitution. This book, as it scans historic and recent leading common law cases across a number of jurisdictions, including the United States of America where a written constitution is central to judicial and legislative decision – making, offers a useful reflection for this debate in New Zealand.

China is known worldwide for its Confucian ancient régime, and now for its remarkable opening up and development in recent decades. China's history, as well as its modern achievements, are testament to the tenacity and innovation of its people and the nation's status as a leading global player in trade and business. *Power of the Rule of Law* comes at an important time during the continued development of Chinese jurisprudence with respect to accordance with internationally accepted standards for justice and the need for certainty in commerce. The cases contained in this text provide a good demonstration of the way that the common law works to uphold these principles in cultural contexts that can be as different as New Zealand and the Hong Kong Special Administrative Region of China.

I commend my friendHuo for the contribution this book makes to the deepening of our appreciation of how different legal systems work, and for ultimately enhancing the shared understanding and positive exchanges of ideas between China and New Zealand and the wider West.

Hon Andrew Little MP

March 2019

前　言

一

以英国、美国、加拿大、澳大利亚和新西兰为主体的英美法系（亦称海洋法系、普通法系、判例法系），在对外关系和经贸互动中越来越受到重视。本书以实际判例入手，以四个经典案例附带四个与华人相关的实例，结合民、商、合同、公司、金融、投资、海外收购以及媒体、选举和监护权法，贯穿以上诸国百余年，上百个各类判例，将英美法系的来龙去脉和各国的司法体系做了一个大致介绍。

在西方社会，法律渗透社会和人们生活的方方面面。以英国以及沿袭了英国体系的澳、新为例，大到每年的中央政府财政预算，小到通过税率给超市香烟或加油站燃油定价，都是通过立法来实现的。

不少人有一种误解，以为找律师，和法律打交道，就意味着"出事了"。这好比去医院，不一定非要有病再去医院，体检，防患于未然，也是现在渐渐为大家所接受的一种保健措施。在涉外和商贸活动中，凡发一谋、举一事必先知己知彼。大家熟悉的"尽调"（due diligence）便是其中一项常规动作。当然，海外华人也常有一种体会，外国人是把律师费花在出事之前（尽职调查和风险规避），而华人往往花在出事之后。

笔者有一位学长，早年从牛津大学获得政治学博士学位。他的体会是，牛津的与众不同很大程度体现在其文化和学术氛围上，俗称"熏"。这本书的主要目的就是通过不厌其烦又信手拈来的详解，尽量将西方国家社会的方方面面、边边角角说透，读这些案例，"熏一熏"，可以知彼知己，不但了解西方的体制，更了解西方人的思路。

二

英美法系起源于中世纪的英格兰，目前世界三分之一的人口生活在英美法系的司法管辖区域或混合民法法系的司法管辖区域中。[1]该法系与大陆法系并称为当今世界最主要的两大法系。

英美法系在中文里也常被译作"普通法系"，取其"普遍通行"之意。的确，在英美法系的诸多国家[2]，其国界和司法管辖权概念模糊。判例共享，法学院的教材和所学内容互通，律师可以比较方便地在这些法系的国家执业。

英美法系的最大特点是判例法（the doctrine of precedent），其核心是遵循判决先例（the stare decisis），例如采用三审制的司法管辖区，下级法院必须垂直地遵循上级的上诉法院和最高法院的判例。而以英、美、加、澳、新为代表的英美法系诸国又共享判例、互为参照，因此一通百通，了解一个判例，可以举一反三；了解一个国家，可以打通另外一些国家。

虽然，判例法的特点是"法官造法"（judge made laws），但并不代表英美法系没有成文法，实际上是判例法与成文法（法典、制定法、单行法）并存。

英美法系的另一特点是审判中采取抗辩制度（adversarial system）和陪审团制度，重视司法程序，即"救济先于权利"（remedies precede rights）。相比较而言，"大陆法是异中求同，偏演绎法；而普通法则是同中求异，偏归纳法"。[3]

---

〔1〕 http://www.britannica.com/EBchecked/topic/188090/English－law；British History：Middle Ages Common Law－Henry II and the Birth of a State. BBC. ［2009－07－23］.

〔2〕 除上述五大国，还包括南非、印度、马来西亚、新加坡、牙买加、肯尼亚等国家。

〔3〕 这段话是美国大法官本杰明·卡多佐说的，见 Benjamin Cardozo：*The Nature of the Judicial Process*（1921）22－23。

三

本书分两大部分，第一部分不厌其烦，以四个经典判例为基础，以期说透判例法的"法官造法"过程和思辨方式，顺带介绍具有司法管辖权的相关国家的司法体制。

第二部分点到为止，以四个与华人相关或华人熟悉的题材，结合判决书原文，以身边的实例来解读判例法。

两部分前后呼应，读者可以各取所需，但出发点是通过渗透社会层面的实际判例，打通西方社会司法体系的脉络。

四

四大经典判例。

判例一，"唐纳秋梅诉斯蒂文森"，也就是著名的"啤酒蜗牛案"。这是英美法系国家法学院的必修课，也是一个被看作历史文化事件来纪念和研究的家喻户晓的经典案例。

事情发生在 1928 年的苏格兰，唐纳秋梅的闺蜜约唐纳秋梅到咖啡店小坐，并请她吃冰激凌加生姜啤酒。喝得差不多的时候，将剩下的姜啤从不透明的瓶子倒进她的玻璃杯，"咕咚"一声，一只已经腐烂的死蜗牛掉到杯子里，唐纳秋梅受不了眼前的景象，恶心想吐，稍一回味便肠胃绞疼。三天后不得不看医生，三周后不得不住院急诊。唐纳秋梅随后便向法院递交了诉状。但谁该成为被告呢？

咖啡店主认为自己是冤枉的，因为虽然是他批发的姜啤，但他哪知道不透明的瓶子里有个腐烂的死蜗牛？！唐纳秋梅状告姜啤生产厂家，厂家也说冤枉，因为他直接向咖啡店供货，况且这是原告的闺蜜请客，原告又没有向咖啡店主购买姜啤，因此原告和生产厂家之间不存在任何合同关系。而合同关系是消费者（受害者）能够诉诸法律的前提。同一时期从姜啤中喝出死老鼠、死蟑螂的情形也时有发生，但诉讼结果都是被告和消费者之间因不具备合同关系而不用承担法律责任。

因此，无论在初审、二审的苏格兰民事法院还是在终审的英国上议院，法官们遇到的问题都是面对这样的案件，既无先例可循，又无法理可依。最终，上议院的法官们根据恕道中的"邻居"概念，创下了一个全新的归责原则——民事"过失原则"。而这个归责原则，在随后的（直到现在）合同法、金融法、公司法以及其他法律领域均起着指导作用。这宗判例所确立的"邻居原则"（The Neighbour Principle），也体现了由"恕道"演变成法律原则的一个思辩模式。

也有不少说法认为，因为这则判例，除听装啤酒外，所有啤酒都改用了透明的玻璃瓶。这一规避风险的做法也延伸到其他领域，如酒店的大堂或洗手间在清洁地面时，一定会竖一个"地滑，小心摔跤"之类的牌子。

有了这则经典案例，我们对判例法"法官造法"的方式和应用会有大致的了解。接下来要解决的便是当今"地球村"和自贸经济框架下的司法管辖权问题。

判例二，"美国雅虎案"，便是为这个问题提供答案的跨成文法和判例法两个不同法系的案例。雅虎总部及其互联网服务器设在美国加利福尼亚，而设在法国的雅虎"拍卖网站"提供平台，用来拍卖德国"二战"期间的纳粹宣传品和收藏品。此举违犯了《法国刑法典》，因为法国法律禁止宣扬和买卖纳粹物品。法国法院基于"损害地"原则，依其民事诉讼法典确定了司法管辖权。但雅虎在美国加利福尼亚上诉，美国第九上诉（巡回）法院综合考量三大因素判定美国法院对此案具备司法管辖权，又提出了"治外法权"和"第一修正案权利"。如果雅虎不在巴黎上诉而在加利福尼亚州起诉，个中"如非"（but for）要素以及美国的司法判例意味着什么？这则判例无疑为互联网时代相关国家就法律如何更新升级的问题，打开一扇窗户。

解决司法管辖权的窗户一旦打开，往里稍加窥探便觉其妙无穷。于是便有了判例三："道琼斯《巴伦周刊》诽谤案"。本案被告是出版《华尔街日报》和《巴伦周刊》的道琼斯。《巴伦周刊》在美国出版，而其文章却通过互联网在澳大利亚维多利亚州被下载和阅读，那么原告能在澳大利亚起诉被告吗？英国 1849 年的判例（诽谤文章发表 17 年后诉讼成功）和健美影星施瓦辛格 2004 年判例（被告就原告，美女原告可以在英国告美国名人）以及加拿大 2005 年《纽约邮报》案（纽约的被告在加拿大受审）对这则案件有何影响？

这些案件本身已经让人眼花缭乱了，而这些国家的州、府、联邦等司法机构也颇令人费解，如纽约州的最高法院和维多利亚州（省）的最高法院，虽冠之以"Supreme"（最高）之名，却并不是全国法院系统中的"最高"（终审法院）。而高院（High Court）这个通常被认定为第三级的法院，在澳大利亚却是最高（终审）法院。

此案的奇妙之处，不单在于国际私法中的冲突法选择，更在于对传统诽谤法的新的界定。例如，依"重复发表"原则，你读了一篇涉嫌诽谤的文章，你转发一次便视同你发表（诽谤）了一次，每转发一次便构成一次新的诉因。但互联网页呢？每刷新或点击一次便构成一个新的诉因吗？

读完本判例，以上问题即可逐一解决。

有了判例一、二、三的基础，便可以考量自媒体时代给传统法律带来的新问题。在华文圈广泛流行的自媒体是 QQ、微博和微信，在"洋文"圈则是脸书、推特等。

判例四之"英国'洋微博'诽谤案"，恰好为这个自媒体时代面临的法律问题和诸多乱象，作了一个全面的注解。

五

以上是了解英美法系绕不开的四大经典判例。当然，既然目标读者是华人，自然需要附加和华人有关的案例。"四大判例"之后，第二部分介绍了"四小案例"，分别是：

上海鹏欣新西兰农场收购案（公司法先例）、上市母公司为倒闭子公司偿债案、诗人顾城之子监护权案、关于彼得斯和华人候选人的一则选举法判例。本书第二部分涉及的案例，附有法院判决书的英文原文，既可供研究人员延伸阅读，也可以使大家对英美法系的法院判决书有一个直观了解。这是本书的另一个特别之处。

更为难得的是，成书之时，作者又以其新西兰国会议员的身份草拟了一份个人立法：《新西兰诽谤法（附条件特权抗辩限制）法案》。这无疑又为读者提供了一个了解普通法系国家判例法与制定法并存现状，以及立法种类和步骤的实际例证。

六

本书的一大特点是用简单通俗的语言，以生动鲜活的方式来解读复杂而玄奥的法律问题。因全书布局和词汇独特，法学研究者能体会到书中作者的学术用心；对机构、企业而言，本书则不失为一本对外交流、贸易法律问题的通俗指南。而对普通读者而言，因为书中涉及的千奇百怪的古今案例以及本书重介绍轻理论的特点，读之仿佛一本分类小说。

七

感谢母校中国政法大学，笔者早年学习法律专业和现在工作、从事学术研究，都离不开当年在学院路小月河边的法大校园所受的法学熏陶。"中国政法大学是中国法官的摇篮"这句话无疑是一种激励。新西兰国会议员的上班时间是早上9:00到晚上10:00，每位国会议员每天平均工作12个小时以上，在这种高强度、满负荷运转的工作环境下，还能想到著书立说，这也是母校激励的效果。

本书脱稿之后，交谢富安伦律师事务所亚洲部主管刘云芳审阅。案件审理和法律适用须经其"测试"（testing），如果通过不了她的测试，我就必须重新修改其中的章节或过于拗口的理论解读。法学和医学有相通的地方，本书所阐述的法学理论和原则，比较偏重于"临床实验"。重实际应用，是贯穿全书的一条主线。

　　Paul Grant、Darrel Mager、Jennifer Zhou、王丽和张颖睿先后参与了本书的文字整理。在此一并感谢！

　　　　　　　　　　　　　　霍建强（Raymond Huo）
　　　　　　　2019 年 3 月 31 日于惠灵顿国会办公室

目 录

第二部　和华人贴近的四则案例

附　新西兰国会议员霍建强个人立法

第一部

影响西方社会的四大名案

案例一　啤酒蜗牛案

——啤酒瓶为什么是透明的："过失原则"的由来

Donoghue v. Stevenson［1932］AC 562

案　名：唐纳秋梅诉斯蒂文森

时　间：案发：1928 年 8 月 26 日

　　　　判决：1932 年 5 月 26 日

地　点：苏格兰

原被告：原告：唐纳秋梅

　　　　被告：斯蒂文森

法　院：初审、二审：苏格兰高等民事法院

　　　　终审：英国上议院

本案案情简介及确立的判例原则

闺蜜在咖啡店请客，唐纳秋梅喝了一杯生姜啤酒，喝了半杯再续半杯时却没想到从深棕色、不透明的玻璃杯中倒出一只粘乎乎的死蜗牛。唐纳秋梅越看越恶心，得了肠胃炎住院治疗。之后向法院起诉了饮料生产商和咖啡店主，但因为是别人请客不是自己掏钱买的，所以她和咖啡店之间没有构成任何合同关系。而饮料生产商是直接供货给咖啡店，它和当事人之间也没有任何合同关系。而合同关系是当时苏格兰（抑或所有"普通法系"）在这种情形下能够诉诸法律的前提。生姜啤酒在当时是一种时兴饮料，因为容易沉淀直观上不好看，所以大多采用不透明的瓶子装（因为不透明，消费者不能直观，只能仰仗生产商的质量保证，责任自然尽在生产商）。同一时期从中喝出死老鼠、死蟑螂的情形时有发生，但判下来的结果，都是被告和消费者（受害者）之间因不具备合同关系而不用承担法律责任。本案终审法院最终以3:2判被告必须对唐纳秋梅承担法律责任，并以恕道中的"邻居"概念创下一个全新的"过失原则"，标志着过失责任原则在英美法系得以确立。从那以后，除听装啤酒外，装啤酒或类似饮料的玻璃瓶都改成透明的。

甲、乙双方即使没有合同关系（如本案中是甲的朋友请客，甲喝下有死蜗牛的生姜啤酒，姜啤不是甲自己买的，因此和卖方没有构成法律上的合同关系），但乙（这里指被告生产商）必须采取合理的谨慎措施，以避免在应注意、能注意而未注意的情形下未尽到自己法律上的责任而给甲方带来损害。英国上议院（本案终审法院）最终3:2判被告必须对唐纳秋梅承担法律责任，并从恕道和《圣经》的"邻居"概念中创设了一个全新的"过失责任原则"。"啤酒蜗牛案"读后引人深思。

　　"Common Law"，中文译作"英美法系""普通法系"，主要代表国家包括英国、美国、澳大利亚、新西兰、加拿大等。与"大陆法系"（又作"罗马法系"或"欧陆法系"）并称当今世界最有影响力的两大法系。英美法系以判例法为主要的法律渊源。判例法（Case Law），顾名思义，就是以个案判例来确定法律原则。即作为判例的先例（precedent）对其后案件具有法律约束力，可以成为断案的基本准则。遵循先例是英美法系主要的司法审判原则。先例也有纵向先例和横向先例之说。

　　英国最早的判例汇编是用拉丁文编写，1865 年成立了专门出版判例的机构。美国各州不同，全国范围内的判例汇编始于 1880 年。新西兰 1883 年起至今一直沿用同一系统出版权威性的判例。澳大利亚高等法院和联邦法院系统以及权威性和非权威性系统各自不同，开始的时间可能是 19 世纪中叶。

　　判例编纂（如分类、细目等）都很讲究，法官判决书的段落、数字序列等等也都有严格的章法。普遍应用的原则是 1863 年确立的"凌力原则"（Lindley Principles），其中第一条就是，关于判决，但凡有结论而无理由及推导过程的，一概不收。至于判例检索、馆藏等，随着互联网的普及，传统做法也受到很大冲击。从法官写判决书、法官在判决中引用先例到权威机构编纂判例，都不断调整风格，以适应判例电子化。

　　既然"啤酒蜗牛案"列为四大名案之首，我们不妨以"唐纳秋梅诉斯蒂文森"为例，看看如何识别判例名目[1]。

---

　　〔1〕　Source：http://www.sclqld.org.au/infofor/schools/case_quiz/pdf/snail.pdf.

| Donoghue v.Stevenson | [1932] | AC | 562 |

这一部分指诉讼当事人（原告诉被告）。比较容易弄混的是上诉以后上诉方列在前面，原、被告次序互换。研究判例比较通行也是比较保险的方法是找到终审判例。总之，原则是越高一级的法院判例越有价值，因为判例法体系是上级法院的判例对下级法院有约束力

这是判决公布的年份。各国判例汇编风格不同，方括号、圆括号代表的意思也不同

这是判例汇编缩写（指哪一级法院的判例），AC（Appeal Cases）指"上诉法院案件"

既然是判例汇编，一本书里就有许多案例，这是本案首页所在的页码

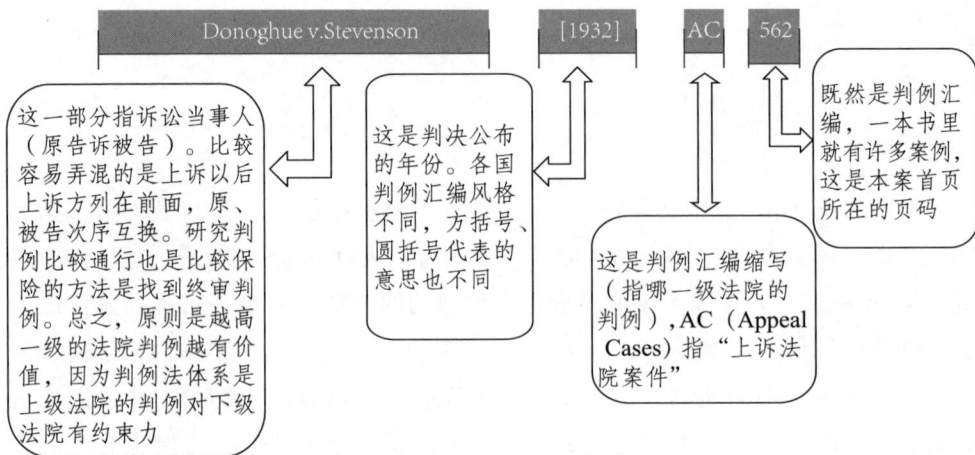

联合王国最高法院依据《2005 年宪制改革法》第三章设立，并于 2009 年 10 月 1 日起开始实施，其前身是创始于 14 世纪的上议院，即本案的终审法院。

很难得见到这么诗情画意的最高法院徽章设计。解读徽章本身，就是了解联合王国的历史和文化。顶部是皇冠，毫无疑问，代表的是君主立宪的君主。下方环绕一行英文字"THE SUPREME COURT"（最高法院）。主体有四种花卉植物，玫瑰（rose）代表英国，韭葱（leek）代表威尔士，紫色蓟（thistle）代表苏格兰，亚麻（flax）代表北爱尔兰。喜欢星相的朋友可能一眼就看出了天秤宫（Libra）造型，代表正义之秤，而希腊字母最后一个字母"Ω"的形状，则代表事情的终结，因为这是联合王国的终审法院。

联合王国最高法院徽章

一、唐纳秋梅

1.1 女主角

1928 年 8 月 26 日，星期天。苏格兰最大的城市格拉斯哥（Glasgow）以东 12 公里左右古色古香的小镇培斯利（Paisley）。此时夜幕悄然降临，我们故事

的女主角刚坐了半小时电车，现在下了车，走在铺满鹅卵石的街道上。她叫梅（May），随夫姓唐纳秋（Donoghue）。这名字看起来平淡无奇。我们现在把这个名字稍微添加一点文学色彩：唐纳秋梅，似乎一下子凸显了一个不太宽裕而踽踽独行的弱女子形象。她本姓麦克阿力斯特（McAllister），时年刚满 30 岁。18 岁嫁给亨利，生了 4 个孩子，活了 3 个，另外一个早产夭折。当时她和丈夫刚分居，那时分居和离异尚属"有碍风化"，所以她仍然保留夫姓。她的职业是"普通店员"。这几乎就是她的全部简历。而正是这样一个普通的弱女子，却使几乎整个普通法系[1]的民法因她而重新改写。

那个傍晚她并非踽踽独行。闺蜜约她到咖啡店小坐。有人说她是自己去的，有人说闺密陪她一起坐电车再一起到了咖啡店。这都不重要。重要的是 20∶50 左右，两人寒暄已毕，闺蜜请客，给唐纳秋梅点了一份苏格兰冰淇淋和一瓶生姜啤酒，给自己点了一只梨和一些冰。生姜啤酒（ginger beer）严格来说不是啤酒，而是纯饮料，不带任何酒精，通常都不经发酵，只是汽水性的饮料而已。当然也有经发酵、含酒精的生姜啤酒，但那是随后好多年的事情。

1.2 咖啡店

敏捷郎（Minchella）是咖啡店主人，敏捷地端来了点好的饮料和冰淇淋。摆在唐纳秋梅面前的是一只宽口平底玻璃杯，里面是冰淇淋，她往上面倒了一些姜啤。姜啤的瓶子呈棕色、不透明，上面标着"斯蒂文森·培斯利"字样（D. Stevenson, Paisley）。唐纳秋梅品了几口，味道不错。闺蜜将剩下的姜啤倒

---

[1] Common Law，又称"判例法系"，"英美法系"或"海洋法系"，近年来称其为海洋法系的越来越少。英美法系，顾名思义，主要代表国家包括英国、美国、澳大利亚、新西兰、加拿大等。与"大陆法系"（又称作"罗马法系"或"欧陆法系"）并称为当今世界最主要和最有影响力的两大法系。曾做过剑桥大学法学院院长、现任新西兰维多利亚（惠灵顿）大学法学院院长的托尼·史密斯教授（Prof. Tony Smith），在他主编的第 15 版《学法》中，对"普通法系"做了比较新颖的解释，大意为①不是来自立法而是来自法官判例的法；②指衡平法（equity）之外的法；③法官行使断案权过程中对包括成文法在内的法律解释。见 Smith, A. T. H, Glanville Williams, *Learning the Law*. 15th ed. London（2013）：Sweet & Maxwell, Thomson Reuters. pp. 22–25, pp. 121–122."普通法系"在中文里指"普遍通行"之意。由此可以想见 Common Law 有时也译作"共同法系"。这里需要指出的是，美国在 1850 年 Brown v. Kendall（"布朗诉肯道尔案"）中首次引入过失责任。及至"唐纳秋梅诉斯蒂文森案"确定的判例，标志着过失责任原则最终在英美法系中正式确立。

进唐纳秋梅的玻璃杯里，这时"咕咚"一声，一只已经腐烂的死蜗牛掉到了杯子里。唐纳秋梅受不了眼前的景象，恶心想吐，稍一回味，便肠胃绞疼，三天后不得不去看医生，三周后不得不住院看急诊，随后便向法院递交了诉状。

这只装姜啤的玻璃瓶呈深棕色、不透明，上下两排大字标着"斯蒂文森·培斯利"的字样，不用说这只"原装"瓶在唐纳秋梅诉斯蒂文森案中被当作一个主要物证。

二、谁该成为被告

2.1 合同关系是诉讼前提

告咖啡店主，敏捷郎说冤哪，我卖的是别人产的姜啤，而且我和消费者一样，面对一只暗棕色、不透明的瓶子，我哪里知道里头有只倒霉而该死的死蜗牛！

告啤酒生产商，斯蒂文森说冤哪，我直接向咖啡店供货，况且是你的闺蜜请客，你又没有向咖啡店主购买姜啤，我们之间不存在任何合同关系！

因产品质量问题而引起的损伤、赔偿，当时的相关法律尚不成熟。在苏格兰和英国以及其他"西方社会"，这类官司通常基于买卖双方因销售而产生的合同关系。但是唐纳秋梅和敏捷郎之间并没有合同关系，因为她没有向敏捷郎购买那瓶姜啤。购买姜啤的是她的朋友，而她的朋友既没有喝那杯姜啤更谈不上因此而遭受任何损伤。而两者均和姜啤制造厂商斯蒂文森不具有任何合同关系。

2.2 啤酒老鼠案

在这样的基础上要想胜诉，必须首先证明被告失职（因被告作为或不作为），原告因失职而致损伤。

那时苏格兰因为姜啤而引发的官司并不鲜见，但两个最近的判例显然对唐纳秋梅不利。"木楞案"和"麦告万案"[1]都涉及生姜啤酒里发现死老鼠。不透明的啤酒瓶里有一只老鼠，这不是明摆着是失职吗？虽然没有直接的证据证明老鼠是在生产过程中装到瓶子里的，难道不可以因此推定制造厂商在法律意义上的"怠忽、失职"（negligence）吗？但是苏格兰高等民事法院的大法官们却不支持这种说法。主审法官中除了一位，其他都认为"怠忽推定"说不能成立，因为生产商对最终消费者的"操心责任"（duty of care）只有在两种情况下产生：第一，他们之间有合同关系；第二，如果产品有危险性而生产厂明知而故意不说（因此可构成诈欺），或者某类产品有特殊的危险成分而生产厂对消费者不加以警示（如炸药）。因此那几个喝了装有死老鼠姜啤的孩子们虽然值得同情，但法律却帮不了他们什么忙，他们的损失赔偿请求，也被法院驳回，因为法官只能依法断案。因老鼠或蜗牛引发的啤酒案，尚没有成文或判例法可资依据。巧的是唐纳秋梅请的，正是在"木楞姜啤老鼠案"中刚刚输掉官司的那位律师。

三、苏格兰法院

3.1 "英国""大不列颠"和"联合王国"

苏格兰属于"大不列颠及北爱尔兰联合王国"的一部分。联合王国（也就是俗称的英国）包括英格兰、苏格兰、威尔士及北爱尔兰。了解其复杂的法律制度之前，得先了解他们因体制和"宪政"规定而产生的不同称谓。托尼·史密斯教授的著作第15版《学法》中介绍了一个让人过目不忘的方法：但凡指英

---

[1] Mullen v. AG Barr & Co Ltd; McGowan v. AG Barr & CO.

国和威尔士的（England 和 Wales）都叫"英国"（England）。将英国、威尔士和苏格兰（Scotland）称为一个统一体的，则叫"大不列颠"（Great Britain）。而将"大不列颠"再加"北爱尔兰"（Northern Ireland）的，就成为我们所熟悉的"联合王国"（United Kingdom）[1]。

联合王国并没有一套统一的司法制度，英格兰和威尔士采用一种体系，苏格兰采用另一种，北爱尔兰又是另一种。但某些方面法律是涵括所有联合王国的，如移民法等等。雇佣（劳资关系）方面的法律涵括范围亦宽，除北爱尔兰之外也是统一的。

3.2 苏格兰法院体系

苏格兰法院体系虽然复杂，但也离不开刑、民两大块。刑事方面包括高等刑事法院、州（郡）法院和地方法院以及特别和"其他"法院（如与未成年人相关的刑事法庭，军事法庭等）及审裁处。州（郡）法院和地方法院这一块正处于改制中，有可能会合并[2]。

需要注意的是，苏格兰高等刑事法院身兼初审和上诉两个职能。初审法院在爱丁堡（Edinburgh），格拉斯哥及其他城市设庭；而上诉法院则只设在首府爱丁堡。上诉法院既受理下一级刑事法院的上诉，也可以受理本院自行初审的案件。对于科刑（sentence）类上诉，有两名法官听审；对定罪（conviction）类上诉，则由三名法官听审。对于刑事案件，苏格兰高等刑事法院是终审法院。这一点与民事法院体系相比有很大不同。

苏格兰民事法院设有州（郡）民事法院（Sheriff Court）以及高等民事法院（Court of Session），日文直接将其译作"民事上诉裁判所"，因为它亦身兼初审和上诉两个职能。具初审职能的高等民事法院通常称作"Outer House"，日文译作"外院"；具上诉职能的叫"Inner House"，日文译作"内院"。内院

苏格兰高等民事法院徽章

---

〔1〕 参见 Smith, A. T. H, Glanville Williams：*Learning the Law*. 15th *ed*. London（2013）：Sweet & Maxwell, Thomson Reuters. p. 2.

〔2〕 The Criminal Proceedings etc（Reform）（Scotland）Act 2007.

受理来自外院的上诉以及来自郡法院、苏格兰土地法院、审裁处以及"纹章法院"的上诉[1]。

对于民事案件,苏格兰终审法院则是联合王国最高法院(Supreme Court of the United Kingdom),其前身是上议院(House of Lords)。

四、上议院(House of Lords)

上议院徽章

联合王国最高法院依据《2005 年宪制改革法》(The Constitutional Reform Act 2005)第三章设立,并于 2009 年 10 月 1 日起开始实施[2],其前身是上议院,也可直译为"贵族院",因为它对应的是"庶民院"(House of Commons)。上议院创始于 14 世纪,1544 年始用"上议院"之名。除立法功能外,上议院在 2009 年 7 月 30 日以前亦行使司法职能,同年 10 月 1 日起其司法职能由联合

---

〔1〕 指"Court of the Lord Lyon",亦称"Lyon Court"或"Lyon Office",主理苏格兰纹章事务。法国人米歇尔·巴斯图罗(Michel Pastoureau)所著《纹章学》中的定义为:纹章在 12 世纪诞生于战场上,主要是为了识别因披挂甲胄而无法辨认的骑士,认为纹章是贵族专利的普遍观点就源于此。从 13 世纪起,无论贵族还是平民,只要遵守纹章术规则,皆可拥有和使用纹章。至今,已融入识别标志,无所不在。参见《纹章学》,谢军瑞译,上海书店出版社 2002 年版。

〔2〕 英国工党政府执政期间,在国会推出《2005 年宪制改革法》,设立联合王国最高法院取代上议院上诉法官(Law Lords,通常称"常任上诉法官")行使其职能以及枢密院司法委员会的部分职能。枢密院司法委员会(Judicial Committee of the Privy Council)是英国的终审法院之一,亦是联合王国海外领地、皇家属地和部分独立英联邦国家的终审法院。我国香港地区在 1997 年主权回归中华人民共和国之前,英国枢密院是最高上诉法院,在主权移交后则改为于本地成立的香港终审法院(Court of Final Appeal)。加拿大在 1875 年成立了加拿大最高法院,并废除了枢密院对该国的刑事案件的终审权。但枢密院对刑事案件终审权到 1933 年才真正终止,对民事案件的终审权到 1959 年才终止。澳大利亚通过 1968 年、1975 年和 1986 年三个立法废除了枢密院对澳洲的终审权。马来西亚于 1978 年和 1985 年分别终止了枢密院的刑、民事终审权。新加坡在 1989 年废除了枢密院的终审权,但涉及死刑案件及民事案件(若双方同意)仍可上诉至枢密院。直到 1994 年,才完全废除了枢密院的终审权。新西兰要废除枢密院终审权的想法在上世纪 80 年代初就有了,但直到工党政府执政期间的 2003 年才通过相关立法,从 2003 年底开始废止枢密院的终审权,并成立新西兰最高法院成为新西兰终审法院。南非是 1950 年废止的,而加勒比共同体成员国则是 2001 年通过废除枢密院之终审权的决定,并由新成立的加勒比法院取代。但贯彻不畅,直到 2005 年在成员国中还有反复。在加拿大、澳大利亚和新西兰,仍有不少业内人士认为废除枢密院终审权有可惜的一面,因为枢密院司法委员会汇集了英国乃至"共同法"领域大法官中的顶尖人物。而反方则认为,多国情形不同,势必会造成价值观、文化及法律拿捏程度之差异。

王国最高法院接管。据 2012 年 10 月 8 日资料，[1]上议院有 760 名议员，与民选的庶民院不同，上议院议员大多非选举产生，其中包括英国国教会的 25 名大主教或主教即"灵职议员"（Lords Spiritual），其他的则称为"俗职议员"（Lords Temporal）。

在联合王国最高法院接管之前，上议院亦行使司法职能，就英格兰、威尔士和北爱尔兰而言，上议院是刑事和民事案件的终审法院。就苏格兰而言，上议院仅为民事案件的终审法院，而刑事案件的终审权则由苏格兰高等刑事法院行使。

常任上诉大法官（Lords of Appeal in Ordinary）自上议院院内选派，行使司法职能。常任上诉大法官不介入政治争端，以维持司法独立。各类上诉案件由各受理上诉委员会（Appellate Committees）负责审理，委员会一般由 5 名上议院大法官组成，成员由首席上议院大法官选定，判决结果于上议院议事厅宣判。任何案件经上议院终审后不可再行上诉，除非事关欧盟法律或欧洲人权公约，则可向欧洲司法院[2]提出诉讼。欧洲司法院的判决较重法益，与上议院有很大不同，但这都是"二战"之后的事了。对唐纳秋梅啤酒蜗牛案最终给一个说法的，就是终审法院英国上议院。

五、一审（1929 年 5 月 21 日）

啤酒蜗牛案的线条已经清楚：

原告：唐纳秋梅。

被告：斯蒂文森，同名商号的啤酒及其他饮料的生产厂商。这是本地一家小家族式的企业，厂址离咖啡店不到 1.6 公里。

原告律师：Walter Leechman，根据音译，我们不妨称他为"立志哥"。

5.1 四个诉讼理由

立志哥很了不起，三周前刚刚输掉的"啤酒老鼠案"（即 Mullen 案）中那

---

[1] 参见英国国会 Guide to the House of Lords。

[2] The European Court of Justice，见 Europa. eu 简介。

几个喝姜啤喝出老鼠的原告，就是由他代理的。虽然刚输了官司，但他并不气馁。他现场勘探，得到结论："啤酒厂车间蜗牛爬行，爬过的粘滑痕迹随处可见。"因此他提出四个诉讼理由：第一，斯蒂文森作为啤酒和其他饮料生产厂商，"欠缺勤谨注意"，也就是说谨慎不足，管理失当，以至于不能保证蜗牛不会爬到或混入饮料瓶中，因此违背了勤谨注意义务。第二，违背勤谨注意义务的直接后果是生产厂商没有一套质保系统，以确保那些不透明的玻璃瓶在装入啤酒和饮料前是干净、无污染的。姜啤是供人饮用的，而这样受到污染的姜啤在市场上流通，消费者唐纳秋梅恰好饮用了这样一瓶姜啤。第三，因生产厂商违背了勤谨注意义务，唐纳秋梅饮用掺有蜗牛的姜啤后恶心、腹痛以致不得不住院治疗直接造成了消费者的损失。第四，装姜啤的是一个深棕色、不透明的玻璃瓶，消费者最终消费前无法判辨，因此即使在当时的法律基础上也应该产生一项"例外性"诉因，原告必须承担欠缺勤谨注意的责任[1]。

在当时提出这样的诉讼理由是不容易的。那时对制造厂商因产品瑕疵或质量问题提出告诉，大抵可以依据"怠忽责任推定"，但推定必须满足两大要件：第一是原、被告及相关当事人之间存在合同关系；第二，被告对产品的危险性故意隐瞒不告或对某些特殊产品其内在危险性（如炸药）没有公开性警示。但这两个要件都不适用于唐纳秋梅案。说到底，姜啤虽然不如意，但它毕竟不是"危险产品"；况且斯蒂文森也不存在主观故意隐瞒。那暗棕色的瓶子是不透明的，鬼才知道里面装的什么！

5.2 敏捷郎解除被告身份

在高等民事法院正式庭审之前，有一个"临时性听审"，是为了解决相关法律问题，以免原、被告正式开仗之后，如果发现没有诉因而缺乏相关法律依据，所产生的费用（双方都得请律师加上法院的人力物力）双方都吃不消。临时听审是在1929年5月21日进行的。有一个小插曲是，唐纳秋梅的律师不但提出500英镑的赔偿外加律师费赔偿，还将咖啡店主敏捷郎列为并列被告，这是6月5日的事。但到了11月19日，原告又取消了对咖啡店主的诉讼，估计

---

[1] Coleman, Clive (20 November 2009): "The legal case of the snail found in ginger bear" (BBC News).

是考虑到两个原因，而这两个原因均成立：第一，唐纳秋梅的朋友为她购买的姜啤，因此唐纳秋梅和敏捷郎之间没有合同关系；第二，敏捷郎虽为咖啡店主，又亲自为唐纳秋梅端上那瓶姜啤并倒给她第一杯饮用，但姜啤的玻璃瓶是不透明的，敏捷郎对瓶中内容（姜啤）和随后倒出来的死蜗牛无从辨识。基于敏捷郎被原告拖进了这场官司，解除其被告身份后，法庭判原告支付敏捷郎律师费。

5.3 一审结论：受污染食品＝"危险产品"

一审于 1930 年 6 月 27 日在苏格兰高等民事法院外院进行。当天作出的裁决十分明确："作为一个基本原则，食物准备过程中有怠忽行为，当事人必须负责。"[1]

一审由法官 Lord Moncrieff 一人独审，他认为销售那些受到污染的食品——尽管理解起来比较牵强——但这样的食品无疑属于一种"危险产品"，而在其制造及销售环节中不得不推导出应尽的责任。失责便导致不同程度的伤害，"而我看不出这样的一个生产商为何不应该承担过失责任，也看不出这样一个生产商为何具备抗辩理由"[2]。

这位法官的判定，实际上推翻了当时英国判例法在处理这类案件的原则，也就是任何因食品质量而导致的伤害，追究责任的前提是当事人之间必须具备合同关系。

他的判决虽然对原告有利，但看得出他的逻辑起点还是在原地打转，只是认为受污染食品属于"危险产品"，因此"推定"责任方之责任不可推卸。在当时那个食品安全及消费者保护法律尚未成熟的年代，这样的推断是难有说服力的。被告因此上诉。

六、二审（1930 年 11 月 13 日）

斯蒂文森向苏格兰高等民事法院内院上诉。庭审的四位法官是裁决"啤酒

---

[1]　关于裁决的具体内容和依据，见 Chapman, Matthew（2010），*The Snail and the Ginger Beer*, *Great Britain*：Wildy, Simmonds & Hill Publishing.

[2]　Donoghue v. Stevenson Appeal Papers：The Appendix（Opinions）. Chapman, Watson & Co.

老鼠案"的原班人马。虽然 3∶1（并非意见一致），但最终结果是对被告上诉予以支持。1930 年 11 月 13 日作出裁决，"木楞案"（即啤酒老鼠案）先例成立，姜啤中的蜗牛和老鼠在性质上并没有区别，所不同之处只是一个是啮齿动物（rodent），另一个是腹足类动物（gastropod）而已。对原告唐纳秋梅来说，现在唯一的希望是向终审法院英国上议院上诉，但困难重重。除去经济原因（请律师在上诉法院这个层级打官司，没有坚实的经济基础是办不到的），更大的障碍在于"木楞案"这样的先例。直白地说，唐纳秋梅想要赢得这场官司，必须首先推翻"啤酒老鼠案"定下的先例。因为英国为判例法国家，确定的先例具有约束力。

七、判例法

7.1 遵循先例

判例法，顾名思义，就是以个案判例来确定法律原则。也就是说，作为判例的先例（precedent）对其后的案件具有法律约束力，可以成为断案的基本准则。法院有上下级之分，原诉讼法庭先前的判例不能约束上诉法庭的判决，但上诉法庭的判决对下级法庭则有约束力。如"木楞案"中四位大法官对"啤酒老鼠案"已作出裁决，该裁决作为先例对随后所有类似的案件均有约束力。

英美法系以判例法为主要的法律渊源，"遵循先例"[1]是主要的司法审判原则。该原则由两个部分组成：第一，上级法院作出的判决或同一法院先前作出的判决，对同一级法院及下级法院均构成具有法律约束力的先例。第二，法院不能够推翻自己的先例——除非有强烈的理由必须推翻，同时从旁系或下级法院判决中参考相应准则。但旁系或下级法院的先例通常称为"说服性先例"，是没有约束力的。

---

〔1〕 拉丁文为"Stare decisis""服从前例原则、遵照先例（指法院对某一类事实确定一项原则，在以后的案件中可适用于同样一类的事实）"，参见薛波主编：《法律英汉词典》，台北五南图书出版公司 2002 年版，第 754 页。

先例也有纵向先例和横向先例〔1〕之说，普通法系大多设初审法院、中级上诉法院和终审最高法院。纵向先例指的是下级法院受上级法院先例的约束。而横向先例则指法官受本院或同级法院先例的约束。

判例法的准则是基于法律的稳定性和可预测性。难以想像类似的两个案子，不但案情相似而且同在一个法律原则框架内，不同的法院会作出大相径庭的判决。所以判例法不但在英美法系诸国和地区建立了一个共同遵循的法，并且在统一性的前提下，替各国司法界和各类当事人也节省了许多精力和时间。当然，也给各国法学院的学生提供了一个"共同法"的平台。在英美法系体系中，学习法律绝不是单纯学习本国法律，本国的成文法固然重要，但包括本国在内的各国判例，无疑使英美法系成为一个跨国界甚至是无国界的资源和智慧共享的法律大一统世界。

7.2 先例、意见和异议

判例法中有三个名词经常出现。第一，"stare decisis"，遵循先例，该先例具有法律约束力。第二，"orbiter dicta"，即法官判决时表达非决定性的附带意见，也就是在断案中由本案引申或发挥的一些观点〔2〕。第三，"dissenting opinions"，反对意见，指同一案件中断案法官之异议。上诉案件通常都由一个以上的法官审理，审判结果少数服从多数。多数派的判决成为先例，而少数派的异议则成为"具有说服力的见解"。在随后判案中可提供新思路而具有参考价值。判决结果固然重要，但形成判决结果的原因同等重要甚至有时更加重要，因为以理服人是法律的前提。在英美法系，每一个案子的判决结果都是公示的，不但是媒体的追踪对象，也是业内人士（律师、学术界）研究和评述的热点，更是法学院学生直接拿来学习的教材。一个法官如果在自己的判决书中（短则几页，长则上百页）语焉不详或逻辑不当，很快就会成为笑柄。但这在各国判例

〔1〕 "纵向先例"，指 vertical precedent 或 verticality；"横向先例"，指 horizontal precedent 或 horizontality。纵向先例，下级法院遵循上级法院先例，这是普遍公认的原则。但横向先例，即同一法院必须遵循自己在相似案件中确定的先例则有争议性。学者罗森教授（Professor Gary Lawson）认为如果先例有悖宪法，如宪法说 X 而先例说 Y，则同一法院非但没有权利去循这个先例并且应尽自己的义务去遵循宪法而不能遵循自己这个先例。

〔2〕 薛波主编：《法律英汉词典》，台北五南图书出版公司 2002 年版，第 539 页。

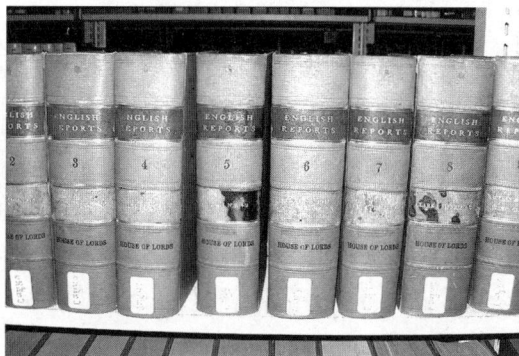

中尚不多见，因为能到法官那个位置，基本都是相关层面的业内精英或学术带头人。成为法官必须有一定年限的执业经验，坐到那个位置以前，已经身经百战，经验老到，或者其许多观点已被别的法官引用过。

因唐纳秋梅引发的啤酒蜗牛案，不但对当时的食品质量法律规范和消费者保护给出了一个明确界定，也因为英国上议院大法官们的精彩判例，在法律、文化、宗教和相关社会层面掀起了一个大波澜。80 多年过去了，这个大波澜引发的余波仍没有消失。培斯利这个当年啤酒蜗牛案发生的小镇，也成为英美法系业界后人朝圣的地方。在这里会定期举办研讨会和各种形式的纪念活动，而咖啡店的原址则竖起了一个纪念碑。和英美法系其他地方一样，在这里法律并不是一个外在的强制性的概念，它是每一个人生活的一部分。

而英国上议院大法官们以 3:2 定下的这个判例，又为何这么不同寻常呢？

八、一波三折

1931 年 2 月 25 日，唐纳秋梅向英国上议院递交诉状。与此同时——并随后得到批准的就是她向上议院请求以"赤贫身份"进行上诉。"赤贫身份"（in forma pauperis）是拉丁文的一个法律名词，指因为自己的经济状况而可以免除诉讼费用的贫民、穷人。用现代语汇来理解，可以说是申请司法援助的一个条件。而无论是现在还是当时，对簿公堂——尤其是商业纠纷案件——法庭费用及输掉官司以后对对方的赔偿，往往是诉讼前要解决的一个重要问题。实战中也不乏这种律师，往往利用"费用担保"作为压对方的一个筹码。双方在法庭开战之前，如果不能提供"费用担保",不但说明没有实力,也很有可能说明没有诚意。

对唐纳秋梅来说,将自己定性为"赤贫身份"也是需要很大勇气的!

御用大律师马丁·泰勒(Martin R. Taylor QC)就曾经感慨,为什么"啤酒老鼠案"没有能够像"啤酒蜗牛案"这样载入史册?多数原因是喝了老鼠姜啤的那几个受害者没有坚持,而喝了蜗牛姜啤的弱女子唐纳秋梅却没有放弃![1]因为她的坚持,食品质量和消费者保护的法律才变得明朗、规范。如果不是她的坚持,还不知道要等多久,我们才能得到这样一则判例。

英国上议院档案:唐纳秋梅签名的请愿状,申请以"赤贫身份"上诉

递交给英国上议院的唐纳秋梅证词的首页[2]

唐纳秋梅申请以"赤贫身份"上诉,这样她可以不用按规定向法庭提供费用担保金。否则一旦上诉被驳回,她是要向对方支付不菲的费用的(律师费或

---

〔1〕 Taylor, Martin R. QC(1991):Donoghue v. Stevenson and the Modern Law of Negligence, Continuing Legal Education Society of British Columbia.

〔2〕 Source:the original in the Records of the House of Lords. English law reports http://en. wikipedia. org/wiki/File:English_ Reports. jpg.

赔偿金）。

在唐纳秋梅的证词上，她写道："我很穷，全部身家加起来还不到5英镑。"[1]牧师和教堂的两位长者为她签字。在解决法庭的"费用担保"问题之后，她的律师团队又同意免费为她打这场官司。

英国西敏宫（Palace of Westminster）

几经波折，啤酒蜗牛案最终来到英国西敏宫（又译作"威斯敏斯特宫"，即 Palace of Westminster），英国上议院于1931年12月10~11日两天开庭，五位大法官共同主审。但差不多半年后，这五位大法官才分别作出判决。

九、终审（1932年5月26日）

9.1 四年等待

唐纳秋梅是1928年8月26日喝下那泡有死蜗牛的生姜啤酒。苏格兰高等民事法院受理并于1929年5月21日进行"临时听审"，6月27日进行一审。第二年11月13日二审，1931年2月25日唐纳秋梅上诉到终审法院英国上议院，12月10~11日两天开庭，而等到1932年5月26日，上议院才作出最终裁决。不但一波三折，而且时间跨度也大，将近四年。

---

〔1〕 证词可以从上议院档案材料中找到：From the original in the Records of the House of Lords。

9.2 法律和道德

读者看到这里，笔者写到这里，可能都有一个共同的感觉：这个案例发展得如此"不痛快"，似乎可以归结为一个潜意识的缘由——无论是当事人，原、被告双方律师还是苏格兰、英格兰各级法官，谁也不知道这个案子会朝着什么方向发展。案情虽然不复杂，类似案件的判例虽然也不如人意，消费者和社会对食品安全虽然也是充满期待，并且因啤酒、饮料中喝出蜗牛和老鼠的情况时有发生，社会上已是沸沸扬扬，大家也都很不耐烦，但如何在法律上"给个说法"，如何通过法律的宏观调控或微观约束，如何通过社会治理达到童叟无欺，买得放心吃得放心，大家心里都没底。此时目光都聚焦在终审法院。而判例法体系的一大特点就是这种"定调子"的判例，往往解决的不仅仅是一个具体事件引发的相关法律问题，更重要的，它能够在社会道义和行为规范上定下一个人人遵守的标准。这样一来，社会就有秩序了，消费者在拧开啤酒瓶的那一刹那，他知道他可以买来一份信任。如此，向社会其他层面辐射开来，信任的力量扩散，善的正能量互相影响，渐渐地可以达到一个童叟无欺的境界。但需要提醒的是，无论是老鼠还是蜗牛，发生在上世纪 30 年代苏格兰的这些案件，中心议题围绕的都是"怠忽"，就是说在生产商没有履行谨慎责任但与最终消费者不具备合同关系的前提下，该生产商对因此遭致伤害的消费者要不要承担法律责任？当时发生的情况，与时下媒体报道中的现象，如用明矾、色素和石蜡给发霉的橙子、橘子打蜡上色，再卖个好价；或是用工业盐泡菜，用加色素的方法将普通醋变成"老陈醋"，用头发造酱油，"化学人造鸡蛋"或是用漂白剂将被黄曲霉毒素污染的大米变成"水晶米""珍珠米"，等等，是完全不同性质和不同范围的问题。

回到唐纳秋梅案，我们可以感觉到，即使是局限在一个"勤谨""注意"或"操心"责任（有别于如今的假、冒、伪、劣产品），也存在一个法律和道义层面上的大震荡，彼时的苏格兰、英格兰，也正在酝酿一场法律和道德领域的革命。因此，五位主审大法官中的一位大法官爱德肯（Lord Atkin），他在判决前 6 个星期在伦敦一所大学的学术演讲，就格外引人注目了。

在题为"法律作为一个教育主题"的演讲中[1]，爱德肯大法官若有所思地说：

法律的限制可以明确界定但却局限在一个有限的范围内，而道德所涵括的却远远超过这些。尽管如此，英国的法根植于一个道义的宣教，并且为人与人之间的交往建立下一个诚实无欺的标准……不要因为自己的怠忽、不谨慎而致自己的邻居受损，这可以涵括很大的一个法律领域。我甚至怀疑，整个民法体系是否都可以包含在"推己及人"的黄金定律中[2]。

9.3 黄金定律和白银定律

"黄金定律"（The Golden Rule）或"互惠规范"（ethic of reciprocity）是一个道义准则。积极面为"推己及人"[3]；消极面——也称"白银定律"（The Silver Rule）——为"己所不欲，勿施于人"[4]。

黄金定律在古希腊哲学、基督教以及儒家、道教中都很普遍。爱德肯大法官据说是"一日三省"，每天都要读几段《圣经》上的文字。旧约《圣经》"利未记"19:18："不可报仇，也不可埋怨你本国的子民，却要爱人如己。我是耶和华。"[5]新约《圣经》"路加福音"6:31："你们愿意人怎样对你们，你们也要怎样待人。"[6]

《论语·卫灵公》中子贡问曰："有一言而可以终身行之者乎？"子曰："其

---

〔1〕 关于演讲的话题和报道，有关文献记载颇多，主要的可参见：(1932) J. of Soc. of Pub. Teachers of Law 27 at 30. Also, G. Lewi's, Lord Atkin (London: Butterworths, 1983)。

〔2〕 中文的"怀疑"用在此类语境中似指肯定，即他认为可以包含在这个黄金定律中。而英文则指否定，所以原文是双重否定，即"我怀疑……不能包含其中"。考虑到阅读习惯，这里意译，直接说出意思而避开双重否定。

〔3〕 原文为"One should treat others as one would like others to treat oneself"。

〔4〕 原文为"One should not treat others in ways that one would not like to be treated"。关于黄金定律积极面、消极面的分析，见 Flew, Antony, *A Dictionary of Philosophy*, London: Pan Books in association with the MacMillan Pres, 1979, p. 134。

〔5〕 Leviticus 19:18："You shall not take vengeance or bear a grudge against any of your people, but you shall love your neighbor as yourself: I am the Lord."《圣经（中英对照）》（和合本·新修订2000标准版），中国基督教会，苏出准印 JSE-0001657 号，第 183 页。

〔6〕 Luke 6:31："Do to others as you would have them do to you." p. 113，同上。这些原话和对这些原话的解读，在爱德肯的判决书上反复出现，对形成判决起到重要作用。

恕乎! 已所不欲, 勿施于人。"〔1〕《论语·颜渊》再次出现"已所不欲, 勿施于人"〔2〕。

所以, "黄金定律"在儒家眼里就是恕道。何为忠, 何为恕呢? 于丹说宋代朱熹对"忠恕"两字解释得非常好, 言简意赅。他说: "尽己之谓忠, 推己之谓恕。"也就是说, 尽自己的心是忠, 用自己的心推及他人就是恕。有人说: "中心为忠, 如心为恕。"朱熹也引用了这个看法, 并且说这个看法也是说得通的〔3〕。

且不论诞生于公元前551年的孔子和诞生于公元前4年的耶稣以及其他先人是如何在恕道上神交的, 爱德肯大法官在唐纳秋梅一案中的判决, 就是源自《圣经》中"爱人如己、推己及人"的思想并且创下了民法体系中的"邻居概念"。

9.4 宠物狗伤人案

这还不够。在"只听楼梯响, 不见人下来"的漫漫等待中, 又恰巧发生了一宗宠物狗伤人的案件。被告将他的一只原本安静而乖巧的狗, 关在车里并将车泊在停车场然后去办事。狗疯了似地又是狂吠又是在车里打转, "哗啦"一声后车窗玻璃被撞碎, 恰巧原告经过, 四溅的玻璃渣命中他的眼睛, 导致一只眼睛失明。英国上诉院判决: 行人路过被碎玻璃渣子击中的概率很小, 正常的人在正常的情况下很难预料并加以防范, 故被告不负法律上的责任〔4〕。

不清楚这宗因狗而导致玻璃渣子伤眼案是哪些大法官判的, 但爱德肯大法官若有所指地说, 一个人最起码的职责是看好自己的宠物或动产, 这样才不至于伤及自己的"邻居"。爱德肯大法官称这种职责为"过失责任原则"(negligence)。〔5〕

---

〔1〕 Book XV, Duke Ling of Wei: Zi Gong asked, "Is there a single saying that one can act upon throughout one's life?" The Master said, "Perhaps the word of Shu (forbearance), which means never do to others what you would not like to do to you." 参见李天辰, 孔凡富, 佟光武, 任国生译:《论语》(汉英对照读本, The Analects of Confucius), 山东大学出版社1991年版, 第249页。

〔2〕 李天辰, 孔凡富, 佟光武, 任国生译:《论语》(汉英对照读本), 山东大学出版社1991年版, 第174页。

〔3〕 于丹:《于丹〈论语〉感悟》, 中华书局2008年版, 第101~102页。

〔4〕 Fardon v. Harcourt-Rivington (1932) 48 T. L. R. 215 at 217 (House of Lords).

〔5〕 Taylor, Martin QC (2004): "An Introduction to Mrs. Donoghue's Journey", p. 11.

9.5 颠覆历史的判决书

1932 年 5 月 26 日，距离听审 5 个月后，英国上议院五位大法官终于作出判决。

爱德肯大法官的判决书很长，他详列了以下五个要点[1]：

9.5.1 距离产生责任

他引用一个先例[2]并加之发挥：如果一个人距离另外一个人或其财产很近，则距离产生责任——他不能因自己的行为导致另外一个人或物受损害。

9.5.2 法律上的"邻居"概念

这里的"邻居"指心理上而非物理意义上的空间概念。就饮料生产商斯蒂文森而言，在给姜啤或其他饮料装瓶的时候，脑子里就应该有唐纳秋梅那样的消费者。唐纳秋梅就是他精神意义上的"邻居"。

9.5.3 过失责任原则

过失责任原则（the liability for negligence）可以有不同的表述方式，如其他法系将之称作"过失"（culpa），即"欠缺勤谨注意"[3]。但毫无疑问，它是建立在公众的道义常识基础上的，也就是说道义上有一个错，则肇事者必须对这个错负责。当然，任何因作为或不作为而导致道义上的谴责，不一定在现实世界都能转换成法律上的权利而使遭到损害的一方得到赔偿。

法律和道德涵括的是不同的领域，法律外延较窄，在此可以界定具体的法律限制，而道德的范围可以延伸很宽。

---

〔1〕 Donoghue v. Stevenson, 1932 S. C.（H. L）31.

〔2〕 Le Lievre v. Gould, 引 Lord Esher 判例。

〔3〕 罗马法中的过失理论对后世各国民法的过失理论有直接的影响。后世法学家将罗马法中的过失分作：过失（culpa）、重过失（culpa lata）、轻过失（culpa levis）等。"欠缺勤谨注意"则指"diligentia"。罗马法泛指罗马国家的法律，它是罗马社会在 1300 多年的历史过程中逐步发展完备的奴隶制社会法律。一般认为，罗马法律史的上限始于公元前 753 年，下限则至公元 565 年。其中公元前 451 年，即《十二表法》（Lex Duodecim tabularum）制定之前，是习惯法时期，以后则为成文法时期。参见江平，米健：《罗马法基础》，中国政法大学出版社 1987 年版，第 287 页，第 1 页。

9.5.4 "爱你邻居" = "不要伤害你的邻居"

作为规则，"爱你邻居"在法律上则变成了"不要伤害你的邻居"。那谁是我在法律意义上的邻居呢？那些在法律意义上和你的距离很近而因此受你的作为直接影响的人就是你的邻居。那么你在引导自己作为或不作为时，就必须合理地把他们考虑在自己的作为或不作为中。也就是说，如果在合理的情形下能够合理地预知自己的作为或不作为可能导致邻居受损，那么就必须谨慎、注意、操上这份心，避免因自己做了某件不该做的事或忘记做某件本该做的事而导致邻居受损。

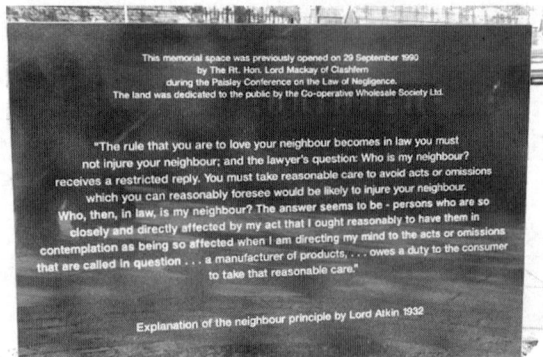

"爱你的邻居在法律上则变成了不要伤害你的邻居"，已经被刻在纪念碑上竖立在咖啡店的原址。[1]

爱德肯大法官引用一宗 1883 年的判例 Heaven v. Pender[2]，一艘船在船侧悬挂一个工作平台，悬挂用的绳索由被告提供。平台是悬挂起来了但却塌了，砸伤了台下干活的工人。调查结果发现，绳索是旧的，以前被火烧过，一使劲就断了，被告显然"没有在合理的情形下合理地事先检查"，被告必须承担法律责任。爱德肯大法官认为这宗案子无疑成为过失责任原则发展的一个先兆，而现有与其原则相悖的案例在对法律的理解上都过于狭隘。连食物中毒这样的案子都不能对制造商诉之以法，这简直是法律的重大瑕疵！

爱德肯大法官进一步发挥，认为如药、肥皂、清洁剂等常见日用品生产商，

---

〔1〕　Source：http://paisleyonline.co.uk/html/paisley_snail.html.

〔2〕　Heaven v. Pender（1883），Ⅱ QBD 503，Court of Appeal.

都必须对这些产品的质量承担民法意义上的责任〔1〕。

我就不信我们的法律制度会如此病态以至于它的原则会和我们文明社会的普通需求变得如此遥远，面临社会上这样一个明显的错误而我们竟不能给他们任何法律上的解救！〔2〕

爱德肯大法官 80 多年前的这番话，如今听起来仍然那么铿锵有力！

9.5.5 包装和责任

对于某一类产品的制造商，如果产品抵达最终用户时的形态是最终用户在合理情形（常规状态下）不能够直接明白其究竟的（如姜啤装在不透明的瓶子里），那么生产商在生产和装瓶过程中没有在合理情形下尽责，则必须对消费者遭受的损失承担合理的责任。

9.6 四大法律原则

实际上，爱德肯大法官借"啤酒蜗牛案"明确了四个法律原则〔3〕：

9.6.1 过失责任

第一，过失责任原则是一类独特的民法（tort），唐纳秋梅判例之后，任何因另一方作为或不作为引起的个人或个人财产损失——而这种损失是因另一方直接、间接或可预见性作为或不作为而引起的——过失责任原则都可以单独作为诉因而无需依附民法中的其他因素。

9.6.2 合同不是要件

第二，合同关系不是要件。

---

〔1〕 区别于合同法和刑法意义上的责任——这是为什么啤酒蜗牛案不仅仅扩大了对消费者的保护范围，更是在民法意义上自创了"邻居原则"和"过失责任原则"。

〔2〕 Ditto.

〔3〕 见 Professor R. F. v. Heuston, "An Overview of the Law of Negligence: 60 Years After Mrs. Donoghue Visit to Paisley" in Donoghue v. Stevenson and the Modern Law of Negligence: The Paisley Papers, (1991), University of British Columbia, Vancouver, 57 at 60-68.

但滑稽的是，唐纳秋梅判例之前，证明原、被告之间有合同关系是诉讼前提，而现代的趋向却是更多的原告选择民法而不是合同法作为诉讼途径和依据，目的是避免合同关系带来的约束。

9.6.3 制造方责任

第三，产品制造方责任。唐纳秋梅判例明确了产品制造方的责任。尽管按现代眼光看来，爱德肯大法官在裁决中采用了一个较窄的测试标准，即姜啤瓶子不透明而消费者无法看清里面装的什么货色，因此在生产和装瓶过程中，生产商因缺乏合理谨慎及质量监督，必须承担由此引起的法律责任。

当然，当时生产商普遍采用不透明的玻璃瓶装姜啤，是因为姜啤容易产生沉淀，沉淀的混浊物——尽管质量上乘——看起来也是怪怪的，甚至让人心理产生不良反应。也有人考证，唐纳秋梅的啤酒蜗牛案以后，除听装啤酒外，但凡玻璃瓶的都一律改用透明的瓶子装啤酒。因为能看见里面的"货色"，消费者指证生产商过失责任的可能就减少了；而一旦出事，生产商能证明自己"合理地注意"的可能性就增大了。

9.6.4 邻居原则

第四，"邻居原则"（The Neighbour Principle）。对于那些在法律意义上和你的距离很近而受你的行为直接影响的人，你在引导自己作为或不作为时，就必须合理地把他们考虑在自己的作为或不作为中。也就是说，在合理的情形下，如果能够预知自己的作为或不作为可能导致"邻居"受损（如养猪专业户在合理的情况下自然可以预见自己养的猪会投放到市场，"不作为"的例子可以是猪得了猪瘟而不采取措施；"作为"的例子可以是在猪的饲料里添加禁用的"瘦肉精"），那么就必须——用现代话说——履行自己的职业道德，尽到自己在法律意义上的勤谨、注意和操心义务，避免因自己做了不该做的事或没有做该做的事而导致法律上的"邻居"受损。

9.7 判决3:2

爱德肯大法官的判决得到另两位大法官的支持，他们在各自的判决中也表达和分析了同样的观点，但遭到剩余两位大法官的强烈反对。反对的理由大致有两个，一是适用面太宽，有可能引起法律层面的无序状态，二是这样的法无疑是社会的倒退，甚至退到了《汉漠拉比法典》时代。但无论如何，以爱德肯为代表的"正方"是三位大法官，而"反方"只有两位，3∶2，唐纳秋梅胜诉，啤酒蜗牛案历时 4 年，一锤定音，成为英美法系一个划时代的判例。

十、"啤酒蜗牛案"的意义

10.1 过失责任原则在两大法系的体现

江平教授在《罗马法基础》一书中说：

罗马私法的原则在逐步摆脱了原始社会的影响之后，于共和国中期确立了过失责任原则。这种过失责任原则既体现着自由资本主义时期简单商品经济关系的要求，也体现着早期资产阶级自然理性的观念，故广为后世资产阶级各国的民法所接受，并成为近、现代民法三大基本原则之一。《法国民法典》第1382 条、《德国民法典》第 823 条、《日本民法典》第 709 条、《瑞士债法》第41 条、《苏俄民法典》第 403 条等等无不如此。即使英美国家，也通过判例法的途径逐步确立了这一原则[1]。

除上述的罗马法系（也称大陆法系、民法法系）国家，江平教授也比照了英美法系国家，认为英美法系通过判例法的途径逐步确立了这一原则。他举的第一个案例是 1850 年美国的"布朗诉肯道尔案"（Brown v. Kendall）[2]，该案首次引入过失责任，并成为其在各州得到承认的标志。第二个案例便是"唐纳秋梅诉斯蒂文森案"，他认为到了 20 世纪，以这个"著名的案例"为标志，过失责任原则最终在英美法中得以确立[3]。

---

〔1〕 江平，米健：《罗马法基础》，中国政法大学出版社 1987 年版，第 294 页。
〔2〕 Brown v. Kendall, 60 Mass, 292（1850）.
〔3〕 江平，米健：《罗马法基础》，中国政法大学出版社 1987 年版，第 295 页。

10.2 美国恶狗案

"布朗诉肯道尔案"因两条恶狗而起。称其为恶狗是因为两条狗互相撕咬，一时间打得昏天黑地。两位狗主人不得不出面拉架。被告用一根棍子来教训自己不听话的狗，没想到失手击中原告的眼睛，"哎哟"一声惨叫，狗的架拉开了，狗主人的架却正式在法庭开打。初审判原告胜诉，法官指示陪审团要解决两个问题：第一，如果制止狗打架必须用棍子抽的话，被告必须证明他行使了"必要的合法行为"，并且小心谨慎地避免误伤；第二，如果用棍子打狗属于一种"可被允许的合法行为"，被告必须证明他的行为不但适当并且"格外小心"以免伤人。

被告提起上诉。上诉法院与初审法院的职能不同，上诉法院要解决的是法律问题。因此摆在上诉法院面前的是两个法律问题：第一，初审法官指示陪审团要分清"必要的合法行为"和"可被允许的合法行为"，并因此而需要证明两个不同的小心程度——需要这么区分吗？怎么才能正确地区分呢？第二，初审法官指示陪审团举证责任在被告，由被告证明他失手（即非故意）打伤原告时，其"小心程度和行使的力度一致"，初审法官这么做对吗？

上诉法院对被告的上诉予以支持将原案发回重审，因为初审法官在引导陪审团时对法律解读有误。

上诉法院就以上两个法律问题作出的结论便成为相关判例：对于失手致伤类的合法行为（注意：如果是故意，那就不是民事诉讼而是刑事公诉了）——无论是必要还是仅仅能被许可——小心程度所必备的标准是一样的，也就是说对这一类失手行为是不用再多此一举分为不同类别的。第二，初审时举证责任在被告，由被告证明他足够小心以免失手；重审时，则将举证责任转移到原告，由原告来证明。（注意：举证责任的转移，无疑代表法律天平的倾斜度明显转移。从初审中可以看到，如果举证责任在被告，被告很难证明自己的行为属于"必要的合法行为并且小心谨慎地避免误伤"）

美国1850年这个案例的重要性，在于对民法意义上的"过失"（fault）概念做了进一步诠释。"无过失"不仅成为民事诉讼的一个抗辩理由，并且举证责任在原告，由原告证明被告行为过失。"无过失"抗辩理由指的是，除非被告被证明行为过失，否则不负法律责任。而证明行为过失，必须考量被告在行使动作时是否在合理情形下行为适当。"合理标准"也在此案中得到明确，从而成为美国早期民法判例中的一个标杆。

"布朗诉肯道尔案"是美国过失责任的一个代表性判例，啤酒蜗牛案比它晚了82年，以爱德肯大法官为主导的多数判决，使英美两国在过失责任法律认定上达成一致。

10.3 别克车轮案

不仅如此，啤酒蜗牛案也在"产品过失责任"上同美国达成了一致[1]。

美国这个案子跟别克汽车（Buick）有关。"麦克弗森诉别克汽车公司案"发生在1916年[2]，原告麦克弗森有一辆1909年款的别克汽车，那时的车轮是木制的，有一个车轮塌了，麦克弗森先生被摔伤了，于是起诉了别克公司。别克公司说汽车是我们制造的，但轮子不是，木车轮是别的公司制造的，别克公司只是拿来组装而已——尽管事后发现木轮制造上确有瑕疵而且稍加检查就能发现毛病。但别克公司否认对该过失负责，因为原告麦克弗森先生是从别的车行买的这辆车，和别克公司并没有构成合同关系（想想啤酒蜗牛案，抗辩理由如出一辙！）。

纽约上诉法院的判决，将过失责任中的合同关系作为要件予以解除。也就是说，如果有过失，并且可预见，责任方必须承担因此而产生的法律责任而不必将合同关系作为前提条件。这在当时也是革命性的。

16年后的啤酒蜗牛案，也使英国和美国在产品过失责任上达成一致，填补了英国法学和法理上的一个空白。

---

〔1〕　Ferrari, Franco, "Donoghue v. Stevenson's 60ᵗʰ Anniversary", *Annual Survey of International & Comparative Law*, Vol. I: Iss. 1, Article 4, 1994.

〔2〕　MacPherson v. Buick Motor Co., 217 N. Y. 382, Ⅲ N. E. 1050 (1916).

十一、唐纳秋梅和她所处的时代

11.1 时过境迁

上诉法院和初审法院的职能是不一样的，上诉法院要解决的是法理问题，英国上议院终审法院解决了这一法律领域的原则问题，因此唐纳秋梅案发回苏格兰高等民事法院重审。

重审的日子定在 1933 年 1 月，这时距离初审已经过了 4 年，距唐纳秋梅喝下那杯恶心的姜啤已经 5 年，许多事已经时过境迁。1932 年 11 月 12 日生产姜啤的厂主斯蒂文森逝世，享年 69 岁。

一年后，斯蒂文森的遗嘱继承人被列为第三方被告，重审没有进行下去，因为双方在 1934 年 12 月庭外和解。最初的诉讼标的是 500 英镑，双方以 200 英镑和解。有趣的是这些细节在几十年后才被披露，可能是当时大家的兴奋点都过了。况且这宗民事案件的意义并不在于谁赢谁输，谁赔给谁多少钱，这宗案子的意义在于当事人不折不扣的"较真儿"，历史应该感谢原告、被告以及他们各自的律师团队、双方的"亲友团"（如为唐纳秋梅做无财产证明的牧师和教会长者）。法律怕就怕"认真"二字，如果任何一方得过且过，那么就不可能在那个时间、那个地点在那个法理命题上追究一个究竟，法制发展就不可能在那个点上得以推进，文明程度也就不会因此而得到提高。许多人会希望踢掉绊脚石的是下一个受害者，而唐纳秋梅却以一个弱女子的身躯促进了一个时代的变革。

11.2 弱女子永不放弃

没理由怀疑唐纳秋梅是个"女强人"，当时喝姜啤喝出老鼠、蜗牛、蟑螂的情形并不鲜见，但只有她坚持了下来，甚至不惜向社会坦白自己的贫穷身份。她终于在 1945 年 2 月和已经分居 17 年的丈夫离婚，她依然是个小店员。1958 年 3 月 19 日，年仅 59 岁的唐纳秋梅因心脏病逝世，她的死亡证书上用的是本姓"麦克阿力斯特"（McAllister），而真正在法律史上永垂不朽的则是她婚后随夫姓的全名：梅·唐纳秋（May Donoghue）。

斯蒂文森的遗孀和儿子继承了他的产业，1950 年 7 月 1 日成为一个有限责任公司，又于 1956 年卖掉了股份。想必是那座城市那个时节也忙着地产开发和城建，因为在 20 世纪 60 年代初期，整个厂区都被推倒，事后并未见工厂搬迁和重建的报道。关于这个公司、这个商号，关注的人和可查考的资料也随着时间的推移而变得越来越少。

敏捷郎也不干咖啡店营生了，咖啡店是 1931 年关的，敏捷郎于 1970 年 3 月 20 日去逝。

当年的咖啡店〔1〕

而和唐纳秋梅一样名垂青史的名律师立志哥，他的儿子继承了父业，也成为苏格兰的一位大律师。唐纳秋梅与斯蒂文森庭外和解的细节，就是他在近些年的国际学术交流中透露出来的。某种程度上替历史解开好多谜团，因为案件发回苏格兰重审，重审后原、被告对基本证词和证物的认定等等，不同文献存在诸多出入，甚至一度还有人怀疑有没有那只死蜗牛，说这故事原本就是一则杜撰的事。好在我们可以不必为这些多思，因为没有必要。

---

〔1〕 Source：The Paisley Museum－http://www.scottishlawreports. org. uk/resources/dvs/mrs－donoghue－journey. html.

十二、后“啤酒蜗牛案”时代

12.1 现代民法判例“三部曲”

爱德肯大法官在“啤酒蜗牛案”中确定的过失责任原则，落实在实际案件中，变成了可以复制和具体操作的“测试标准”。值得注意的是，80多年以来英国上议院这宗判例所确定的原则，从未被随后的上议院（现改为英国最高法院）判例动摇过。当然，有很长一段时间业内担心“邻居”概念过宽，会引起诉讼中的滥用和混乱，但从随后的典型案例来看，不同的案情也在不同的程度上对标准的应用尺度进行调整，而这正是判例法的精妙之所在。许多不明朗的法律问题，都在不同时间和社会背景下得到认真分析和考量。公认的、经得起时间考验的判例就延续下来，经不起时间考验的判例在随后的判例中得到修补、完善或被全盘推翻。

在英美法系——和大多数法系一样——订立一部成文法耗时耗力耗程序，而判例法却在“法官造法”的有时近似于学术推演的传统和实践中，发现社会问题并通过调控（如政策导向）和司法干预使之得到解决。社会是纷繁复杂的，立法总归赶不上犯法，永远是滞后的。

从19世纪中叶开始收集、出版的各国判例不但在整个英美法系扩展了法律基本原则的统一性，也起到及时应对社会新现象、新问题的作用。

12.2 孕妇死婴案

“啤酒蜗牛案”之后比较值得注意的案例首推1943年的“孕妇死婴案”[1]。案情好比一个电影场景。孕妇B女士下了有轨电车，风驰电掣的Y先生驾驶摩托车从其身边经过，一声巨响，摩托车和一辆汽车相撞，Y先生当场死亡，而当B女士走过时，尸体已经被移走但地下留下一滩鲜血，惨状可想而知。B女士受到惊吓随后产下一个死婴，于是告了Y先生的遗嘱继承人，她认为她和死

---

〔1〕 Bourhill v. Young〔1943〕AC92.

者构成法律上的"邻居关系"。但法院驳回了她的起诉，因为原、被告在事故发生时并未构成任何法律上的关系，也就谈不上谁该为谁负责。

12.3 少年犯和第三方责任

1970 年的有关英国内政部[1]和少管所的案子[2]涉及被告内政部要不要为第三方（少年犯）行为负责的问题。

少管所（属内政部编制）监督一群少年犯在一个岛上劳动。一天夜里，少管所的官员们忙了一天也累了便娱乐一晚，于是这帮少年犯中的 7 人趁此机会偷了一艘船逃跑，结果撞上一艘豪华游艇，游艇主人遂起诉内政部失职，因为少管所官员未尽职守。初审原告胜诉。但被告内政部提起上诉，申请法院将诉讼驳回，因为原告所告的是不良少年犯们的"独立行为"。

在上诉法院内政部继续败诉。上诉法院法官以 4∶1 判决内政部监管不当、疏于职守，内政部（少管所）必须为第三方（少年犯）的行为负责。理由是内政部因其监管责任而形成与当事人之间的法律关系；同理，因其职业性法律关系而产生监管责任。

原告胜诉的原因，是因为内政部（少管所由内政部领导）处在一个监督第三方的位置，因此构成必须对其负责的法律关系。对少年犯监督不当会酿成祸害，这一点是可以预见的。上议院大法官在本案中还否定了一件纽约相似案件的判例，该判例对逃犯行为赋予监狱看守人员豁免权。而因英国上议院这宗判例，可以说类似的豁免权在英美法系从此就被推翻了。

12.4 小偷撞死人，公交车不负法律责任

同样涉及第三方行为，1993 年的"伦敦郊区公交公司案"[3]就得到完全不同的结果。公交车司机倒班，上一班的司机将一辆"迷你巴"停在公路旁的一个停靠点，车门没有锁，车钥匙挂在引擎点火器上专等接班的司机。上一位

---

[1]　"Home Office"，习惯被称为"内政部"，是英国政府处理内部事务，包括警察和监狱等事务的政府机构。除此之外，内政部主要负责移民、边境和"军情五处"事务。

[2]　Home Office v. Dorset Yacht Co Ltd［1970］AC1004；［1970］2All ER 294.

[3]　Topp v. London Country Bus［1993］，WLR 976 CA.

司机离开下一位司机在规定的时间没有来。上班的没来但小偷却来了，不幸的是小偷开车撞上了一位骑车的女士，女士被撞死，其丈夫告到法院。法院判决公交公司对第三方行为没有法律上的责任。公交车被小偷偷走并撞死一位骑单车的女士，在法律意义上没有可预见性。

请注意，这里讨论的是本案的民事部分，至于小偷的法律责任不在本书的讨论范围。读者不要误解，公交公司作为第三方在本案中不用承担法律责任，并不代表小偷也不用承担法律责任。

12.5 广告公司被客户"蒙"，客户银行不负责

以上案例大多涉及人命，"黑得利广告代理诉银行案"〔1〕则是纯粹经济损失。原告黑得利是一家广告代理公司，开始对其一个客户的财政状况起了担忧，万一付不起广告费，黑得利得承担经济损失。慎重起见，黑得利找到客户的银行（即被告），打听它的财政状况如何、现金流如何等问题。被告银行向原告提供了报告，说这家公司名声不错、履约有望、经营无误等等，并在报告的首页上附上一行话："供您私用，本银行及其职员不因此负责。"黑得利因此打消了疑团，但很快这家客户就倒闭了，欠了他 17 000 多英镑（这在 1963 年算是一笔不小的数目了）。黑得利遂起诉了这家银行，因为其提供误导性报告而直接导致原告经济损失。

法院要解决的问题是，如果一个人依赖一个"无辜却误导"（甚至是有过失责任之嫌）的信息（银行报告）而致经济损失，他能不能以及在何种情形下可以追究对方责任并要求赔偿损失？这里用"无辜"这个字眼，意思是这份报告是你原告主动要的，不是被告要故意"蒙"你的。

上议院大法官的判决很明确：依本案案情，被告没有过失责任，因为，第一，被告是因为客气才给你一个回复；第二，在回复时双方彼此都很清楚：我给你一份小报告但"仅供参考"，报告说的很清楚，这是给你私下看的，本银行概不负责，云云。因此，被告的"免责声明"起到免责作用。大法官还细心地给大家支招儿：以后遇到这种"请你帮帮忙"的事，别太顾及面子了，可以

---

〔1〕 Hedley Byrne v. Heller & Partner Ltd〔1964〕AC465；〔1963〕2 All ER 575.

有三个选择：不理；理；理但附一个免责声明。

但是上议院在本案中无疑开了一个口子：如果原、被告双方之间形成了一个"特殊关系"，一方向另一方寻求专门意见，另一方答应给专门意见，双方都知道索求方会依赖这个专门意见——那么在这个前提下原告因依赖这个意见而致经济损失，被告必须承担过失责任的可能性就很大了。

"啤酒蜗牛案""黑得利广告代理诉银行案"和"内政部少管所案"并称现代民法过失责任判例三部曲。

12.6 屋主诉市政府案

而 1978 年的"屋主诉市政府案"[1] 则将这三部曲的法律立场做了一个新的推演。Anns 等人在伦敦拥有一幢房产，但存在结构性问题，起因是地基不牢，没有依规章建造，显然市政府质检部门有失察之责[2]。上议院大法官认为，啤酒蜗牛案三部曲事实上确定了在"合理预见"前提下的归责原则，是否归责取决于有没有"公众政策"考量因素，也就是说如果没有这样的公众政策等因素来否定这样的归责原则，那么被告方必须负责。这就是由本案设立的著名的"两段测试"，显然这位大法官将当事人之间法律上的"距离"以及危害和损失的"合理预见"等同划之。

屋主 Anns 等人起诉市政府部门，因其质检疏忽，导致屋主们花费很大的代价和精力对房屋进行维修。建筑质量问题也严重影响了住户的身体健康，而这方面的法律就是用来保护公众健康的。也就是说并没有"公众政策因素"来否定和阻止这样的归责原则[3]，市政部门必须对自己的失察负法律责任。

这个判例引起很大争议，它设立的"两段测试"标准过宽。12 年后，上议

---

〔1〕 Anns v. Merton London Borough Council〔1978〕AC 728；〔1977〕2 All ER492.

〔2〕 在英国、澳大利亚、新西兰等国，地方政府的职能包括对民宅进行质量监督。建筑过程中市政府有关部门分阶段检查并在完工后签验房证。

〔3〕 可以借助其他一些案例，来理解为什么需要有"公众政策"考量因素。例如能容纳 1 万人的足球场却涌进来 1.5 万人，显然管理部门失职，结果一个看台塌了，压死了人，死者家属寻求赔偿，胜诉。同时现场有人亲眼目睹这血淋淋的一幕，精神大受刺激，诉诸法庭，也获得赔偿。既然现场目击者精神受到损伤，可获得赔偿，那么看电视现场转播的呢？听收音机现场解说的呢？等等。法院受理此类案件时，自然要考虑到案件的涉及面及对社会实际和潜在的影响——这些都是"公众政策"考量因素。

院推翻了这个判例，把归责原则的适用又带回到渐进方式。而这个判例就是1990 年的 Caparo 案[1]，我们不妨根据案情称其为"大股东诉会计师案"。

12.7 大股东诉会计师案

甲方看好一家制造电器的上市公司。该电器公司在 1984 年 3 月向股东发出预警，说市场不好股值可能减半，5 月公司的执行董事在财政年度报告中公布了初步数据，证实了公司的状况，股票继续下跌。甲方有意抄底，目的是全盘接管。到了 6 月，公司向股东公布了年度财政报表。那时甲方已经持股 29.9%，看到财务报告后依当地上市公司的相关规定向其他股东出价收购了剩下的股份，最终控股。控股后发现公司的实际状况比了解到的要糟得多。甲于是起诉那位负责财务报表的会计师，认为会计师失职，向其提供了一份"怠忽性报表"，甲方索赔公司目前的市价与依财务报表公司显示所值之间的差价。甲方的理由是他是依据这份财务报表来进行的大规模收购，报告显示公司有大量财政盈余，而实际上恰恰相反公司存在巨额亏损。

法院要解决的问题是，依甲方所描述的情形，被告（会计师）对甲方有没有法律上的"谨慎责任"。确定了这个责任，才能判定违背这个责任而造成的财产损失要不要赔偿。

一审说没有责任。二审说有责任，理由是如果甲方是单纯的外来投资者便没有责任，但当时甲方是以小股东身份出现，而作为股东他有权利依赖公司提供的财务报表并相信财务报表的准确性。但这个观点被上议院驳回。

上议院判定没有责任，理由如下：

第一，原告（甲方）无论是作为现任股东还是潜在的投资方，出具财务报表的那一方对他都不构成法律上的责任。"怠忽性报表"成为诉因的前提取决于提供报表的人对原告依赖报表的程度和性质有主观认知，而这种认知是需要双方对彼此有明确意思表示的。公司会计师也好，审计师也罢，在准备和公布这份报表时，无从知道甲方会依据报表所提供的数据来决定收购整个公司（即购买所有剩下的股票）。

---

[1] Caparo Industries plc v. Dickman [1990] 2 AC605；[1990] 1 All ER 568.

第二，针对公司，英国（和其他国家一样）有专门的法律条款要求公司的报表依会计制度制定、审计制度审核，其中心目的是供公司内部管理而不是给外部投资人提供数据分析。

这里，如第一条所列，公司的会计师、审计师并不知道有人要通过收购股票来接管公司。上议院引用新西兰 1978 年的一个判例[1]，案情相仿，新西兰的法官引英国早先的"黑得利广告代理诉银行案"，但强调当事人之间的"特殊关系"：假定一方自愿为另一方提供专业意见，便构成"自愿承担责任"。这种情况下，双方如果都明确无误的认为一方会依赖这个意见作出生意上的判断，由此招致经济损失，提出意见的那方势必要承担法律责任。

有趣的是，新西兰上诉法院这三位大法官当中一位叫库克（Robin Cooke 1926~2006）的大法官，还将民法与合同法上的损失进行了比较。面对经济损失，他认为民法下的法律救助，意在恢复或挽回损失掉的那一部分；而合同法下的法律救助，则在于实现原本想通过履约而达到的目的。

这个判例确定以后，对于这一领域的法律认知，新西兰的法官们（和其他国家的法官们一样）取得了一致。这是上诉法院的判例，在当时上诉法院是新西兰境内的最高法院，因为终审法院是英国枢密院。值得一提的是，库克大法官在新西兰做了二十几年大律师（1964 年成为"御用大律师"Queen's Counsel）、继而做了二十几年大法官之后，又在 1996 年以 75 岁的年纪，成为英国上议院一名大法官。他出生在惠灵顿，他的爵号依他在惠灵顿的出生地，称为"Baron Cooke of Thorndon"（崧盾库克男爵）。"崧盾"的附近就是使馆区（中国驻新西兰大使馆就在这里），再旁边便是维多利亚大学，他在维多利亚大学法学院获得法学位。在全球法学院前 500 强中，维多利亚大学法学院排第 19 位；而前 40 强中，新西兰的法学院占了三位[2]。新西兰法官成为英国上议院坐拥爵位的大

〔1〕 Scott Group Ltd v. McFarlane〔1978〕1 NZLR 553.

〔2〕 见 QS World University Rankings by Subject 2013—Law。其中哈佛、剑桥和牛津分别占前三名。新西兰的维多利亚大学法学院列第 19，奥克兰大学法学院列第 24，南岛的奥塔哥大学法学院列第 32 名。亚洲国家中，东京大学法学院列 37，中国的北京大学法学院 41，清华大学法学院 43，台湾大学法学院 62，韩国首尔大学法学院 67。前 100 强法学院里有新西兰基督城的坎特伯雷大学、汉密尔顿怀卡托大学和美国华盛顿大学、瑞士的苏黎世大学。前 150 强里面有中国的中国政法大学、复旦大学，日本九州大学、西班牙巴塞罗那大学、英国的格拉斯哥大学，爱尔兰的都柏林大学，芬兰的赫尔辛基大学和加拿大的维多利亚大学。需要提醒的是，这一类排名是按照不同标准或具有不同侧重（如论文及学术成果被引

法官，也说明"共同法"体系下，法律无国界，智慧和知识共享的一个现象。

回到本案，上议院在判定被告会计师没有法律责任的同时，也确认上市公司的会计师、审计师在"某种情形下"必须对股东负责以维护公司的正常管理，但就股东而言，其利益的保护在于公司本身，股东以自身的权利（即因股东身份产生的权利）告公司的会计师、审计师，这种情形尚属罕见。

"大股东诉会计师案"推翻了"屋主诉市政府案"中将"距离"与"可预见性"等同视之的先例。但凡经济类案件，"大股东诉会计师案"确定的原则为后来的法院所广泛引用。上议院为这个原则确立了三个测试准则（即"Caparo three-stage test"）：（1）对原告造成的经济损失可否合理预见？（2）因当事人之间法律上的距离是否产生法律上的关系？（3）让被告承担法律责任是否公平、正义、合理并且符合公众政策原则？

这三个测试标准前两个直接来自于"啤酒蜗牛案"中的"邻居原则"，后者则从"屋主诉市政府案"中引申——尽管那个案例作为判例被推翻，但去伪存真，正确的地方还是要保留和吸收。这也是判例法的一个妙处：不仅整块的肉可以令人大快朵颐，即使"下水""边角料"也都有价值。"大股东诉会计师案"中的三段测试，就是从二审结论中得来的，尽管二审的判决被三审否定但它的逻辑推断是有价值的。二审判例以及"屋主诉市政府案"，都被收集在"判例汇编"中，供律师和法官引用、学者研究、法学院学生学习。因为断案不仅在于结论，更重要的是形成结论的理由和推理方法。记得笔者在奥克兰大学法学院学习时，老师们反复强调："因此被告有罪"不会得分，"因此被告有罪是因为以下理由"才能得分。

"大股东诉会计师案"中确定的三个测试标准从 1990 年至今，成为这类案件审判的公认准则。二十多年来，诸多大小案件均依照这个判例确定的原则断案。最近也是最有轰动效应的当属英国 2011 年的"夜总会持刀伤人案"[1]，肇事者被判无期徒刑——这是刑事部分，不在本案讨论之列。本案涉及的是民事

（接上页）用的次数就是标准之一）。这些标准多以英语国家和地区的体例和习惯来制定，对非英语国家的法学院显然有"不公平"因素。因此这种评级，从某种角度看，并不能代表一个法学院的综合实力，尤其是将法系和各国法律实践的差别作为考量因素。

〔1〕 Everett and another v. Comojo (UK) Limited (t/a the Metropolitan) and others [2011] EWCA Civ 13.

部分，受害方诉夜总会失职，必须对第三方（肇事者）的行为负责。

12.8 夜总会持刀伤人案

原告（受害方）两人去伦敦一个高档夜总会，与人发生争执，结果遭第三方（肇事者）刀砍。事发前女招待发现情形不妙，便向经理报告。原告认为女招待应立即向门口负责安保的人报告，这样保安可以冲进来避免这场血淋淋的事故。

法院要解决的是两个法律问题：第一，夜总会是否要为第三方的行为负责？第二，如果夜总会法律上必须为第三方的行为负责，在本案中夜总会是否有违自己的法律责任？

一审原告败诉。后原告提起上诉，上诉法院作出以下判决：

第一，这家夜总会对场地和过往客人行使管理权，况且这是一家"会员方可入内"的夜总会，门口有保安检查会员身份。管理方和消费方（客人）之间的法律关系足以构成法律上的责任。客人有权期待夜总会提供一个安全的消费场所。夜总会为管理而做的"危险因素分析"也确认，因酒精饮料消费有可能导致失控和暴力行为。因此，不能说发生一个客人滋扰另一个客人的概率低而可以忽略。

第二，赋予管理层民法上的责任是公平合理的。况且议会 1957 年通过的居者责任法（Occupiers' Liability Act 1957）已经明确界定了夜总会作为"居者"和客人之间的法律关系。[1] 英国这部 1957 年的立法，将民法领域这一类成文法和判例，汇编成一部通过议会订立的单一法律，确定"居者"（通过所有权或租赁权）因其不动产（建筑物、房屋）而对来访者应尽的责任。这些责任是多方面的，如建筑物建筑本身的瑕疵或内部陈设或其他状况引起的危险因素。"居者"包括承租人，但如果租约条款规定房东负责公共区域如楼梯的维护，则房东和承租人共同承担"居者"法律上的责任。"内部陈设"引起的责任，比较典型的例子是客人在地毯上被绊倒以至摔伤等等。回到本案，如果管理方或"居者"（夜总会）在法律上可以因客人在地毯上被绊倒摔伤胳膊而承担责任，

---

〔1〕 英美法系为"判例法"或"普通法"系，并不代表就没有成文法。相反，民法、刑法、商法、合同法等各领域法典性质的法律法规十分周详。

却不用为客人被刀砍伤而承担责任——而这种事故是可以预见的—— 这显然是不合理的。

第三，尽管以上两点均成立，对"责任范围"的确立却必须是公平合理的。本案中女招待虽然判断情况不妙，有可能发生暴力事件，但她却不可能判断暴力事件发生的精确时间。她选择向值班经理报告而不是原告所说的向保安报告，并不因此招致夜总会承担法律责任。

法院判定夜总会管理方对第三方的行为应负法律责任，但因上述具体情形，夜总会并没有违背这一法律责任。上诉法院驳回上诉，维持原判。

12.9 三段测试

这宗案件虽然原告没有胜诉，但也引起不小的波澜。在法律上，英国上诉法院 2011 年判定的本案，再次确定了 1990 年"大股东诉会计师案"中所确定的判例，并且严格遵循了"大股东诉会计师案"中的三段测试。经"夜总会持刀伤人案"后，这个三段测试更加得到证明与完善。

第一，距离产生关系。这家夜总会是一间高档会所，正可谓夜夜笙歌，名流出入。管理方对夜总会行使控制权，只有会员才能进入。会员（客人）对夜总会的管理有合理期待并依赖夜总会提供一个安全甚至是隐密的社交场所。况且夜总会（如吧台）和客人因消费而进一步产生经济上的法律关系。因此其法律上的"距离"和"关系"使得双方产生法律上的"谨慎责任"，夜总会必须对会员（客人）负责。

第二，事故可预见。尽管对这种高档会所式的夜总会而言，暴力事件尚属罕见，但消费酒精饮料后"喝高了"寻衅，这是可以预见的。会员制夜总会与向社会开放的夜总会相比，这种事情发生的比例相对较低，因此，危险与防范之间的度需要合理把握。

第三，公平合理原则。无论成文法还是判例都确认了夜总会的法律责任。但通过责任范围和行使的度来确定责任的程度——而这必须体现公平及合理原则。[1]

这一判例确定了夜总会在法律上必须为第三方的行为负责。而判例中对

---

[1] 参见 Sole, Emma: "Liability for the Criminal Actions of Third Parties", Farrar's Building.

"度"的解读，无疑使 2011 年后英国——乃至整个英美法系国家和地区——从事夜总会行业的相关公司和机构，对自身的营业性质和安保措施进行调整，从而达到"度"在法律上的要求。"度"体现得越靠近这一判例所确定的原则，尔后遇到相似事故时面临的法律责任就越小。

12.10 涟漪效应

这样的判例，往往在社会层面会产生"涟漪效应"。经常见到那些地板由大理石铺就的大厅，会醒目的摆放一个牌子标有"滑，谨防摔倒"等类似字样。香烟盒上不但印着那些恐怖、令人心理产生不良反应的人体器官癌变图片，更有"吸烟致癌""请勿吸烟"等字样。这些不是商家好事，而是各类不同法律规定和判例所引发的连带效果。

也有人认为，"啤酒蜗牛案"直接导致了几乎所有装啤酒的玻璃瓶子都改为透明的[1]，但"啤酒蜗牛案"引发的不仅是自上世纪 30 年代以来行业习惯的改变，它的意义更在于为处理道德和法律问题提供了在法理层面上的全新视角。这也是为什么"啤酒蜗牛案"在法学界成了一个真正永垂不朽的案例，因为它不仅解决了当时围绕食品质量而引发的民法领域的困惑，更重要的是英国上议院通过爱德肯等大法官们的判例，使后人知道了"恕道"竟成为"邻居概念"和"归责原则"的一个逻辑起点。

无论成文法还是不成文法，法律条款和各类判例皆浩如烟海。但追求社会的正义、公平、秩序，唤醒世人的良知、诚信和真爱，这一点是亘古不变的。苏格兰培斯利这个小镇，也没有想到一个小小的死蜗牛，居然酿出了这么多的故事，产生了如此大的效应。

十三、培斯利朝圣——法的精神在人心中

培斯利在律师、法官和法学院学生的心目中有一个特殊的位置。在这里业

---

[1] 近些年因保鲜、储藏和环保（减少因运输而产生的碳排放原因），有一种呼声是多用听装啤酒。见 Olmsted, Larry："Craft Beers Say Hello Cans, Goodbye Bottles: An Aluminium Revolution", www.forbes.com。

界会定期甚至每年都举行世界范围的不同形式的研讨会和纪念活动。1990 年以加拿大律师协会为主导的"朝圣",是迄今最具规模的一次。加拿大律师协会在这之前就举办了各种形式的研讨会和模拟法庭。1990 年 9 月各路人马汇合,齐聚苏格兰的培斯利,和其他国家的同行一起举行纪念活动,仅来自加拿大的就有 200 多名法官、律师和学者,为纪念这次"朝圣",还专门出版了"培斯利论文集"〔1〕。御用大律师泰勒(Martin R Taylor QC)在研讨会演讲了主题论文"唐纳秋梅诉斯蒂文森案与现代过失责任法"〔2〕。

2012 年当地政府在当年那家咖啡店的原址,竖起这样一个纪念碑,标题是"啤酒蜗牛案",正文是案件的简要说明,中间的那段文字是这样的:这就是咖啡店的旧址,因为在这里发生的一个小小事件却成为一个标志性判例的基础。至今,这宗案件仍全球闻名。原先的纪念碑稍小,这是 1990 年"朝圣"期间在现代民法研讨会上落成揭幕的。2012 年"啤酒蜗牛案"80 周年纪念时,在原址上换上了一个较大的纪念碑。

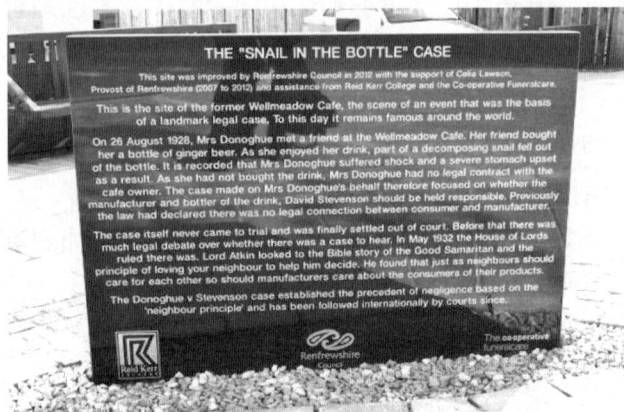

当地政府在咖啡店原址竖起的纪念碑〔3〕

---

〔1〕 见 Sandy Wylie QC 2004 写的序文:"An Introduction to 'Mrs Donoghue's Journey'""《唐纳秋梅的旅程》序"。

〔2〕 见 Martin R Taylor QC:"Donoghue v. Stevenson and the Modern Law of Negligence" 以及 "The Paisley Papers——The Proceedings of the Paisley Conference on the Law of Negligence"。

〔3〕 Source:The Paisley Museum:http://paisleyonline. co. uk/html/paisley_ snail. html.

BBC（英国广播公司）在报道中用了这样一个标题："改变世界的那只蜗牛"[1]。培斯利当地的历史学家埃伦·法魔（Ellen Farmer）接受采访时说，唐纳秋梅因喝姜啤喝出来蜗牛而将饮料厂商告上了法庭，在这之前没有什么法律可以保护消费者。消费者的权益无论怎样被损伤，真能诉诸法律获得保护的几乎没有可能。而这个判例之后，对于饮料厂这样的制造商而言，让他们在法律上负他们应尽的责任，从此有了法律依据，消费者有法可依了。"当年的那间咖啡店已在 60 年代被拆除，但它和由它引起的法律案件，它的遗产在法律史上将被永远载入史册。"[2]

十四、"啤酒蜗牛案"的背后和未来

"人事有代谢，往来成古今"。[3]代谢之后，沉淀了什么？我们至少认识了苏格兰上世纪 30 年代的一个普通得不能再普通的小职员唐纳秋梅。不寻常的是，和她同一时期喝姜啤喝出死老鼠的人都忍下来了，但她喝出死蜗牛后没有忍。从一审、二审到英国上议院终审，这三审审出了英美法系民法过失责任的一个全新判例。在她之前没有这样的保护消费者权益的法律，即使有，也绕不开"合同关系"的基本前提。在她之后，便有了一个明确的、全新的法，并且被许多其他新奇古怪的案件所引用。

14.1 大法官爱德肯男爵

还有一个人我们不会忘记的就是爱德肯大法官（James Richard Atkin，Baron Atkin）。

他是威尔士人，父母早年移民澳大利亚"圈地养羊"。一年多的时间父亲从马上摔下受了重伤，从此弃羊从政。爱德肯出生于布里斯班，4 岁多一点又随母亲回到英国（父亲不久在澳洲去世）。他受祖母"平等主义"的影响很大，

---

〔1〕 见 "The Slug that Changed the World" by Stephanie Todd，BBC News Online Scotland.
〔2〕 见 "The Slug that Changed the World" by Stephanie Todd，BBC News Online Scotland.
〔3〕 见孟浩然（689-740）"与诸子登岘山"，《唐诗鉴赏大全集》编委会：《唐诗鉴赏大全集》，中国华侨出版社 2010 年版，第 47~48 页。

从小就受不了伪善和社会的不公正。爱德肯在牛津大学接受高等教育，24 岁时开始从事律师工作，1913 年 46 岁时成为一名法官。

大法官爱德肯男爵（1867. 11. 28–1944. 6. 25）[1]

为他写传记的作家杰弗里·路易思在书中披露了其许多鲜为人知的一些生活细节[2]，如爱德肯大法官上班总是坐公交车，有一次赶车还从行进中的车上掉下来——那时他已经是赫赫有名的上诉法院的大法官了。他爱读侦探小说，喜欢骑自行车而且蹬得飞快。但和"啤酒蜗牛案"相关的一个爱好恐怕是他每天都要习惯性地读几段《圣经》。

14.2 邻居

他创立的归责原则中的"邻居"概念，很有可能直接取材于《新约全书》中路加福音第 10 章第 25～28 节"善心的撒玛利亚人"[3]。

有一次，一个律法师问耶稣如何才能永生。"摩西的律法怎么说，你又怎么解释呢？"耶稣反问。律法师答道："要尽心、尽性、尽力、尽意去爱主你的上帝，又要爱邻居如同自己。"耶稣说："你答得对，照着去做就永生了。"那位律

---

〔1〕 Source：http://en.wikipedia.org.

〔2〕 Lewis, G (1983). Lord Atkin. London：Butterworths.

〔3〕 "Luke 10, The Parable of the Good Samaritan". Holy Bible. 中国基督协会（2000），第 126 页。

法师又追问："那么，谁是我的邻居呢？"

耶稣举了个例子：有一个人从耶路撒冷到耶利哥城去，途中遇劫，被抢一空还被打得半死，丢在路边。一个祭司路过，看见他就绕道而走；有一个利未人路过，也绕道而走。只有一个撒玛利亚人看见他，动了慈心，替他包扎伤口并护送到客店照应，临走还拿出来银子交给店家，说："你且照应他，如果不够我回来必还你。"耶稣问："这三个人当中，谁是遇劫者的邻居呢？""那个同情他的撒玛利亚人。"耶稣说："对了，你照样去做吧。"[1]

14.3 一生三大判例

爱德肯大法官一生中有三个判例在法律界极具影响力。"啤酒蜗牛案"在英美法系被广为引用——尽管美国的情形和民法的发展有很大不同。另外两个判例，一个成为合同法的经典判例[2]，另一个是"二战"期间一个轰动一时的判例，所不同的是，他在这个判例中代表异议（少数派）观点。这个 1942 年的案子，涉及战争状态下政府有没有权力，将涉嫌危及"国家安全"的人士在未经审判的情况下逮捕拘禁。多数派观点认为有，并表示如果国会立法时语焉不详，可以在庭审时通过司法干预，将国会的立法原意体现在判例上。而爱德肯大法官在"反方意见"中强调，无论出于何种状态，立法、司法、行政三权分立是立国基础。他说：

> 身处战乱中的英国，法律并不沉默。法律或许被更改，但无论是战争还是和平，法律都用同样的语言说话。[3]

这样的措辞，在硝烟弥漫的当时自然让许多人难以接受。负责审判的子爵大人还亲自给爱德肯写了一封信，让他对文字加以修改。他回答了一个字："不。"

直到 1980 年，英国的法官们表示，当时代表多数意见的上议院大法官们有

---

〔1〕 "Luke 10, The Parable of the Good Samaritan". Holy Bible. 中国基督协会（2000），第 127 页。

〔2〕 见 Bell v. Lever Brothers Ltd〔1931〕UKHL 2.

〔3〕 原文是这样的："In England, amidst the clash of arms, the laws are not silent. They may be changed, but they speak the same language in war as in peace." Liversidge v. Anderson〔1942〕AC 206.

可能受情势所迫。现在看来，"他们是在一个完全可以理解的情形下错判了，而爱德肯一个人的意见却是正确的"。[1]

十五、结论

英国上议院在"啤酒蜗牛案"中确定的判例，将"过失责任原则"引入民法体系，也意味着以"啤酒蜗牛案"（唐纳秋梅诉斯蒂文森）与"美国恶狗案"（布朗诉肯道尔）为标志，"过失责任原则"最终在英美法系得以确立。

案发时，1928年代的苏格兰、英格兰和其他"普通法系"的国家和地区，喝饮料喝出死老鼠、死蟑螂、死蜗牛并不鲜见，但诉讼的结果很少能判被告（生产厂商）应负法律责任，因为那时这类案件的诉讼基础是原、被告之间必须具备合同关系。本案原告唐纳秋梅是闺蜜请客，喝了那瓶倒出死蜗牛的生姜啤酒，她和生产厂商斯蒂文森之间没有合同关系，因此在苏格兰高等民事法院的初审和二审，均判她败诉。

从民法角度看，此案之前涉及民事侵权行为领域的法律（tort）大体有两个方面：（1）对原告身体直接或间接造成伤害。直接造成伤害叫"trespass to the person"，分三类，第一类（assault）和第二类（battery）都可以译成"攻击""殴打""施暴"。区别是，构成第一类伤害需要和肢体直接接触，构成第二类伤害不需要身体直接接触。第三类则指"非法监禁"（false imprisonment）。（2）任何除（1）之外可以诉诸法律的行为（trespass on the case）。这是一个防止遗漏的保底式法律定义。总之，从一瓶姜啤里面喝出死蜗牛等这类恶心的东西，并不能在以上两个民法概念中构成民事侵权。因此，唐纳秋梅并不能依据当时的法律伸张权利、寻求赔偿，因为无法可依。

而终审法院英国上议院另辟蹊径，基于恕道和《圣经》中的"邻居"概念创立一个新的法律原则。这一原则不但确定了法律上的"邻居"定义，也推导出一系列全新的过失责任原则，如法律上的"距离"产生法律上的责任，生产厂商本身的责任以及由包装形态带来的责任，合同关系不必成为要件，等等。

---

[1] 见 I. R. C v. Rossminster Ltd and others［1980］AC 952.

从此，判断当事人之间是否存在这种法律关系就有了直观的、举一反三功效的逻辑起点：原、被告之间有没有法律上的"谨慎责任"关系？

被告在应注意、能注意而未注意的情形下是否尽到应尽的责任？未能尽责是否导致对原告的损害？从"啤酒蜗牛案"之后的案例当中就可以看到这一判例所起到的作用。也比较容易理解为什么 1943 年的"孕妇死婴案"中，原告和已经死于车祸的被告之间并没有法律上的"邻居"关系。而 1990 年的"大股东诉会计师案"中，尽管会计师提供的报表有误但最终被判定不用承担法律责任，因为他和原告之间并没有产生特殊的职业关系。针对上市公司有专门的法律和规章要求公司的报表依会计制度制表、审计制度审核，其中心目的是供公司内部管理而不是给外部投资人（尽管本案中的投资人是股东之一）提供数据分析以抄底控股。最近也是最有轰动效应的是 2011 年英国"夜总会持刀伤人案"，更是将"大股东案"中确定的三段测试进一步完善。

正如"啤酒蜗牛案"，直接或间接导致了饮料玻璃瓶的"透明化"，"夜总会"和诸多同类性质的判例，则导致了在公共地带清洁地面时，我们常常会见到"滑，谨防摔倒"的牌子以及香烟盒上印着令人心理产生不良反应的人体器官癌变图片以及"吸烟致癌"等字样。这些固然是规避风险的小举措，但也看得出法律的效果和威严。

唐纳秋梅诉斯蒂文森这宗"啤酒蜗牛案"，之所以成为影响西方世界的十大名案之首，除了它在英美法系民法领域中引入了一个全新的过失责任外——而这个归责原则，在随后几十年合同法、金融法、公司法以及其他领域起着指导作用——同时，它引领的"邻居原则"，也成为"恕道"演变成法律原则的一个思辨模式。就法院、法官而言，最难的可能不是各种千奇百怪的案件，而是在没有成文法和判例的指导下从何下手，或是面对形形色色的社会如何在法律和道德上把握好尺度。

无论是何种体系，社会问题和犯罪现象多半出现在法律规范之前。这也使得如何判断犯罪行为构成要件、如何量刑变得尤为困难。"啤酒蜗牛案"能够让方方面面都平静下来，因为我们从中看到，建立一个法律原则不是那么容易的，所以别着急，慢慢来。

案例二　美国雅虎案

——美国雅虎在法国被告

LICRA v. Yahoo!

法国部分

案　名： 法国反种族歧视联盟和犹太学联诉美国雅虎公司 Ligue contre le racisme et l'antisémitisme et Union des étudiants juifs de France c. Yahoo! Inc. et Société Yahoo! France（LICRA v. Yahoo!）

时　间： 2000 年 5 月

地　点： 巴黎民事高等法院（Tribunal de grande instance）

美国部分

案　名： 美国雅虎公司诉法国反种族歧视联盟和犹太学联 Yahoo! Inc. v. La Ligue Contre Le Racisme et l'antisémitisme（Yahoo! v. LICRA 433 F 3d 1199（9th Cir 2006））

时　间： 2001~2006 年

地　点： 加利福尼亚州地方法院（初审）；美国联邦第九上诉法院（二审、终审）

本案案情及确立的判例原则

2000 年初，雅虎"拍卖网站"提供平台，拍卖德国"二战"期间纳粹宣传品、纪念品和收藏品。此举在法国引起轩然大波，法国两家民间组织将雅虎（公司法人）告上法庭，另一民间组织则将雅虎首席行政总裁（自然人）告上法庭。巴黎高等法院依《法国民事诉讼法典》行使司法管辖权，并于 2000 年 5 月、8 月和 11 月三次颁布法庭判决，勒令雅虎通过技术手段过滤 IP 地址，使法国境内用户不能登录有关拍卖网站；并勒令雅虎删除相关照片、数据和调整美国境内的服务器。如果不能在规定期间完成，则每天判罚 10 万法郎并逐日累计。

雅虎于 2000 年 12 月 21 日向加利福尼亚州北区联邦地方法院递交诉状，请求法院宣告法国巴黎法院判决书在美国无效。在美国变成被告的这两家民间组织则请求加利福尼亚州地方法院撤销雅虎诉状，因为加州法院不具备司法管辖权。雅虎随即抗辩，认为法国判决违反《美国宪法第一修正案》，而第一修正案赋予的言论和出版自由与法国法院要求调整服务器进行信息和内容审查相冲突。

加利福尼亚州地方法院行使司法管辖权并宣告法国判决在美国无效，不得执行。被告上诉，美国联邦第九巡回上诉法院 3 位法官主审，以 2:1 裁定美国法院在此案中不具备司法管辖权，撤销地方法院原判。雅虎再上诉。第九巡回上诉法院由 11 位法官主审，扑朔迷离的是，11 位法官中 8 位裁定加利福尼亚州地方法院具备司法管辖权，但 8 位当中 3 位认为此案不具备"诉讼成熟"的条件应予驳回，5 位法官认为诉讼成熟。最后表决以 6:5 裁定撤销加利福尼亚州地方法院原判。而雅虎对于伸张第一修正案权利的内国法性质与治外法权性质的辩论，也在法官判决中逐步明朗。

本案确立了以下两个原则：

（1）巴黎法院判定美国雅虎公司因"雅虎拍卖网站"拍卖纳粹物品，其行为——尽管并非出自本意——在法国境内对原告造成了损害。基于"损害地"原则，依《法国新民事诉讼法典》第 48 条确定司法管辖权，巴黎法院裁定雅虎通过过滤 IP 地址等方式使法国境内用户无法登录拍卖网站，雅虎必须采取一切必要措施禁止在其网站上提供能够登录与纳粹物品相关的网页及链接，限期为3个月，否则每天罚款 10 万法郎并每日累计。

（2）美国第九上诉法院综合考量三因素，判定美国法院对此案具备司法管辖权，即法国被告在加利福尼亚州司法管辖区内的直接活动和联系；雅虎作为原告提出诉讼及诉讼之性质；巴黎判决对雅虎造成的影响以及潜在影响。第九上诉法院确定了"诉讼成熟"两大基本原则。就美国宪法第一修正案权利问题的争辩，认为如果巴黎法院对雅虎的要求仅涉及在法国的用户，而这样的要求并不涉及对美国境内用户的上网/登录限制，那么雅虎只是伸张一种治外法权意义上的第一修正案权利。如果巴黎法院对雅虎的要求仅涉及在法国的用户，但其结果却不可避免地限制了美国境内的用户，那么雅虎对于第一修正案权利之伸张辩论就会同时既有内国性质也有治外法权性质。

一、美国的雅虎为何在法国被告?

1.1 Yahoo! 雅虎

雅虎（Yahoo!）是一家美国跨国互联网上市公司，是由杨致远（Jerry Yang）和大卫·费罗（David Filo）于 1995 年 3 月 1 日成立的公司，总部设在美国加利福尼亚州。它提供综合互联网服务，包括门户网站、搜索引擎、雅虎邮箱、雅虎新闻、雅虎财经、雅虎广告、雅虎拍卖及网上地图和视频共享等等，其规模和影响力在世界居显著位置。据媒体报道，每个月大约有 7 亿人访问雅虎网站[1]。雅虎自己也声称，其以 30 多种语言提供的各种服务平台，每个月从全球吸引 5 亿多用户造访。[2]据美国互联网数据分析公司"控思过"（comScore）[3]显示，雅虎在 2013 年 7 月期间美国访客数量达到 1.96 亿人次，这是自 2011 年 5 月第一次超越谷歌网站的访客人数。雅虎的美国访客数量一年内增加了 21%。[4]

1.2 "YaHoo!"名字的由来

雅虎在英文里应写作"Yahoo!"，因为"Yahoo"这个字已经被其他行业的公司注册成商标。"Yahoo"是首字母的缩略词，指"Yet Another Hierarchical Officious Oracle"。拆开这些字，"Hierarchical"指雅虎数据库按不同分支来安排；"Oracle"原意与古希腊神话有关，有"神谕宣示所""智者、哲人"的意思，这

---

[1] Swartz, Jon（November 7, 2011）, "Yahoo's latest moves baffle some" USA Today（Washington DC）.

[2] Yahoo!（2012），这里引用的是其 2012 年数据。

[3] "控"，借用网络新词，如"围脖控""小说控""冰山控"。据互动百科的释义（www. baike. com），"控"取 complex "情结"之引申。但这里"com"应该指通讯，而"score"是"得分、刻痕"的意思。总之，是通过观察流量和其他数据分析来判定互联网的覆盖程度，将其译作"控思过"是借音意结合式翻译，幽默大于实际意义。

[4] "Yahoo Tops Google for US Web Traffic in July, ComScore Says", August 22, 2013.

里主要指"真理与智慧之源";而"Officious"传统上有"过分殷勤、好管闲事、非官方"等意思,这里引申为互联网时代办公室文员网上冲浪,凭借雅虎数据库获取信息。[1]所以,"Yahoo"合起来指的是"又一个另一层级化殷勤之万事通"。但雅虎创始人曾一度坚持,说取这个名字不过是喜欢这个字的原汁原味儿,主要是指大卫·费罗老家路易斯安那州"那些笨笨的带几分粗鲁的南方佬"。[2]

但是,"Yahoo"这个词和英国及爱尔兰作家乔纳森·斯威夫特(Jonathan Swift)[3]的小说《格列佛游记》(Gulliver's Travels)有关。小说共分成四个部分,分别记载了格列佛的四次冒险旅行:小人国游记、大人国游记、诸岛国游记和慧骃国游记。慧骃即"Houyhnhnm",是一种智马。格列佛再次远航时,雇来的水手叛变,将他丢到一个岛上。岛上当家作主的就是智马慧骃。据说"Houyhnhnm"读作"慧—以—能",是模仿智马的发音而来。岛上的另一种动物叫做"犽猢",就是"Yahoo"了,被视作低等畜生,被智马用来拉车、做工甚至宰来当食物吃。这些犽猢是岛上最低劣、粗鲁和野蛮的动物,完全不可驯服和调教,除了有高度智慧的慧骃可以驾驭它们,其他动物对它们都避之唯恐不及。但格列佛发现,这些犽猢就是人类。以至于格列佛辗转回到英国,他已经无法忍受和社会上甚至包括家人在内的"犽猢"们相处,结果他在家里养了两匹马并每天花上几个小时与它们沟通。[4]

"犽猢"在《格列佛游记》中的本意,想必是激发了杨致远和大卫·费罗创新、冒险、率真和叛逆的诸多精神,这也是他们将自己的创业命名为"Yahoo"的原因之一。[5]

---

〔1〕 Gurnitsky, Joanna "What Does 'Yahoo' Stand For? 见 about. com Retrieved via Wikipedia. or. September 14, 2013.

〔2〕 见 wikipedia. org/wiki/Yahoo!。另,美语方言体现在不同地区比较明显,南方地区的方言尤其浓厚并富有特色。

〔3〕 乔纳森·斯威夫特(1667-1745),讽刺文学大师,以《格列佛游记》和《一只桶的故事》等作品闻名于世。《格列佛游记》被改编成多种形式的文艺作品。最新的电影版本是 2010 年制作的,引进了许多"现代成分",如智能手机等。

〔4〕 参见维基百科《格列佛游记》繁体字版,这里采用"慧骃"的音译。最后访问时间:2013 年 9 月 14 日。

〔5〕 Gurnitsky, Joanna;About. com。参见 "The History of Yahoo!"–How It All Started. Filo and Yang insist they selected the name because they liked the general definition of a yahoo:"rude, unsophisticated, uncouth"。见 http://docs. yahoo. com/info/misc/history. html.

格列佛在小人国即"厘厘普"（Lilliput）的见闻也颇有"警世意义"。1699年的厘厘普有两大政党，以鞋跟高低分为低跟党（the Slamecksan Party）和高跟党（the Tramecksan Party）。现任皇帝较倾向于低跟党。而低跟、高跟两党政见如此不同，乃至他们吃不到一起、喝不到一起，真正地老死不相往来。该国原本信仰大蛋端（即鸡蛋较大的那一端），但现任皇帝的曾祖父因皇储敲蛋时不慎受伤，而下令全国改从蛋的小端敲蛋，但此举却使厘厘普人与一海之隔的另一国势如水火。[1] 斯威夫特也是借小说影射当时支持低教会权和高教会权的各派势力以及天主教及英国国教。

1.3 为何在法国被告

回到本案，美国的雅虎在法国被告，是因为"雅虎搜索引擎"和"雅虎拍卖网站"为拍卖德国纳粹纪念品提供了平台。拍品涉及上千件纳粹的军旗、军服、徽章、宣传品、回忆录及当时"纳粹鬼子"对自己歌功颂德的各类纪念品。雅虎（Yahoo!）并没有在"雅虎法国"（Yahoo! France）网站上就拍卖刊登广告，但雅虎法国网站提供了链接，可以直接登录提供拍卖服务的美国 Ya-hoo.com 网站。因此，原告认为总部设在美国的雅虎公司不但触犯了《法国刑事法典》第 R645-1 条，并且伤害了被纳粹法西斯所摧残的所有人的感情。雅虎在法国被告上法庭。

二、法国巴黎的判决

2.1 法国反种族歧视联盟和犹太学联

2000 年 5 月，"反种族歧视及反排斥犹太人联盟"（Ligue Internationale Contre Le Racisme et L'Antisemitisme，"LICRA"，以下简称"反种族歧视联盟"）[2]

---

〔1〕 参见维基百科《格列佛游记》繁体字版。最后访问时间：2013 年 9 月 14 日。

〔2〕 英文全称为：The International League Against Racism and Anti-semitism，成立于 1926 年，致力于反对种族歧视及"hate crime"（"仇恨类罪行"）方面的犯罪，指针对某一特定社会群体（包括种族、宗教、性取向、族群、国籍、年龄，等等）的歧视性犯罪行为。

和"法国犹太学生联合会"（Union des Etudiants Juifs de France，"UEJF"，以下简称"犹太学联"）〔1〕将雅虎公司及雅虎法国公司同时告上法庭。

2.2 法国的法院组织结构

法国的法院组织结构与英美法院系统有很大不同。法国设"特别最高法院""行政法院""冲突法院"。在刑、民两大机构中，刑事方面设最高法院、重罪法庭、上诉法庭、轻罪法庭、警察法庭、儿童管辖法院（如未成年人专门法庭，未成年人重罪法庭）以及专门管辖法院（如国家安全法院、军事法庭和海商法庭）。民事方面设普通法院和专门管辖法院两部分。普通法院有最高法院、上诉法院、民事法院、治安法庭；专门法院有商业法庭、劳资调解委员会、养老金法庭、租金裁判法庭、儿童法庭和监护法庭，等等。〔2〕

2.3 三次庭审

受理雅虎案的是巴黎民事法院，共进行了三次庭审，并于 2000 年 5 月 22 日、8 月 11 日和 11 月 20 日分别作出判决。被告雅虎，即 Yahoo!（"雅虎美国"）和 Yahoo! France（"雅虎法国"），三次均质疑法国法院的司法管辖权，但巴黎法院在第一次判决中驳回被告质疑，因此后两次裁定主要针对判决执行问题。

原告认为，尽管"雅虎法国"并没有在网站上刊登拍卖的广告，也未参与与拍卖相关的任何活动，但是任何身在法国的人都可以通过登录雅虎网站（不管网站分布何处）参与拍卖，而拍卖任何与纳粹相关的收藏品和纪念品，这种行为都是触犯法国刑法的。

被告抗辩，认为原告所声称的违法行为发生在美国，因为雅虎网站的服务器设在美国，所有与拍卖相关的商业行为皆以美国境内的雅虎网站为载体，依据行为发生地原则，法国法院不具备司法管辖权。

---

〔1〕 法国犹太学生联合会成立于 1944 年，以帮助那些在集中营和从大屠杀中幸免于难的年轻犹太人。

〔2〕 参见薛波主编：《法律英汉辞典》，台北五南图书出版股份有限公司 2002 年版，第 996 页。

但巴黎民事法院支持原告的观点，得到的结论是雅虎公司因其拍卖行为——尽管并非出自本意——在法国境内对原告造成了损害。[1]也就是说，法国法院是基于"损害地"原则，确定其司法管辖权，因此依《法国新民事诉讼法典》[2]第48条对本案具备司法管辖权并予以裁定。

2.4 过滤 IP 地址

鉴于原告的意图是阻止拍卖，法院考量的主要是如何通过司法干预实现这一诉求。于是，法院给雅虎两个月的时间完成技术操作，要达到的效果是法国境内的用户无法登录该拍卖网站。但雅虎辩称，认为没有技术手段可以阻止法国境内的用户登录"雅虎法国"之外的雅虎网站。

新西兰法官大卫·哈维（Judge David Harvey）在他关于互联网法律的专著《新西兰互联网法》internet. law. nz 中指出[3]，新西兰主营哈瓦那雪茄的网站（www. havana-house. co. nz）在当时就具备并引用了这项技术，使其网站在符合新西兰法律的基础上继续运行。新西兰国会对《1990年禁烟环境法》[4]进行修订并于2003年12月3日通过新法，对幼儿园、学校（室内及操场）以及对包括购物中心、体育俱乐部、办公大楼等"室内"场所全面禁烟。除此之外，法律规定禁止向未成年人出售香烟并禁止香烟广告。雪茄属于"香烟"的法律界定范围内，自然受到限制。因此，该网站采用对 IP 地址[5]过滤的方法，阻止新西兰境内用户登陆有违法内容的网站，并将他们引导到符合新西兰法律的网站。

鉴于雅虎公司的态度，法国法院于2000年8月要求成立一个技术工作小

---

〔1〕　LICRA & UEIF v. Yahoo! Inc & Yahoo! France Order in Summary Proceedings by the Superior Court of Paris, 22 May 2000。

〔2〕　The New Code of Civil Procedure。

〔3〕　哈维法官是笔者在奥克兰大学法学院读书时期教授互联网法的老师。为了不影响他的法官工作，他的课都安排在上午8点。每次他都带一罐热咖啡，"两眼放光"地讲两个小时，然后自己驾车去40公里外的南区法庭上班。他是互联网法律专家，据说他连最新的各种电子游戏都统统熟悉。他给自己的专著起了一个别致的名字：internet. law. nz。2003年初版以来已再版三次。见 Judge Harvey, David: internet. law. nz（third edition），LexisNexis, 2011；Wellington. p. 57。

〔4〕　The Smoke-free Environments Act 1990。

〔5〕　即 Internet Protocol，中文译作"网际协议"，目的是根据源主机和目的主机的地址传送数据。

组，来寻找解决办法。该工作小组得出结论：通过识别 IP 地址，并要求上网登陆的用户声明自己的国籍，可以过滤 90% 的法国用户。因此，法院限定雅虎 3 个月内遵从这个要求。2001 年 1 月，雅虎总部宣布终止纳粹物件拍卖。但同时，在美国启动诉讼程序，诉请美国法院宣告法国法院对雅虎案不具有有司法管辖权，同时阻止法国法院的判决在美国执行。

三、Yahoo! v. LICRA 〔1〕——美国加州的判决

3.1 雅虎成原告

雅虎在美国加州法院所寻求的是一个"宣告式判决"〔2〕，诉请美国法院宣告法国法院要求雅虎过滤法国用户登录的判决不能强制执行。

在法国的原告（"反种族歧视联盟"和"犹太学联"）在美国则变成被告，被告认为美国联邦法院应驳回雅虎提起的诉讼，因为美国联邦法院不具备司法管辖权。这里的司法管辖权指的是"personal jurisdiction"，意思是法院对诉讼当事人具备司法管辖权，与"subject-matter jurisdiction"相对，指的是按诉讼标的物确定的管辖权。加州法院受理的雅虎案，不涉及标的物的司法管辖权，只涉及针对当事人的司法管辖权。也就是说，除非存在国际礼让〔3〕，否则法国巴黎法院的判决不能在美国境内执行。

---

〔1〕 Yahoo, Inc. v. La Ligue Contre Le Racisme et L'Antisemitisme et al 145 F. Supp. 2d 1168（ND Ca. 2001）。

〔2〕 即 declaratory judgment，也有人简称为 declaration，法院在宣告式判决中，对不同当事人所处的法律地位进行陈述。这一类"宣告式判决"近些年变得时兴，尤其是欧盟国家，往往是原告和被告抢着看谁先跑到法庭。有一种策略是被告抢先到法庭，申请法庭对其做"无罪"宣告，以先发制人，阻止原告诉讼。

〔3〕 Comity，或 comity of nations，即国际礼让，国际上的互相尊重，指在某些情况下，一国法院承认并适用另一国法律之惯例，参见陈庆柏，王景仙译：《英汉双解法律词典》，世界图书出版公司北京公司 1998 年版。

3.2 司法管辖权："一般"和"特定"

根据判例[1]，美国地方法院对非居民被告具备司法管辖权。这种司法管辖权分为"一般管辖权"（general jurisdiction）和"特定管辖权"（specific jurisdiction）。一般管辖权可以是推定的或者自行行使——尽管诉因与被告在管辖区的作为没有关系——只要能证明被告与管辖区的接触是"实质性或连续性且系统性"的[2]。但是，如果被告的行为不能满足以上一般管辖权要件，则仍然可以依特定管辖权来行使。而特定管辖权的条件，取决于被告在管辖区内与诉因相关的接触之"本质及特质"[3]。

理解这种区分，美国联邦第九上诉法院在 2000 年作出一个判例[4]。这个案例涉及网站域名侵权问题，但法院要解决的首要问题是原告所在的加利福尼亚州地区法院对乔治亚州的被告有没有司法管辖权。第九上诉法院驳回地区法院没有司法管辖权的判决，认为加州地区法院尽管对被告没有"一般司法管辖权"，但如果具备以下三个条件，该法院仍可以行使"特定管辖权"。这三个条件是：第一，非本地居民的被告，在原告所在辖区必须行使了一定"动作"，而被告有意识地通过这些动作利用原告司法管辖区内的法律保护自己的利益。第二，法院所受理的诉讼事由必须与被告上述活动相关或因上述活动而引起。第三，司法管辖权的行使必须具备合理性。[5] 当然，如果一个案子涉及非本地居民被告，而该被告质疑司法管辖权，举证责任（burden of proof）在原告，由原告证明司法管辖权的合理性。

就美国法庭对法国被告是否具备一般管辖权的问题，原告雅虎并未深究，但雅虎坚持加州法院对被告具备特定管辖权。

---

[1] 加州地区法院这里主要沿用了两个判例：Data Disk Inc v. Systems Tech Assoc Inc（1977）557 F 2d 1280（9th Cir1977）和 Helicopteros Nacionales de Colombia, SA v. Hall 466 US408（1984）。

[2] "substantial or continuous and systematic"，引自 Helicopteros Nacionales de Colombia 案，同上。

[3] "The nature and quality"，见上述案例。区别"本质"和"特质"是有一定法律前提的，在此不赘述。

[4] Bancroft & Masters Inc. v. Augusta National Inc 223 F 3d 1082,（9th Cir. 2000）.

[5] 同上 Bancroft & Masters Inc. 案，p. 1087。

3.3 法国反种族歧视联盟和犹太学联的"动作"

2000 年 4 月 5 日，法国反种族歧视联盟和犹太学联向设在美国加州的雅虎总部发出一封"禁止信"，信中强调，如果雅虎不立即在美国的拍卖网站上终止纳粹纪念品的拍卖，法国反种族歧视联盟和犹太学联将在"合适法庭"提出告诉，勒令雅虎遵守法国法律。当初在巴黎对雅虎提出诉讼时，这两个组织委托美国法警局向设在加州的雅虎送达法律文件。巴黎法院作出裁决后，原告也是委托美国法警局向雅虎送达了法庭判决书。

因此，在加州法庭，雅虎作为原告作出如下声辩：

第一，法国反种族歧视联盟和犹太学联目的明确、有意识地利用美国加州司法管辖权内的美国法律来保护自身的权益。他们向雅虎公司总部发"禁止信"；他们要求雅虎公司总部在美国境内通过干预服务器的方式达到禁拍的效果；他们委托、利用美国法警局送达法律文件。

第二，法国这两家组织对雅虎所在的司法管辖地的"联系"，不是"随意、轻忽或武断的"[1]。

第三，法国这两家组织的行为直接针对设在加州的雅虎总部，而行动目的是实现他们所想达到的效果。雅虎强调，效果之一是强迫雅虎对其服务器内容进行"审查"，而言论及表达自由在美国是受宪法保护的。

3.4 效果测试标准

"效果"（effect）在这里是个关键词。加州地区法院的法官认为，以"效果测试标准"（the effect test）来衡量本案以确定加州法院的司法管辖权，不但符合由先例确定的这一测试原则，并且合乎传统的司法管辖准则和相关国际法。"在外国提出告诉并以当地法律来裁决，这可能是完全合适的。但就本案来说——站在美国法院的角度来看——这宗诉讼案有可能是错误的，因为它的目

---

〔1〕 原话用的是"random, fatuous or opinionated"。注意这些措辞，律师在起草文件和法庭抗辩书时，需要引用相关判例来证明自己的观点。这些关键词大多从判例中来，仿佛训诂，否则难有说服力，也难引起法官的注意。

的或想达到的效果是剥夺一个美国居民[1] 宪法意义上的权利。"[2] 诚如原告雅虎所申辩的，被告的所有行为直指设在加州的雅虎总部，因此法官认为将被告引入加州法院，由其在加州法院为他们在巴黎法院所得到的判决抗辩，这是完全合理的。

加州地区法院的法官实际上是引用了联邦第九上诉法院 2000 年在 Bancroft & Masters Inc. 案中确立的判例原则。上述分析确定三要件中的第一个要件已经得到满足，即被告在加州司法管辖区域内的行为是实质性的、直接的而且具备可预测性结果。第二个要件是原告诉讼请求是由被告在原告所在的司法管辖权区域内的行为引起的。作为原告的雅虎需要证明，是一个"but for"（如非）要素。也就是说，如果不是被告到加州来要这要那，雅虎根本不需要到法庭来申请一个宣告式判决。第三个要件是司法管辖权的行使具备合理性。判例已经明确表明，合理性的举证责任在原告。但加州地区的法院对这一要件的解读更细一步：一旦作为原告的雅虎证明被告已经有意识地利用原告所在地的法律保护和伸张自己的利益，举证责任则转移到被告，由被告（法国反种族歧视联盟和犹太学联）来证明原告所在地的法院行使司法管辖权的不合理性。

3.5 行使司法管辖权七要件

但无论针对原告、被告，在国际法意义上行使司法管辖权，都必须综合考量以下因素[3]：

第一，被告在原告司法管辖区内的有意行为达到什么程度？

第二，如果是被告就原告，那么被告来这里抗辩将承受多大的负担？

第三，与被告国家的法律冲突将会是什么样的程度？

第四，原告所在地的法院受理此案并作出裁决，对原告所在地的管辖权和利益会产生什么影响？

---

[1] 自然人或法人。

[2] Yahoo! Inc v. La Ligue Contre Le Racisme et L'Antisemitisme et al 145 F Supp 2d. p. 1175（ND Ca 2001）.

[3] Judge David Harvey 在 internet. law. nz 第二章第三节中，专门总结了雅虎案（加州部分）司法管辖权的综合考量因素，见 Judge David Harvey（2011）：internet. law. nz（3rd edition）. Wellington：LexisNexis，pp. 55–65。

第五，最有效率的司法解决方案是什么？

第六，原告索求最方便、最有效率的司法解救——由原告所在地的法院行使司法管辖权对这一索求的重要性如何？

第七，是否存在另一个法院可供原、被告选择？

重要因素理清楚了，法庭要做的就是在各要素之间取得平衡。

关于被告在加州的"行为"的程度问题，加州地区法院认为原告登录美国境内的雅虎网站、发律师信、用美国法警送达文件，寻求司法途径勒令雅虎对设在加州的服务器进行技术干预，等等，综合考量，这些因素自然将天平偏向由加州地区的法院行使司法管辖权。至于因此是否给被告带来应诉负担，法庭注意到现代多媒体科技的发展，尤其是电话、传真、电子邮件和法庭视频的应用，使得原告、被告即使是远距离"对薄公堂"也变得可能和便捷。这使跨国诉讼不再因联系不便而受阻。另一重大理由是雅虎此案不会涉及太多的取证工作，纠纷双方就本案陈述的事实并没有争议。

3.6 司法主权

因为是跨国诉讼，自然涉及两国司法意义上的主权问题。雅虎作为加州地区法院的原告，提出的请求只有一个：美国法庭是否应该认可法国法庭的判决并在美国强制执行判决——而判决是为了制裁雅虎在美国本土提供的服务并使雅虎服从法国刑法？从法庭角度看，两国的主权利益必须平衡，尤其是涉及对美国居民受宪法和其他法保护的利益和权利。两者相权，自然倾向由加州地区法院行使司法管辖权。况且，加州地区法院也有义务对本辖区内的居民提供法律上的救助、匡正和保护。通俗来说，本地的法院不为本地人做主，"面子上"也过不去。

从法理上看，针对法国判决能否在美国强制执行的问题，也只有美国的法庭才能予以裁断。从技术上看，现代科技（多媒体的应用）使抗辩双方对薄公堂以及取证、作证没有阻碍。而原告提出的问题，本质上只有加州法庭才能予以解答。

综合以上理由，加州地区法院对法国被告提出的管辖权异议予以驳回。也就是说，加州地区法院认为自己具备司法管辖权，雅虎作为原告对法国被告提出的诉讼成立，官司得接着往下打。

3.7 一波三折

一波三折，但后两折都发生在美国联邦第九上诉法院。上诉法院先是撤销了加州地区法院的原判，认为加州不具备司法管辖权。但对上诉法院的判决再次上诉后，法官们的意见分成两派，一部分认为不具备司法管辖权；另一部分认为具备管辖权但"诉讼不成熟"，不宜在法院裁判，所以驳回。

在细看第九上诉法院的判决之前，我们先看看美国的司法系统以及联邦巡回审判区是怎么一回事。但是，在讨论美国法院组织系统之前，得先了解建立这个系统的依据和源头：美国宪法。

四、美利坚合众国宪法

4.1 世界上首部成文宪法

联邦律师协会（Federal Bar Association）[1]这样介绍美国法院的组织系统：

"我们的立国先人懂得司法独立之必要，《美利坚合众国宪法》（Constitution of the United States）第3条建立了独立的司法。司法是联邦政府三权分立的一个组成部分，另外两个是立法和行政。"

《美利坚合众国宪法》规定，联邦政府的司法权属于包括最高法院以及在国会所设立的各个下级法院在内的联邦法院系统。从技术层面看，《美利坚合众国宪法》第3条明确设立的只是联邦政府的最高法院，其他各个下级法院仍需要国会（立法机关）再通过立法规定或设立。

《美利坚合众国宪法》是世界上首部成文宪法，是美国的根本大法，奠定了美国政治制度的法律基础。这部宪法在1787年9月17日费城召开的制宪

---

[1] 见 www.fedbar.org，最后访问日期：2013年10月1日。

会议上获得代表们的批准，并在此后不久为当时美国拥有的 13 个州的特别会议所批准。1789 年，美国宪法正式生效。根据这部宪法，美国成为一个由各个拥有主权的州所组成的联邦国家，同时也成立了联邦政府以为联邦的运作而服务。从此，联邦体制取代了基于邦联条例而存在的较为松散的邦联体制。"邦联"和"联邦"有很大不同。易中天先生在《费城风云》[1]中这样描述：

　　那时的"美利坚合众国"甚至不是"1 个"国家，而是 13 个"半国家"的联合体，即"邦联"。她是由这些各自独立的"半国家"通过契约联合起来的。这个联合体虽然后来由邦联变成了联邦，但"联合"的概念没有变，联合的方式（通过契约）也没有变，只不过那"契约"由"邦联条例"变成了"联邦宪法"而已。而且，正因为她是一个联合体，所以美国人从不称其为美国（America）。要简称，也称作"合众国"或"联邦"（US），比如联邦政府、联邦法院、联邦调查局。

　　"美利坚合众国国玺"，上部的拉丁文是"E PLURIBUS UNUM"，英译为："Out of Many, One"，中译为："合众为一"。

---

　　[1]　易中天：《费城风云——美国宪法的诞生和我们的反思》，广西师范大学出版社 2008 年版，第 42~44 页。

《美利坚合众国宪法》原稿第 1 页

《美利坚合众国宪法》序言〔1〕

We the people of the United States, in order to form a more perfect union, establish justice, insure domestic tranquility, provide for the common defense, promote the general welfare, and secure the blessings of liberty to ourselves and our posterity, do ordain and establish this Constitution for the United States of America.

我们合众国人民，为建立更完善的联邦，树立正义，保障国内安宁，提供共同防务，促进公共福利，并使我们自己和后代得享自由带来的幸福，特为美利坚合众国制定本宪法。

---

〔1〕《美利坚合众国宪法》序言，只有一句话，52 个字。中译引自易中天所著《费城风云》扉页。

4.2 立法、行政、司法三权分立

美国立法、行政、司法三权分立。

国会徽章

立法。《美利坚合众国宪法》第 1 条规定了立法机构即美国国会的权力和组织构架。美国国会包括众议院和参议院两部分。

美国总统大印

行政。《美利坚合众国宪法》第 2 条创立了三权分立中的行政权，由总统、副总统和由总统任命的其他行政官员行使。第 2 条中的第 4 部分规定了对政府官员（包括总统、副总统和其他官员）的弹劾（impeachment）及免职程序。

美国联邦
最高法院大印

司法。《美利坚合众国宪法》第 3 条确立了司法机关（联邦法院系统），规定要建立一个"最高法院"，最高法院以下级别的法院由国会设立。

4.3 美国宪法六大基本原则

美国宪法是世界上第一部成文宪法，其确立基于六大基本原则[1]：

第一，民治政府，主权在民，一切权力归人民，人民才是一切权力的渊源，美国宪法序言概括了这一原则。

第二，有限政府、宪法至上、法律面前人人平等。政府的职能和权力是有限的，也就是说人民的某些基本权利政府是不能碰触的——这在尔后的修正案中有更多、更具体地体现。宪法作为母法，是万法源头，而政府、总统、官员、民众等都受法律约束。

第三，立法、行政、司法三权分立。制定、掌握和执行法律必须经过立法、行政和司法三方面的认可，这种分权使得各部门难以因专断而滥用权力。立法、行政、司法三个部门三权分立、各司其职。国会有立法权，但没有执法权，联邦法律由国会通过，但由总统签署；法官断案，但需行政部门来执行；总统为代表的行政机构有执法权，但没有立法权更没有司法权和解释权；法官有司法权、解释权但没有执法权。

第四，权力及部门间相互制衡。光有三权分立还不够，分立靠制衡起保障和监督作用。典型的例子是国会，对政府可行使投不信任票机制。而政府则可以解散国会。具体的事例是总统任命，譬如中央情报局局长或联邦法官，参议院可以确认或否决——这不是参议院没事找事，而是参议院在遵守宪法原则前提下的职责。同理，美国宪法规定，副总统兼任参议院议长。通常情况下，副总统兼任的议长不具有投票权，仅当参议院议员表决为平局时，副总统兼任的议长才能投票。这一票不但打破僵局，而且有实际决定权。

第五，司法审查（judicial review）。司法审查作为一个专有名词，有两个基本含义。一是指法院对行政决定进行的复审；另一个就是泛指高级法院对下级法院在断案有误的情况下，对案件进行复查。而谈论美国宪法意义上的司法审查，则离不开美国最高法院1803年带有标志性的一个判例——"马伯里诉麦迪

---

[1] McClenaghan, William A., Magruder's American Government, Needham, MA：Prentice Hall, 1996。见 www. whc. net. Retrieved October 2, 2013。

逊案"（Marbury v. Madison）[1]。

这桩案子是庄园主马伯里诉国务卿麦迪逊。老马获得一个"太平绅士"（Justice of the Peace）的头衔，但由于上届政府的疏忽迟迟未发委任状，而继任政府的国务卿麦迪逊拒绝下发委任状。根据 1789 年《美国司法法》的规定，最高法院对此具有初审管辖权，于是老马作为原告直接向最高法院提出诉讼。（此处请注意，最高法院作为最高上诉法院是不受理初审案件的，况且最高法院在当时刚刚创立不久，既无实权，也不知自己权限有多大）在由首席大法官约翰·马歇尔主笔的判决书中，最高法院首先肯定马伯里被任命为太平绅士是合法的，有权获得司法救济；但同时认为马伯里不能向联邦最高法院寻求司法救济[2]，理由是根据《美国宪法》第 3 章第 2 节第 2 款的规定，最高法院对此案并不具备初审管辖权，仅具有上诉管辖权，故随即又将案件撤销。

这宗案件的重要性，并不在于马伯里有没有或该不该得到委任状。这宗案件的重要性在于确立了美国联邦最高法院的违宪审查权，即法院有权判定国会的立法是否与宪法的精神相违背，从而可以宣布国会的立法符合宪法或者违宪无效。这一判例也确立了法院审理具体案件时，可以对宪法进行解释并运用到实际判决中。这样一来，不同时期的判例，可以反映不同时期政治、经济、文化和社会的发展变化状况，因此也使得美国宪法在不进行修改的情况下，运用司法审查的"微调"，具有适应社会发展的弹性。

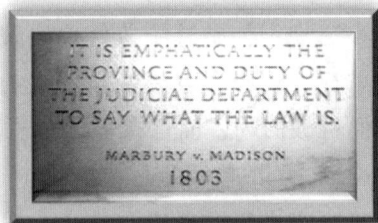

刻在最高法院墙上首席大法官约翰·马歇尔在"马伯里案"中的判词：**毋庸置疑，由司法部门来说法是什么，这是我们的权力和职责**。这句话其实概括了司法审查的概念。

---

[1]　Marbury v. Madison, 5 U. S 137（1803）。

[2]　《美国司法法》的规定使得马伯里能够直接向最高法院递交诉状。这实际上延展了《美国宪法》第 3 条赋予最高法院的权力，这个条款本身是违宪的，因此该条款无效。

第六，联邦性。联邦制作为一种政治形式，体现在国家由半自治省或州组成的联邦，并有一个中央联邦政府。所谓的"美利坚合众国"最初来源于各自独立、互不相属的松散型地方政治实体。《独立宣言》发表以前，北美大地并没有什么国家，只有一些殖民地，其中有一些属于大英帝国，叫"英属殖民地"，从北到南共有 13 个。所谓美国，最先就是由这 13 个殖民地联合而成的。这些殖民地虽然都以盎格鲁-撒克逊人为主，也号称英属，但互相之间并没有什么关系，每一个殖民地都是以个案的方式建立起来的，政治权利直接来自英国国王的特许。

1753 年建成的美国独立大厅，位于宾夕法尼亚州的费城市中心。《独立宣言》与《联邦宪法》均在此讨论通过。[1]

易中天先生在《费城风云》中是这样描述的：

1620 年，在荷兰的部分英国分离派教徒，乘五月花号轮船，计划到弗吉尼亚去安家。可是，他们在海上漂流了 66 天后，到达的不是弗吉尼亚，而是马萨诸塞。这些苦难而勇敢的人在船上发誓，要制定对殖民地人民最合适、最方便的法律、规则和条例。这个《五月花公约》就成为第一个体现主权在民的文件；而马萨诸塞州则成为美国独立思想和运动的发源地。[2]

---

〔1〕 Source：http://zh.wikipedia.org/wiki/File：Independence_ Hall.
〔2〕 易中天：《费城风云——美国宪法的诞生和我们的反思》，广西师范大学出版社 2008 年版，第 4~6 页。

所以，美国的联邦制就是一个中央政府和若干区域政府权力分散又联盟的一个模式，也可以称作平行和垂直的联邦制〔1〕，因为这根本就是在一个严密中央集权政府和松散邦联（confederation）之间取得的妥协，而美国宪法原则也正是体现了这种妥协。

难怪易中天在《费城风云》的简介中这样开笔：

200多年前，蛮荒大陆上的一群乡巴佬齐聚费城，为了制定世界上第一部宪法吵得不可开交。……制宪代表的原则也很简单——依法治国、三权分立、保护公民生命权、自由权和追求幸福的权利——惟其简单，才是底线；也惟其简单，才可坚守。〔2〕

宪法有了，依宪法而建立的最高法院也有了，我们现在来看一看美国的法院架构。

五、美国法院架构（之一）：州法院

介绍了《美利坚合众国宪法》，我们知道了州（state）和联邦（federal）的区别。美国的法院架构可以分成州法院（state courts）和联邦法院（federal courts）两大版块。

5.1 州最高法院是初审法院

美国各州法院系统是各州根据本州的宪法和法律设立的法院系统，与美国联邦法院平行、重叠又保持独立，并根据本州法律审理案件。州法院一般分成三级：初审法院、中级上诉法院和州最高法院。

初审法院在这里指"a state trial court"，对民事和刑事案件均具有初审权。但是法院的正式名称，通常叫"superior court"（"较高的""高级的"或"在上的"

---

〔1〕 Horizontal and vertical federalism，见 McClenaghan, William A, ibid。

〔2〕 易中天：《费城风云——美国宪法的诞生和我们的反思》，广西师范大学出版社2008年版，第4~6页。

法院）——人们对此极易混淆。更容易令人混淆的是，有的州称它为"巡回庭"（circuit court），而纽约州居然称其为"最高法院"（New York/Supreme Court）[1]，但也有的州老老实实地称其为"地方法院"（district court）。总之，五花八门。那么，这样的"高级法院"是比谁高呢？比它下一级的"专门"初审法庭高，这样的专门法庭是指交通法庭、家庭关系法庭（亦称家庭法庭或少年法庭）、遗嘱公证法庭（有些州称为遗嘱认证法庭、孤儿法庭，是一个专门处理遗嘱、遗产继承和管理、未成年人或无民事行为能力人监护的专门法庭），等等。这些法庭可以是单独的，也可以是具有一般司法管辖权的初审法院的分庭。加利福尼亚州于1998年进行了改革，将所有下一级法庭全部纳入"高级法院"（Superior Courts of California），下级法庭仅成为替上级法院行使行政管理职能的分支机构，这样法院就无所谓高级和低级之分，名称虽延用"superior"，但仅仅是为了保留传统而已。

5.2 州中级上诉法院

有了上面的解释，我们就明白了这里的"高级"指的是具有一般司法管辖权的"最高一级"的"初审"法院，因为在它上面还有一个"中级"法院。这里的中级指的是"中级上诉法院"（intermediate appellate courts），是介于初审法院和终审法院之间的中级上诉法院，绝大多数案件最终都是由这些中级上诉法院进行最终审判的。目前，50个州中有40个州有中级上诉法院。有些州还不止一个，如阿拉巴马州（Alabama）各有一个民事和刑事中级上诉法院。

5.3 州最高上诉法院

再往上就是州最高法院（state supreme court）了，有些州也称之为上诉法院、最高司法院、最高上诉法院，总之是州法律的终审法院。只有涉及联邦法律的实质法律问题，才能继续上诉到美国最高法院，这里是指美利坚合众国联邦最高法院。需要注意的是，州最高法院属于地方法院，其不隶属于联邦最高

---

[1] 纽约州的62个初审法院均称作"最高法院"，而纽约州（State）的终审法院则是纽约上诉法院（New York Court of Appeals）。在用词混淆程度方面和纽约州有一拼的大概要数澳大利亚了，为了避免更令人迷惑，在此不提。忍不住的读着，可一睹下一章节："美国道琼斯《巴伦周刊》诽谤案"。

法院，各州最高法院的组成方法和司法领域彼此也不尽相同〔1〕。

总之，理解美国州法院系统，也可以分两大块来看。一大块是由市、县和"当地"（权限有限）的法庭构成。市法院具有审理来自市镇法庭和治安/警察法庭转来的上诉案件的管辖权；而县法院则只有一般管辖权，审理民事或者其他违法案件。"当地法庭"包括市镇法庭和治安/警察法庭，前者由地方行政官主持，后者由治安法官主持。

5.4 州初审法院和上诉法院

在州那一级，可笼统分成初审法院和上诉法院两部分。初审法院分成巡回法院（不要和联邦巡回法院混淆）、地区法院、高级法院和衡平法院。上诉法院包括中级上诉法院、高级刑事上诉法院（只有某些州才设立）、最高法院（不要和联邦最高法院混淆）。

5.5 特别管辖和一般管辖类法庭

美国是世界诉讼大国，各类案件五花八门，各级法院也是应接不暇。分门别类的法庭不要说会令其他国家的人晕头转向，就是美国人自己，州法庭还是联邦法庭，带陪审团还是不带陪审团〔2〕，也往往不是很清楚。有人〔3〕想出好方法，用司法管辖权加以区别。对绝大多数州法庭而言，有两种司法管辖权：特别管辖和一般（全面）管辖。特别管辖类法庭，也称县法庭、地方法庭、警察法庭等等，处理的是交通类案件、青少年案件以及轻度民事、刑事案件。一般管辖类法庭涉及面比较全面，这类法庭又称作巡回法庭、高级法庭（甚至是

---

〔1〕 参见 Benesh SC，Martinek WL，"Context and Compliance：A Comparison of State Supreme Courts and the Circuits"，Marquette Law Review，Vol. 2009.

〔2〕 Jury（陪审团）随机抽样从公民中产生，也就是说由普通百姓组成。被抽到的公民，到法庭还得经过一个程序叫"voir dire"（预备讯问），由法院和律师讯问以确定是否适合做陪审团成员。陪审团分成"小陪审团"（a petit jury）和"大陪审团"（a grand jury）。小陪审团由 6~12 名成员组成，民事陪审团可以是 6~12 名，但刑事陪审团必须由 12 名成员组成。大陪审团由 16~23 名成员组成。这里为了避免混淆，不单独介绍陪审团制度。

〔3〕 见 Jacob Silverman："How the judicial System Works."http://people. howstuffworks. com. Retrieved October 3, 2013.

最高法庭）等，处理较大的民事、刑事案件。每个州都有自己的上诉法院和州终审法院。也就是说，在州这个层面，既有最基层的初审法院，也有州上诉（终审）法院。美国全国约95%的案件都在州法院得到解决。

每个州的法官任免制度也不尽相同，有的是由州长任命，有的则是经选举产生。

之所以不厌其烦地介绍美国联邦和州的司法系统，是因为雅虎案所涉猎的范围，不仅涉及跨国司法管辖权问题，而且涉及联邦第九巡回法院的两个判决，更涉及美国联邦司法体系和美国宪法以及宪法修正案的核心精神。

理解了美国州法院体系，我们现在来看联邦法院体系。

六、美国法院架构（之二）：联邦法院

美国联邦律师协会（Federal Bar Association）将联邦法院系统分成五大领域：最高法院、上诉法院、地方法院、破产案件法院，以及特别司法管辖权法院[1]。

6.1 联邦最高法院——宪法渊源

美利坚合众国最高法院[2]　　　　　美国联邦最高法院大印[3]

第一部分是美国联邦最高法院。《美国宪法》第3条第1款规定："合众国的司法权属于最高法院及国会随时制定与设立的下级法院。最高法院与下级法

---

[1] www. fedbar. org. Retrieved October 3, 2013.

[2] Source：www. supremecourt. gov.

[3] Source：www. supremecourt. gov.

院的法官毋忝阙职时，得终身任职，于规定期间应受职务的报酬，该报酬于任期内不得减少之。"[1]

联邦最高法院根据《美国宪法》这一条款创立，并于 1790 年 2 月 2 日组建。《美国宪法》第 3 条第 2 款赋予的最高法院司法权"涵括所有案件"，包括普通法与衡平法[2]的案件，发生于本宪法及合众国各种法律上的案件，根据合众国权力所缔结的条约及涉及大使、公使和领事的案件，涉及合众国为当事人的诉讼，州与州之间的诉讼，等等。

有趣的是，最高法院作为美国的终审法院是不受理初审案件的，但宪法赋予其直接受理"涉及大使、公使和领事"的案件。从技术上看，所有这些案件必须先递交至最高法院，再由最高法院转交下一级法院受理。

如前面所介绍的，只有最高法院的创立直接渊源于宪法，其他各级法院则是通过国会和不同立法的授权。

---

〔1〕 The Constitution of the United States of America in Various Foreign Languages：Chinese. 《美利坚合众国宪法》，选自《宪法学习参考资料》，北京大学法律系 1977 年版，第 8 页，见美国国会图书馆 Library of Congress Catalog Card No. 87–619879。

〔2〕 "衡平法"（equity）是与"普通法"并行发展起来的使普通法更公平的英国法律制度。衡平法可用这样一句格言来总结："公正不会让在没有救济的情况下蒙受一种冤屈。"（"Equity does not suffer a wrong to be without a remedy."）见 English–Chinese Bilingual Law Dictionary 2nd ed Peter Collin Publishing（1992）。衡平法应该是华人在英美法系学习法律遇到的最大难题之一。衡平法是与普通法相对的。"关于这两个概念的理解，比较典型的例子是所有权（title）在普通法和衡平法意义上的区分。前者指拥有权，后者指使用权。例如家庭信托，托管人在法律上拥有房产（产权）而受益人则拥有使用权。两个权利之间的渊源以及毁损后的'补'和'偿'（remedy and restitution）都是不一样的。"参见霍建强：《海外创出四重天——在新西兰做国会议员、律师、记者和诗人》，北京师范大学出版社 2011 年版，前言。衡平法源自古代英国，法院均以普通法（这里指写成条文的法律）审理案件。由于普通法只重条文和程序，很多人单单因为未能符合程序导致案件超过了诉讼时效，而得不到公平对待。于是，单独设立一个法院叫"衡平法院"，以"公正、良心"来断案。因此，普通法和衡平法的案件必须由不同的法院审理。典型的例子是，根据与银行签订的合约逾期不还房贷，银行便可拍卖房子来抵债。房主（借贷方）千里单骑带着金币来还钱，但途中遇洪水，桥被冲垮结果比规定的时间晚两小时到，但房子已被拍卖。这时，他可以到衡平法院申诉，衡平法院很有可能将房产再判回给他。由衡平法派生出来的一系列概念，实际上都是本着这一精神。英国的普通法院与衡平法院尔后得以合并。在此不赘述。在美国衡平法的发展，可能更多地在法律救助和补偿上与普通法不同。譬如，甲的奶牛跑到邻居家被邻居扣着不还，而甲想通过司法途径得到的"救助"是邻居将奶牛退还而不是简单地赔钱。这就涉及普通法和衡平法救助上的区别。在美国，普通法和衡平法合并之后，法院吸纳并沿用了诸多衡平法法院程序，因衡平法法院程序比普通法法院程序要灵活许多。在法庭上用的较多的共诉、反诉等，都源自衡平法院。见 Douglas Laycock, *Modern American Remedies*, 3rd ed, Aspen Press, 2002, p.370。

约翰·马歇尔，1801～1835 年任最高法院首席大法官。[1]

6.1.1 合众国终审法院

最高法院有 9 名大法官（Justices）[2]，因为是整个美利坚合众国的终审法院，其作用和权力可以想见。正因如此，每次围绕大法官的提名，总会成为全国关注的焦点。大法官的提名以及他们任内的作为，也引起广泛关注。目前的 9 名大法官中，首席大法官约翰·罗伯茨（John G. Roberts Jr.）是 2005 年由小布什总统提名的。

根据《美国宪法》第 3 条，法官"毋忝厥职时，得终身任职"。自"二战"以来，美国 11 位总统共任命了 28 位最高法院大法官，其中共和党任命了 17 位，民主党任命了 11 位。

最高法院作为终审法院，其影响力毋庸置疑，尤其体现在司法审查以及对下一级法院的导向作用中。

6.1.2 司法审查

司法审查（Judicial Review）最先源自 1803 年的"马伯里诉麦迪逊案"，首

---

　　[1]　这尊雕像是 1920 年初的作品，马歇尔身着法袍，神情严肃而怡然，坐落在华盛顿的约翰·马歇尔公园里。如同本书第一章中的纪念碑，苏格兰人肯为一宗"啤酒蜗牛案"竖纪念碑，美国人将首席大法官当明星来追捧，都体现了他们对法的信仰。Source：United States District Court.
　　[2]　"Justice"和"Judge"同为"法官"之意，但大致的区别——因不同司法体制用法不同——judge 指地区一级的法官，而 Justice 指高等法院或上诉法院以上的法官。不少新律师经常将两者混淆。

席大法官马歇尔也在判决中创下首个先例："一部法若违宪则不是法。"[1]而
1954 年的"布朗诉教育局案"[2]则创下另一个划时代的判例原则。在"布朗
诉教育局案"中，最高法院以 9∶0 全票通过，宣布白人和黑人学生不得进入同
一学校的种族隔离在本质上就是一种不平等。因此，涉及种族隔离的法律因为
剥夺了黑人学童的入学权利，而违反了《美国宪法》第 14 条修正案中所保障的
同等保护权。这是最高法院在美国历史上非常重要的具有标志意义的判例。这
个判决，从法律上终止了在美国存在已久的白人和黑人必须就读于不同公立学
校的种族隔离主义。

从这两个判例可以看出，司法审查大致涵括了三大领域：一是如果法律违
宪最高法院可宣告其无效；二是联邦法律或国际条约如果与州和地方立法不同，
最高法院可判定哪个法优先；三是对《美国宪法》做权威性解释。

除此之外，因判例对下级法院有拘束力，加之最高法院对宪法、法律和先
例具有解释权，最高法院对各级法院无论在实体法上还是程序法上均有导向作用。

美国最高法院设在华盛顿，周一至周五上午 9 点到下午 4∶30 对公众开放。
根据法律规定，最高法院每年 10 月的第一个星期一到第二年 10 月的第一个星
期一办公。每年有上万件案件递交至最高法院，但每年经最高法院裁定的不足
200 件[3]。

6.2 联邦上诉法院（巡回上诉法院）

第二部分是联邦上诉法院，又名巡回上诉法院（Circuit Courts），是美国联
邦司法系统中的中级上诉法院，主要裁定来自各联邦司法管辖区内对于地方法
院的判决。称其为"中级上诉法院"，是因为其介于终审最高法院和初审地方
法院之间。因为是上诉法院，所以不用陪审团也不传唤证人（主要解决的是上
诉中的法律问题）。

联邦上诉法院是美国司法系统中最具影响力的法院群，他们直接受理地方
法院的上诉，作出的判决成为判例，对美国的司法制度和政策有极大影响力。

---

[1] 原话是："A legislative act contrary to the Constitution is not law."

[2] Brown v. Board of Education 347 U. S. 483 (1954).

[3] 参见 www. maxwell. syr. edu.

最高法院每年裁决的大案不到 200 件，因此大多数联邦案件的终审判决都是由上诉法院来承担的，其中不到 1% 会上诉到最高法院。

6.2.1 联邦 11 上诉法院

从"上诉法院和地区法院区划图"中可看到共标有 11 个上诉法院，这些法院都是按数字来命名的。其余两个上诉法院，分别是首都哥伦比亚特区联邦巡回上诉法院和美国联邦巡回区上诉法院。因此，美国 50 个州、首都华盛顿特区加境外领土（美国大陆以外）被划分为 13 个审判区，设有 13 个巡回上诉法院。

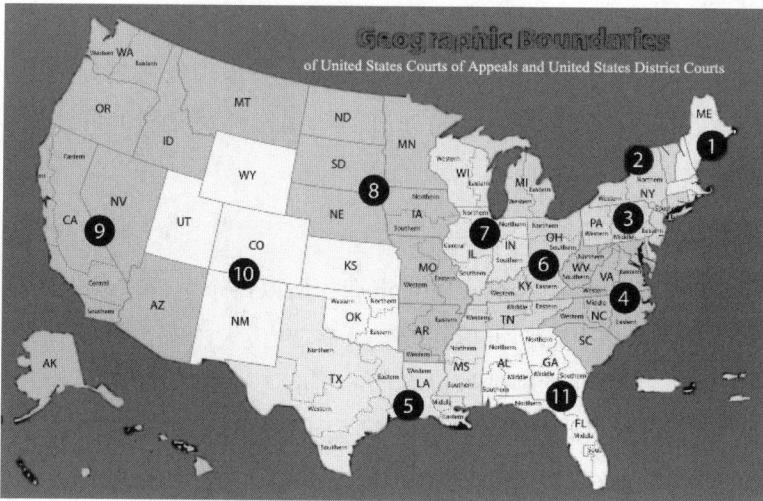

上诉法院和地区法院区划图〔1〕

美国 11 个按数字命名的上诉（巡回）法院

1. 波士顿（辖 5 个州）	5. 新奥尔良（辖 3 个州）	9. 旧金山（辖 11 个州，含阿拉斯加州、关岛和夏威夷）
2. 纽约（辖 3 个州）	6. 辛辛那提（辖 4 个州）	
3. 费城（辖 4 个州，含维京群岛）	7. 芝加哥（辖 3 个州）	10. 丹佛（辖 6 个州）
4. 里士满（辖 5 个州）	8. 圣路易斯（辖 7 个州）	11. 亚特兰大（辖 3 个州）

---

〔1〕 Sources：http://www.fedbar.org. Retrieved October 1，2013 and also www.uscourt.gov. Retrieved October 3，201，见美国联邦律师协会网和美国法院网。

6.2.2 哥伦比亚特区联邦巡回上诉法院

哥伦比亚特区联邦巡回上诉法院（United States Court of Appeals for the District of Columbia Circuit, D. C. Cir）对哥伦比亚特区联邦地区法院拥有上诉管辖权，可直接审查首都各联邦政府机构的政策、法规和决策，"直接审查"指的是不必由初审法院听审才能上诉。根据《美国行政程序法》的规定拥有一般司法管辖权，可以直接受理涉及其他行政机构的行政诉讼案件。[1]

6.2.3 美国联邦巡回区上诉法院

美国联邦巡回区上诉法院（United States Court of Appeals for the Federal Circuit, Fed. Cir 或 C. A. F. C）是位于首都华盛顿的一个联邦上诉法院，是根据1982 年的《美国联邦法院改善法》创设。与其他按地理区域划分的上诉法院不同，它是按标的物司法管辖创立，将原有的联邦关税及专利上诉法院以及美国索赔法院中的上诉部门合并而成。

6.2.4 大法官共审制

上诉法院的案件一般由 3 名大法官审理，所以每个上诉法院设 4 到 26 位大法官，值得注意的是第九巡回上诉法院，共有 29 位大法官，是所有联邦上诉法院中规模最大的，并且非常独特地设有"en banc"制度，即某一件上诉案件必须接受全体大法官出庭审理——正是这个原因，我们才必须不厌其烦地介绍美国的司法制度，只有这样才能说清楚"雅虎案"，以及伴随它的实体和程序问题。但是近些年来，伴随第九巡回上诉法院法官和辖区太多、太大的问题，"en banc"的应用也引发许多争议。在其他巡回法院，"en banc"意味着所有现任法官加参与过原始案件的高级法官共同主审——尽管这在理论层面意义居多，因为"en banc"在其他上诉法院所用极少，但第九巡回上诉法院因为法官人数较多，不可能做到每遇"en banc"便人人事必躬亲，所以不得已而为之地形成一个折衷方案，即随机抽出 11 名大法官而非全体主审。这就出现了三个问题：首先，这不是真正的"en banc"，因为反映的不是全体法官的意见；其次，因是随

---

[1] John G Roberts, Jr. "What Makes the D. C. Circuit Different? A Historical View", *Virginia Law Review*, 2006, 92: 375.

机抽选，原来断案而了解具体案情的那 3 位法官未必能抽选上；最后，也是争议最大并涉及整个 "en banc" 理念的，就是如此一来众多法官按见解分为不同 "派别" 各出判词，对法律的稳定性、严肃性会产生不利影响。

也正是由于以上诸多原因，本书才必须不厌其烦、一环套一环地介绍美国司法制度，因为只有这样才能说清楚 "雅虎案"。

6.3 联邦 94 个地方法院

以上第一部分、第二部分着重介绍了美利坚合众国最高法院和联邦上诉法院。第三部分是地方法院，地方法院是联邦法院系统中的初审法院，全国共有 94 个联邦地方法院，也就是在全国共设 94 个联邦司法管辖区，至少保证每个州设一个司法区。国会依规模、人口及案件数量来决定司法管辖区。有些州有一个地区法院，有的如纽约州、加利福尼亚州则各有 4 个。在这 94 个地方法院中，每院设两名法官（judges），大的区则多达 24 名法官。每个辖区内还设有处理破产事务的法庭。地区法院受理的刑事案件涉及触犯联邦刑法之类的违法行为，而民事案件则涉及联邦民法或不同州公民之间的民事纠纷。也就只有在这一级联邦法院，才会动用大陪审团。

6.4 破产法院

第四部分是美国破产法院（受理破产案件的法院），全国 94 个联邦司法区内设有破产法院——与破产法相关的案件是州法院不能受理的。《美国法典第11 部》（Title 11 of the United States Code）是美国破产法的主要渊源。在法庭使用较多的条款是第 7 条（清算）、第 11 条（重组）和第 13 条（偿债），目的是在保护债权人的前提下，通过重组使公司和业主能够跌倒了再重新爬起来。

6.5 特别司法管辖权法院

第五部分是美国 "特别司法管辖权法院"，涉及军事法庭，国际贸易、税务法庭及审理跨区诉讼案件的法庭，等。

七、"雅虎案"：美国联邦第九上诉法院（第一轮）

7.1 立法和国民教育谴责大屠杀

案情发展至此，许多细节也凸显出来。如本章开始所介绍的，雅虎平台提供"二战"德国纳粹收藏品和纪念品拍卖。"雅虎拍卖"网站列出的拍品被越来越多的人知道，"雅虎聊吧"（chat room）也开始有人聊起这个话题。《法国刑法典》禁止宣扬和买卖纳粹物品，对那些替战争犯罪开脱的人，一旦定罪会被处以有期徒刑（可达 5 年）和巨额罚款。在法国和其他国家，对战争和纳粹大屠杀（holocaust）的憎恶深入人心，尤其是立法和国民教育，也使民众对和平与战争、正义与邪恶有深入骨髓般的认知。2000 年 4 月初，法国反种族歧视联盟和犹太学联，发现可以在法国登录雅虎总部的美国网站（www.yahoo.com）浏览列在拍卖网页上的纳粹纪念品。2000 年 4 月 5 日，法国反种族歧视联盟向雅虎美国总部发送律师信，禁止雅虎在网络上陈列这些拍品。4 月 10 日和 20 日法国反种族歧视联盟和犹太学联相继在巴黎法院对雅虎提出告诉，并依《海牙公约》委托美国法警向雅虎送达法庭文件。雅虎在巴黎应诉挑战巴黎法院司法管辖权，但巴黎法院依《法国新民事诉讼法典》行使司法管辖权。

7.2 巴黎法院的判决

2000 年 5 月 22 日，巴黎法院作出判决勒令雅虎：（1）销毁在服务器上存储的所有与纳粹相关的短信、图像、文字说明尤其是纳粹军旗、徽章和一切对德国纳粹歌功颂德的宣传材料。（2）删除雅虎网站上的登录指南和一切与纳粹拍品相关的导引及标题。（3）雅虎必须"采取一切必要措施"禁止在其网站提供能够登录与纳粹物品相关的网页及相关链接，巴黎法院指出，仅仅是浏览这样的内容也触犯法国法律——以上各条如果不能执行，雅虎将被每天罚款 10 万法郎（约 13 300 美元）。2000 年 11 月 20 日，巴黎法院作出第二号判决令，除重申 5 月 22 日判决外，法院给雅虎 3 个月的时间来遵守和执行第一号判决令，并强调违令则罚款每日累计。同上次一样，判决书也是由法国原告委托美国法警局送达。

7.3 雅虎不在巴黎上诉而在加利福尼亚州起诉

雅虎选择不在巴黎上诉，其上诉权也于 2001 年 2 月 7 日到期失效。此时雅虎按照巴黎法院的要求对服务器和网站做了诸多调整，删除了许多内容但并没有完全达到巴黎法院的要求。

2000 年 12 月 21 日，雅虎在加利福尼亚州北区联邦地方法院递交诉状，请求法院作出裁决，宣告法国法院 2000 年 5 月 22 日及 11 月 20 日两份判决书在美国"不被认可"或"不能执行"。法国反种族歧视联盟和犹太学联随即向加利福尼亚州法院提出异议，依联邦民事诉讼规则，请求法院撤销雅虎诉状，理由是加利福尼亚州地方法院对法国这两家组织没有司法管辖权。雅虎又紧随其后递交了另一份诉状，请求法院作出"即决判决"[1]，理由有二：一是法国法院的判决违反了《美国宪法第一修正案》[2]；第二，法国法院的罚款是每日累计的而雅虎并没有执行（或曰完全执行）巴黎法院的判决[3]。加之巴黎法院禁止向"法国雅虎"收取罚款而"法国雅虎"是雅虎在法国的唯一资产——这样一来法国法院的判决和罚款只可能在美国执行，因此加利福尼亚州法院可以作出即决判决。

7.4 加利福尼亚州地区法院判决巴黎判决无效

加利福尼亚州地区法院作出以下判决：（1）加利福尼亚州地区法院对法国这两家组织可行使司法管辖权，因此驳回法国被告撤销雅虎诉讼的请求；（2）依雅虎请求作出即决判决并宣布在美国执行法国法院之判决违反了《美国宪法第一修正案》；（3）次日，加利福尼亚州地区法院又颁布了经修正的判决书，宣布法国法院 2000 年 5 月 22 日和 11 月 20 日两份判决书在美国没有约束力，均不

---

〔1〕 "Summary judgment"，一般指原告认为被告提不出任何合理抗辩，原告因此请求法庭对自己所申请的案件立即进行判决。

〔2〕 "First Amendment"第一修正案禁止美国国会制定任何法律以妨碍宗教信仰自由、侵犯言论自由或出版自由，以及剥夺公民和平集会和向政府请愿伸冤的权利。第一修正案于 1791 年 12 月 15 日获得通过，是美国权利法案中的一部分。

〔3〕 雅虎对自己网站作出的多项调整是"自发"的而非出于执行巴黎法院的判决。

得执行。

法国反种族歧视联盟和犹太学联上诉，在司法管辖权不具备、诉讼不成熟及地区法院未能因前两个理由而拒审三个方面，挑战加利福尼亚州地区法院。

7.5 上诉法院撤销地区法院原判

2004 年 8 月 23 日，美国联邦第九巡回上诉法院以 2:1 裁定，美国法院对法国上述两个组织没有司法管辖权，因此撤销加利福尼亚州地区法院原判。[1] 两位持"多数派"意见的法官颁布了长达 34 页的判决书，而代表"少数派"的那一位法官出具了一份 23 页的"反方意见"。考虑到本书篇幅，对联邦第九巡回上诉法院这一轮的裁决，不展开说明。

八、"雅虎案"：美国第九巡回上诉法院（第二轮）

8.1 扑朔迷离的 6:5

这一轮由联邦第九巡回上诉法院全体（en banc）法官共同审理，但由于第九巡回上诉法院规模过大，所谓"全体"也只是象征性地抽选 11 位主审法官来代表。扑朔迷离的是这 11 位法官中，8 位认为加利福尼亚州地区法院对法国这两家组织（本案在美国的被告）有司法管辖权，3 位法官认为没有。但就第二个法律问题即此案是否符合"诉讼成熟"的标准[2]，5 位法官认为符合诉讼成

---

〔1〕 第九巡回上诉法院对加利福尼亚州地区法院的判决逐项分析并从既有判例中得出不具备司法管辖权的结论。因为不具备司法管辖权，上诉法院认为其他两个法律问题（诉讼不成熟、法院未能拒审）可以不议。

〔2〕 "成熟"这里指 ripeness，在美国司法实践中经常碰到。如果一宗案件在诉讼上不成熟，法庭则不予受理。经常举的例子是，如果一部法律语焉不详、模棱两可但从来没有在实践中适用，那么试图引用或挑战这部法律的诉讼案很有可能不被法庭受理。这种情况下如果有各种原因法庭必须受理，法官通常会找来当时国会的辩论记录，从辩论中了解当时立法的来龙去脉，判断立法原意，并根据立法原意——因为只有国会才能立法——进行解释以便能够有效适用相关条款。受英国传统影响，澳大利亚、新西兰、南非等国均设"翰洒"（Hansard）桌面，国会议员在国会讲的每一句话都被逐字逐句自动记录下来，定期汇编成册。翰洒汇编通常是个很好的资料库，帮助了解立法环境和意图，尤其是涉及几十年前或上百年前的立法。当然，媒体和民众也经常阅读这些汇编，从中找到国会议员讲话的漏洞。经常"曝料"的是某某国会议员十几年前说了如何如何但十几年后观点又变了云云（"不信你看翰洒记录"）。

熟标准（即法庭可以受理），3 位认为不符合而另 3 位则认为此案尚未触及这个问题，因为加利福尼亚州地区法院不具备司法管辖权。投票的结果是 6:5，6 票认为此案应驳回。少数服从多数，因此撤销地区法院原判。因为是上诉法院裁决，此案被发回初审法院但不是重审而是直接撤销。

8.2 法官们如何形成 6:5

我们不妨再梳理下这 11 位法官是如何裁定并投票表决的：8 位法官裁定加利福尼亚州地区法院具备司法管辖权，这 8 位法官当中，有 3 位（包括首席法官）认为此案诉讼不成熟应驳回，但有 5 位认为诉讼成熟。另 3 位则认为应驳回此案，理由是地区法院对法国被告不具备司法管辖权。综合考量，虽然原因不同（诉讼不成熟或不具备司法管辖权），但裁定驳回此案的法官占 6 位，6:5 因而成为本案的最终裁决。[1]

8.3 律师信、送达文件和暂行判令构成"联系"

在长达 50 多页的判决中，第九巡回上诉法院引经据典详细分析了原、被告双方提供的法律依据和抗辩要件。上诉法院裁定加利福尼亚州地区法院具备司法管辖权是基于法国被告在加州的联系达到"足够的最小标准"（地方法院判决依据之一就是法国两组织在加州的活动达到"联系"在法律程度上的要求）。法国反种族歧视联盟和犹太学联在加利福尼亚州的"联系"主要集中在三个方面。第一，向雅虎总部发律师信，要求雅虎按照巴黎法院的判决去"禁"和"止"（cease and desist）其特定行为。第二，在加利福尼亚州司法管辖区内送达法庭文件。第三，在此期间又向巴黎法院申请并获得两份"暂行判令"[2]，而这两份判令都是引导雅虎在加利福尼亚州为执行法国法院判决而"采取一切措施和行动"，否则将以每天累积的方式课以重罚。

第九巡回上诉法院认为，单纯前两种"联系"或许还不足以构成司法管辖

---

〔1〕 Yahoo Inc v. LICRA No. 01-17424, Argued and Submitted March 24, 2005-January 12, 2006.

〔2〕 "Interim order"，又称暂行判令、临时命令、临时判决，指在案子审理过程中颁布的有效命令与判决。

权基础，但第三种"联系"，合并前两种，足以构成司法管辖权基础。

8.4 "效果测试"先例

1984 年美国最高法院在"考而得诉琼斯案"〔1〕中确定了"效果测试"标准，而"最小限度的联系"则是前提。最高法院裁定，一个佛罗里达州的出版商发表一篇诋毁在加利福尼亚州的原告的文章，被告的行为是明确地针对加州原告，而原告在加州能够感受到被告诽谤之伤害，那么加利福尼亚州法院对佛罗里达州的出版商〔2〕有权行使管辖权。

回到本案，"效果测试"标准的前两个要求是：第一，法国被告实施了一个故意行为；第二，该行为明确地针对原告所在地司法管辖区。显然，这两点依测试标准都是符合的。第三个要求则针对"伤害"，而被告知道对原告造成的伤害发生在原告所在地。

8.5 法律意义上的伤害

对"伤害"要求的分析有点复杂。因为雅虎在法庭上承认，尽管雅虎对拍卖网站做了诸多调整，也删除了诸多纳粹宣传品图片，但这些并不是依法国判决的要求而做，许多层面上完全是自主行为。即使将这些调整看成是雅虎所经受的法律意义上的"伤害"，但"伤害"并非由法国法院的判决直接造成。同时，雅虎也承认，即使做了以上调整，法国法院的判决只要一天有效，雅虎便是处于违反法国法院判决的状态。无独有偶，法国被告也认为雅虎撤掉了许多纳粹宣传品、删除了诸多图片，只要这样有效地调整下去，巴黎法院的判决精神便得到领会贯彻，如此则不必强制执行法院的命令。雅虎的辩词也有说服力：无论法国这两家组织怎么说，毕竟剑悬其首，法院判决只要一天有效，法院判决就要执行，雅虎还是照样要被制裁、罚款。总之，原告和被告各说各的，而所说的既互相矛盾又彼此切合。

---

〔1〕 Calder v. Jones 465 U. S. 783（1984）.

〔2〕 这里用的是 publisher（出版商）这个统称，因为诽谤文章的作者和出版/发表这样文章的责任人，如报社、电台、电视台、网站，均可列作被告。

8.6 司法管辖权三理由

这是造成以上分析复杂的原因。但是综合考量以下因素：（1）法国被告在加利福尼亚州司法管辖区内的直接活动和联系；（2）雅虎作为原告提出诉讼及诉讼之性质；（3）巴黎判决对雅虎造成的影响以及潜在影响等，第九巡回上诉法院判定美国法院对此案具备司法管辖权。

8.7 诉讼成熟两方面

至于"诉讼成熟"说，其基本原则来自两个方面：（1）《美国宪法》第3条涉及的司法限制；（2）法庭拒绝行使司法管辖权之法理理由。[1] 就相关问题，初审法院加利福尼亚州地区法院认为巴黎判决对雅虎造成的影响，足够使本案在《美国宪法》第3条意义上构成一个诉讼命题或诉讼争议。这一点得到第九巡回上诉法院的认同。但第九巡回上诉法院却不认同地方法院关于此案具备成熟诉讼条件的结论。关于成熟条件，上诉法院着重考量两大因素：（1）对本问题进行司法裁定的适当程度；（2）不予裁定对诉讼当事人造成的"艰难"程度[2]。

8.8 内国性质还是治外法权

经过法官们抽丝剥茧般的分析论证，许多问题变得明朗：第一，法院不确定关于宪法第一修正案的问题是否会以及以何种形式提交法庭考量。如果法国法院认为，雅虎调整网站政策以及其他相关动作——哪怕是自愿和自主行为——已经使雅虎在很大程度上达到巴黎法院的要求，那么第一修正案问题便不成其为问题。如果巴黎法院对雅虎进行调整的额外要求仅涉及在法国的用户，而这样的额外要求并不涉及对美国境内用户的登录限制，那么雅虎只是伸张一种治外法权意义上的第一修正案权利。如果巴黎法院对雅虎进行调整的额外要求仅

---

〔1〕 参见 Nat'l Park Hospitality Ass'n v. DOI 538 U.S 803，808，123 S. Ct 2026，155LEd 2d 1017（2003）案中确定的判例。

〔2〕 参见判决书第Ⅲ部分第三自然段。

涉及在法国的用户但其结果却不可避免地限制了美国境内的用户，那么雅虎对于第一修正案权利之伸张辩论就会同时既有内国性质也有治外法权性质。

第二，从整个案件的进展角度看，在美国境外需要强制执行巴黎法院判决的必要性和可能性都极小。鉴于雅虎已经在自愿前提下调整了自己的网站，而这一系列动作已经使巴黎法院的判决在很大程度上得到贯彻，因第一修正案侵权对雅虎带来法律意义上的损伤或许根本不存在。假定雅虎并没有在很大程度上贯彻巴黎法院的判决，雅虎违反责任只是体现在对法国境内用户登录限制的不够。当然，如果因不足而需要加强但最终结果又可能涉及美国境内用户，但这种可能性在这一点上目前只是推测，而这正好证明：（1）雅虎因此有可能被招致的"损伤"是不确定的；（2）不确定的损伤程度不足以改变这一不定事实。因此，本案达不到诉讼成熟的条件。

8.9 诉讼成熟反方意见

对"诉讼成熟"持反方意见的法官也陈述了自己的观点：（1）法国法院的"暂行判决"违宪，所以对此案其他事实部分的发展和陈述法院无须考量；（2）如果需要考量，上诉法院会将此案发回初审法院。

对这种复杂案件，正、反方意见都需认真领会。法学院老师常给学生说的一句话是：法律有时并不是说对和错，断案也不是非白即黑（从本案按投票决定结果可见一斑），法理及论证方法往往更有意义，只有这样，才能更加接近事实。也是因为这个原因，本书避免武侠小说般的那种写法，描述某个法庭判某个被告多少年让读者过瘾，而是不厌其烦，尽量介绍法官们是如何用他们的逻辑思辨，将法律应用在现实具体案件中。

九、三个插曲

9.1 法国：雅虎总裁被告

在巴黎法院对雅虎案公布判决后的两个月，法国另一家人权组织（主要由那些经受纳粹大屠杀和集中营罹难的受害人家属和相关人士组成）又将雅虎首席行政总裁蒂姆·苦哥（CEO Tim Koogle）告上法庭，这次是依据刑法控告苦哥"为战争和对人类的罪恶开脱"。如果罪名成立，法庭定罪，被告将被处以最高 5 年有期徒刑以及 43 000 美元的罚款。显然，这样的指控是针对自然人而不是法人。诉苦哥的标的为 1 法郎（约 15 美分），象征意义显而易见。这其实是从不同角度控诉法西斯罪行并杜绝纳粹犯罪有任何死灰复燃的可能。尽管雅虎只是提供了一个拍卖平台，但是法国民间组织和国家法院旗帜鲜明的立场，也使任何有可能沾上纳粹边的人和公司（哪怕是技术性或中立性提供一个拍卖平台）变成过街老鼠！不仅如此，艺术家们也用作品让人类记住战争的黑暗，像《辛德勒名单》《钢琴家》《拯救大兵瑞恩》这些出自艺术大师之手的作品，真正地抑恶扬善！这些艺术家连同他们的作品，也更加值得人们的尊敬。一个健康的民族也因为这些健康的、抑恶扬善的作品而变得更加健康。

9.2 德国：澳大利亚籍德国人被判有期徒刑

2000 年 12 月，德国联邦宪法法院驳回费雷德里克·拖奔（Fredrick Töben）的上诉，拖奔出生在德国但生活在澳大利亚并取得澳洲国籍，他在澳大利亚的网站上发布一系列文章并发行小册子否认"二战"纳粹大屠杀。在初审法院，他被定罪并被判处 10 个月有期徒刑。拖奔提起上诉，理由是其网站上的内容及印发的小册子均在德国境外发表和发行，因此不受德国法律的约束。

德国宪法法院裁定，任何人出版、发行任何对德国纳粹歌功颂德或为其战争犯罪开脱的人，无论其国籍和刊发地点，均受德国法律约束。就本案而言，否定大屠杀和为纳粹开脱的资料、信息尽管储存在德国境外的服务器，但德国境内用户可以登录相关网站接触这些资料信息，因此适用德国反纳粹、反法西斯法律。[1]

德国联邦宪法法院标志

德国宪法法院是根据德国基本法特别设立的最高宪法法院。其中心任务是行使司法审查权，类似美国最高法院。但不同的是，它不是普通法院系统的一

---

〔1〕 见 Pinsent Masons：www. out-law. com，p. 1245. 最后访问日期：2013 年 10 月 10 日。

部分，而是一个独立的司法机构。根据德国宪法，联邦宪法法院共设法官 16 名，任期 12 年，必须年满 40 周岁，且必须是经验丰富、训练有素的法学专家，年届 68 岁必须从法官位置退休。本案由联邦宪法法院审理，是因为它涉及刑事审判中被告的人权问题，而人权问题是由宪法法院审理。德国法院系统复杂，一般来说分为普通法庭、行政法庭、税务法庭等。[1]

9.3 美国：俄罗斯电脑高手在美国被抓

第三个插曲与法国、德国及"二战"统统无关，将我们的视野转到俄罗斯。这是一个互联网时代多媒体技术领域涉及知识产权的一个"猫抓老鼠式"的案件。

"美国诉爱尔控公司案"[2]是一桩美国政府诉俄罗斯一家软件公司的案件。该公司雇员斯嘎雅罗夫是一位电脑高手，他为公司写了一套软件，可以将 Adobe 加密的电子书解密，然后变成常见的 PDF 版本。

"奥多比"标识

Adobe（中文译作"奥多比"）是总部设在美国加利福尼亚州的一家跨国公司，创建于 1982 年。奥多比开发的系统产品，如"Adobe Photoshop"（图像处理软件）以及"PDF—Portable Document Format"（便携式文件格式），不但是多媒体时代不可缺少的工具，并且是这个领域国际标准的制定者和技术先驱。[3]斯嘎雅罗夫的软件实际从技术上破解了电子书的加密系统，使"文抄公"在网上大动手脚更加便利。此举直接触犯了美国版权法以及《千禧年数字版权法》。奥多比公司向美国政府投诉。2001 年秋，斯嘎雅罗夫赴美参加学术研讨会，他要主讲的题目是电脑安全及加密技术。但是他一入美国国境，便遭联邦调查局（FBI）逮捕，

---

〔1〕 参见 Bell, John, *Judiciaries Within Europe: A Comparative Review*, Cambridge University Press, 2006.

〔2〕 United States v. Elcom Ltd 203F. Supp 2d 1111 （N. D. Cal. 2002）.

〔3〕 见 Orion, Egan. PDF 1.7 is approved as ISO 32000. The Inquirer. 2007-12-05. 另见新浪科技 2009 年 7 月 3 日："9 月 1 日起 PDF 格式成为中国国家标准"，引自 http://zh. wikipedia. org. 最后访问日期：2013 年 10 月 10 日。

依据是他触犯包括《千禧年数字版权法》在内的美国法律。尽管此案的最终结果是对被告（自然人斯嘎雅罗夫和法人爱尔控公司）的指控均不成立，但此案既是一个小标志也是一个大警示：斯嘎雅罗夫的行为符合俄罗斯法律（为公司写这样的软件是合法的），但涉嫌触犯美国法律，在美国境内还是难免囹圄之灾，而且一关就是 5 个月。[1]

十、结论

"美国雅虎案"历经法国巴黎法院、美国加利福尼亚州地区法院、美国联邦第九巡回上诉法院等初审、上诉几轮审判，不同的人有不同的期待。对审判结果的满意程度也是因人而异，归根结底，法国反种族歧视联盟和犹太学联是真正的赢家。[2] 无论雅虎对网站的调整（包括删除纳粹纪念品图片、关闭拍卖纳粹纪念品的网页等）是出于自愿还是法国法院判决的威慑，不争的事实是，法国这两家组织对雅虎的诉讼，迫使总部设在美国、服务器也设在美国的雅虎，不得不重视法国的内国法律。《美国宪法第一修正案》赋予的言论自由、出版自由等对雅虎来说是神圣不可侵犯的，但这一权利与外国反法西斯立法相冲突时（既然言论自由那么理论上说就应该是免于内容审查的），一个外国法院的判决能否在本国被强制执行，显然因雅虎案而被推到社会前台。这已经不是一个单纯的学术命题，而是活生生的现实。而第九巡回上诉法院关于美国加利福尼亚州地区法院对法国被告具备司法管辖权的判例，无疑为类似的案件在不同司法体制下得以实践铺平了道路。

综合分析[3]，以下几点值得注意：

第一，互联网作为一个无国界的"新世界"，其行为受到有国界的不同地区、不同法系的法律规范。"雅虎案"要解决的是司法管辖权问题，而司法管辖权问题的核心是一国判决能不能在另一国强制执行。

---

〔1〕 Greenberg, Marc, "A return to Lilliput: The LICRA v. Yahoo! Case and the Regulation of Online Content in the World Market", *Berkeley Technology Law Journal*, Vol. 18, 1191, p. 1249.

〔2〕 这方面的观点，参见 Roger Alford (2006)："Ninth Circuit En Banc Dismisses Yahoo! Case"。

〔3〕 参见 Judge Harvey, David, *internet. law. nz*, 3rd *edition*, Wellington: Lexis Nexis, 2011, pp. 65~70。

第二，互联网诚然没有疆界，但从不同的关于司法管辖权的判例中可以看出，不同的司法管辖区也竖起了不同的"围墙"，而法院则充当起"守门员"角色来决定通向管辖区的大门是关还是闭。从拍卖物件到知识产权的传播，互联网以数码方式，通过电脑和网络在全球范围将这些物权进行转移和交换。毫无疑问，各种体系之间的法律冲突，将在一个全新的领域得到前所未有的发展和诠释。

第三，互联网因其渗透力、全球化和即时性，已经改变了传统的广告、物流、营销行业。生产和消费的中间环节越来越少，超市、银行、纸媒等几乎无时无刻不被网上购物、电子金融和多媒体所挑战。因此，电子商务以及其引发的一系列变更，将是不可避免的社会现实。

第四，服务器的地点、ISP 的设置以及各类 IP 地址，不再受地理位置和行政疆域的限制。如"雅虎案"所显示的，服务器设在美国，法国的用户既可以登录"雅虎法国"网站也可以登录"雅虎美国"网站或其他形形色色的网站，本国或特定区域的法律不再是唯一的法律渊源——那么互联网应该成为新的国际公法和私法的分支吗？

第五，如德国联邦宪法法院判例所显示，对网站内容的监督、审核，不是由传播方（如澳大利亚）而是由接受方（德国）来实施。这个问题随着对未成年人保护的急切程度越来越受到重视（如保护他们免受色情网站的危害），已经成为跨越国家、文化、法律、道德领域的一个全球命题。

第六，对 IP 地址进行过滤以达到遵守法律的效果，是雅虎案留下的一个行之有效的先例。但雅虎案中，过滤的责任留给被告雅虎来承担。对于雅虎这样的"文明被告"可以如此为之，但对于那些不文明、不可控的被告呢？如何在查封该查封的网站（如涉及未成年人的色情网站、种族歧视网站等）和不该查封的网站之间取得平衡？

第七，涉及名誉诽谤类案件，互联网对传统民法提出了诸多挑战。施虐者既可匿名在网上"贴大字板"，更可以借互联网的渗透力和无疆域性，轻按"回车"便流毒四溢。即便法庭作出判决，但网上谣言已出，覆水难收，而且申冤要花数年（尤其是跨国、跨区诉讼案）。似乎互联网时代的窦娥更冤！

这似乎已经远远超出了雅虎案所涵括的范围，也不像雅虎案刚发生的时候，某些业界人士所轻视的那样，说这样的案例无非如斯威夫特小说里暗喻的那般——无非是"大蛋端"与"小蛋端"或"高跟党"与"低跟党"之间的琐事。无论如何，互联网已经成为我们生活的一部分。如何规范，如何在民、商、刑等法律领域得到体现并使传统法律得到"版本升级"，这是每个国家、每个司法体系所应共同承担的责任。

案例三 美国道琼斯《巴伦周刊》诽谤案

——文章电子版下载地澳大利亚法律的适用

Dow Jones & Co Inc. v. Gutnick〔2002〕210 CLR 575, 194 ALR 433（HCA）

案　名: 1. 初审：澳大利亚维多利亚州最高法院，"嘎特尼克诉道琼斯"

Gutnick v. Dow Jones & Co Inc〔2001〕VSC 305（28 August 2001）

2. 终审：澳大利亚高等法院，"道琼斯诉嘎特尼克"

Dow Jones & Co Inc. v. Gutnick〔2002〕210 CLR 575, 194 ALR 433（HCA）

原被告: 1. 原告：澳大利亚商人约瑟夫·嘎特尼克

2. 被告：出版《巴伦周刊》和《华尔街日报》的美国道琼斯公司

本案案情及确立的判例原则

2000 年 10 月 28 日，美国道琼斯公司（以下简称"道琼斯"）旗下的《巴伦周刊》以"君子爱财，取之无道"为标题，图文并茂地发表了一篇文章。澳大利亚商人嘎特尼克认为该文章对他构成诽谤，将道琼斯告上澳大利亚维多利亚州最高法院。最高法院判定，虽然《巴伦周刊》纸媒和"巴伦在线"互联网版本在维多利亚州发行量和阅读面均有限，但维多利亚州读者在登录网站、下载并阅读那篇文章开始，该文章便构成在维多利亚州法律意义上的发表。文章的发表构成诉因。原告名誉被损害地即诽谤行为发生地在维多利亚州，维多利亚州法院有权行使司法管辖权。被告道琼斯上诉，认为文章的"传递"和"下载"理当剥离，并且传递是发表的前提，既然传递发生在美国，那么发表自然就不在澳大利亚。道琼斯认为维多利亚州法院不具备司法管辖权，此案应在美国法院审理，否则媒体和出版商对在互联网上发表的每一篇文章都得提心吊胆。鉴于互联网的无国界性，如果被告就原告，今后每发表一篇文章，从阿富汗到津巴布韦都有可能蹦出一个原告来，势必造成被告跟着原告满世界跑，这将对新时代的新闻自由和大众传播造成极大混乱和不定因素。

澳大利亚终审法院 7 名大法官全体一致，驳回道琼斯要求撤销原告诉讼的请求，对初审法院的判决予以支持。

本案确定的判例原则是：英美法系现行诽谤法，依涉嫌诽谤内容的接受地确定司法管辖权。这一原则同样适用通过互联网为媒介的传播方式，尽管互联网和现代科技使新媒体相比传统媒体有本质的区别。本案涉及的诽谤文章，虽然在美国撰写、编辑、上传以及在服务器存储，但其互联网版本可在澳大利亚下载、阅读，因此构成法律上的发表，民事侵权地在澳大利亚，澳大利亚法院具备司法管辖权。美国的被告必须在澳大利亚应诉。

此案从 2000 年事发到 2002 年审理，引起全球媒体普遍关注，是涉及互联网新媒体诽谤案的最具有影响力的典型案例之一。其判例原则被美国、英国、加拿大和新西兰法院广泛引用，但是也引起了极大争议。尤其是涉及下载构成发表、新的发表构成新的诉因，是否意味着互联网页每刷新一次、带有诽谤内容的文章每点击一次，便构成一个新的诉因呢？

澳大利亚高等法院的法官们呼吁，必须通过国会立法方式，来完善判例法对新技术和新问题的解读。尤其是"美女告名人""女影星择优而告""《华尔街日报》有惊无险"等诉讼案件之后，以英国为代表的英美法系国家，对互联网时代的诽谤法体系进行了大手笔的更新和改革。其间，加拿大和新西兰更从不同角度，展现了互联网时代诽谤法作为民事侵权在法理和应用层面的全新体验。

一、道琼斯为何被告？

1.1 道琼斯

道琼斯是一家闻名全球的提供财经信息和服务的美国老牌出版公司。1882年由三位记者在美国纽约华尔街创立，公司的名字由前两位记者的姓——"道"（Charles Dow）和"琼斯"（Edward Jones）——合并而成。像《纽约时报》和《华盛顿邮报》一样，公司虽然是公共交易，但由私营管理。鲁伯特·默多克（Rupert Murdoch）控股的新闻集团（News Corporation）于 2007 年以 50 亿美金（约每股 60 美金）收购了道琼斯公司[1]。

道琼斯旗下出版众多的专业性报刊，包括美国发行量最大的日报《华尔街日报》（The Wall Street Journal），据 2013 年 3 月数据，其发行量达到 240 万份（包括 90 万份电子阅读订户）。[2]《华尔街日报》创刊于 1889 年，是侧重金融、商业和市场等领域的全球发行的日报。1996 年始，道琼斯以 WSJ.com 为域名，推出互联网版本。

与本案相关的是道琼斯出版的《巴伦周刊》。

1.2 《巴伦周刊》及"巴伦在线"

《巴伦周刊》创刊于 1921 年，内容涵括美国及世界其他主要地区的财经信息、市场动态及基金证券、技术革新等方面。自 2002 年 1 月 14 日起，每周分四大部分刊出："技术一周"（大型技术公司一周要闻综述）、"市场一周"（上周市场回顾和分析）、"共投基金"（也称投资基金、信托基金、共同基金、证券投资基金等，主要是这方面基金的信息和专业分析）以及"综述"（主要是

---

〔1〕 Perez-Pena, Richard："Shareholders Back Dow Jones Sale", The New York Times.（2007.12.13）.

〔2〕 Total Circ for US Newspapers, Alliance for Audited Media. Retrieved June 9, 2013.

分析和展望类专栏）。这是继 1999 年 1 月分类推出三部分专栏和 1994 年 3 月 7 日推出两部分分类专栏之后，对杂志的一种与时俱进甚至超前发展式的调整。除此之外，《巴伦周刊》还推出电子版并相继推出适合手机下载的 iPhone 版本、iPad 版本等。

《巴伦周刊》是以喀莱伦斯·巴伦（Clarence W. Barron, 1855-1928）的名字命名的，巴伦先生是道琼斯公司历史上的一位传奇人物。他是记者出身，被公认为现代财经新闻的鼻祖。1903 年 3 月，他在道琼斯公司创始人之一的道先生过世之后，以 130 000 美金买下道琼斯公司。1912 年，他任命自己为董事会主席（他一直担任此职直至去世）。1921 年，他创立了《巴伦国家财经周刊》，这便是《巴伦周刊》的前身。那时的《巴伦国家财经周刊》每期定价 10 美分，到 1926 年发行量飙升至 3 万册，自那时起，《巴伦周刊》便是投资者和财经专业人士的必读刊物。[1] 据 2011 年数据，《巴伦周刊》的发行量在 305 494 册。

值得注意的是《巴伦周刊》的读者群及其职业背景。根据周刊 2010 年的读者调查，《巴伦周刊》的读者中 90.8% 是男性，平均年龄 54 岁，43.8% 有大学学历，94% 为高管，平均个人收入为 282 000 美金，而且平均已阅读《巴伦周刊》8 年。[2]

道琼斯网络版本是 1996 年推出的，域名为 WSJ. com，需付费才能阅读电子版本。在本案发生时，年费为 59 美元，但对《华尔街日报》和《巴伦周刊》的纸媒订户，年费只需 29 美元。没有缴年费的用户，只要事先注册、键入用户名和密码，也能登录阅读"巴伦在线"。

2000 年 10 月 28 日"巴伦在线"版本（以及发行的标明日期为 2000 年 10 月 30 日的纸媒印刷版本）均刊登了一篇文章，标题为"Unholy Gains"（且译成"君子爱财，取之无道"），文章多处提到一位名叫嘎特尼克的先生。嘎先生认为文章有关章节对他构成诽谤，遂将道琼斯告上澳大利亚维多利亚州最高法院。

在继续案情以前，我们得先简单介绍一下澳大利亚的法院系统。

---

〔1〕 数据参见 http://en. wikipedia. org. Retrieved 2013. 10. 13.

〔2〕 Barron's 2010 Print Subscriber Survey. Barronsmag. com.

二、澳大利亚的法院系统

2.1 联邦和州

澳大利亚的法院系统和美国相仿，也是分成联邦和州两大部分。州法院分成三级：初级地方法院、中级地区法院和州最高法院。需要注意的是，这里的最高法院（Supreme Court）指的是州（也有人习惯称省）最高法院。既然是最高法院，自然具有上诉职能，上诉部门称为"最高法院民事上诉法院"和"最高法院刑事上诉法院"。在"雅虎案"中介绍美国司法制度时说过，在州和联邦法院系统应用名称上，大而乱、可与美国有一拼的，当属澳大利亚。所以在引用判例时，要格外小心，因为纽约州的最高法院或维多利亚州（省）的最高法院，虽冠之以 Supreme（最高），但并不是全国法院系统中的终审法院，只是那个州的最高法院而已，或者指那个州的最高初审法院。

联邦法院的主要职能是受理与公司财团、商贸纠纷、移民、破产等与联邦法律相关的案件。联邦法院对这些方面的案件具有初审权，同时也具有上诉权。但与之并行的还是一套"家庭法院"系统，顾名思义，家庭法院是用来受理跟家庭相关的案件，如父母、子女、离异、领养，等等。受理上诉案件时同州（省）法院一样，一般由"全院上诉法院"来受理，即由 3~5 名法官同时受理。

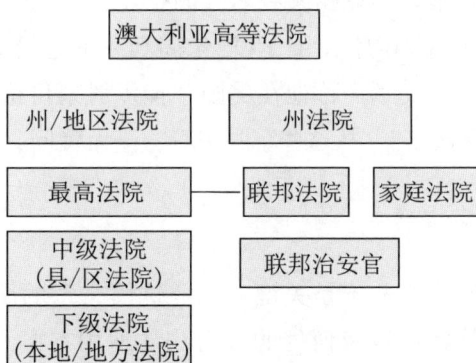

澳大利亚法院系统

2.2 高等法院最高

从上图可以看出，澳大利亚的终审法院是"澳大利亚高等法院"（High Court of Australia）。澳大利亚高等法院是依《澳大利亚宪法》第 71 条设立的，其判例对全国所有法院均有约束力。

终审法院受理的上诉案件有限，而且必须得到高等法院的批准——这种批准不是轻易给出的。因此，各州最高法院以及联邦法院设立的上诉法院，基本上是大多数案件的终结法院。

在"啤酒蜗牛案"中提到过，和其他大英国协成员国一样，澳大利亚最初的终审法院也是英国枢密院。但澳大利亚于 1968 年、1975 年和 1986 年分别以三部立法，几乎完全割断了与英国枢密院的关系。说"几乎完全"是因为根据《澳大利亚宪法》第 74 条的规定，涉及联邦与州之间的法律纠纷，在高等法院批准的前提下可以向英国枢密院上诉，但这只是在理论上成立，因为高等法院明确表示，高等法院"拟不做批准"。

简单介绍了澳大利亚的法院体系，可以看出，道琼斯能够直接上诉到澳大利亚高等法院，本身就说明了此案的力度。

三、"道琼斯案"第一回合：嘎先生诉道琼斯

嘎先生是澳大利亚维多利亚州颇有名气的企业家，在美国也有自己的产业，多年从事慈善业。2000 年 10 月 28 日，《巴伦周刊》的这篇文章，图文并茂，还配了一张嘎先生的照片。文章声称他在美国"操纵股票价格"，并且和美国一位洗钱及逃税高手"过从甚密"。从这些字眼来看，毫无疑问，文章诽谤意味很浓。

3.1 文章在何处发表

就本案来说，诽谤内容并不是关键，刊登这篇文章的所在地点才是，因为这决定了本案的司法管辖地以及何处的诽谤法才适用本案。所以，需要着重强调的是，这篇文章的作者是在《巴伦周刊》的总部纽约撰写文章并上传到道琼斯网站，而网站的服务器设在新泽西。道琼斯网站并不是一个向公众开放的网

站，而是一个专业性、只对自己收费用户开放的网站。根据当时的统计，全球的缴费用户达 550 000 人，但澳大利亚境内全部加起来不过 1700 个用户，维多利亚州内只有几百个用户。当然《巴伦周刊》的纸媒印刷版在澳大利亚也有销售，但数量有限。[1]

嘎先生将道琼斯告上维多利亚州最高法院。鉴于道琼斯在澳大利亚境内并没有公司，嘎先生依维多利亚州最高法院规则，在其司法管辖区外向被告道琼斯送达传票。原告依据两个法律原则：第一，被告的侵权行为发生在维多利亚州；第二，因为被告的侵权行为，原告在维多利亚州的名誉受到损害。也就是说，虽然文章在美国刊登，但在维多利亚州下载后，在维多利亚州构成法律意义上的"发表"。

法庭对这个问题进行了详细的分析。原告强调，用户只要登录道琼斯网站，输入密码并阅读"巴伦在线"上的文章，这些文章（包括这篇有诽谤嫌疑的文章）在下载并出现在电脑屏幕上之时，便构成了法律意义上的发表。这完全符合诽谤法传统意义上的构成三要件：（1）诽谤内容；（2）诽谤内容针对原告；（3）针对原告的诽谤内容已经发表。所谓发表，指的是第三方听到或者读到诽谤内容的那一刻这三个要件符合，则侵权成立，诉因成立。

原告也指出，传统意义上的诽谤内容的发表与互联网时代的发表有诸多不同。但万变不离其宗：只有在第三方听到或者读到的那一刻，诉因就能成立。原告引用了 1934 年的一个判例：对于文字诽谤，其内容构造本身并不构成可起诉的侵权行为，对诽谤内容的发表才构成。只有在这样的内容传导给读者之时，才构成对名誉的侵权。[2]

3.2 互联网服务供应商（ISP）

法庭分析并引用了若干涉及互联网司法管辖权的判例。比较突出的是英国 2001 年一个涉及 ISP 的判例。ISP 即 Internet Service Provider，中文常译作"互联网服务供应商""网际网络服务提供者"或"互联网服务供应商"，即提供互

---

[1] Gutnick (2002) 194 ALR 433 (Callinan J).
[2] 见 Lee v. Wilson (1934) 51 CLR 276 所确定的判例。

联网登录（Internet Access）相关服务的供应商。也就是说，只有通过他们将个人电脑连到互联网络上，我们才能上网。早年的拨号连线，近些年来发展的宽频和光纤 Modem（中文译作"调制解调器"），都是围绕如何快速上网进行。ISP 可大可小，可以是纯商业化运作以营利为目的，也可以是不营利或社区性的。

3.3 "歌德弗莱案" 解读网上 "发表"

英国的 "歌德弗莱诉待盟互联网案" 中的被告就是这样一个互联网服务供应商[1]。它为用户提供一个分布式的互联网交流系统，用户可以在系统里发帖、上传文章等。这些帖子、文章或其他信息，按不同层次存储在服务器里。这样的服务器，通常可以再转发给其他服务器，滚雪球式越滚越远、越滚越多。英国这件案子里，被告的服务器一般将这些信息存储两周。一位不提供姓名的"路过"人士，在"新闻组"（这里指网络意义上不同层次的分类，与传统意义上的新闻不同）"soc. culture. thai"上发帖，内容对原告构成诽谤。原告通知被告，要求被告将这篇诽谤帖子删除。被告原本可以很容易地按要求删帖，但却没有这么做。原告于是诉诸法律，被告在法庭提出三个抗辩：第一，他不是这个帖子的"发表者"；第二，他采取了合理的必要措施；第三，他不知道也没有理由相信他的行为促使这篇诽谤帖子的发表，也就是说帖子的发表跟他没有关系。原告则请求法庭将被告以上三个抗辩驳回。但被告强调，根据 1996 年《英国诽谤法》，"发表"不能成立。

但法官得到的结论如下：任何在服务器上存储的信息（帖子）在传导给登录的用户后，便构成对那位用户的发表。传播过程好比书商将书卖给图书馆，图书馆提供给读者。

其次，在原告通知被告帖子含有诽谤内容之后，被告便有了主观上的认知。在这之前，被告本可以依"无辜传播"抗辩，根据英国这部成文法，如果被告可以证明以下三点，便可做如此抗辩：（1）他不是这则有诽谤嫌疑文字的作者、编辑或出版者；（2）就这则内容的发表，他采取了必要谨慎措施；（3）他

---

［1］ Godfrey v. Demon Internet［2001］QB201at 204,［1999］4All ER 342（QB）at 343-344.

不知道也没理由相信自己之所为促使了诽谤内容的发表。

法官专门比较了美国的相关判例，并指出：在英国诽谤案件中适用美国判例需要小心谨慎。美国宪法第一修正案带来的影响，使英美两个司法体系在处理诽谤案件时有很大不同。例如，就"无辜传播"来说，英国法要求被告（发表者）证明自己的无辜；而美国法则要求被诽谤的原告来证明被告（发表方）不是无辜的。[1]

从英美两国的判例和断案立场来看，在美国诽谤法下诉讼成功的门槛显然要比英国高。也就是说，因美国宪法第一修正案影响，在美国的诽谤诉讼，更有利于被告开脱而不利于原告追究。"歌德弗莱案"确定的判例，使所有互联网服务供应商都必须小心。虽然是第三方匿名"路过"，但留下一堆诽谤"垃圾"，是要由供应商来"清扫"并承担责任的。法官得出的结论，便是这则判例的核心：在服务器上存储的信息，在传导给登录的用户后，便构成对那位用户的发表。这跟英国早年的判例，确定一位老板向自己的秘书口述一封信，便构成对那位秘书的发表如出一辙，只是发表的方法和技术层面不同而已。

3.4 被动传送和谷歌搜索引擎

但令互联网服务供应商稍为宽慰的是另一则判例。2006 年英国的这件判例（Bunt v. Tilley）[2]，也是涉及互联网上的聊天室，有所不同的是，原告不但告了互联网服务供应商，并且连电话公司、线路公司以及和互联网传送相关的公司全告了，因为被告不但在聊天室涉嫌发帖诽谤，而且这些帖子随着互联网的传播，越传越远，越传越离谱。但法院认真考量了"主动诽谤"和"被动媒介"的区别，认为将普通法意义上的诽谤责任，归咎于电话公司这类被动性传输媒介不妥。此案与"歌德弗莱案"的区别是，前者对诽谤内容有主观认知（因为原告事先通知被告并要求被告删帖），而本案中互联网服务公司仅起到被动传输的作用，因此不能够被认定为普通法意义上的发表者。

互联网服务供应商如此，那么搜索引擎如谷歌（Google）呢？

---

〔1〕　Godfrey v. Demon〔2001〕QB 201 at 204.

〔2〕　Bunt v. Tilley〔2006〕EWHC 407（QB），〔2006〕3 All ER 336（QB）.

英国 2009 年还真有这么一件诉讼案。[1] 第三方在网上搜索, 从谷歌中搜出诽谤内容, 谷歌能否因 "发表" 了这些诽谤内容而被起诉呢? 法庭认为, 在这种情形下, 谷歌作为被告实在是 "有点过了"。要谷歌承担法律责任, 第一, 需要类似于 "犯意" 那样的主观认知, 即知道这部分内容有诽谤成分; 第二, 谷歌在其中起到的作用连 "被动传输" 都算不上, 充其量只是为客户 "提供方便" 而已。

这两件案子对 "歌德弗莱案" 中互联网服务供应商扮演的角色和有可能承担的责任, 进行了不同层面的分析和认定。需要注意的是, 应具体问题具体分析。互联网服务供应商或搜索引擎, 在某些情形下不用承担法律上的责任, 并不代表它们在任何情形下都不用承担法律上的责任。随着网络法律的发展, 在不同的诉讼案件中, 互联网服务供应商或搜索引擎被判有责, 或被勒令交出有关客户的 IP 地址, 类似情形比比皆是。总之, 责任轻重取决于它们在事物和情节链中起到的作用和扮演的角色。

3.5 道琼斯的文章发表在维多利亚州

原告律师引经据典无非是为了证明一个论点: "巴伦在线" 在维多利亚州的用户, 在键入密码、登录并阅读这篇文章的那个时间点开始, 便构成这篇文章的发表。就本案而言, 文章在维多利亚州发表, 因此适用维多利亚州的法律。该观点的中心意义在于, 维多利亚州的读者在电脑屏幕上读到文章的那一刻, 便意味着文章下载后内容传输给读者, 文章因发表而将文章 (文字和图片) 的实际意义传输出去。原告也指出, 就 "发表" 而言, 其文字本身的意义和诽谤法界定的意义有很大不同。只有在一个诽谤内容传输给一个受众之后, 这样的 "发表" 才能构成法律上的诉因。

Lee v. Wilson 是一个 1934 年的判例, 它确定的原则是, "就文字诽谤而言, 是该文字的发表而非该文字的组合构成一个诉因。信息被公而告之, 但接受该信息的人通常不是作者 (而是他人如读者)。诽谤引起的名誉损毁, 由该信息对其读者产生的效果而产生"。[2] 原告嘎特尼克在法庭的诉讼主张以及所确定

---

〔1〕 Metropolitan International School Ltd v. Designtechnica Corp〔2009〕EWHC 1765, 〔2010〕3 All E. R. 548 (QB).

〔2〕 Lee v. Wilson (1934) 51CLR276.

的原则，在维多利亚州最高法院得到支持。

3.6 被告道琼斯抗辩

被告道琼斯向法院申请将诉讼驳回，主要依据三个抗辩理由：第一，维多利亚州法院没有司法管辖权——因为该文章不是在维多利亚州发表的。第二，被告质疑法庭对相关规则的解读和适用，因为这些规则的解读和适用导致被告在这种情形下被送达诉状。第三，"法院审理不便"原则（Forum Non Conveniens，常缩写为 FNC）——但被告表示第三条只有在第一条司法管辖权抗辩不成立时才被引用。"法院审理不便"是普通法关于冲突法适用的一个法律原则。其中心思想是，如果另一个法院更适合审理，那么在这种情形下，当前法院可以拒绝审理。

3.7 "法院审理不便"原则

道琼斯案发生时的澳大利亚，因 2002 年的一个判例，确定了澳大利亚在适用 FNC 原则时，采用"明确不恰当法院"作为法律测试标准。也就是说，法院在判定这个命题时，要判断该法院是不是"明确不恰当的法院"。

澳大利亚高等法院同时也表示，尽管在一个案件的审理过程中，即使需要适用外国法律，澳大利亚法院也不会因此而变成"明确不恰当的法院"。从中可以看出，这个判例所确定的法律原则，在冲突法原则前提下，是注重考量平衡点的。澳大利亚高等法院受理的那宗 2002 年的案件还与华人有关。Regie National des Usines Renault SA v. Zhang[1]案中，原告是一位张姓（音译）先生。他于 1986 年到澳大利亚，但在 1991 年初去了距澳 1000 多公里的法属新喀里多尼亚（New Caledonia），目的是到设在首府努美阿（Noumea）的澳大利亚总领馆申请永久居民身份。在新喀里多尼亚期间，他租了一辆雷诺（Renault）轿车，但因车失控出了严重车祸，脊柱受伤，他在努美阿住了 14 天医院，随后转回悉尼医院，一住数月，落下残疾。

张先生向雷诺公司索赔，将其告上新南威尔士州最高法院。雷诺公司在新

---

〔1〕 Regie National des Usines Renault SA v. Zhang［2002］HCA10（14 March 2002）.

南威尔士州抑或整个澳大利亚都没有公司和业务关系，因此张先生在管辖区外向被告送达传票和法院文件。被告雷诺公司以新南威尔士州"法院审理不便"为由，申请法院驳回诉讼。初审法院依此驳回，上诉法院拒绝驳回。原、被告互换身份再诉到高等法院〔1〕，由5位法官共同审理，判定：根据澳大利亚冲突法原则，民事侵权行为发生地的法律为适用之法律——不管该侵权行为是发生在澳大利亚还是海外。最终结果是雷诺赢而张先生输，得原告就被告，侵权行为发生地之法律即法国法，作为适用和断案之法律。

张先生案所确定的判例，适用于道琼斯案（记住"侵权行为发生地"这个关键词）。当然，2005年《澳大利亚民事诉讼程序法》出台后，因判例而形成的普通法立场有所改变——这是后话，为避免混淆，在此不赘述。

3.8 被告抗辩有创意

说被告在法庭这种场合"抗辩有创意"，实际上是一句文明的骂人话。因为法庭上要以理服人，这个理指的就是法理和判例上的依据，没有依据的抗辩，用大白话说就是"瞎掰"。法官除了经常引用法律和判例外，还有权威性的教科书或学术文章。这也是为什么法官的判决书公布后，精彩的青史留名（如爱德肯大法官在"啤酒蜗牛案"中的判决），拙劣的遭人晒笑，除可能被选作教材外，更是学术、媒体、各类团体组织等各路人马从不同角度分析和考证的对象。这也是司法接受公众监督的一种方式。对法官如此，对辩护律师更甚。道琼斯的律师有创意的抗辩有以下几项：

其一，文章的发表地不在维多利亚州，而是上传到网络服务器的那个地点。同时，就民事诽谤法层面而言，对该文章的"理解"不属于"发表"（"publication"）的一部分〔2〕。显然被告将"发表"从法律意义上撇开，只单纯强调"发表"一词在语言学上的单一含义。尽管如此，这种解读似乎也很勉强。我

---

〔1〕 从案例名中可以看出，初审张先生是原告，是 Zhang 诉 Renault，上诉后双方调换了身份，变成 Renault 诉 Zhang。

〔2〕 道琼斯的律师的原话是："…that understanding or comprehension was not a part of publication for the purpose of the tort of defamation." 见 Gutnick v. Dow Jones & Co Inc〔2001〕VSC 305（28 August 2001）at〔21〕。道琼斯的律师这一观点是自创的，没有任何法理和判例依据。

们不妨看看权威词典是如何解释"Publication"这个词的。《剑桥》〔1〕和《牛津》〔2〕以及梁实秋的《远东英汉大辞典》〔3〕对"发表"都有比较详细的解释。从中可以看出，道琼斯的律师似乎只采用了这个词的表层含义，用现代网络语言说，就是看到一个热贴，"转得好——我收了"，为收帖而收帖却全然不顾该帖内容，即不看此贴内容单凭标题而判定其好——那看标题本身是否对此帖（或此帖的一部分）构成"阅读而理解"这个行为呢？毕竟，"视"而不"见"在文字传播过程中难以实现。而道琼斯的律师似乎强调，"视"可以不"见"，因此对文章的理解则不构成法律意义上的发表。读之再三，不知所云。

法庭其实也是这样分析的，只是我们换成网络语言戏说一番而已。因为法庭自始至终〔4〕，对"发表"给出的定义，都是指将带有诽谤意义的内容传导给读者，〔5〕而这种传导只有在这则内容被读到之后才可以实现。道琼斯的律师将"发表"语言学上的意义和法律意义剥离，不但牵强，而且如同硬要将"波"和"浪"分开一样，此抗辩"创意"之一也。

其二，道琼斯的律师将"传递"（delivery）和"下载"（download）分开。何为传递？道琼斯的律师说，当设在美国的服务器对用户的指令作出反应时，便发生了"传递"。与此相对，当文章在维多利亚州"使读者索取变成可能"之时，便构成"下载"，但下载的动作是独立的——因此被告不应对此负责。道琼斯为论证这个观点，引用了1849年和1820年的两个判例，第一个判例是Duke of Brunswick v. Harmer（1849）。原告在文章发表17年后提出诉讼。诉讼时效不成为阻碍，因为在这期间刊有这篇文章的报纸在反复流通。第二个判例是

---

〔1〕 Publication：noun［u］，"the act of making information or stories available to people in a printed or electronic form；a book，magazine，newspaper，or document in which information or stories are published"．见Cambridge Advanced Learner's Dictionary & Thesaurus，Cambridge University Press．cambridge. org。

〔2〕 Publication：noun［u］［c］，"the act of printing a book，a magazine etc，and making it available to the public；a book，a magazine，etc. that has been published"．参见Oxford Advanced Learner's Dictionary．Oxfordlearnersdictionaries. com。

〔3〕 发表：名词，"出版物、发行物；出版、发行；发表、公布"．参见梁实秋：《远东英汉大辞典》，商务印书馆、远东图书公司1991年版，第1674页。

〔4〕 这里的"始"可能源自1891年的判例Pullman v. Walter Hill & Co［1891］（QB524（CA）。法庭引用这个判例，意在法律层面解释"发表"含义。

〔5〕 这里指"文字诽谤"（libel）、"言语诽谤"（Slander）传播给听众和观众的载体不同，另说。现代诽谤法已经很少进行文字、言论诽谤区分。

R v. Burdett（1820）。写有诽谤内容的信未被蜡封，法庭判定诽谤内容不必实际传导而构成诽谤。法官对道琼斯这一立场连同引用的两个判例一并驳回。[1] 道琼斯的律师是希望借"传递"和"下载"的剥离，证明传递是发表的前提，既然传递发生在美国，那么发表自然就不在澳大利亚。但法官更直截了当：如果道琼斯这一立场正确，即传递是发表的前提，那么法官认为传递实际上在服务器（美国）和家用电脑（维多利亚州）同时发生。

3.9 初审判决

初审法官从"歌德弗莱案"中受益良多，认为任何一个第三方，在网上"看到"对原告诽谤的帖子之时，该帖对其便构成法律意义上的发表。初审法官得出的结论是，第一，诽谤法已经存在了好几个世纪，公认的原则是，当诽谤内容（无论是口头还是书面）被人听到、看到、读到以至知晓其内容，彼时彼地便构成发表。第二，被告的抗辩是没有法律依据的，信息被传递而不被知晓（即中文常说的"视"而不"见"）是说不过去的。因此可以得出的结论是，当道琼斯在维多利亚州的订户在缴完费、办完手续可以登陆上网并将文章下载之时，便构成了文章在维多利亚州的发表。

初审法官还认为现代科技在明辨法理上没有太大关系，万变不离其宗，他倾向以传统意义来定义"发表"，并将此案与"歌德弗莱案"相提并论。但需要注意的是，"歌德佛莱案"中网上聊天室是对所有公众开放的，发帖与读帖非常自由。而本案中道琼斯"巴伦在线"只对自己的用户开放，且有事先缴费、输入密码等一套标准和要求。将两者相提并论不加区分，这也是初审法官判决中有瑕疵的地方。道琼斯案初审时，还传唤了一位专家级证人，这位博士对法庭解释，说互联网是"一个电信网联接另一个电信网"，与传统通讯相比其最大的不同是，互联网的这种特性使得"史无前例的人众使用史无前例的装备，以多重数据格式在一个没有国界的领域互相交流"。[2] 这位专家的陈述，也让人联想到不少"专家"在关键时刻出场说理或者"辟谣"的场景。只是少

---

〔1〕 法庭不是驳回（否定和推翻）这两个判例所确定的原则——关于 Duke 案，本章最后一节也有分析。法庭是驳回道琼斯律师引用这两个判例所证明的观点。

〔2〕 见 Dow Jones and Company Inc v. Gutnick［2002］HCA56；210 CLR575 第 14 段。

了一份严肃，多了一份滑稽。道琼斯此时要争辩的不仅是司法管辖地问题，作为被告，他必须弄清楚另一个所有诽谤法领域都绕不开的问题：既然"发表"已经成立，那么是单一发表还是重复发表？如果是重复发表，那么一共发表了多少次？因为根据传统的诽谤法，每发表一次便构成一个新的诉因。在互联网时代，每点击或刷新一次，便构成一次新的发表——这在理论上是完全成立并且有最近的案例支持的。道琼斯决定上诉并获准直接向澳大利亚终审法院——澳大利亚高等法院上诉。

澳大利亚高等法院徽章

四、"道琼斯案"第二回合：道琼斯上诉

4.1 高等法院判决书

澳大利亚高等法院由首席大法官领衔，共七位法官听审。判决书共203个自然段外加236条引文和注释，累计30 336字。最终结果是道琼斯的上诉被驳回。但结果似乎并不重要，重要的是这个案件确定的判例和解决的法律问题。这也是普通法（判例法）美妙的地方。无论是被告道琼斯公司出资还是原告嘎特尼克先生自己掏腰包，他们是以自己的官司来完善判例和法理，以解决新技术和新时代带来的新的法律问题。用中文语汇说，他们是以自己的精力、财力和麻烦，来参与和完善一个社会抑或整个共同法系的法制建设。

判决书中涉及的法律问题主要有：国际私法，诽谤法（哪国法律适用），司法管辖权及司法管辖地，法庭文件送达规则，文章是否发表以及在何处发表，如果原告名誉遭毁损那么毁损地在哪里，以及被损伤的名誉主要和哪些地方相关联。

但受理上诉案件，高等法院的主要考量归根结底还是两大问题：第一，文章在何处发表？第二，澳大利亚的法院是否为受理本案最适合、最方便的法院？

澳大利亚高等法院7位法官全体意见一致，支持初审法院的结论（这在上诉案件中尚不多见），并作出判决：文章在维多利亚州下载后构成发表；受理此诽谤案，澳大利亚法院作为最合适、最方便的法院具备司法管辖权。

4.2 道琼斯喊冤

道琼斯重申在初审时的立场，并强调，《巴伦周刊》发行量（纸媒）达30万份，99%在美国发行。"巴伦在线"付费订户也多达50万户，只有极少数订户在维多利亚州。

道琼斯首先从技术上进行分析：信息传播的那个载体在传统意义上称作"文件"（document），在互联网意义上称作"网页"（web page）。运行相应软件并使那个文件得以传播并为用户获取的电脑设备叫"网络服务器"（web server），而使用电脑发出指令并获取这个文件的叫"互联网浏览器"（web browser）。不用说，以上步骤得以实施是因为最初有那么一个人将文件"放"到电脑系统中，这个动作叫"上传"（uploading）。上传后用户想找到一份文件得输入电脑网址，即所谓的资源定位——IT行业俗称的URL即Uniform/Universal Resource Locator，译作"统一资源定位符"，实际上，是关于网页地址的一个记号。

道琼斯的《华尔街日报》和《巴伦周刊》编辑部设在纽约，"巴伦在线"及《华尔街日报》网站（WSJ. com）也设在纽约。文章写好后先是储存到编辑部电脑，再传到设在新泽西的电脑中心。道琼斯在新泽西有两个这样的数据处理中心，一个设有6台服务器，另一个则起中转作用。

"巴伦在线"的文章是在编辑完毕、上传到新泽西的服务器上才成为文章的，因此文章在新泽西发表——这是道琼斯在法庭上一直坚持的观点。沿着这个逻辑，道琼斯认为一个在互联网上发表文章的人（姑且称作"出版商"）应该依据其网络服务器所在地的法律来规范自己的行为，当然这样的服务器所在地应与公司业务和所在地相关，并且具备一定的稳定性。随机或投机选择的服务器地址不在考虑之列。

诸位看官，是不是觉得这些话听起来挺绕的？可能在理屈而词不穷的时候，往往会出现这种情形。但站在道琼斯的律师的角度，他们想表达的是他们将服务器选择在新泽西不是偶然的：他们是当地的纳税大户，他们是当地严肃、认真而成功的产业，其企业文化与当地水乳交融……所以，有什么法律问题可以来这里说清楚嘛！"服务器所在地"说保证了互联网时代出版商遵纪守法的可靠性和稳定性。否则，被告跟着原告走，在互联网无国界的现代社会，原告在地球无论哪个角落下载一篇涉嫌诽谤的文章，被告出版商都得接受那个地方的法律制裁，于情于法都说不过去。喊冤之余，道琼斯抛出了一个观点：澳大利亚法院应采纳和适用"单一发表规则"。

4.3 "单一发表规则"和"重复发表"

这些规则与诽谤法的特点和性质有关。但是在介绍"单一发表规则"之前，不妨先看看传统诽谤法对相关概念是如何解读的。

传统的诽谤法早在1849年的一个判例中[1]就允许原告在诽谤文章发表17年后（因为那时他才发觉），将被告告上法庭。传统的诽谤法对"重复发表"也有成熟而系统的界定，英国1964年的一个判例确定，一份报纸如果发表（如转载）另一份报纸已经发表过的诽谤言论，并不代表后发表的就不用负责或责任较轻。既然已经重复发表，自然因此构成新的一个诉因（见本章附录）。因为诽谤对受害者的折磨，仿佛杀人不见血，不能说别人已经捅了一刀或者反正已经有人先捅了，我再捅一刀或打打黑拳没什么了不起。

但从出版商角度，也存在两大问题：第一，一本书发行上万册，一份报纸发行几十万份，电台或电视的一则新闻靠电波或者卫星传送出去，又被刻成若干份光盘……这些构成重复发表吗？如果构成重复发表，那么如何裁定因重复发表而导致的新的诉因呢？报纸发行几十万份意味着几十万个诉因吗？第二，

---

〔1〕 Duke of Brunswick v. Harmer。

诉讼时效。诽谤法的诉讼时效（一般一到两年，各国、各地区不同）从哪个时段起算？——从第一份报纸印好还是最后一份卖完？如果第一份印好和最后一份卖完因特殊原因而间隔时间太长呢？解决不了这些问题，出版商随时随地都有可能吃上官司。

20 世纪 80 年代美国的两个判例使这些问题的解决变得明朗。

4.4 成人杂志诽谤案

第一个案子是成人杂志《阁楼》的发行人诉另一份内容更成人的成人杂志（Keeton v. Hustler Magazine Inc）[1]，这些所谓的成人杂志内容及图片大多已经从"乐而不淫"发展到"露骨销魂"，但偏偏这样的"专业杂志"也惹上诽谤官司。但惹上官司的不是图片上的男女主角，而是出版这些杂志的男女老板们。诽谤内容自然离不开那些老套路，考虑到本书篇幅，在此不展开。与本章有关的是法院如何裁定诉讼管辖地。

原告来自纽约，但却跑到与加拿大魁北克省接壤的新罕布什尔州（New Hampshire）提出诉讼。理由很简单：新罕布什尔州的法律，诉讼时效为 6 年（比其他州和其他国家要长得多），并且本州适用的"单一发表规则"在考量侵权赔偿时，可将被告全国发行 50 个州内的收入一并核算。

原、被告两家都是出版成人杂志，且实力相当、口味相投，真正的谁也不怕谁，官司一直打到美国联邦最高法院。

美国联邦最高法院所要解决的法律问题就是：来自外州的原告，诉全国发行的杂志（被告）并在新罕布什尔州提起诉讼，联邦法院对此案有无司法管辖权？最高法院判决：联邦法院具备司法管辖权，因为法律从未要求原告对提请诉讼的这个州行使"最低程度接触"作为司法管辖的前提条件，更何况被告作为全国发行的杂志的确在本州有商业行为，也就是说被告在本州有"最低程度接触"，这是在本州诉讼的逻辑起点。

听起来拗口，但意思很明确，这类诉讼案可以被告就原告，原告有权选择诉讼管辖地。

----

〔1〕 Keeton v. Hustler Magazine Inc 465 U. S. 770 （1984）.

4.5 女影星诉娱乐杂志

"花开两朵，各表一枝"。与"成人杂志案"前后脚的另一个案子是 Calder v. Jones〔1〕案，原告是位女影星，被告是全国发行的一份娱乐商业杂志。该杂志刊登了一篇文章说这位女影星"酗酒"。女影星一怒之下，一口气不但告了杂志、杂志发行人，索性连作者和总编都"一勺烩"全告了。原告来自加利福尼亚州，而被告（总部）在佛罗里达州。

与上一个案子不同的是，上一个案子的原告选了一个第三方地界打官司，而这个案子的原告将被告引进自家后院。她说这份娱乐杂志在全国每周的发行量为 500 万份，而其中至少有 60 万份是在加利福尼亚州，单凭这一点，加利福尼亚州法院也应该行使司法管辖权。

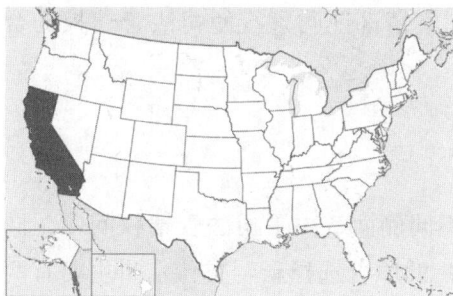

加利福尼亚州在美国的位置〔2〕　　　　佛罗里达州在美国的位置〔3〕

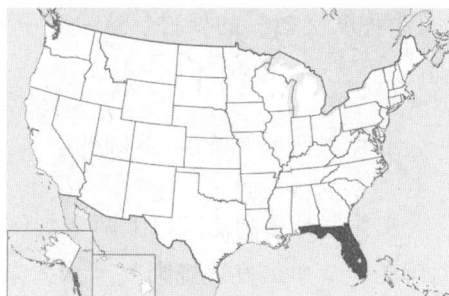

对此杂志发行人没有异议，但作者和总编表示反对。为此在加利福尼亚州的初审法院、中级法院和上诉法院折腾了几个来回，最终官司打到美国联邦终审法院。双方抗辩理由不一。被告说如果把他们从佛罗里达州拉到加州参加诉讼，允许加州法官行使司法管辖权，势必对宪法第一修正案所保护的言论自由权产生负面影响。而此时的作者和总编则将手中的笔幻化成"电焊枪"，并在最高法院打比方：自己就是电焊工，在佛罗里达州焊接一个锅炉，锅炉在加利

---

〔1〕　Calder v. Jones 465 U. S. 783（1984）.

〔2〕　Source：www. ca. gov.

〔3〕　Source：www. myflorida. com.

福尼亚州爆炸，固然生产商应该为在加利福尼亚州发生的产品质量事故负责，但作为电焊工，怎么可以为在佛罗里达州焊接的部件而到加利福尼亚州尽责呢？

巧舌如簧至此，法官就差当头棒喝。最高法院的法官说，就算你们是电焊工，佛罗里达州的电焊工是不会有意识地锁定身在加利福尼亚州的目标的。可惜你们不是电焊工而是大笔一挥下笔千言的写手。作为总编，你不可能不知道你们的娱乐周刊在加利福尼亚州发行量之大，而原告生活、工作在加利福尼亚州，诽谤言论在加利福尼亚州流传，原告名誉在加利福尼亚州受损，民事侵权行为发生在加利福尼亚州，所以加利福尼亚州行使司法管辖权当之无愧。至于被告搬出宪法第一修正案，法官说那是针对言论自由的抗辩，不是针对司法管辖权的抗辩。

这两个案子，一个是发行量之众（加利福尼亚州），在民事侵权所在地影响深重；一个是发行量虽小（新罕布什尔州），但作为被告已满足在司法管辖地"最小程度接触"的要件。这一左一右不同案情都证明了行使司法管辖权的合理性。

4.6 基本规则的一个例外

美国联邦最高法院以上两个判例，从不同侧面解决了司法管辖权问题，同时阐明了"单一发表规则"。"成人杂志案"的原告选择新罕布什尔州主要有两个目的，一是诉讼时效长，二是赔偿金按全国发行收入核算，对原告有利。但是从这个判例演化出来的"单一发表规则"，却派生了当时无法预测的诸多效果。

所谓"单一发表规则"，指的是诽谤案中原告对被告所出版的批量出版物，只能行使一次诉讼主张。也就是说，涉嫌诽谤的书、杂志或报纸，不是每印一本便导致一次诉因。但是诽谤法的基本规则——至少是"道琼斯案"发生的时候依然如此——都是指诽谤内容每传播一次（不管是传播给同一个人还是不同的人）都构成一个新的诉因。"单一发表规则"可以看作是这个基本规则的一个例外。

"成人杂志案"中的判例将这一例外进一步明确：第一，诉讼主张只能一次；第二，发生在所有司法管辖地的所有侵权赔偿，可在一次诉讼主张中得到解决；第三，根据案情对原告作出的胜诉或败诉判决，对原、被告在所有其他司法管辖地的同一诉讼起到禁止作用。换句话说，同一诉讼只要判决了，此事不可再议，换地方、换法院、换律师都不行。[1]

这是该判例具有重大意义的原因所在。尤其在互联网时代，纯理论的推理是，对于诽谤内容每点击一次，便构成一个新的诉因。美国最高法院的上述判例，使世界上主要几个司法体系面对互联网时代的类似问题，都或轻或重地打消了一些顾虑。普通法体系不用说，判例、经验和智慧是共享的。欧洲大陆法系（如德国、法国）尤其在欧盟框架下，对判例法的借鉴与引用亦越来越多。但互联网正在以一个我们从未体验过的速度改变着我们的生活、我们的世界。要解决纷繁复杂的具体问题，一个判例是不够的。当澳大利亚高等法院的大法官们考量"道琼斯案"时，当道琼斯的律师们请求他们引用美国"单一发表规则"，并就具体问题作出更新的司法解释时，澳大利亚的大法官不无感慨地说，我们还是各司其职吧，我们负责断案，立法的事留给国会。

的确，"道琼斯诽谤案"之后，许多国家在互联网时代诽谤法领域都有诸多深层的思考和大胆的动作。因为互联网对司法管辖权和诉讼时效这两个原本很清楚的法律课题，带来了极大地挑战。

4.7 例外之例外

从以上判例可以看出，"单一发表规则"对诉讼时效的规范，实际上取决于对"发表"何时起算。对传统媒体，判断起算的时间比较容易。当诽谤的话传到第三方耳中，诉讼时效的计时表便开始跳动。报纸杂志出版后通过各种渠道传到千家万户，当第一份这样的报纸、杂志在市场上出现，诉讼时效的计时表便开始跳动。同理，诽谤言论在互联网上首次出现（发表）后，诉讼时效也开始起算。因为这个"单一发表规则"，不是说在网页上每刷新一次便构成一个诉因。（关于"刷新构成诉因"的案例，本部分有专门段落讨论）"单一发表规则"的主要意图是在保护言论自由的大前提下，取得原、被告间利益的平衡。各地区、各国对诽谤法诉讼时效的规定不一，但大致都是 1~3 年。比较特殊的如"成人杂志案"中的新罕布什尔州，应该是目前所遇案例中最长的，为 6 年。

---

[1] Keeton v. Hustler Magazine, Inc, 465 U. S. 770（US1984）.

但"单一发表规则"不是绝对的，它原本是传统诽谤法基本准则中的一个例外，但例外之中还有一个例外，就是"再发表"（republication）。这是美国地方法院 2006 年确定的一个判例。[1] 这个判例源自一个破产案。既然是破产案，又涉及双方的不愉快，相争无好言，便惹上了诽谤官司。这个判例确定"再发表"为"单一发表规则"之例外。即如果涉及重新编排、重新发表或以一种新的方式发表的诽谤内容，则诉讼时效重新起算。这个案例是在 2002 年美国另一案例的基础上，将这个规则进一步推进的。

Firth v. State 案[2]，从案名就看得出这是一个"民告官"的案子，告的是美国政府。原告是政府环保部门执法处的一名主管，一份对他的管理方法及政府采购之账目等问题有诸多非议和抨击的报告被贴到政府网站上，1 年后原告起诉，但政府律师请求法院驳回起诉，因为过了当地法律规定的 1 年诉讼时效。法院判定当一份文件（如案中所涉报告）在网上首次发表时，诉讼时效起算。用户下载或网页调整并不改变诉讼时效的起算时间。纽约最高法院上诉庭维持了初审法院的以上判决。但原告声辩说，发表原报告的网页重新调整并增添了新内容，因此构成重复发表。但纽约最高法院上诉庭判定网页虽有调整，但增添的内容跟原报告无关，因为对原报告没有产生内容上的影响，诉讼时效仍按原报告首次在网上发表的时间起算。超过了诉讼时效，内容不议，原告起诉被驳回。从原告角度看是够冤的。这也令人联想到在西方社会流行的一句话："不要让权利睡着了。"什么"大人不计小人过""君子以德报怨"之类，遇到诉讼时效等法律问题，需慎重对待。这个判例唯一比较可惜的是，原告提出被告在网页调整过程中，还在其他网站提供了这份报告的网址链接，提供链接是否构成重新发表？但纽约最高法院上诉庭拒绝对这一抗辩进行考量。所以链接问题只能留到下一个新的案例中再做考证。法官、律师和学术界有的时候是盼着有一些新奇的案子出现，非此不能解决诸多新奇的法律问题。但这个判例却对"再发表"这一例外做了清楚的阐述，并表示"再发表规则"的目的是对原告

---

[1] In re Emory M. Davis and Carol D. Davis, Debtors、Emory M. Davis and Carol C. Davis, Appellants, v. Frank Mitan, Appellee. Civil Action No. 06-88-C. United States District Court, W. D. Kentucky, Louisville Division. August 14, 2006. 347 B. R. 607 (2006).

[2] Firth v. State 287 A. D. 2d 771, 731 N. Y. S 2d 244 (N. Y. Ct Claims 2001), aff'd, 98 N. Y. 2d 365, 775 N. E. 2d 463, 747 N. Y. S. 2d 69 (2002).

起到进一步保护作用，假定被告"重新编辑、重新传输并且其目的是为了扩大新的受众"，则"再发表"构成，诉讼时效从新的发表之日起算。就互联网而言，哪怕网页未动，但违章内容有较大篇幅改动，也构成"再发表"。

4.8 澳大利亚法官眼中的"单一发表规则"

道琼斯的律师团队请求澳大利亚高等法院采纳"单一发表规则"，但被驳回。高等法院的法官们在判决书中从第29~37页整整9大段来分析"单一发表规则"的历史及发展现状。判决书说，美国有包括纽约、加利福尼亚州和宾夕法尼亚州等在内的27个州，通过立法（成文法）或判例确定了"单一发表规则"。澳大利亚高等法院将单一或多重发表做如下总结：

第一，除以下第二种、第三种情形，同一诽谤嫌疑人传导给第三方的诽谤内容，每传导一次便构成一个单独的新的发表。第二，一次传导但被两个或两个以上第三方同时听到则构成一次发表。第三，一本书或一份报纸或电台、电视台的一条新闻或一部电影及任何批量性质的传播内容，其同一版本的任何一次传播视作一次发表。第四，"单一发表规则"有三：（1）原告请求赔偿只能行使一次诉讼主张；（2）发生在所有司法管辖地的所有侵权赔偿，可在一次诉讼主张中解决；（3）根据具体案情对原告作出的胜诉或败诉判决，对同一原、被告在所有其他司法管辖地的同一诉讼起到司法禁止作用[1]。

澳大利亚高等法院驳回道琼斯"单一发表规则"的请求。驳回理由很简单，因为单一发表规则的主要意义在于决定诉讼时效期何时起算，而诉讼时效在本案没有争议，有争议的是文章在何处发表以确定司法管辖地。

4.9 英国判例

同一时期英国的一个判例[2]也明确表明，英国在互联网领域不适用"单一发表规则"。这个案子的原告从事国际贸易，英国一家老牌日报撰文说他和国

---

〔1〕 Dow Jones and Company Inc v. Gutnick（2002）HCA 56；210 CLR 575；194 ALR 433；77 ALJR 255（10 December 2002），para29（1）（2）（3）（4）.

〔2〕 Loutchansky v. Times Newspapers Ltd（No. 2）〔2001〕EWCA Civ 1805；〔2002〕1 All ER 652.

际犯罪团伙有染，又涉嫌洗钱和走私核武器。不难想象原告火大了，告了报社、总编和分别写了两篇报道的两位记者。第二次的诉因是同一篇文章在报社网站上重发的电子版本。案情很复杂，但与本文有关的是电子版本的同一篇文章，是否因"单一发表规则"而不构成新的诉因。在 2001 年和 2002 年那个时间，英国和澳大利亚在这个问题上的认知是相同的，即美国式的"单一发表规则"不在英国和澳大利亚适用。

反观那一时期的相似案例，法官这样断案是有法理和社会基础的。那时关于互联网传播和网上诽谤的案例尚不多见，诽谤手段以及原、被告双方的反应程度，也没有累积到使法律进入大幅度革新的状态。但 10 年后的今天就不同了，正是由于"道琼斯案"这样的判例，已经使互联网大环境下的诽谤法，到了成熟的、可以将传统的规范重新梳理一番的时候了——这是后话。

五、澳大利亚高等法院"道琼斯案"判例的意义

5.1 嘎兄何许人也

澳大利亚高等法院七位法官全体一致支持初审法院的原判并于 2002 年 12 月 10 日颁布判决书。至此，因道琼斯旗下"巴伦在线"2000 年 10 月 28 日一篇《君子爱财，取之无道》的文章引起的官司，几经周折终于落下帷幕。道琼斯的上诉被驳回，赢家仍然是原告嘎特尼克。

嘎特尼克何许人也？他的别名是"钻石乔"，从名字上就可以看出，他是矿业大亨，并且是宝石和金矿大亨。是一名犹太人、慈善家和一名"拉比"——梁实秋的《远东英汉大辞典》将其译成"犹太教牧师""法师""教师"[1]。据说，早在 1988 年，另一位具有传奇色彩的犹太教牧师面授机宜，告诉他在西澳大利亚找到金矿的准确地点。[2]

---

〔1〕 梁实秋：《远东英汉大辞典》，商务印书馆、远东图书公司 1991 年版，第 1706 页。

〔2〕 见 Long, Stephen（5 June 2003）. "The World Today-Profile of Joseph Gutnick". Retrieved 10 February 2010. Quoted from en. wikipedia. org as at 9 November 2013。

5.2 谁是赢家

可见嘎特尼克不是好惹的，他有知名度，有财力、人力和物力。也正是因为如此，道琼斯旗下的《巴伦周刊》才会招惹他。从这个意义上看，"嘎特尼克诉道琼斯案"至少有两个赢家。一是原告嘎特尼克，他被"平反昭雪"，被告道琼斯被迫在法庭一字一句地收回文章中的指控。虽然律师费不菲，但对嘎兄来说不是问题，他和自己的公司更火了，不但恢复清白，而且在法律领域青史留名。另一个赢家是被告，道琼斯的产品是媒体，媒体怕的是无人问津，不怕的是街头巷尾扬名。在澳大利亚法院系统的这几个来回，不但使《华尔街日报》更加有名，《巴伦周刊》也从"阳春白雪"的高端领域拓展到普通阶层，就"巴伦在线"而言，惹上官司在法庭上打上几仗，全球大小媒体跟进，这何尝不是一次广而告之？

时代不同了，不管是时尚还是"感冒"，只要流行起来就会在舆论和商业领域产生价值（且不论这价值的正面或负面性）。随着时代的发展，媒体也越来越趋向"商业化、产品化"。从美国、欧洲、澳洲和全球其他区域的发展情况看，媒体倾向私有化、集团化和垄断化，它们也是需要营利的公司，也要上市融资，只要进入这个流程，就必须按行规运作。因此——尤其是伴随互联网的发展和对生活的渗透——滋生了一批具有"窥阴癖"习性的人，打着媒体的旗号，去挖隐私、造谎言、弄是非，他们不是"新闻记者"意义上的媒体，只是传播病菌的载体而已。

好在此案中的原、被告嘎先生和道琼斯都是商界的正人君子——法律在很大程度上，原本就是给守法的人制定的！所以这个案子的第三个赢家实际上是我们，是我们这些普普通通的芸芸众生。互联网带来的冲击不仅是一次或两次浪潮，它不动声色地宣告传统上一切持恒的东西，在现代社会或许变得不再持恒。正是像一个又一个类似"道琼斯案"这样的判例，才能从不同角度、不同层面帮我们在现代社会的浪潮中，梳理我们的脉络，升级我们的运行程序，为我们装上各种防火墙和杀毒软件。所以，借这个机会再次提醒一下，判例法的价值不仅仅在于一个判决的结果，更重要的是各级法院在确定判例的过程中，对法理的理解、对逻辑的推导以及对现实个案的适应，这才是判例法真正的精华。也需要反复提醒的是，不要一看到"十大名案"这样的字眼，就不可遏制地联想到"十大名捕"之类，既而期待能在这本书中读到武侠小说式的情节并大快朵颐。这本书只是试图在能被允许的范围内，用直白的语言还原判例法断案的原貌。试想，无论民法、刑法，都是关乎一个人（无论自然人还是法人）的吉凶祸福甚至生死。没有一个判例是可以拿来轻松改编成小说和电影的。但了解了这"十大名案"，对判例法大致就有了一些轮廓认识。这些都是题外话。那么，澳大利亚高等法院的判例究竟有什么意义呢？

5.3 澳大利亚高等法院的判决

如前文所述，判决书很长，也阐明了诸多法律问题。但作为判例，以下五大要点尤为重要：

第一，现有的诽谤法原则要求提出告诉的地点是诽谤信息接收地点而非传送地点。这一原则同样适用于互联网传播的信息，尽管现代科技和互联网传播与传统媒体相比性质不同。就本案而言，涉嫌诽谤的信息是在美国的互联网上传但在澳大利亚维多利亚州下载、阅读，行使司法管辖权受理本案的法庭应该是维多利亚州的法院。

第二，维多利亚州是原告嘎特尼克的主要居住地和"名声所在地"。因此，维多利亚州是原告名誉被损害地。诽谤行为并非在发表之时发生，而是在一个任何第三方接触到（读、听、看到）诽谤内容并受诽谤内容影响而对原告因此产生"轻视想法"之时。

第三，高等法院判决中的实际效果是，澳大利亚的原告可以就互联网诽谤案的任何一位被告提出告诉，而不用管被告所处的地理位置。也就是说，因互联网诽谤信息"接受地原则"，被告就原告，被告得跟着原告满世界转。针对这一司法管辖地原则，七位法官中有一位说了一番颇耐人寻味的话：

人们为了商贸或其他事由去不同的国家，住在不同的国家，使用不同国家的基础设施。既来之则安之，既安之则受当地法律法规约束。事实上，诽谤信息的"发表"，因互联网的传播有可能变得在世界每个角落漫天飞，但不意味着从此法不责众而找不到一个地方将其绳之以法。在不同司法管辖地的"重复发表"，对像澳大利亚这样的联邦政府来说，自然不是什么新奇的事。[1]

第四，"被告就原告"，是否意味着出版商对互联网上发表的每一篇文章都得提心吊胆呢？道琼斯的律师很煽情：因为互联网的无国界性，今后每发表一篇文章，从阿富汗到津巴布韦都有可能蹦出一个原告来，大众传播业岂不因此就乱了?!

这一论点被法院驳回。法官们说，除非是特别得不能再特别的案子，否则十之八九都可以有效识别文章所针对的人物（即诽谤对象），找到了诽谤对象便可确定被诽谤的原告所将倚仗的法律体系和司法管辖地。也就是说，原告"名声所在地"才是原告所在意的。如果在阿富汗或津巴布韦，没有人知道原告是谁，诽谤造成的后果微乎其微，原告诉诸法律的可能性便变得很小。

也就是说，"名声所在地原则"，从不同侧面确定了诽谤法的"属地性"（即名誉遭到毁损所在地）。正是因为这个特点，才有效地限制了被告责任无限制性（即在所有互联网流通地区皆可被告）的想象和理论推导。

关于这一点，法官判决中的附带意见（"obiter dicta"[2]）也值得注意：

（1）就互联网而言，判例法中被告的抗辩元素（被告可资抗辩的理由）有待发展。言下之意是，相比传统媒体，互联网时代被告的抗辩依据尚不完备。（2）被告侵权责任与原告名誉被损之间的平衡点需要合理把握。侵权赔偿的前提是诽谤内容发表地为原告名誉所在地。（3）原告在司法管辖地之外提出诉讼的可能性不大——除非判决对原告确有实质性价值。（4）除非极其特别的案件，否则对诽谤侵权对象（原告）的有效识别，可判定司法管辖地及其相

---

〔1〕 见 Dow Jones & Co Inc v. Gutnick （2002）210 CLR 575，194 ALR 433 （HCA）判决书第 186 段。这是法官 Callinan J. 说的。原文是："If people wish to do business in, or indeed travel to, or live in, or utilize the infrastructure of different countries, they can hardly expect to be absolved from compliance with the laws of those countries. The fact that publication might occur everywhere does not mean that it occurs nowhere. Multiple publication in different jurisdictions is certainly no novelty in a federation such as Australia. " 这里为了中文阅读习惯，没有直译。

〔2〕 这是法庭常用的拉丁文术语，意思是"判决中的附带意见、附带判词"。法官断案中常就事论事或借题发挥，发表一些观点或感概。这些是判决中的一部分但不是判决中的有机体或组成部分，因此不能形成判例。但对适用和理解该判例以及在未来案件推导过程中都有重要的参考价值。尤其是级别较高的法院如上诉庭以上的法院，即便是"附带意见"，对平级和下级法院审理案件都有较大的参考价值。

应法律。[1]

第五，法院以多数意见驳回"单一发表规则"，无论是传统媒介还是以互联网为载体的相关传播，该原则均不适用。说是"多数意见"是因为七位法官中，有四位（包括首席大法官）联合出具判决书，但有一位[2]出具了自己单独的判决书。在单独判决书中，他得出的结论虽与其他法官相同，但是推导的过程和思路不同。他认为传统判例法在诽谤法领域已经非常成熟和完备。因此，专门为一项新型科技（如互联网）而制定一套新的规则不妥，因为规则是中性的。"单一发表规则"存在诸多问题，在确定新的一套符合互联网等新技术发展的新规则之前，得找到针对"单一发表规则"问题的解决办法。总体而言，这涉及一整套规则和体系的更新和改革，靠单一判例是解决不了问题的。因此，涉及互联网和现代科技给诽谤法带来的挑战，只能靠国会立法机构寻求新的立法，才能得以解决。由此可见，法官们拒绝引用"单一发表规则"，并不代表传统规则有多周密或"单一发表规则"有多糟糕，而是彼时彼地尚没有找到一个既符合新技术发展又能被普遍接受的规则。从随后的各类评价来看，澳大利亚高等法院的判决，虽然以极大的力度解决了一个重大而复杂的法律问题，但字里行间和总体气氛，总夹带着一股山雨欲来的气息。法官们也极大地暗示和配合了这种气息：互联网时代来临了，传统的诽谤法体系从四面八方受到冲击。许多问题都是实质性的：诽谤文章在何处发表？——这决定了司法管辖地、官司在何处打；诉讼时效期从何时起算？——这决定了诉讼案能不能成立。这时间、空间两大层面的困惑，也足以使法官感叹，伴随着一个新时代的来临，判例法和成文法必须左右开弓，从微观和宏观两大角度，找到各类问题的答案。

5.4 极大争议

从以上判例以及法官的表述可以看出，"道琼斯案"是在当时成文法及判例法所具备的条件下，作出的较为完备的判决。尽管如此，澳大利亚高等法院的

---

[1] 以上总结见 Judge David Harvey, *internet. law. nz*, 2nd *ed*, Wellington：LexisNexis, 2011, p. 609。

[2] 法官 Kirby J. 。

这个判决，在全球司法界引起了极大轰动。这不是因互联网引发的第一个跨国诽谤法案例，却是最大也是最具争议性的一个。因此判决一出，便引来全球范围研讨一片。甚至以"个人请愿"的名义，被投诉到联合国[1]。但热议也罢、请愿也罢，法院判决是有约束力的。2004年11月15日，此案得以了结。原告嘎特尼克在法庭澄清了《巴伦周刊》这篇文章对自己的诽谤内容，还自己一个清白，道琼斯还为他支付了部分律师费。

别忘了，刊有这篇文章的纸媒《巴伦周刊》，从美国新泽西州寄到澳大利亚的只有区区5份，并且据说因各种原因，这5份报纸并没有送到澳大利亚的读者手中。换句话说，在维多利亚州或澳大利亚其他地区，没有人读过那篇文章。这正是为什么原告律师以"巴伦在线"互联网上的电子版本（而非纸媒）为诉讼依据。"巴伦在线"全球有550 000个订户，具体不清楚澳大利亚有多少订户，但从信用卡付款数据看，也只有1700个订户而已。具体不清楚究竟有多少人在互联网上读到《巴伦周刊》上的那篇文章，想必即使有也寥寥而已。但这不重要，重要的是这个判例已经明确地起到警示作用：媒体写文章骂人痛快，骂完了是要负责任的！写文章骂人只要几个小时，上传只要几分钟，但给自己、给所属媒体带来的法律上的麻烦，要几个月甚至几年才能了结。有人甚至会因此而倾家荡产。

美国律师协会《传媒法季刊》2003年第4号，刊登了墨尔本一家知名律师事务所合伙人的一篇文章[2]，直言"嘎特尼克诉道琼斯案"意义重大，尤其是针对美国被告，因为美国的诽谤法"对被告友善多了"。而本案判例的实际效果是原告可以选择对自己有利的诽谤法体系提出告诉，而原告可以不必居住在那个司法管辖地。文章提出，国际律师协会于2002年10月在南非德班（Durban）提出的"德班原则"草案，或许可拓展为一种新的模式。

"德班原则"有三大要点：第一，涉及互联网诽谤诉讼案，符合下列三种情形中任何一种的法庭便可受理：（1）是原告所在地法庭；（2）是被告所在地法庭；（3）原、被告均认同并具备合理条件受理的法庭。第二，涉及因互联网

---

〔1〕 根据联合国与人权相关的4个条约而成立的4个专门委员会，负责受理个人投诉和请愿。

〔2〕 见 Peter Bartlett：" Gutnick Shows Need for New International Jurisdictional Principles"，*Communications Lawyers*，*American Bar Association*，*Winter 2003*，Volume 20 Number 4，pp. 16–18。

网站内容而引发的诉讼，受理法庭须适用与该互联网网站联系最为密切的司法管辖地之实体法，而不必考究冲突法。如果该网站不涉及货品或服务业，只提供发帖之类的内容信息，确定司法管辖权则通过"何处决定将文章发表"的那个所在地来定，而不必考虑该司法管辖地是不是文章的上传地或存储地。也就是说将"编辑地"和"上传地或存储地"明确区分开来。第三，如果互联网网站接到原告投诉并在 24 小时内在网站公示并提供投诉内容链接，互联网网站此举则可成为诉讼案中的有效抗辩。换句话说，互联网网站只要摘开自己，声明某某内容有诽谤之嫌，已经被投诉了，并提供可以下载投诉内容的链接，网站即可免诉讼之灾。这听起来挺公平，反正互联网站仅需要维持一个技术上的中立。但诽谤内容并没有因此被删除，反而有可能被重复或激活了。连这篇文章的作者自己也承认，"德班模式"并不能阻止嘎特尼克在澳大利亚起诉道琼斯，但可以有效防止那些并不居住在澳大利亚的"机会主义"分子，到澳大利亚"死缠烂打"。别忘了，美国的诽谤法体系对被告友善，被告抗辩机会和余地大，道琼斯这样的被告自然是希望官司在美国打。而原告嘎特尼克则是希望官司在澳大利亚打，因为澳大利亚的诽谤法倾向传统和保守，较偏向原告。

5.5 严格责任

为了对判决介绍的尽量全面和周到，必须看一看法官如何解读澳大利亚诽谤法以及澳大利亚诽谤法"传统"到什么程度。判决书第 25～28 段专论"诽谤"，第 25 段开始便掷地有声：

> 作为民法的诽谤法——至少在澳大利亚是这样理解的——关注的是导致名誉毁损的出版物，在民法上属严格责任主义，也就是说被告或许终当承担法律责任，即使被告对名誉毁损并没有主观故意并且在过程中具备合理注意。[1]

---

〔1〕 原文是这样的："The tort of defamation, at least as understood in Australia, focuses upon publications causing damages to reputation. It is a tort of strict liability, in the sense that a defendant may be liable even though no injury to reputation was intended and the defendant acted with reasonable care." Dow Jones and Company Inc v. Gutnick〔2002〕HCA 56, 210 CLR 575, 194 ALR 433, 77 ALJR 255（10 December 2002），last updated 5 February 2003, p. 25。

当然法官也指出，如果书商或报纸销售商在自己正常的销售过程中，不知道也没有理由怀疑书报中有诽谤内容，他们的业务行为不应视作并构成法律意义上的"发表"而因此承担责任。名誉毁损指的是因毁损而招致诉因。判决书第 26 段强调：

当诽谤出版物发表并被读者读之、听者听之、观者观之，则构成名誉毁损。之前，没有毁损。从这个意义上看，将出版物之发表当作出版人之单一行为是错误的。这是双向行为——发表者授之，第三方解之。[1]

为阐明上述观点，法官引用的是 1934 年的一个判例[2]和 1887 年的民法教科书[3]。由此可以看出，判例法（或译普通法、共同法）法理的历史传承，具有相当的稳定性和历史厚重感。

"Strict Liability" 一般译作"严格责任"或"后果责任"，指的是被告（实际加害人）对所犯错误、罪行承担全部责任，而不管有错无错。有学者则将其定义为："严格责任不依赖于实际加害人的过失或故意，但以违反保证他人安全的绝对义务为基础。严格责任常适用于高度危险活动或产品责任案件。也称为绝对责任、无过错责任。"[4]

民法和刑法均适用严格责任，指的是在损害发生的情况下，即使不存在故意或者过失，也需要承担损害赔偿责任。民法上常举的例子有两类：一类指"产品责任"（product liability）——除非被告能证明产品瑕疵是因为原告的行为（如操作失误）而非产品本身；另一类指狮子、老虎、毒蛇之类的饲养中心，动物跑出笼子咬了人，主人是要承担责任的，这和主人是否故意没有关系。在刑法上常见的例子是驾车超速，肇事司机（被告）是否知道自己在行驶路段超

---

〔1〕 原话是这样说的："This being so, it would be wrong to treat a publication as if it were a unilateral act on the part of the publisher alone. It is not. It is a bilateral act-in which the publisher makes it available and a third party has it available for his or her comprehension." 考虑中文阅读习惯，这里没有直译。同上，p. 26。

〔2〕 Lee v. Wilson & Mackinnon〔1934〕HCA 60.

〔3〕 The Law of Torts（1887）at 210 as Pollock said.

〔4〕 周杰："严格责任与无过错责任之源流初探——用比较的视角看两大法系侵权法的发展"。北大法律网法律在线，http://article. chinalawinfo. com/Article_ Detail. asp? ArticleID=34816，最后访问时间：2013 年 12 月 17 日。

速并不重要，公诉人只需要证明被告驾车超速就可以了。

判断这类责任有时可以直接参考成文法。如果国会制定法律将"犯意"（mens rea）要素故意排除，公诉则不需要证明犯罪意图，适用的显然是严格责任原则。

但需要注意的是，不能将"严格责任"与"无过错责任"简单地加以等同视之，尤其是英美法系和大陆法系在侵权法归责原则上，有各自的发展过程以及理解和表述。中国学者周杰在其论文中指出：

严格责任与无过错责任分别系英美法系与大陆法系侵权法上至为重要的归责原则。二者得以确立均经历了从结果责任到过错责任/过失责任再到严格责任和无过错责任的过程。由于两大法系业已存在的固有差异及当下相互吸收、借鉴的趋向，严格责任和无过错责任在发展、确立的过程中，既存在内涵外延、适用范围、抗辩事由上的区别，又在哲学基础、配套机制等方面趋同。对严格责任和无过错责任的源流及发展加以探索，为中国侵权法的立法发展走向提供了参考和启示［……］〔1〕

5.6 2005 年《澳大利亚诽谤法》

2006 年 1 月 1 日起，澳大利亚各州实行新的诽谤法，取代了 1899 年澳大利亚《诽谤法》，如果涉嫌诽谤的内容在 2006 年 1 月 1 日及其之后发表，则诉讼时效依新法为 1 年，从发表日起算。如果能向法庭证明不能够合理地在 1 年内提出告诉，经法庭批准可以延期 3 年。

如果诽谤行为发生在 2006 年 1 月 1 日以前，则仍依 1889 年的法律，诉讼时效为 6 年，从产生诉因的那天起算。

2005 年《澳大利亚诽谤法》对原、被告的界定，诽谤诉因及抗辩等要件均有明确规范，在此不赘述。

---

〔1〕 参见周杰："严格责任与无过错责任之源流初探——用比较的视角看两大法系侵权法的发展"。北大法律网法律在线，http://article.chinalawinfo.com/Article_Detail.asp? ArticleID=34816，最后访问时间：2013 年 12 月 17 日。

六、后"道琼斯案"时代

6.1 澳大利亚最新案例：2012 年"推特诽谤案"

从目前所接触到的案例来看，发生在澳大利亚最新的当属 2012 年的"Twitter 诽谤案"。说"Twitter 诽谤案"实在有点牵强，因为它不过提供了一个互动平台。

Twitter 作为一个单词，原意是指小鸟"吱吱喳喳、喋喋不休"的意思。顾名思义，它提供的社交网站及微博客服务可以让各类"网虫"和

Twitter"推特"标志

"大鸟小鸟们"不断发帖、不断更新、不断抒发。中文多音译为"推特"[1]，以此发的文"tweet"叫"推文"，一次发帖推文不能超过 140 个字。推特是 2006 年 3 月 21 日创立的，总部设在美国加州旧金山，部分服务器和办公室设在纽约。

墨尔本的艺人、作家和版主 Marieke Hardy（以下简称"哈迪"）2011 年在推特上发帖，义愤填膺地指出同在墨尔本的 Joshua Meggitt（以下简称"老麦"）就是一篇诽谤她的"仇恨博文"的作者。这桩案子涉及三方：哈迪、老麦和推特。哈迪自认为是受害者，但老麦证明哈迪弄错了人，结果是推特被老麦起诉诽谤。

这是推特第一次在澳大利亚被告诽谤，但值得注意的是诉因并非源自推特自己的诽谤行为，而只是因为推特提供了发表涉嫌诽谤信息的平台。仅此一点，就足够让微信、Facebook 和 YouTube 等密切关注。

学术界对此热议颇多。昆士兰科技大学法学院高级讲师布莱克认为此案有三点特别值得注意：

第一，高等法院在"道琼斯案"中定下的判例，将对此案原、被告双方的

---

[1] 见"新浪科技：Twitter 简体和繁体中文版正式上线"，2011 年 9 月 15 日。

法律思辨起主导作用。道琼斯远在美国，但这不影响嘎特尼克在澳大利亚将其告上法庭。所以，这个判例可以理解为"诽谤法诉因从所有发表地而起"，沾上了就甩不了。何况哈迪、老麦两个主角加上推特这个平台都在澳大利亚！因此，虽然推特远在硅谷，但因在澳大利亚发表的信息而承担法律责任是有判例依据的。尽管"道琼斯案"在美国倍受争议，但在澳大利亚却是被广泛接受的判例法。

第二，推特在自己的网站上有郑重的"免责声明"（disclaimers），但免责声明能否提供法律责任上的豁免？一般来说，免责声明可以提供一定的法律保护但并不是绝对的。就本案而言。老麦的观点颇有说服力：即使免责声明可以针对推特用户的侵权诉讼主张对推特起到保护作用，但是，这样的免责声明对非推特用户的侵权诉讼主张是没有保护作用的。因为这样的免责声明作为"用户条款"，自然只对用户起作用。

第三，这也是第一起提供发帖和交流的平台（推特）被告，而不是涉嫌诽谤的作者被告。这已经让美国人大跌眼镜了，因为美国有成文法[1]对类似的平台提供法律责任的豁免[2]。

澳大利亚没有类似的专门立法，只能从其他成文法（如民法、电信法或信息交流法）及判例法中去找到原、被告认为对各自有利的依据。如果对信息平台的法律责任要求过严，业界的说法是这对信息产业的发展（技术和社会层面）均为不利因素。比较合乎情理的是，首先要让发诽谤言论的那个人负法律责任。对"中间人"和提供平台的人来说，只有在当事人进行交涉并要求删帖但却无动于衷者，才令其承担法律责任。无论如何，案情的发展值得注意，十年后的今天，"推特案"俨然又是一个"道琼斯案"力度的案件，尽管相比而言，"推特案"似乎是"道琼斯案"的一个袖珍版。

6.2 施瓦辛格在英国被起诉

"安娜诉施瓦辛格"[3]，是一个曾轰动一时的明星案。

---

〔1〕 指的是 Communications Decency Act，其中第 230 条有明确规定。

〔2〕 见 Black，Peter："Will Marieke Hardy's Twitter case change Australian law forever?" 17 February 2012。http：//thecoversation. com. 最后访问时间：2013. 11. 18 日。

〔3〕 Richardson v. Schwarzenegger〔2004〕EWHC 2422（QB）

女主角叫安娜·理查森（Anna Richardson），男主角是时任美国加利福尼亚州州长的大明星阿诺德·施瓦辛格（Arnold Schwarzenegger）。1947年7月30日出生的施瓦辛格从15岁开始便接受举重和健美训练。20岁便获"宇宙先生"称号，从此一发不可收拾，共夺得"宇宙先生"5次，"奥林匹亚先生"7次，以及"欧洲先生""世界先生"等多项荣誉称号。施瓦辛格被公认为世界健美史迄今最显著的重要人物。从1970年开始，他先后在30多部动作大片中担任主角。从健美明星到电影明星，施瓦辛格是很多人心目中的英雄。

2003年加利福尼亚州发生州政府财政危机，时任州长面临加州选民弹劾公投。根据州宪法，罢免公投的同时需补选一位新州长。故公投需要选民投两张选票：第一张票决定是否罢免时任州长，第二张票是罢免确定后补选新州长。施瓦辛格就是在这次"罢免选举"（Recall Election）中被补选为州长的。2006年底补任期满后他再度投入州长大选，再获成功，于2007年至2011年任加州第38届州长（完整任期）。

2004年10月29日英国高等法院"皇座法庭"（Queen's Bench），开庭审理安娜·理查森诉施瓦辛格一案。这个案件的性质，与他最初竞选加州州长时遇到的麻烦如出一辙，都属"乱摸门"（"Gropegate"），广东话习惯称"咸猪手"。也有我国香港地区的朋友考证，说这里的"咸猪手"并不是指猪的手，而是前臂即猪肘子。手也罢肘子也罢，老施惹下的就是这一类麻烦，并且碰巧的是这些麻烦都是在大选如火如荼、临近投票时被媒体爆料。至少有6位女子相继出现，在媒体上陈述她们各自被"咸猪手"之类的故事。这些故事出现在选举敏感时段，其政治色彩和动机自难淡化和开脱。但法庭感兴趣的是证据以及不同案件所面对的不同的法律问题。

英国这位美女电视主持人，此前声称在2000年12月对老施在伦敦的一次采访过程中，被他的"咸猪手"摸了。此事在大选前再掀波澜，《洛杉矶时报》（Los Angeles Times）也做了报道。施瓦辛格的发言人代表他回应了记者的提问，并坚定而彻底地否认了这一指责，强调这是"编造"的"一个小政治伎俩"而已。美女主持人不干了，认为施瓦辛格发言人的这番话，实际暗含着她"别有用心并不诚实地编造"，其言下之意对她构成诋毁，对她在英国的名声造成损害。

值得注意的是，刊登这篇报道的《洛杉矶时报》并没有成为被告，而三个被告中除"主事人"施瓦辛格外，第二被告是那位发言人，第三被告是他竞选班底中负责公共关系的经理，此其一。其二，《洛杉矶时报》是美国的报纸，州长选举也远在加利福尼亚州，但原告是在伦敦将老施等人告上法庭，法理依据就是澳大利亚高等法院在"嘎特尼克诉道琼斯案"中定下的判例。

长话短说，原、被告是于2006年8月庭外和解并通过联合声明的方式广而告之。尽管和解之前双方又"剧透"了不少细节，引全球无数媒体打了鸡血似地笔墨云雨几番——自然是大大提高了报纸的发行量、网站点击率，兴许还因此挽救了几家濒临破产的小报。时下这样的剧透，不仅不是可有可无的噱头，而是吸引大众阅读严肃文献的有效方法之一。

这些都不重要，重要的是伦敦法院要解决的三个问题以及由此而确定的判例。这三个问题是：

第一，被告认为原告应到加州法院提出诉讼而不应该在伦敦提出告诉，因此法庭应驳回原告的诉讼请求。

第二，据加州当地法律，第二、第三被告作为候选人的发言人及竞选团队的成员，对媒体做如此发言是受"豁免保护"而应免于起诉的。就英国法庭而言，此案涉及的是一个外国报纸刊登的一个外国地方政府候选人的一桩涉嫌风化的"历史性动作"而已，真正的非今事而是故事也。

第三，因判决执行问题，原告请求"禁止性补救"（Injunctive Relief）是否妥当？

第二个、第三个问题相对容易解决。法庭的结论是，"司法豁免"是基于综合因素考量，因而不宜以简易听审的方式解决——因此反而加大了在伦敦法院受理的合理性。而第三个问题是涉及法庭判决的异地执行，但无论如何，至少可以保证在取得禁止令的前提下，涉嫌诽谤的报道不能在英国司法管辖区重复发表。

而第一个问题则是所有问题的核心。法庭依"道琼斯诉嘎特尼克"判例[1]

---

〔1〕 Dow Jones & Co. Inc v. Gutnick，这是澳大利亚高等法院接受道琼斯上诉后的案例。此前在维多利亚州法院则列为 Gutnick v. Dow Jones & Co. Inc.，在本书中考虑到中文阅读习惯，"嘎特尼克诉道琼斯"及"道琼斯诉嘎特尼克"均指高等法院终审判例。

以及包括美国法院的其他判例〔1〕作出如下推导：（1）原告是英国公民；
（2）她的居住地和工作地均在英国；（3）她在英国家喻户晓；（4）她和包括美
国在内的其他司法管辖地没有任何关系；（5）可以推定她的名声在英国受到损
害；（6）事发地在英国；（7）英国法适用于在英国的出版物；（8）被告应对其
言行负责，而言行的"再发表地"在英国；（9）《洛杉矶时报》纸媒在英国有
售，其电子版本通过互联网可在英国下载和阅读。

英国高等法院判决：驳回被告撤销原告诉讼的请求，文章的发表地在英国，
原告名誉在英国受损，英国是合理而公平的司法管辖地。

尽管原、被告双方庭外和解，但不影响法庭判决，而由此案定下的判例依
然是有效的。也因此可见澳大利亚"道琼斯案"判例之影响深远。

6.3 影响远及加拿大

2005 年判定了这样一个案件〔2〕，原告是加拿大一支著名的曲棍球队的前
总经理，被告是《纽约邮报》（New York Post）〔3〕。报纸刊登了一篇关于这位
前总经理的"斗殴"性八卦新闻，互联网版本远及原告及球队所在的加拿大西
南部的不列颠哥伦比亚省。

不列颠哥伦比亚（British Columbia，简称 B. C）1871 年成为加拿大的第六
个省，这个名字是英维多利亚女王（Queen Victoria）在 1858 年命名的，因为原
本就是英属哥伦比亚殖民地。很多人一听到"英属哥伦比亚"以为是讲英国而
不是加拿大。本章为方便起见，将其称作"不列颠哥伦比亚"简称为"不哥"。
首府是大家不太熟悉的维多利亚，但该省最大的城市是大家熟悉的温哥华
（Vancouver）。

---

〔1〕 如 Calder v. Jones.

〔2〕 Burke v. NYP Holdings, Inc., 2005 BCSC 1287.

〔3〕 《纽约邮报》是美国历史最悠久的报纸之一，创刊于 1801 年，现属默多克新闻集团，"其报道
风格以煽情、八卦而闻名"。在 1960 年代后半期，日发行量达 70 万份，现虽下降到 41.8 万份，但仍是
纽约地区最有影响力的报纸之一。见维基百科中译版。最后访问时间：2013 年 11 月 25 日。

Outline of Canada's Court System

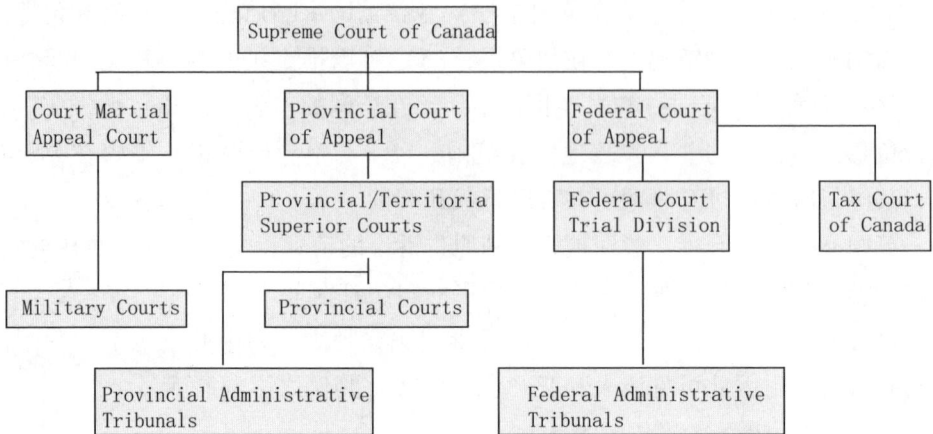

```
                  ┌─────────────────────────┐
                  │ Supreme Court of Canada │
                  └─────────────────────────┘
      ┌──────────────────┬──────────────────────┐
┌──────────────┐  ┌──────────────┐      ┌──────────────┐
│Court Martial │  │Provincial Court│    │Federal Court │
│Appeal Court  │  │of Appeal     │      │of Appeal     │
└──────────────┘  └──────────────┘      └──────────────┘
                  ┌──────────────┐      ┌──────────────┐  ┌──────────────┐
                  │Provincial/Territoria│ │Federal Court │  │Tax Court     │
                  │Superior Courts│     │Trial Division│  │of Canada     │
                  └──────────────┘      └──────────────┘  └──────────────┘
┌──────────────┐  ┌──────────────┐
│Military Courts│ │Provincial Courts│
└──────────────┘  └──────────────┘
        ┌────────────────────────────┐    ┌────────────────────────────┐
        │Provincial Administrative   │    │Federal Administrative      │
        │Tribunals                   │    │Tribunals                   │
        └────────────────────────────┘    └────────────────────────────┘
```

加拿大法院系统

从图中可以看出，加拿大法院系统也分成"省"和"联邦"两部分。终审法院是加拿大最高法院，需要注意的是——可参阅"美国雅虎案"中关于美国法院系统的介绍——省一级的初审与上诉法院亦称作"最高法院"。本案中涉及的就是不哥省最高法院的诉讼案。不哥省最高法院是省内最高的初审法院，既可初审也接受下级法院的上诉。不哥省最高法院的上级法院则是"上诉法院"，是本省终审法院，再往上，便是全国的最高法院。

本案案情与其他诉讼案大同小异。需要解决的问题是，远在美国纽约的报纸刊登涉嫌诽谤的文章，原告是否可以在加拿大的不哥省提出告诉？不哥省最高法院确定了一个"两部曲"测试标准：（1）本法庭与被告或诉讼主题是否具备"真实和实质"上的关联；（2）本案是否可以更方便地在其他司法管辖地受理。

法院在判决中列出以下理由作为依据：

第一，涉嫌诽谤报道的互联网版本在不哥省下载、传阅，因此民事侵权行为发生在不哥省；

第二，报社可以预见——当报道在互联网发表后，报道便"跟随原告"来到不哥省，因为，（1）原告在本地的名望；（2）因其名望而引起民众对这则报道的关注程度；（3）名誉毁损绝大部分发生在本地。

不难看出，加拿大的法院是依据澳大利亚高等法院在"道琼斯案"中确定的判例，得出结论：名誉受损地即诽谤发生地，就互联网而言，诽谤内容下载地便构成名誉受损地。因此，原告可以在加拿大不哥省地方法院起诉被告《纽约邮报》。

"《纽约邮报》案"可以看作是澳大利亚"道琼斯案"在加拿大的浓缩版本。而"道琼斯案"判例，在邻国新西兰被推到了一个新的高点。新西兰的法官们不仅适用了该判例之精神，并且将不听话的被告直接送进监狱。

6.4 新西兰奚陌案：入狱三次

本案主角叫文森·奚陌（Vincent Siemer），1956 年出生于美国，曾是一个成功的商人和地产经纪。1999 年举家移民新西兰，2002 年入籍。2000 年左右文森·奚陌以购买股份的方式入主一家公司，不久与另一董事发生商业纠纷，从此开始了漫长的诉讼之路。从普通的商业纠纷，衍变成民事侵权、名誉诽谤、刑事诉讼、藐视法庭……又从一般的民事诉讼各自对簿公堂，发展为公诉人（检察院）[1] 提出公诉，从 2000 年底打到 2013 年中，从高等法院打到上诉法院，再打到最高法院，并以个人请愿方式投诉到联合国人权委员会[2]。有人说他是英雄屡败屡战，有人说他是另类，专做一般人不肯做或不敢做的事。譬如，2003 年 10 月，他就告了自己的出庭律师，因为他认为律师有"职业性过失"[3]；在他认为蒙冤受屈、力曝"司法黑幕"之时，他创办了网站"www.kiwifirst.co.nz"，并于 2005 年 4 月在奥克兰商业中心竖起大广告牌，让

---

〔1〕 新西兰沿用英制，Attorney-General 叫"检察总长"，行使刑事案件政府公诉人的职能。检察总长从国会议员中产生，其副手是 Solicitor-General，为理解方便可译作"副检察长"，由任命产生而非从国会议员中产生。无论 Attorney-General 还是 Solicitor-General 大多由有律师背景的人担任，通常都是"御用大律师"（QC）一类的资深律师。本案就是"副检察长诉奚陌"，属于刑事公诉案件。检察总长在新西兰国会的另一职能是，所有立法草案（法案，即 Bill）在进入国会立法程序之前，需要检察总长确认是否和人权法精神一致。因为从国会议员中产生，检察总长自然带有政党色彩。这也是为什么设"副检察长"（不从国会议员中产生）而独立地专精业务的原因。请注意：Attorney-General 在美国则指司法部长。

〔2〕 United Nations Human Rights Committee Communication No. 2072/2011.

〔3〕 见 High Court CIV 2003 404 5782.

大家上网看他爆料[1]；2008 年 12 月 3 日他在新西兰上诉法院出庭时，浑身上下着"爱丽丝漫游奇境记"装束，讽刺法庭并宣告"事实不再要紧"[2]……他还挑战最高法院首席大法官，说她与诉讼当事人有"利益冲突"，必须回避[3]。在打遍新西兰所有四级法院之后，又以个人请愿方式投诉到联合国。当然，最具戏剧性的是他 2012 年 8 月回美国，见一拖车便飞奔追赶，一路狂喊"我爱这车，我爱这车"。警察以酗酒闹事的名义逮捕了他，并惊奇地发现被拖的车并不是他的。[4]

在十多年的漫长诉讼过程中，他的家被警察突袭搜查；因名誉诽谤罪名成立，他被判给付原告近 100 万新西兰元。并于 2007 年 7 月，2009 年 7 月和 2010年 5 月因"藐视法庭罪"（Contempt of Court），三次被判入狱。

"奚陌案"可谓跌宕起伏、纷繁复杂。但总体来说，可以分成两大部分。第一部分是起因，原本并不复杂的商业纠纷。但因商业纠纷和由此派生的人际关系和法律关系（如他和律师及公司债务清算人之间的关系），使案件变得扑朔迷离。期间，又因自办网站爆料，引起诽谤官司——这还属于他自己的麻烦。2010 年 12 月 9 日，新西兰法庭受理一件刑事案，法官颁布了一份预审判决，并在首页强调，预审判决内容不得在任何媒体（平面、网站或其他媒体）报道。但奚陌先生却无视法官判决，将预审判决在自己的网站上做了报道并提供判决内容的链接。当然，预审判决也引起了司法界学术讨论，即法院有没有权力禁发自己的刑事判决书[5]——这是题外话。这两大部分，题内的民事和商业纠纷只是让他丢财失物；而题外的藐视法庭，却让他惹上刑事官司。这也是公诉人、检察院出场的根本原因。新西兰最高法院在 2013 年 7 月 12 日的判决中指

---

[1] Sunday Star-Times, dated: April 17, 2005, Author: Sheeran Garry. Quoted from Wikipedia. org. as at November 26, 2013.

[2] Media Law Journal 和 TV3 News "Appeal Claimant Wears Alice in Wonderland Costume". Quoted from Wikipedia. org. as at November 26, 2013.

[3] Solicitor General v. Siemer SC48/2009 [2010] NZSC 12.

[4] Greenberg, Pierce, "New Zealand legal rights activist arrested in Nashville after alleged drunken run", The City Paper published August 23, 2012, Retrieved November 26, 2013.

[5] 新西兰最高法院在 2013 年 7 月 12 日的判决中认定新西兰法院具备这种权力。尽管 1985 年《新西兰刑事审判法》第 138 条对这种权力加以限制。且这种权力对人权法赋予的公平审判不具有负面影响。

出："上诉人（被告）明知自己违背法庭禁令，他应该意识到藐视法庭可能招致的后果。……他的行为构成藐视法庭罪——这不是因为他对法官判决的批评，而是因为他对法庭判令的公然违抗。"〔1〕判决书的最后一段客气地说，下级法院的判决是对的，得以维持。奚陌先生必须于 2013 年 7 月 15 日上午 9 时到奥克兰高等法院报到——言下之意是，报到完毕您直接去监狱。读者或许好奇，堂堂刑事判决写得如此文明礼貌！那么，如果他偏不在规定时间去报到呢？如果拍电影的话，下一幕就是警笛声，接下来就是常见的场面了。

以上是奚陌案的来龙去脉，铺垫这么多，是为了说明"道琼斯案"判例是如何在本案中适用的。

哈维法官在他的专著〔2〕里感概：如果此前新西兰法官们对适用"道琼斯案"判例尚有一丝犹豫的话，那么，"奚陌案"中便已经十分明朗了。法官们对"道琼斯案"判例是这样认定和略加发挥的：

第一，随着互联网的到来，对电子媒介出版物的发表及其连续性和不间断性，法庭是颇为敏感的。就互联网上的出版物何时、何地发表的问题，有些案例已经探究过了，并且都指向了同一个方向——涉嫌侵权的内容被下载和阅读的彼时彼地，确定为诽谤内容被发表的时间和地点。美国许多州因为"单一发表规则"，以上诸多判例不称其为法，但在英国、澳大利亚和新西兰却是法。这里，法官特别强调，是因为他们在此案中适用了这一判例，这一判例才正式在新西兰被确认为法。

第二，涉嫌诽谤的内容由被告上传或存储到互联网上，这是初始动作。为调阅而获取这些信息（数据），则完成了"发表"这一过程。本案是公诉人起诉奚陌，当公诉人将诽谤内容下载到他们的电脑并阅读时，"发表"动作完成。尽管被告强调其互联网服务器均设在海外，这对本案没有任何影响——因为诽谤内容在新西兰下载、在新西兰阅读。

第三，被告抗辩认为以上因素并不能构成发表，因为公诉人自己也不能确定在电脑上获取的文件是否"源自隐含存储器"〔3〕。但法庭认为被告这个抗

---

〔1〕　Vincent Ross Siemer v. the Solicitor-General SC 37/2012, [2013] NZSC 68, par238.

〔2〕　Judge David Harvey, *internet. law. nz*, 3rd *ed*, Wellington: LexisNexis, 2011, pp. 613-614.

〔3〕　"Cache" 指高速缓冲存储器。

辩理由不能成立，因为诚如英国"歌德弗莱案"所阐明，即便内容处在一个被动的存储状态，但文件内容只要能被索取和浏览，则构成发表。

"奚陌案"明确认定澳大利亚高等法院在"道琼斯案"中所确定的判例，在新西兰已经成为其判例法的一部分。

七、对"道琼斯案"判例的修正

7.1 《华尔街日报》在英国的有惊无险

《华尔街日报》互联网版本刊登了一篇文章，文章中列了一份名单，原告"榜上有名"。这篇文章说的是本·拉登及其恐怖组织的资金来源，任何名列清单的人都有可能沾上赞助恐怖主义的恶名。原告因此将出版《华尔街日报》的道琼斯告上英国法庭。

道琼斯在高等法院申请将诉讼驳回，理由是被告在英国并没有对原告构成任何"真实和实际"的侵权，但高等法院不予支持。道琼斯上诉，这次却得到英国上诉法院的支持，上诉法院驳回诉讼，判定原告"滥用司法程序"。理由是，尽管原告证明被告《华尔街日报》互联网版在英国有超过 5000 个订户，但只有 5 个人读到这篇文章，其中 3 位来自原告自己的律师团队。

上诉法院要解决三个问题：第一，面对以互联网为载体的全球性出版物，原告选择一个出版量极小的国家，并认为这里的法庭能使他在全球范围内澄清自己——原告这样做合理吗？第二，这样的诉讼案要进展到何种程度才能达到澄清自己的效果？第三，因出版物数量的限制，名誉遭到毁损的程度因此也受到限制——同理，靠诉讼澄清自己的力度也受到限制。况且，诉之法庭耗时耗资，这与数量有限的诽谤出版物相比，显然不成比例。

因此在这宗 Jameel（Yousef）v. Dow Jones ［2005］QB 946（CA）中，道琼斯有惊无险。惊的是原告实力雄厚，一开打就打到英国高等法院。不像"嘎特尼克案"在澳大利亚所陷极深，此次在英国打到上诉法院便奇迹般解脱了。这也是继"嘎特尼克案"之后，第一宗以"侵权极小"作为测试标准驳回原告诉讼请求的判例。业界认为，2005 年英国上诉法院的这则判例，至少让那些打算到英国"择优而告"的人三思。[1]

7.2 2013 年《英国诽谤法》

仿佛回应澳大利亚高等法院的法官们当年在"道琼斯案"判决中的感概，英国立法机构果然通过成文法，系统解决了许多判例法无法解决的问题。2013年《英国诽谤法》于 2013 年 4 月 25 日接受"御准"（Royal Assent）[2]依既定程序于 2014 年初正式生效。该法最重要的特征，是将"言论自由"和"名誉保护"的平衡点向言论自由方向偏移，标志着英国在诽谤法领域开始偏向美国的司法理论和实践。而美国诽谤法一向是亲被告疏原告，也就是说因宪法第一修正案的缘故，美国诽谤法对被告较为友善。

2013 年《英国诽谤法》考量了许多澳大利亚"道琼斯案"中出现的问题，许多判例原本来自英国。毕竟是判例法的源头，英国以成文法的方式，在诽谤法领域跟进和更新了现代社会许多法律实践、经验和概念。从这个角度看，可以说判例法的发展是"一以贯之"的——"万物虽殊，而其情可类，所谓一以贯之者"[3]。因此，需要反复强调的是，读判例法，贵在"得其意而忘其形"。得"意"忘"形"，也是本书写与读之根本。各种案例千奇百怪，症状不同下的药也不同。但归根结底，道理是一样的，结论所依据的法理也是一样的，这也是为什么 100 多年前的案例照样有用，甚至被后世法庭否定的判例也依然被拿出来作为参考例证。大快朵颐、饱餐一顿，最后再加块甜点——"吃饱"是因为咽下的每一口，不能是最后一个烧饼让我吃饱了，便感慨之前的纯属多余。许多华人学生初涉判例法，在拿到教科书的那一刹那会觉得绝望，因为大多数教科书不是按中国式的"定义""名称解释"或"概念"来展开，而是开篇便是案例，由案例来剥笋撕皮式展开，再考据式地通过判例依据来支持自己的

---

[1] 见 Pearson, Roger, "Court ruling could block claims for online libel." PressGazette：February 09, 2005, Retrieved November 26, 2013。

[2] Royal Assent, "御准，御批"，指英国女王在议案上签字，确定法案成为法律。御准制在英国通常以"英王制诰"等较为正式的书面方式进行，有时也会举行正式而详尽的仪式。在其他大英国协成员国，如澳大利亚、加拿大、新西兰，"御准"由总督代为签署。御准是国会立法，是"法案"（Bill）变成"法律"（Act, Law）的最后一个步骤。

[3] （宋）韩滤：《涧泉日记》，见《汉典》，www.zdic.net，最后访问时间：2013 年 11 月 27 日。

结论。

大致说来，2013 年《英国诽谤法》有以下四大特点：

第一，诽谤言论定义加入"严重损害"要素。第 1 条规定，"一则陈述不构成诽谤，除非其发表对原告名誉造成或有可能造成严重损害"。

第 1 条"严重损害"要素引发了两大问题：新要素导致诽谤概念新的定义还是施加原告额外的法律要素才能证明诽谤成立？英国律师界对此争论颇多。以大律师评头（Pinto）为代表的一方认为，"严重损害"说是在原有概念基础上的额外成分。也就是说，原告需要证明涉嫌诽谤的言论：（1）对原告名誉造成或可能造成严重损害；同时（2）招致——举例来说——①原告在社会上思维正常的人眼里被看低；②其他人对原告的态度有重大的负面影响[1]。

因这一额外成分，实际效果是证明诽谤言论的门槛有可能被提高，诉讼案件谈不上锐减，但起码可以预测，许多原先想打官司的原告现在有可能打退堂鼓。还有两种情形也会受到影响：第一种是针对发行量不大的出版物（诽谤影响小则纠错力度小，因此不必诉讼）；另一种是原告名声原本就很差，如何证明原本就已毁损的名誉因诽谤言论而"严重损害"呢？——当然，我们可以拭目以待，看今后案例。

第二，区别以上所说的自然人，对法人名誉侵权而言，新法加入了一个"严重经济损失"要件。由此有可能产生两种效果。其一是法人作为原告诉讼起点被抬高，而且在诉状中必须列明"严重经济损失"（以及经审计的财务报表或其他证据），否则被告有可能依新法这一条款申请法院驳回告诉。其二，本着"上有政策、下有对策"的全球通行理念，预计不少法人会将对公司的诽谤视作对公司领头人（如总裁、CEO）的诽谤，从而绕开"重大经济损失"要件而变成自然人性质的诉讼。大的公司如苹果，谁能将苹果和乔布斯分开呢？小的公司更不用说，骂店铺与骂掌柜原本就是一回事[2]。

第三，跟"嘎特尼克诉道琼斯案"最贴近的，就是新法第 8 款确定了"单

---

〔1〕 见 Pinto, Timothy："Defamation Act 2013-Taylor Wessing analysis"，May 1, 2013, NB_ 001165_ 05.13.

〔2〕 见 Pinto, Timothy，同前注，p.2。

一发表规则"。前文提及过一个 1849 年的案例[1]，原告是在相关文章发表 17 年后才知道有这么一篇文章，然后去博物馆和报社档案室索要刊有这篇文章的报纸，随后告报社诽谤。这个案件判下了著名的先例，即每新的一次发表便构成一次新的诉因。

与 1849 年这个案例同样有"花开两朵、各表一枝"效果的，是 2001 年的一个案例[2]，这则判例确定了在互联网上发表的文章，每"点击"（hit）一次便构成一次新的发表，因此构成一个新的诉因。而诉讼时效的起算也因此不断更新——尽管新的赔偿额应该随着读者群的递减而递减。

这实际上造成了互联网时代大众媒体界极大的不确定性。这一点，在澳大利亚高等法院法官们的论证中已经表达得十分明确。这也是为什么法官们呼吁，只能靠国会立法，才能在宏观上综合调节新技术带来的新问题。

英国新法将"单一发表规则"纳入成文法，规定诉因从第一次发表之时起算（以此推算诉讼时效）。除非在首次发表之后，涉嫌诽谤的内容有"重大的"或"实质性的"不同，否则皆为一次发表。当然，新法中保留了 1980 年《英国诉讼时效法》赋予法庭的裁决权，即视具体案情，法庭有权延展诉讼时效。

第四，除传统抗辩理由外，新法规范了互联网时代因新的技术和实践带来的新的抗辩因素。如，作为提供平台的纯中间人技术性媒介（某种程度上"微博""微信"属于这种平台），如果这样的中间人媒介能证明自己不是诽谤言论的作者、编者、发表者，并且采取合理措施以及对导致该诽谤言论的发表没有实际认知或可能合理的认知，则抗辩成立，免于承担法律责任。

与 2013 年的"谷歌案"相比[3]，新法将责任焦点从"平台"转移到"平台使用者"。

但业界认为[4]，鉴于"谷歌案"判例，责任位移的尺度以及相关领域技术和法律的互动发展，尚有待观察。无论如何，英国最新的诽谤法，如同其判

---

[1]　见 Duke of Brunswick v. Harmer，同前注。

[2]　见 Loutchansky v. Times Newspaper Ltd [2001] EWCA Civ 1805。

[3]　Tamiz v. Google [2013] EWCA Civ 68，谷歌平台上被贴诽谤言论，谷歌接到原告通知后的 5 个星期才撤下诽谤内容，谷歌被判承担诽谤责任。

[4]　见 Agate, Jennifer, "The Defamation Act 2013-Key Changes for online", *Farrer & Co*, September 2013。

例法，在英美法系抑或全球诽谤法领域，起到了一个龙头作用。

八、结论

本案归根结底涉及的还是在互联网无国界前提下，如何确定司法管辖地的问题。不同体系下的法律，对原、被告各自立场和利益均有不同侧重。同一时期英国的法官就如此感慨过：美国宪法第一修正案带来的影响，使英美两个司法体系在处理诽谤案件时的出发点有很大不同。例如，就"无辜传播"来说，英国法要求被告（一般指诽谤言论的发表者，但互联网时代有可能也包括纯技术平台提供方如谷歌、微信等）证明自己的无辜；而美国法则要求被诽谤的原告，来证明被告不是无辜的。显然，在美国诽谤法前提下诉讼成功的门槛比英国高。因宪法第一修正案的影响，在美国的诽谤诉讼，更有利于被告开脱而不利于原告追究。

澳大利亚高等法院受理此案要考量的核心问题有两个：其一，诽谤文章在何处发表？——因为这关系到民事侵权行为发生的地方。其二，澳大利亚法院是不是受理本案最合适、"最方便"的法院？这两大问题都涉及司法管辖权问题。

澳大利亚高等法院旁征博引、纵横古今，尤其是参考对比了英国、美国、澳大利亚和其他体系的成文法和判例法后，得出结论：现行的诽谤法依涉嫌诽谤内容（文章、书籍等）的"接受地"（而非"发送地"）来确定司法管辖权。这一原则同样适用以互联网为媒介的新的传播方式。因此，道琼斯旗下的《巴伦周刊》和"巴伦在线"，尽管是在美国境内采编、上传并在服务器上存储，但其电子版本借互联网在澳大利亚境内被下载和阅读后，便构成在澳大利亚境内的发表，民事侵权行为发生在澳大利亚，澳大利亚法院有权行使司法管辖权。就像在随后的加拿大"《纽约邮报》案"中不列颠哥伦比亚省的法官所解释的，当诽谤言论在互联网上发表后，诽谤言论便"跟随原告"来到原告名声所在地。原告自然会关注自己的名誉在这里被损害的范围和程度。由此看来，"被告就原告"非但不是什么深奥的法理，倒是人之常情或普通常识。

澳大利亚高等法院（终审法院）在本案所确定的判例，已经在英美法系被普通接受和引用。但十多年过去了，互联网和新科技带来的挑战，又从不同角度给我们带来新的问题，比较突出的至少有两个：第一，"单一发表规则"如何更好和更公平地判断诉讼时效期的起算点以及刷新网页或网上点击等不算构成新的"发表"？第二，为网上聊天和发帖提供技术平台的"纯中间人"——如 Facebook、Twitter，YouTube、微信和微博等——所扮演的角色应该或可能承担的法律责任是什么？这些都是新技术、新时代所带来的不可避免的问题和现象。

2013 年《英国诽谤法》以成文法的方式已经提供了不少答案。除了英国这个判例法的源头，其他英美法系大家族的成员如美国、加拿大、澳大利亚、新西兰等也都从各自的角度来分享新时代的法律经验。新技术和新时代扑面而来，澳大利亚"道琼斯案"恰到好处地折射了其中几组画面。

案例四 美女、政要、贵族：英国"洋微博"诽谤案

——社交媒体上的几个字和一个表情符号

McAlpine v. Bercow〔2013〕EWHC 1342（QB）

案　名： 麦考潘诉白扣"洋微博"诽谤案

原被告： 原告：麦考潘勋爵，曾在撒切尔夫人任首相期间任保守党要职

　　　　　被告：萨丽·白扣，英国下议院议长夫人

地　点： 英国、意大利

法　院： 英国及威尔士高等法院（皇座庭）〔1〕

---

〔1〕　英国及威尔士高等法院（皇座庭），High Court of Justice of England and Wales，Queen's Bench Division。英国及威尔士高等法院（又译成"英国及威尔士高等司法院"）由三部分组成：皇座庭、衡平法庭和家事法庭。第一，皇座庭（the Queen's Bench Division，其判例汇编缩写为QB，如果是王座，则缩写为KB——本书引用的判例中常见这样的缩写）主要有两大职能：审理范围很宽的民商法案件及对下级各类法院的督导。皇座法院另设商务法庭、海事法庭和行政法庭。第二，衡平法庭（the Chancery Division，也译作"大法官法庭"），主要审理遗嘱、合伙、税务和破产等案件。第三，家事法庭（the Family Division），顾名思义，主要审理婚姻及父母子女方面的案件。高等法院案件上诉，如果是民事案件一般上诉到上一级上诉法院，个别重要的有可能直接上诉到最高法院；但如果是刑事案件，则直接上诉到最高法院。

本案案情及确立的判例原则

2012 年 11 月 4 日，英国广播公司（BBC）重量级的晚间新闻播出北威尔士性侵未成年人丑闻，英国独立电视（ITV）也相继播出 20 多年前在儿童收养中心性侵未成年人的专题报道。虽未点名，却含沙射影指向"前保守党高官""撒切尔夫人的顾问和亲信"，涉嫌性侵和猥亵收养中心的儿童。社交媒体更是推波助澜、以讹传讹，网上贴标语、造谣言、打黑拳，比比皆是。名人萨丽·白扣此时发推特一则："麦考潘勋爵为何热门？＊一脸无辜＊（表情符号）。"麦考潘遂采取法律行动，BBC 和 ITV 两大电视网分别赔偿 185 000 英镑和 125 000 英镑。麦考潘将这些赔款捐给儿童慈善机构，并要求那些重复了诽谤内容、推特用户"朋友圈"关注人数在 500 人以下的人通过向儿童慈善机构小额捐款便可获庭外和解。萨丽·白扣认为自己的推文虽指名道姓但却无诽谤之意。双方为此对簿公堂。法官认真考量了相关判例并逐一解释诽谤法"重复发表"原则、"中性报导"以及诽谤法判例和成文法可以成立的抗辩。法官将字词含义的判断集中在"原本含义"和"影射、暗讽"两类，以"合理测试"为标准，将推文七字和表情符号结合当时的媒体环境做综合判断，得出推文七字构成诽谤的结论。

本案确定了这样的判例原则：判断字词含义无非两个方面：第一，字面或原本含义；第二，影射、曲笔和嘲讽。"原本含义"除顾名思义之外，也包含那些可以推断出来的含义，但区别在于一个普通读者只需要一般而非特别的认知即可。与之相对的影射和嘲讽，不是从一般字词中可以推断出来的，而需要借助外部事实。经典的例子是指某某行为不轨，因为他刚从"那幢房子里出来"，而那幢房子是一所地下妓院。这便是"圈内人"知道的外部事实，不是一般或所有读者都知道的。同时判断字词含义要结合上下文综合判断，合理性测试为前提。表情符号作为推文一部分将媒体报导的新闻串联起来，构成诽谤并适用"重复发表"原则。

一、美女、政要和贵族以及惹祸的"洋微博"

1.1 美女和政要

美女是本案的主角萨丽·白扣（Sally Bercow），从事公共关系和广告业。她的政要光环除了她自己，也来自她的先生约翰·白扣（John Bercow），现任英国下议院议长（Speaker of the House of Commons）。

英国国会由三大部分组成：君主、上议院（又称贵族院）和下议院（又称庶民院）。下议院的历史可追溯到 14 世纪。我们现在所看到的英国下议院，是经由民主选举产生的国会议员组成，目前下议院共设 650 席。所谓的"全国大选"指的就是选举这 650 位国会议员（Member of Parliament，MP），任期 5 年。由占多数席位的政党组阁，首相就从执政党的国会议员中产生，[1]政府各部长（除极个别例外）也是从国会议员中产生（这和美国的国会与政府的关系有很大的不同），英国政府对下议院负责。由此可见，下议院的权力和影响力，远远超过上议院，而根据 1911 年《英国国会法》[2]，上议院驳回议案的权力被削弱为仅仅拖延议案通过而已。国会每届任期 5 年，只有不信任投票或 2/3 的多数决议才能解散国会，提前大选。"不信任投票"（votes of confidence）是英国威斯敏斯特宪政制度的一大特点，其原则是作为"行政"（executive）部门的政府，必须取得作为"立法"（legislature）部门的下议院的信任，方能执政。如果不能获得立法机构的多数支持（"多数"指的是哪怕多出一票也可），政府则

---

　　[1]　自 1902 年开始，除一位外，所有的英国首相都是从下议院国会议员中产生。唯一的例外是 1963 年 10 月至 1964 年 10 月，亚历山大·道格拉斯-霍姆（Alexander Douglas-Home）出任英国首相一职。他是迄今最后一位来自上议院的首相，也是最后一位由英国君主指定委任的首相。但他随后还是放弃贵族爵位，再以补选途径进入下议院。他任首相仅一年，1964 年 10 月大选，英国工党获胜执政，他所在的保守党成为反对党。

　　[2]　本法主要是规范上议院与下议院的职能及彼此之间的关系，需要和 1949 年《英国国会法》合并对待，当作规范英国国会的立法。

不能执政〔1〕。但从另一方面来看，如果一个政党不能在国会获得多数席位，该政党最初也就不具备组阁能力〔2〕。这一点听起来挺拗口，尤其是生硬地理解孟德斯鸠的"三权分立"概念就更加混淆。但是在英国威斯敏斯特宪政制度下（包括澳大利亚、新西兰等），国会议员（立法）和在国会占多数席位的政党中产生的政府（行政），两者是"一套人马两套招牌"，国会议员既行使立法职能又行使行政职能，首相或总理〔3〕及政府部长就是从国会议员中产生的，当选首相或总理的前提是当选为国会议员。这和美国的体制有很大区别。

约翰·白扣 1963 年 1 月 19 日出生在一个犹太家庭，大学时代就活跃于右翼政党英国保守党。1997 年全国大选中当选为白金汉区（Buckingham，位于英格兰中南部）的国会议员。2009 年起担任下议院议长。1996 年他角逐党内国会议员提名时，必须一天在保守党的两个安全选区赶两场提名会。于是他花了 1000 英镑雇直升飞机两头赶，结果功夫没有白费，获得了白金汉区的提名。他说这是他"这辈子花得最值的 1000 英镑"〔4〕。

尽管是三个孩子的母亲，萨丽·白扣的敢说敢做是远近有名的。她的先生当选下议院议长之后，她参加明星真人秀，出场费是不菲的 15 万英镑，她承认她的丈夫对她此举甚为不满却又无可奈何，"做议长的夫人就得像个议长夫人的样儿？我看不见得！"——她不但这么说，还一五一十地对媒体算账如何合理分配这笔出场费：10 万英镑捐给慈善机构，2 万交公关费用，3 万自个儿留着。〔5〕别忘了 2013 年英国国会议员的年薪也不过 66 396 英镑（不算其他补贴）〔6〕，首相是 142 500 英镑，议长年薪比首相稍微少一点，是 142 162 英镑〔7〕。而英

〔1〕 参见 http://www.parliament.uk/documents/commons-information-office/m07.pdf.

〔2〕 在两院制国家（如英国），这种意义下的"国会"指下议院；在一院制国家（如新西兰），"国会"指众议院（House of Representatives）。

〔3〕 英文里都是"Prime Minister"，在英国称首相，在澳大利亚和新西兰等则称总理。

〔4〕 Wheeler, Brian, "The John Bercow story", *BBC News*. Retrieved November 30, 2010, quoted December 23, 2013.

〔5〕 见 http://www.bbc.co.uk/news/uk-politics。

〔6〕 2013 年基本工资，见 http://en.wikipedia.org/wiki/Salaries_of_Members_of_the_United_Kingdom_Parliament。2018 年，英国国会议员的工资涨到 77 379 英镑。首相涨到 150 402 英镑。

〔7〕 参见英国国会"分类问答"：http://www.parliament.uk/about/faqs/house-of-commons-faqs/members-faq-page2/。

国大学毕业生的平均工资是 2 万英镑多一点[1]。列出这些年薪数字，对比随后判付的赔偿额，也能看出此案的力度。当然近些年各方面工资都有涨幅。之所以列出 2013 年的数据，是因为这和此案发生和法庭判决的时间接近，比较有参考价值。

1.2 贵族

这里的贵族是男爵阿莱斯戴·麦考潘（Alistair McAlpine, Baron McAlpine of West Green），在正式场合如判决书和媒体报道中常称为"麦考潘勋爵"（Lord McAlpine）。1942 年出生在伦敦，已退休，现居意大利[2]。麦考潘勋爵 1975 年与保守党领袖撒切尔夫人相识，撒切尔夫人随即任命他为保守党司库（treasurer），他担任此职一直到 1990 年，为保守党筹集大选经费立下了汗马功劳，深得首相撒切尔夫人赏识。1979～1983 年，任保守党副主席[3]。1984 年晋封为男爵。2010 年，他辞去贵族院（上议院）议员席位。[4]

麦考潘勋爵家道兴旺，从曾祖父那一辈开始就从事建筑业。他 16 岁就在家族企业就职，21 岁当选为董事开始管理公司。1960 年前后到西澳大利亚发展，从事五星级酒店的开发。到 20 世纪 80 年代，开始重振布鲁姆[5]计划，投资 5 亿澳币，给布鲁姆旅游业带来生机。至今，在布鲁姆海滨还树立着当地人为麦考潘勋爵塑铸的真人大小的铜像。

---

〔1〕 http://www.thecompleteuniversityguide. co. uk/careers/what-do-graduates-do/what-do-graduates-earn/.

〔2〕 引自 "Non-dom Tory peer quits Lords". *Daily Mail* (London). 10 June 2010. Retrieved 4 November 2012. For Lord retirement lists see also "Tory donor Lord Ashcroft gives up non-dom tax status". *BBC News*. 7 July 2010, quoted from http://en. wikipedia. org/wiki/Alistair_ McAlpine, _ Baron_ McAlpine_ of_ West_ Green。

〔3〕 "Profile: Lord Midas, his zenith and nadir: Lord McAlpine, party treasurer for Mrs Thatcher". *The Independent* (London). 19 June 1993.

〔4〕 参见 "Non-dom Tory peer quits Lords". *Daily Mail* (London). 10 June 2010. Retrieved 4 November 2012. For Lord retirement lists see also "Tory donor Lord Ashcroft gives up non-dom tax status". *BBC News*. 7 July 2010, quoted from http://en. wikipedia. org/wiki/Alistair_ McAlpine, _ Baron_ McAlpine_ of_ West_ Green。

〔5〕 布鲁姆（Broome）是西澳大利亚州金伯丽地区的主要城镇，也是著名的旅游胜地，曾是世界上重要的珍珠生产中心。该镇位于西澳首府珀斯（Perth）北部 2200 公里处，城镇常住人口约 15 000 人，但旅游旺季时每月递增近 5 万多人。

布鲁姆海滨树立的麦考潘勋爵的铜像

1.3 晴天霹雳

2012 年 11 月，平地一声雷，麦考潘勋爵被无端卷入"北威尔士性侵未成年人"丑闻[1]。英国广播公司（BBC）重量级的《晚间新闻》[2]和英国独立电视台（ITV）《晨报》[3]，相继播出关于多年前在北威尔士儿童收养中心儿童遭性侵的专题报道，含沙射影指"前保守党某高管""撒切尔夫人的顾问和亲信"，涉嫌性侵和猥亵收养中心的儿童。社交媒体如"洋微博"（Twitter）等，更是以讹传讹、添油加醋，网上贴标语、造谣言、打黑拳的比比皆是，一时间晴天霹雳、黑云压城，虽然英国广播公司和英国独立电视台以及社交媒体上的散户，都没有指名道姓，但彼时彼刻的舆论空间，大家都心照不宣，知道所指的"前保守党某高管"就是麦考潘勋爵。

〔1〕 David Leigh（10 November 2012）. "The Newsnight fiasco that toppled the BBC director general". *The Observer*（London）. Retrieved 13 November 2012. Quoted from http://en. wikipedia. org/wiki/Alistair_ McAlpine, _ Baron_ McAlpine_ of_ West_ Green, January 3, 2014.

〔2〕 David Leigh（10 November 2012）. "The Newsnight fiasco that toppled the BBC director general". *The Observer*（London）. Retrieved 13 November 2012. Quoted from http://en. wikipedia. org/wiki/Alistair_ McAlpine, _ Baron_ McAlpine_ of_ West_ Green, January 3, 2014.

〔3〕 Mark Sweney（22 November 2012）. "ITV to pay Lord McAlpine £125, 000 in damages". *The Guardian*（London）. Quoted from http://en. wikipedia. org/wiki/Alistair_ McAlpine, _ Baron_ McAlpine_ of_ West_ Green, January 3, 2014.

1.4 两大广播网

英国广播公司（BBC）1922年10月18日成立，不仅在英国本土有渗透力，而且其影响力远及全球。说BBC是全球公共电视媒体的典范（指新闻力度、拨款方式及自主模式等），应毫不为过。

"BBC《世界新闻》"（电视）是1991年3月推出的，24小时滚动播出。BBC电台就更早了，1932年起就以短波向全球播报，目前播报的语言达28种，据2009年的数据，"BBC《世界新闻》"（广播）平均每周收听人众达1.88亿。[1]

"BBC《晚间新闻》"以时事和政论为主，1980年开播以来，一直以主持人的犀利和时常让接受访谈的政要下不了台而著称。

独立电视台（ITV）1955年9月22日开播，是英国第二大无线电视网，它的成立初衷就是为了与英国广播公司竞争，避免英国广播公司一家独大。

---

[1] "BBC's international news services attract record global audience of 238 million"。加上电视观众，BBC全球观众和听众人数每周达2.38亿。

有这两家大哥大级别的媒体挑头，众散户在社交媒体推波助澜，性侵儿童，似乎是未经审判却早已定罪了。这时，萨丽·白扣也手痒痒地，于是她发了一个帖子。

1.5 七字千金

萨丽·白扣是在推特（Twitter）上发帖的。推特 2006 年 3 月在美国加州旧金山创办，截至 2013 年 2 月，推特共有 2 亿"活跃用户"[1]，加上其他用户，估计全球范围有 5 亿之众[2]，这些用户每天发表数亿推文。同时，推特每天还会处理约 16 亿的网络搜索[3]。到 2012 年，推特公司收入已达 3.17 亿美元[4]。目前已成为全球受访最多的十大网站之一[5]，足见其发展之快。

推特是一个不折不扣的社交网络。推特可以让注册用户发表推文（含静止和动态图片），注册用户可以跟帖，非注册用户只能看，每次发文不超过 140 个字，还有诸多表情各异的符号渲染气氛。无论是用智能手机还是普通电脑，推特用起来都十分方便。推特还有一个功能，就是"即时潮流识别"，在推特网屏的显著位置设一个专门板块，上列标题"Trends"，按网络语言，可译成"新潮""热门"之类。据推特解释[6]，这一功能是为了识别时兴、新潮和热议的话题（包括人、物以及地点等）。这是按计算机程序采集排列的，推特用户也可以自己设定，关注推特的潮流方向和热议话题。与其他类似功能不同的是，

〔1〕 "Celebrating #Twitter7". Twitter. 2013-03-21. Originally retrieved 2013-03-21.

〔2〕 Twitter Passed 500M Users In June 2012, 140M Of Them In US; Jakarta 'Biggest Tweeting' City". *TechCrunch*. July 30, 2012.

〔3〕 Twitter turns six Twitter. com, March 21, 2012. Retrieved December 18, 2012.

〔4〕 Jeremy Quittner（October 3, 2013）. "Twitter Unveils IPO Papers; Includes ＄317 Million in 2012 Revenue". *Inc*. Retrieved November 14, 2013. Quoted from http://en. wikipedia. org/wiki/Twitter, January 3, 2014.

〔5〕 Twitter. com Site Info. Alexa Internet. Retrieved 2013-12-01. Quoted from http://en. wikipedia. org/wiki/Twitter. January 3, 2014.

〔6〕 见判决书第 5 段 The Lord McAlpine of West Green v. Sally Bercow〔2013〕EWHC 1342（QB）。法官首先分析这一功能，是因为通过此帖的跟帖数量、关注密集度和引发的热议程度，可以判断此帖的影响力，这样在确定"诽谤构成"的前提下，可参考量刑决定赔偿额。法官引推特解释：Twitter explains that this list is generated by an algorithm which "identifies topics that are immediately popular, rather than topics that have been popular for a while or on a daily basis, to help you discover the hottest emerging topics of discussion on Twitter that matter most to you. You can choose to see Trends that are tailored for you."

"最新潮流"识别和排序的是"即时潮流",而不是按每天或已经流行一阵子的热议话题。其目的是发现和挖掘与用户有关的新兴的、有可能热议的话题。这其实是网络营销的手法之一,只有源源不断地制造新鲜话题,大家才会恋恋不舍、欲罢不能,这样点击率和刷新频率才会提高,广告才会在不知不觉中被随之关注,网站收入才会提高。

萨丽·白扣发了一个帖,共 7 个字:

*Why is Lord McAlpine trending? * Innocent face ** (表情符号)

依网络语言,似乎可译成:"麦考潘勋爵为何热门? *一脸无辜* (表情符号)"。

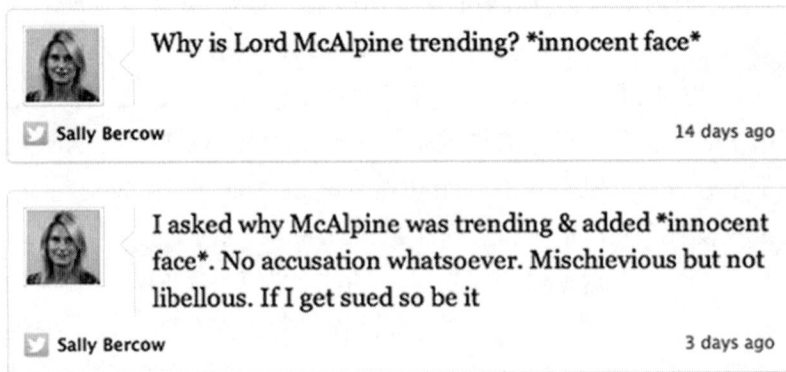

> **Why is Lord McAlpine trending? *innocent face***
>
> Sally Bercow   14 days ago

> **I asked why McAlpine was trending & added *innocent face*. No accusation whatsoever. Mischievious but not libellous. If I get sued so be it**
>
> Sally Bercow   3 days ago

就为了这 7 个字,麦考潘勋爵将萨丽·白扣告上了法庭。从随后的判决来看,萨丽·白扣为这 7 个字可是付出了昂贵的代价。但是法官首先要解决的、全世界对这个案件有所关注的人以及整个推特社区所好奇的,就是这 7 个字构成诽谤吗?

二、麦考潘勋爵反击

2.1 BBC 和 ITV 先行落马

BBC《晚间新闻》"未成年人遭性侵"的专题报道是 2012 年 11 月 2 日周五播出的。一般来说,在周四、周五播出此类新闻,其用心主要是为了在周末引发一个大波澜,涟漪效果能辐射下周甚至随后更长的时间。从媒体角度看,无论是新闻力度和市场营销都是成功的，但对当事人（主要是受害者）来说，无疑要忍耐整整一个周末的煎熬。这跟司法界不少人习惯在周五发传票或律师信一样，除非万不得已，很大程度上看是不必要的。用中文说，那不厚道！但英文里似乎很难找到一个十分确切的词来表达"厚道"的意思。

BBC 在播出新闻后第 13 天，便在法庭上向麦考潘勋爵正式道歉、赔偿 185 000 英镑外加一笔不菲的律师费损失。

所谓的"北威尔士性侵未成年人丑闻"，虽未指名道姓但却含沙射影"前保守党高官""公众人物""撒切尔夫人的顾问和亲信"，加上有鼻子有眼地直指"多年前在北威尔士儿童收养中心"并采访当年的受害者。一时间麦考潘勋爵成了人人唾弃的、有恋童癖之嫌的人民公敌。

但明眼人看得出，如此令人耸动的大新闻，既没有实际证据（接受采访的受害者事后坦言"认错人了"），也没有针对当事人采访的平衡报道。从节目本身来看，雷声大、风格犀利，大有不经审判而强行定罪之势。这也可以算是现代社会媒体审判的一个特例。好在大牌媒体有大牌媒体的气度，就这则报道，BBC《晚间新闻》犯错快认错也快。但后果严重，不但节目组接受 BBC 内部和独立外部机构的双重调查，BBC 总监也因此不得不引咎辞职。

但大家不要忘了，BBC 作为国际上数一数二的综合媒体，就资金来源而言，它是个不折不扣的"公器"。2012～2013 年 BBC 的资金收入共计 51 亿英镑，而其中 37 亿英镑是英国政府通过"电视执照费"的方式直接拨款[1]。英国电视执照费是 1946 年 6 月 1 日实行的，实际上是另一种形式的税收。私家媒体靠广告，而不依赖广告的公共媒体自然靠政府拨款。但凡有电视的家庭，必须缴纳执照费，这是法律规定。违法者，轻则罚款重则遭起诉。电视执照费在英联邦国家并不鲜见，但近些年发展趋势是尽量让这些公共媒体多发掘包括广告在内的收入来源，以减轻纳税人的压力。

ITV 版"未成年人遭性侵"的专题报道比 BBC 晚差不多一周，是 2012 年 11 月 8 日在《今晨》栏目播出。需要注意的是，《今晨》栏目主持人还向当时接受访谈的英国首相卡梅伦出示了一份性侵"嫌疑人"名单。尽管在实况节目

---

〔1〕 参见 BBC 2012～2013 年度财务报表。"BBC Full Financial Statements 2012/13"．BBC. Retrieved 22 August 2013。

中名单一晃而过，但人们可以通过录制的节目用"暂停"键，清楚地看到名单上的个别嫌疑人的名字（包括麦考潘勋爵）。这是受害人名誉受损的原因之一。原因之二，则是那些闲来无事或别有用心的好事之徒，通过转播、重放或借推特这样的社交媒体，扩散谣言、推波助澜。

ITV 向麦考潘勋爵作出"毫无保留的正式道歉"，赔偿 125 000 英镑外加律师费[1]。ITV 的正式道歉是在媒体上公布的，为表诚意，ITV 通过律师在法庭上再郑重地宣读了一遍。

麦考潘勋爵的律师也表示，和 BBC 及 ITV 的官司虽了，但此事远没有结束，因为利用社交媒体散布谣言的"散户"，对两大电视网的败诉无动于衷，依然乐此不疲、"毁人不倦"。

2.2 推手全被起诉

麦考潘勋爵起初是将所有在推特上发布或转发这则谣言的人全都告上法庭，随后调整战术，将诉讼集中在"追随者"在 500 人以上的用户上，并与他们庭外和解，他们也以每人付出小额赔款的方式，免对簿公堂之祸。而麦考潘勋爵则将这些小额赔款集中起来，捐给保护儿童的慈善机构。

显而易见，麦考潘勋爵的律师团队采取各个击破的方式，尽快和散户庭外和解，因为他们集中精力，目标锁定了萨丽·白扣。

三、目标锁定萨丽·白扣

3.1 萨丽·白扣的 7 字帖

萨丽·白扣在推特上的发帖不算标点英文共 7 个字，译成中文是："麦考潘勋爵为何热门？＊一脸无辜＊。"

法庭首先确定，被告萨丽·白扣也接受的，是其发贴暗示麦考潘勋爵在 11 月 4 日（即两大电视网相继作出性侵报道的敏感时段）"热门"了。而"＊一

---

〔1〕 参见 ITV to pay Lord McAlpine £125, 000 in damages By Mark Sweney theguardian. com, Thursday 22 November 2012 13. 51。

脸无辜 * "则相当于微博、微信中经常用到的情绪脸谱小符号。表达的是两重意思：表现在萨丽·白扣脸上的是真诚的，指"我一脸无辜，不知道麦考潘勋爵为何热门"。反射在原告麦考潘勋爵脸上的则是不真诚或具讽刺意味的，指"一脸无辜，不知道为何热门"。这样的春秋笔法自然不是出于为尊者讳、为亲者讳或为贤者讳，萨丽·白扣反话正说，其意义十分明确，貌似中性的语言之外，似乎有个小声音的不断叽叽喳喳：装什么蒜！装什么蒜！

在确定 7 字帖明指热门、暗示装蒜之后，法官要解决的是这样的语境在彼时彼刻是否构成诽谤？构成或不构成诽谤的法理依据是什么？成文法对此如何解释、判例法如何适用？

3.2 萨丽·白扣的推文背景

法官在法庭上强调，要判断萨丽·白扣推文这 7 个字是否构成诽谤，必须清楚这 7 个字在法律上的含义，而理解、分析或推断其法律上的含义，首先得了解推文发表时的背景和媒体环境。然后法官所要做的，便是撇开所有"事后诸葛亮"式的信息（包括事实和结论），将推文完全置于彼时彼地，依当时的环境来分析和判断推文在文字和法律意义上的含义。只有这样，才能对原告、被告作出一个客观、公正的判定。

BBC《晚间新闻》是 2012 年 11 月 2 日播出的。关于上世纪 70~80 年代发生在北威尔士儿童收养中心的性侵事件，是由受害人史蒂夫·米申爆料的。收养中心发生的对男童性侵事件是令人发指的。针对那些年发生的大小事件，政府进行了专门的调查。如 1996 年的专项调查，就传唤证人多达 575 人，140 多起赔偿案结案。但在 2000 年公布的报告中，却有 28 位涉嫌人员的名字从名单上被抹去。而此前 1991 年的调查，虽然有包括收养中心工作人员在内的 7 名嫌疑人被法庭定罪，但调查的力度和范围皆难服众。而米申所揭露的都不在前几次调查范围内。毋庸置疑，米申在儿童收养中心被性侵是公认事实。他在 BBC《晚间新闻》中，将矛头指向"当年保守党高官""撒切尔夫人时代知名的保守党政客"……

不幸的是，米申认错了人。当年造下罪孽的不是米申在电视采访中暗指的那个人。米申年少时遭遇的不幸，却酿造了一个新的不幸：有人被冤枉了，而这个人正是麦考潘勋爵。连法官也表示，尽管那个人是谁与本案无关，也不会影响法官对本案的裁定——因为本案是裁定白扣的推文是否构成诽谤——但为了公平起见，法官还是强调，本案中的原告麦考潘勋爵已经坚决而彻底地否认与性侵案有任何牵连。社会大众也都接受了这一事实，即麦考潘勋爵是无辜的[1]。被告在 11 月 4 日之后也承认原告麦考潘勋爵是无辜的事实。

需要注意的另一细节是，BBC《晚间新闻》并没有公布米申所指的那位"保守党高官"的姓名，在节目结尾，主持人说"我们没有足够证据指名道姓"。但尽管如此，还是吃了官司，赔了大笔名誉损失费和律师费——当然这是后话。

BBC《晚间新闻》播出后，不仅使舆论哗然，更使媒体跟风，一时间风云突变，对麦考潘而言，简直就是黑云压城。

3.2.1 《卫报》亮相

《卫报》（The Guardian），创刊于 1821 年，英国全国性的综合类日报。无论是其发行量还是影响力，《卫报》在英国都位居前列。

《卫报》2012 年 11 月 3 日的大标题是："一男声称被保守党政客性侵"[2]。导语是这样写的："上世纪 70 年代北威尔士儿童收养中心性侵事件受害者，呼吁首相重新展开调查并声称被当时保守党高官性侵。"报道笔锋一转："据电视4 台新闻，那位资深政治人物并没有在报道中被点名，但据传是撒切尔夫人时代的一位知名人物，但他已经十分强烈地否认了这一指控……"

3.2.2 《每日电讯报》跟进

2012 年 11 月 3 日《每日电讯报》（The Daily Telegragh）首先在网页上发表跟进报道。《每日电讯报》创刊于 1855 年 6 月 29 日，是英国发行量最大的报纸之一。同时出版姊妹报《星期日电讯报》，报道的内容倾向互为犄角、彼此帮衬。该报的政治立场比较倾向保守党，所以报导的口吻与《卫报》不同。

导语直接援引 BBC："《晚间新闻》称虐童事件系'保守党资深政客'所为。"

---

〔1〕 法官 Justice Tugendhat 判决第 16 段。

〔2〕 "Man claims he was sexually abused by Tory politician", *The Guardian*, 2012. 11. 3.

注意，文中将"保守党资深政客"加了引号，是为了表明新闻来源于 BBC《晚间新闻》而非自己，这也是媒体避免惹火上身的基本技巧之一。报导的后三段仍然引用了 BBC 节目交代事件的时间、地点以及史蒂夫·米申的陈述。从第四段开始角度变了，指出 BBC《晚间新闻》对这则新闻的处理"已遭批评和非议"，尤其是其中一位受访者在推特上发文，称 BBC 该节目"将暴露保守党一位恋童癖高官"。

《每日电讯报》指出，上述言论借推文社交媒体散布未经证实的流言，引发民众猜测，已经有好几位保守党资深政治人物被怀疑是节目中受害人所指的恋童癖者。BBC《晚间新闻》并未指名道姓。而处于是非旋涡中的那位保守党资深政治人物已经坚决否认了这一指控。"这位资深政治人物在接受《每日电讯报》采访时表示，BBC《晚间新闻》的报导完全不属实……我从未踏入那位受害人住所半步。如果报导矛头针对的是我，我将诉诸法律——他们第二天清晨就会接到我的诉状，我不会迟疑半分钟。"

这也是这位"保守党资深政治人物"在 BBC 节目播出后，第一次直接在媒体上亮相。他自然会选择一份对本党理念有倾向且自己信得过的报纸说出自己要说的话。

3.2.3 吉米·萨维尔

这里必须再交待一个背景，一个明星和魔鬼合二为一的人物：吉米·萨维尔（Jimmy Savile）。他的名衔全称是 Sir James Wilson Vincent Savile，有人译作"骑士"，有人译作"爵士"，他的确在 1972 年和 1990 年两次获得英女王勋章，以表彰他在电视娱乐传媒和慈善公益事业方面所作出的贡献 [1]。正是他，引发了英国历史上最大的对儿童性侵系列事件的大揭秘。

吉米·萨维尔生于 1926 年 10 月 31 日，卒于 2011 年 10 月 29 日，是 BBC收视率颇高的招牌节目"吉米帮你搞定"（Jim'll Fix It）和"流行音乐排行榜"（Top of the Pop）的主持人。一生募得善款 4000 万英镑，捐给医院、学校等机构。其间他获得荣誉博士学位并可自由出入受其捐助的医院。有趣的是，在一向严谨得趋向保守的英国，医院居然也借他的"Dr"（荣誉博士）在医疗场所

---

〔1〕 见 The Landon Gazette, p. 141。

称其为 "Dr"（大夫）。除此之外，他是家喻户晓的电视大明星，许多追星一组（尤其是年轻女子）用热吻换他的签名也是常有的事。

就是这样一个虽举止疯癫却光芒四射的名人，2011 年后不久便遭四面讨伐，被曝猥亵、性侵，而且魔爪常常伸向孩童甚至精神病院的病人。受害人年龄从 2 岁到 47 岁不等[1]。不少事件发生在 BBC 演播中心和医院。有一位 14 岁的女生，以追星心态被带到演播厅，中途被他带到化妆间便遭"上下其手"[2]。几十年一贯如此，受害人也不断投诉甚至报警。但许多投诉不是证据不足被撤诉，就是投诉人所说情节不为人相信。一个在电视节目中举止疯癫之人，只要套上明星的光环，疯癫则不为疯癫而成"狂士"了。并且如此"狂士"也知道用法律武器保护自己。萨维尔在 2008 年 3 月将《太阳报》（The Sun）告上法庭，因该报文章称萨维尔涉嫌性侵儿童[3]。BBC《晚间新闻》制作专题，对萨维尔展开调查，该专题原定于 2011 年 12 月 7 日播出却因故取消，取而代之的是 2011 年圣诞节播出的另一专题，却是对萨维尔的感谢和称颂。真相大白之后，BBC《晚间新闻》被揭是由于"内部高管"干预，那位高管早已引咎辞职，因为 BBC 另一节目组[4]对《晚间新闻》进行调查，并播出了 BBC 的内部丑闻。政府部门随机展开对萨维尔的调查，多地警局封存良久的档案也被一一打开。许多被猥亵、被强暴的受害人纷纷指证。被名流光环掩盖几十年的真相终于大白于天下。

吉米·萨维尔造价不菲的大理石墓碑，在公墓仅仅显赫了 19 天便遭损毁，最终被迁走。以他名字命名的 BBC 演播厅改名。他的遗产由遗嘱执行人冻结，考虑到投诉案件以及受害人的数量，被冻结的财产在法院结案后可依判决赔偿。

这便是麦考潘勋爵一案媒体报导的大背景中的一幕。吉米·萨维尔留在民众心头的阴影，无疑给北威尔士性侵案和相关报道增添了更多疑团以及令人后背发凉的寒气。

---

〔1〕 参见 Quin, Ben 2012.9.28。

〔2〕 Jimmy Savile The Power to Abuse.

〔3〕 参见 Goswami, Nina（17 March 2008）。

〔4〕 Panorama，即 BBC 时事电视节目《广角镜》，1953 年开播，是世界上寿命最长的时事记录电视节目。

3.2.4 《每日邮报》网上曝料

1896 年创刊的《每日邮报》（Daily Mail）是继《太阳报》之后英国的第二大报刊。风格上属小报，典型的特征是小版面、大照片，配耸人听闻的大标题。其网上版本更具特色，从屏幕上方往下浏览，囊括要闻、体育、保健、理财、科技、女性等各色新闻话题，不用说娱乐及八卦新闻是其主打产品，而且图片和录像居多。

"邮报在线" 2012 年 11 月 4 日凌晨 0 点 45 分抛出重磅炸弹："保守党强奸犯告诉我胆敢报警就杀了我……"接着描述了一些细节。

报导接着引用米申的话，说当地警官已经和他取得了联系。警察当局定在《晚间新闻》播出后着手调查这一案件的。文章指出，尽管指控众多，但"《晚间新闻》一再强调未获足够证据点那位政治人物的名"，引发对《晚间新闻》的指责，认为 BBC 又重蹈覆辙，秘而不宣，掩盖真相。

这篇报导还引用了两则推文，第一则是诘问式："揭恋童癖隐者，《晚间新闻》再藏猫腻？"第二则是煽风点火式："猜测谣言满天飞。"

除了这两则推文外，"邮报在线"还以照片方式刊登了欧凹屯早些时候的一则推文。欧凹屯指 Iain Overton，他在发这则推文之前任新闻调查局（The Bureau of Investigative Journalism）总编。发了这则推文后被迫辞职，可见祸从口出并惹祸不小。新闻调查局于 2010 年在英国成立，是独立的非盈利机构，由慈善机构筹资建立，专职深度新闻调查。和 BBC《广角镜》《晚间新闻》及其他媒体合作密切，独立或合作调查采集的新闻或专题片，在 BBC 或其他有影响力的媒体转播，获得不少新闻大奖。这是英国的首创。现今社会，媒体为了生存——无论是自愿还是被迫——越来越趋向迎合。迎合之中的一个很大特点就是倾向性，或曰偏见，这是利益使然。只要媒体有生存需要，这种迎合和偏见便是与生俱来而难以抗拒。因此，这种独立的、非盈利性的以探究真相为己任的新闻调查模式，不失为公正新闻的一个出路。

欧凹屯的推文发表在《晚间新闻》播出之前，属预告式的煽风点火："《晚间新闻》热点，资深政治人物将被挖恋童性侵丑闻。"

欧凹屯为何如此卖力呢？因为《晚间新闻》的这个专题就是新闻调查局和 BBC 合作采编的。

"邮报在线"凌晨赶发的这篇文章代表了当时的一种倾向，就是BBC继吉米·萨维尔性侵事件之后，似乎又要重蹈掩盖真相的覆辙。因此舆论的压力在于公布那位"政治人物"的真实姓名和身份。毕竟萨维尔丑闻事件刚过，制作待播的新闻专题被封杀，BBC不至于在这么短的时间内再犯一个同样的错误。

而"邮报在线"这样的同行，既然站在一个道德制高点上，自己又不用承担什么责任，因此发表的文章大气磅礴，大有不逼BBC说出人名誓不罢休的架势。

3.2.5 帮腔媒体

跟着帮腔的媒体可谓层出不穷。《周日电讯》（The Sunday Telegraph）更进一层，不但点出事件发生的地点，而且指出身为"撒切尔夫人朋友"的嫌疑人不是一个而是两个并且"虽退休但活着"（见法官判决书第24段）。

《每日镜报》（The Daily Mirror）2012年11月3日发文，除包含上述所报内容外，还引用一位曾经在《晚间新闻》工作的业内人士的话，说他和新闻的中心人物取得了联系，这位人士已经向他确认BBC并未联络这位嫌疑人，指桑骂槐却不敢联络，BBC葫芦里卖的什么药呢？于是这位业内人士也发表推文一则："被指桑骂槐的政治人物否认指控并表示将状告BBC。"

主唱也罢，帮腔也罢，因BBC《晚间新闻》引发的媒体大战，不仅主角呼之欲出，而且火药味已经很浓，大战一触即发。

3.3 萨丽·白扣的推文发表

正是在这样硝烟弥漫的大背景下，萨丽·白扣发表了她的7字推文。虽只有7个字，却引起了轩然大波。

主审法官在细阅原告、被告提供的法庭文件之后，就推文发表前后的态势做了一个小总结：第一，为数不少的人看了《晚间新闻》专题节目；第二，到11月4日的时候，在英国和威尔士为数众多的人阅读了一篇或多篇上述媒体的报导；第三，在观看了电视专题和阅读了上述报导的人群中，很多人读了那则推文。

诚然，如果原告麦考潘勋爵"热门"——被告的推文用的就是这样的字眼——那么推特上一定有不少推文认定他"热门"，否则不会被推特电脑系统依"热门"与否而自动排序归类。被告列举了这样的其他推文，有不少也是直接点了麦考潘的名字。法官表示略去未直接点名的，那些点名的推文也只是与《晚间新闻》报导相关。

回到被告白扣的推文，原告认为无论是依其推文中的原本意思还是被告所用的暗讽式"春秋笔法"，都是指麦考潘是个恋童癖并且对受害人所说的性侵事件负责。而被告则否认她的推文构成诽谤。她认为自己的推文是"中性"的，只是提一个问题罢了，即使有暗示，暗示也只不过停留在麦考潘为何"热门"而已。依推特功能，是否"热门"是由中性的、不带感情色彩的电脑程序来自动排定的，电脑程序不构成诽谤，为什么她的推文就构成诽谤呢？

法官要做的，是先看看诽谤法及有哪些判例可以引用，再结合本案判定被告的推文是否构成诽谤。

四、诽谤法的经典判例及应用

4.1 诽谤的法律构成

依判例法断案，仿佛解数学题，答案固然重要，但更重要的是要详细列出求证和推导的过程。判决书上鲜见我们经常看到的"依什么法多少条多少款判被告有（无）罪"这种文字。相反，法官需要给出自己的结论，列出分析过程并提供司法判断的依据，即常说的"authority"，指的就是法律渊源和判例。

无论是成文法还是判例法，诽谤法的概念都是清楚无误的。构成诽谤的三要素：存在诽谤言论；该诽谤言论针对原告；针对原告的诽谤言论已经发表。那么什么样的言论构成诽谤言论呢？很简单，针对原告并且诋毁和破坏原告的名誉，这样的言论构成诽谤言论。本案法官在判决书第36段给出以上定义，只是英文中加了一个"substantially"这个字，意思是"重大地、实质地、严重地"。这是受近些年成文法和判例法的影响，将这一因素列于构成诽谤的要素之中。只是中文"诽谤"二字流于语言学层面其含义过于精炼，如"诽"字常指背地议论，而"谤"字则指公开指责，加在一起自有"实质地、严重地""诽"和"谤"的属性。这是需要略为啰嗦一下的。

本案中被告的言论针对原告，因为她的推文点了被告的名。推文借推特这一社交媒体发表和传播。因此，诽谤言论针对原告、针对原告的诽谤言论已经发表这两大要素已经得到证明。剩下只需要求证推文是否构成诽谤，以及构成诽谤的程度（即轻度诽谤还是严重诽谤）。当然，如果能直接证明推文的意思是指原告"性侵儿童"，性侵儿童是严重刑事案件，构成的诽谤自然具有严重诽谤的性质。

法官首先引用一则 1964 年上诉法院的判例：路易斯诉《每日电讯报》[1]。被告有两个，《每日电讯报》和《每日邮报》，两报皆刊登头版头条新闻，称路易斯和他的公司"遭欺诈专案组调查"。初级法院判这样的报导虽弦外有音，但不构成诽谤。路易斯上诉，上诉法院的法官以 4:1 驳回上诉，维持原判。以 4 名法官为主导的"多数意见"将这种有诽谤之嫌的言论分为以下层级：第一级是说某某"被调查"；第二级或许可采取法律行动但取决于文字被怀疑的程度。而第一级可诉诸法律的基础很弱。任何比较理性的人，在报上读到某人或某公司被调查，一般都会作出比较合理的判断而不至于听之信之或无边想象，认为既然被调查就一定有事、就一定犯法。此处涉及三个层面，第一层是被调查这件事（有没有被调查？），第二层是被调查的原因（为什么被调查，有什么合理理由？），第三层则是被调查之后被证明有罪。需要注意的是，涉及公司（法人而非自然人），公司的"情感"是不会受到伤害的，公司只有经济上遭受损失。因此，财政收入和无形资产是衡量损失的两大考量因素——这是题外话。

法官还举了一个形象的例子，说："某某进入一幢房子"和"某某进了妓院"。要证明第一种说法构成诽谤则需要连同"房子"以及任何相关的暗示一起证明，如果弦外之意是某某进入那幢房子并非去打桌球而是去干点别的事并且能够让人浮想联翩地扯出其他事，那么离诽谤的敏感地带就不远了。

在这个案例基础上，2003 年英国一则判例也列出言语涉嫌诽谤的三个层面（程度）[2]：第一是指原告的行为"构成严重的刑事犯罪，如谋杀"；第二是言语带出的意思指"有合理的理由来怀疑原告犯了谋杀罪"；第三，言语带出的意思是"有合理的理由来怀疑原告可能因上述犯罪嫌疑而被调查"。回到本案主题，无论原告、被告各自如何解读和坚持那则推文的意义，法庭大可不必理

〔1〕 Rubber Improvements Ltd and Lewis v. Daily Telegraph Ltd［1964］AC234.

〔2〕 见 Chase v. Newsgroup Newspapers Ltd［2003］EMLR 218,［2002］EWCA Civ 1772 at 45。

会，因为——法官毫不客气地说——你们说的都做不得准，得是由我领会的意思才算数。

法官接着快速地考量了"重复发表"这个规则，即重复他人的诽谤言论视作自己发表的诽谤言论，并列举英国最高法院2012年的最新判例和2008年的一本权威著作作为法理依据[1]。

"重复发表"规则在这里似嫌多余，因为原告、被告都懂这个规则，也不会说BBC《晚间新闻》先报导的，我重复一下不算什么。但法官还是需要重申一下这个规则，否则审理就不算周全。但这一规则却引出了另一概念，即"reportage"。"Reportage"指的是"中性报导"。个别汉英词典将其译作是"报告文学"，这在法律上是不确切的。法律上这个字指的是对某个事件或传闻的报导尽量贴近事实或传闻本身，既不添油加醋，更不在报导和语气上流露出对传闻的肯定。也就是说记者和编辑的立场是中性的，对新闻事件冲突中的一方不能有偏袒。这倒不是要求媒体直笔谠论、公正报导——因为西方媒体有自己的立场——"公正"的解读自然取决于各自的立场和导向。"Reportage"是有明确的法律界定，"中性"的程度将决定媒体作为被告时能不能依"qualified privilege"原则提出抗辩。"Qualified"这个字有两个基本含义：第一，"有资格的、合格的"；第二，"有限制的""附条件的"。"Qualified privilege"指的是"附条件的特权"，是一种授予性特权。在诽谤法意义上指被告如果符合一定条件（包括所做之陈述即报导不带有主观恶意），则被告免受诽谤诉讼，这是诽谤法中对被告的一种保护，也就是说被告在惹上诽谤官司时可依据这一原则在法庭提出抗辩。但这是"附条件的"。与之相对的是"absolute privilege"，即绝对特权，常见的是国会议员（MP）在国会的辩论以及法官在法庭上的陈述。国会议员和法官在这种情形下，言论受"绝对特权"保护，不管说什么，都免受诽谤诉讼。

说到这里，可以看出本案法官采用了一种排除法，先考量有哪些抗辩因素，然后再抽丝剥茧式地逐步分析本案被告所发的几个字是否构成诽谤。分析之前，当然还要考量原告、被告律师各自提出的理由，然后由法官作出裁决。

---

〔1〕 见 Flood v. Times Newspaper Ltd〔2012〕UKSC 11；〔2012〕2AC 273 para〔5〕。那本专著是 Gatley on Libel and Slander 11th ed（2008）para 11.4。

但在进入这个步骤之前，法官说，且慢，我们还得认真回顾和分析一下诽谤法近些年的发展，以便从经典判例和单行成文法中找到解决问题的方法和依据。

4.2 诽谤法经典判例老三篇

源自美国、澳大利亚和新西兰以及爱尔兰和英国的这三个经典判例，是解决诽谤法问题的必经之路。这三宗大案——实际上是四宗——解决了诽谤法发展道路上的许多问题，但随着社会发展和科技革新引发的多媒体冲击，这些经典判例因其经典和权威性，也派生了许多问题，制造了若干困惑。

4.2.1 老三篇之首："萨利文诉《纽约时报》案"

这是美国终审法院联邦最高法院的判例，原告是萨利文（L. B. Sullivan），被告是《纽约时报》（New York Times），因为是最高法院接受被告上诉的判例，因而案名写成了 New York Times Company v. Sullivan[1]，被告的名字在前，原告的名字在后。这是查阅和研究判例原文时需要注意的。

萨利文是阿拉巴马州（Alabama）首府蒙哥马利市（Montgomery）的警察总监。有趣的是他告《纽约时报》不是因为其新闻报道，而是其刊登的一则广告。

蒙哥马利市人口中黑人（现在比较流行的称谓是"非洲裔美国人"）占一半以上。蒙哥马利市在美国南北战争、美国民权运动和罢乘"黑白分座"公共汽车运动中扮演了重要的角色。1960 年 3 月 29 日，《纽约时报》刊登整版广告，声援马丁·路德·金（Martin Luther King Jr，1929. 1. 15–1968. 4. 4）。这则广告是由支持马丁·路德·金的一个委员会出资刊登的。广告不但为这一民权运动领袖的正义行为募款，并且指出当地警察局以"暴力手段镇压民权运动"。萨利文并没有在广告中被点名，但身为警察总监，他认为广告中列举的诸多例证与事实不符。譬如，广告中指责当地警察将马丁·路德·金逮捕达 7 次之多，但萨利文说我们警察才抓了他 4 次嘛！算上其他方面的不符点，萨利文起诉《纽约时报》名誉诽谤。

---

〔1〕 （1964）376 us 254；11 L Ed 2d 686；84 S Ct 710.

这位警察总监想必是那种视名誉为生命的血气男儿，他不但要倚仗法律替警察讨个公道，而且在法庭上向被告索要"惩戒性损害赔偿"（punitive damages）。阿拉巴马州法律针对公职人员的诽谤案是禁止惩戒性赔偿金的，除非原告首先向被告提出书面要求，对发表的内容更正或收回，如果被告拒绝，则可向法庭提出惩戒性赔偿。萨利文于是致函《纽约时报》提出收回或更正的要求。但是《纽约时报》没有及时更正或收回，而是回了一封信，问"你依据什么理由来判定广告上列举的指的是你呢？"

这位警察总监自然是懒得回复报社那封信，而是直奔法院，法院判《纽约时报》败诉，并罚 50 万美金的惩罚性损害赔偿金。

《纽约时报》上诉，最高法院于 1964 年 1 月 6 日庭审，3 月 9 日作出判决，以 9∶0 判《纽约时报》胜诉。最高法院的判决书本身也充满了自由、民权的气息。第一，阿拉巴马州法院的判决存在着宪法意义上的瑕疵，因为它没有尽到保护言论自由的责任，而这份责任是由宪法第一和第十四修正案所赋予的；第二，就本案而言，即使将言论自由的保护考虑在列，向法院提供的证据本身，也不足以判萨利文胜诉；第三，宪法第一修正案保护出版自由，针对公职人员的言论，即使发表有误，除非被证明有"实际恶意"（actual malice），否则不承担法律责任。

"恶意"字面上的意义指的是出于坏的动机故意干坏事或有刑法意义上的"犯意"。落实在诽谤法上则指被告明知是假的是错的但还是照样发表。要注意的是，具体抗辩时，实际恶意要素指的是作者/出版方对发表物的"明知"或是对耸动性传闻缺乏必要的核查而径直发表。但诚如断案的法官所言，"实际恶意"这一要件是抽象而捉摸不定的，既难证明亦难反驳。总之，从随后类似案件的发展趋势来看，法庭着重考量的要点大体上有两个：一是被告对假的实际了解程度，即"明知"；二是对真的不闻不问，因各种目的或动机将假的内容发表，即"故犯"。鉴于这一概念的抽象性，法庭普遍认定，只要能够证明作者（泛指出版人）明知是假的却仍然发表，即可构成"实际恶意"。

"萨利文诉《纽约时报》案"无论是具体诉讼还是学术研究，都引起了极大轰动。"实际恶意"作为一个概念虽非本案独创，却是第一次以如此分量被赋予《宪法》意义，从此一改美国诽谤法的格局，使新闻自由与名誉保护的平衡得到前所未有的调整。法律的天平明显偏向新闻自由。这在当时的美国是有实际的政治背景的，尤其是在南方几个州，民权及反种族隔离运动此起彼伏。新闻报道自然处在运动的最前沿。在最高法院这宗判例之前，发生在南方诸州新闻界诽谤诉讼案之标的额就达3亿美金之多。新闻界对民权运动及其他有可能惹上官司的报道，极尽谨小慎微之能事。但最高法院设立的"实际恶意"标准，却极大限度地将天平偏向了新闻自由，从此对民权运动和公众人物的报导和评述，其自由度和抗诉讼性便大大提高。由于证明媒体"实际恶意"标准的门槛太高、太难，针对媒体的诉讼案失败者众而成功者寡。这也是法治国家法院和判例对社会运作起到无形调节作用的一个实例。

但"实际恶意"的标准又引发对"公众人物"概念的解读。何为"公众人物"？单纯指担任公职并以公职身份作出言行的人物呢，还是在公共领域活跃因而变成公众关注的人物呢？"公共人物"作为概念其外延太宽，难免引起司法认定的混乱和不确定性。

总之，"实际恶意"作为要件，实际的效果是要求原告必须证明一篇报导的不真实性，而不是被告必须证明这篇报导的真实性。这一要件在美国因为最高法院的这一判例而变成法律原则。但在英国、澳大利亚、加拿大和其他英联邦司法体系中，却在不同案件中遭到不同程度地质疑。尽管言论自由和名誉保护在人权的大框架下基本原则相同，但在美国和英联邦两大司法体系，反映在大小诽谤诉讼案件中，也体现出各自发展的路径[1]。

无论如何，1964年的这一判例是革命性的。2014年恰逢"萨利文诉《纽约时报》案"50周年，《纽约时报》刊登社论纪念。社论重申了最高法院这一判例的革命性，并表示美国对新闻自由的认知以及对政府和公共人物监督的重要性的理解，绝大程度来自于这个经典判例的认知和理解。社论也强调，虽然互联网在全球范围几乎将每个人都变成记者、作家和出版商——因为手指那么一按，文章或图片就发表了——但围绕宪法第一修正案对言论和出版自由的原则认定是没有改变的。

---

〔1〕 见 Derbyshire County, Hill, Grant, Theophanous。

4.2.2 老三篇之二（澳大利亚案）：朗宜诉澳大利亚广播公司案

老三篇之二涉及两宗判例，原告均为新西兰前总理大卫·朗宜（David Russell Lange，1942.8.4—2005.8.13）。第一宗诉澳大利亚广播公司案是由澳大利亚的终审法院澳大利亚高等法院判定的，而第二宗则由新西兰上诉法院及当时的终审法院英国枢密院裁定的。在判例法体系，这两宗判例不能不说是最高司法判决。这两个案例对笔者来说关系比较接近。朗宜是笔者服务的新西兰工党的前领袖、政府总理。在国会他被称为辩才第一，每星期二上午国会召开工党国会议员决策会，会议室的入口处悬挂着朗宜的油画肖像，进出会议室，不经意间会感觉他那双睿智的眼睛，透过厚厚的镜片看着你。

而第二宗诉讼案的被告阿特金森教授，则是笔者当年在奥克兰大学政治系读硕士时的老师。如果画漫画，首先映入眼帘的应该是他高耸而饱满的前额和一双同样充满智慧的眼睛。当时我随他读了一本书：《是电视看你还是你看电视？》，还隐约记得他说的一些话，尤其是西方媒体大多已经"好莱坞"化，报导的处理都是把对象分成"好人"和"坏人"两大类，然后以此渲染和展开故事。

大卫·朗宜

大卫·朗宜在奥克兰南区出生并接受教育。他的父亲是名德裔医生。奥克兰南区是相对落后、收入较低人口的密集区。朗宜所上的小学、中学算不得条件和质量较好的学校，他却凭天分考上奥克兰大学法学院，靠在肉联厂的冷库打工完成学业，毕业后成为很有影响力的律师，常为那些贫困人士免费打官司。他一生为体胖所困扰，从小在学校常遭人欺负和嘲弄。据他自己说，他的辩才和反应快就是在无数次反嘲弄中训练出来的。1985 年他在牛津大学关于无核政策的辩论，被公认为是世界级最高水准的辩论之一。他脱口而出应答对手："哈，我能嗅出你口中的铀味儿！"[1]成为常被引用的例证。因为他和工党的立场，无核化已成为新西兰以立法形式确立的国策。

朗宜 1977 年在他生活的南区当选为国会议员，直到他 1996 年离开政坛。

---

[1] Lange，David："Nuclear Weapons are Morally Indefensible".

1984 年他以反对党领袖身份，带领工党在大选中以压倒性的胜利击败国家党。工党执政，朗宜出任总理，时年 41 岁，成为新西兰 20 世纪最年轻的政府总理。

卸任的国家党政府留下了巨额国债，迫使朗宜和他的财政部长立即着手展开大胆的、前所未有的经济改革，其中包括减少政府对产业的控制以及出售国有资产（国有企业）用于偿债。这样的经济改革触动了工党诸多原则性问题，导致工党内部因理念不合而分歧，不少人退党成立了"新工党"。由于财政部长更激进、更右倾的经济改革主张（包括备受争议的"单一税制"等）导致党内意见分歧，于是财政部长脱离了工党，成立了极右的"行动党"（ACT）。新工党后来又与联盟党结盟，成立了极左的一个党。若干年后，因为《海岸海床法》[1]触动了一些毛利人的利益，工党中走出了一个毛利国会议员成立了毛利党。所以目前（截至 2014 年 9 月 20 日大选）在国会占有席位的 8 个大大小小的政党中，极左极右党和毛利党均从工党派生，也反映出工党作为百年大党，的确是包容性强又十分丰富多彩的一个政党。

澳大利亚广播公司旗下的时事电视节目《四角》（Four Corners），在 1990 年 4 月播出一个专题，声称朗宜总理领导下的工党政府实际上是被大企业和财团控制，而作为回报的是这些企业和财团则以政治献金的方式，为工党 1987 年的大选提供竞选经费。涉及朗宜总理，该报导称这些公司和财团以政治献金的方式换取政策优待并控制政府，让政府出卖国有资产以中饱私囊，以及贪腐、行政管理不当，等等。

要证明这些言辞和指责构成诽谤，澳大利亚高等法院必须解决一个关键的法律问题，即诽谤法与"默示政论自由"之间的互动关系。而所谓的"默示政论自由"，又源于高等法院自己于 1993 年创下的一个判例。

澳大利亚版本的"萨利文"

Theophanous v. Herald & Weekly Times Ltd（1993）案 182 CLR 104 涉及报纸

---

〔1〕 许多毛利人认为，根据习惯法和《怀唐伊条约》，毛利人对海岸海床拥有所有权（a rightful calim to title）。工党政府依上诉法院判例通过了《海岸海床法》（Foreshore and Seabed Act 2004），在法律上确定了海岸海床的所有权国有。工党毛利支持者众，推出这样的立法颇为不易也颇为毛利人不解，国家党毛利支持者较少，但在 2008 年大选时（当时是反对党）表示，如果当选则废止这部法律。

发表的一封类似读者来信的文章，指责澳大利亚联邦一位国会议员"对希腊移民存有偏见和歧视"。报社于是被起诉诽谤。被告律师不是以传统的"真相""诚实观点"和"附条件特权"进行抗辩，而是另辟蹊径，认为在议论政府和政治人物时，澳大利亚联邦宪法赋予媒体一种"默示政论自由"，而这种自由在遭诽谤诉讼时可用以进行有效抗辩。

澳大利亚高等法院的 7 名法官以 4:3 确定这种默示权利成立，被告不用承担法律责任。法官中多数派意见主要集中在对媒体赋予的新闻自由度的考量，担心过多的限制令会形成对媒体的桎梏，以至于失去对政府和国会议员的监督。尽管如此，持多数派观点的法官中也只有一位认为这种权利是绝对的，类似美国最高法院在"萨利文案"中所确定的程度。而持少数派观点的法官也旗帜鲜明地对法庭确定的这种"默示自由"提出质疑，并担忧这样的权利会影响判例法针对言论自由与名誉保护之间的平衡。

7 名法官以 4:3 最终定案，不能不说这对原告和被告而言都是挺悬的一桩案子。法官之间的意见分歧显而易见。因为是终审法院确定的判例，其他法院只能遵守不能违背，解铃还须系铃人，4 年后终于等来了"朗宜案"。

朗宜诉澳大利亚广播公司

"朗宜诉澳大利亚广播公司案"[1]最值得注意的一点，是将言论自由与名誉保护的平衡点，从宪法高度重新拉回到判例法高度。对此与"萨利文案"对美国宪法第一修正案、第十四修正案的认定相比较，可以体会到英美法系中诽谤法发展两大板块的各自定位。

澳大利亚高等法院推翻了上述 1993 年的判例，否定了宪法赋予的默示权利，但同时又确定了一项新的权利。这就是当澳大利亚公民接受有关政治人物履职表现的信息并对此加以评论时，该信息之性质及评论对象足以构成诽谤诉讼时"附条件特权"之抗辩理由。也就是说媒体的言论自由，是由判例法附条件特权原则来保护，而非源自澳大利亚宪法的默示权利。

但这并不表示这种默示权利不存在。这种权利是存在的，并且是持续性的现在进行时——并不局限于选举期间。赋予这种权利的目的是对政府和民主体

---

[1] Lange v. Australian Broadcasting Corporation（1997）189 CLR 520.

制进行有效的监督，而任何有效监督都取决于选民和民意代表之间交流的畅通。但这种默示权利是一种"被动权利"而非"主动权利"。

高等法院对"附条件特权"的要件进行了修订，因为现有的"附条件特权"作为一种抗辩/防卫依据并不能有效地适应政治交流过程中的默示权利。对于政府职能和政治事件的报道，选民/民众有知情权而媒体有发表和广而告之的义务。在这种情况下，媒体发表信息（包括社论、报道、读者来信甚至广告等），倘若蹚了雷区，发表的信息可能有诽谤之嫌，但媒体人在处理过程中审时度势，在行使媒体职责过程中具备合理因素，则可依此抗辩。那么怎样才构成"合理性"呢？法庭列举了以下几个因素：（1）出版人有合理理由相信有诽谤之嫌的这则信息是真实的；（2）出版人是否采取合理步骤对这则信息的准确性进行核实；（3）出版人对此是否不相信不是真实的？（4）对受影响的那一方出版人是否寻求回应或是寻求回应不必要或不现实？[1]

总之，最高法院得出的结论是澳大利亚宪法并不赋予这种默示权利，默示权利作为一种防卫性抗辩在此案中不具备，因此被告对新西兰总理的个人名誉造成了损害，诽谤成立。

4.2.3 老三篇之二（新西兰案）：朗宜诉阿特金森案

"朗宜诉阿特金森案"[2]可以说是新西兰诽谤法判例中最具权威性也是最具争议的大案，从高等法院[3]、上诉法院直到英国枢密院，所有的法院皆领教一遍，但结果却是越判越不明朗。这宗判例争议性之大，连一向沉得住气的新西兰法律委员会（Law Commision）也专门为判决结果发布了一份意见报告。法律委员会是独立于政府之外、由国会立法设立的权威机构，其职能是对新西兰的法律进行系统审核、修订，主要目的是通过对法律的追踪修订，达到既不

---

〔1〕 参见 Winterton，G，et al。

〔2〕 Lange v. Atkinson（1997）2 NZLR 22，（1998）3 NZLR 424（HC and CA）；PC 71/98，1999. 10. 28.

〔3〕 新西兰与澳大利亚法院体系不同，除专业法庭和仲裁机构之外，新西兰法院在取消英国枢密院为终审法院前为三级：初级法院、高等法院、上诉法院。2003 年 10 月《新西兰最高法院法》在国会通过三读并于 2004 年 1 月 1 日生效，以此为标志，新西兰最高法院正式成立，同时废止英国枢密院为终审法院。2003 年 12 月 31 日以前就法院作出的判决仍可上诉至英国枢密院，之后则由新西兰本土最高法院行使终审权。

断完善，又维持法律稳定的作用。委员会成员大多是法律界的学术带头人和法官。[1]

高等法院和上诉法院

阿特金森教授在新西兰杂志《南北》（North and South）上撰文，对朗宜担任总理期间的表现大加讨伐，并对朗宜就该时期诸多重大事件的陈述提出质疑。朗宜将阿特金森和《南北》杂志告上法庭。被告引用澳大利亚1993年那宗判例，认为文章属于对政治人物的评述，默示权利构成防卫基础，因此要求法庭将诉讼驳回。

高等法院和上诉法院均拒绝引用美国"萨利文案"和澳大利亚上述案件的宪法意义上的抗辩先例，但确认"附条件特权"式抗辩。美国"萨利文案"以及澳大利亚版本的"萨利文案"都是从宪法角度来确定言论自由权。新西兰有《权利法案》，其中第12条、第14条与美澳宪法相对条款具备同样效力，但新西兰高等法院和上诉法院的出发点放在判例法渊源上。不同的是，高等法院法官详尽分析了新西兰新的MMP即"混合代表比例"选举制，而上诉法院则更侧重判例法的发展。与澳大利亚高等法院相同，新西兰上诉法院也遇到同样的尴尬，因为在1992年的一个判例中[2]，法院判定"附条件特权"不取决于合理性要素测试。意味着现在要依判例法裁断，此前的逻辑起点和得出的结论需要重新认定，简单地绕开是不可能的。与此相关的便是"公众人物"这个老话题。法官们承认，在咖啡店或餐厅听到一个传闻便不假思索或幸灾乐祸式地重复，不能说不是恶意传播。而关于公众人物本身并不公众的事情（如家庭或私生活），难道也能因为是关于公众人物而可以免吃诽谤官司吗？虽感慨如此，判例法"附条件特权"作为防卫抗辩是成立的，并且上诉法院没有回避此前判例的尴尬，而是维持了这个尴尬。于是朗宜的律师将此案送到了伦敦，向新西兰当时的终审法院英国枢密院上诉。

---

[1] 笔者在任新西兰第49届国会议员时，担任工党法律委员会发言人，和法律委员会大多数委员都打过交道，为他们法律学识的渊博而折服。

[2] 指 South Pacific Manufacturing Co Ltd v. New Zealand Security Consultants & Investigation Ltd［1992］2 NZLR 282。

碰巧的是，英国的大法官刚刚审判了"雷诺兹案"[1]。如果用时下的网络语言且原谅在这里的用词不恭，英国枢密院似乎是"不作不死"，对朗宜的律师说，"雷诺兹案"已判，汝等可比照领会。直接将此案发回新西兰上诉法院。而那时新西兰朝野议论最多并将付诸行动的，是通过立法将英国枢密院在新西兰法院体系中取缔，不再行使终审法院职能。

但有两点英国枢密院的观点是有很高参考价值的。一点是"附条件特权"抗辩不应局限于政治人物，在现代社会，不仅仅是政治人物拥有"特权"，所以这一抗辩外延要拓展。这一点是枢密院直说的。另一点是枢密院没有直说，但新西兰法律委员会在报告中为其做了概括——概括得非常直率——"附条件特权"抗辩时要有测试标准的，尤其要衡量有诽谤之嫌的新闻报导之本质、状况和来源，只有在公众利益要求以及非恶意发表的前提下，这一防卫抗辩才能成立。

法律委员会在特别报告的最后一页[2]不留情面地说，英国枢密院拒绝接收新西兰上诉法院作出的决定——言下之意是这样的结论与他们刚刚判下的"雷诺兹案"确定的判例不符，不能纳入判例法体系，因为新西兰上诉法院的判决是排除合理性要素测试标准的。没有这个测试标准（即条件限制），不能不说这个判例是有重大瑕疵的。

27年过去了，新西兰最高法院已取代英国枢密院成为终审法院。要改变上诉法院在"朗宜案"中作出的判例，只能等最高法院借一宗新案对其重新审核不可——因为英国枢密院出于我们目前尚无法揣测的原因，拒绝驳回新西兰上诉法院作出的判决。但枢密院这种类似中国清代皇帝在一些奏折上批阅"知道了"的方式发回上诉法院——而非作出明确决定，实乃令人疑惑和感到遗憾。

新西兰法律委员会在特别报告的前言里举了一个假设的例子：

一位叫张三的国会议员候选人，在大选前被爆料是个恋童癖，而且被多次指控并被定罪。张三君自然是落选了，而且身败名裂。但事后真相大白：那位有恋童癖的坏人是张三同名同姓的远房表哥。记者敬业有加，又一心要发

---

〔1〕　见"老三篇之三"。
〔2〕　见 Preliminary Paper 33, Par 27.

个全球独家，因而听风就是雨才引发了这么个葫芦案。但有一点是肯定的，就是报社并不是出于恶意。根据上诉法院在"朗宜案"定下的判例，作为一个国会议员候选人，关乎其品行的报导自然属于"公众人物领域"，在没有"恶意动机"的前提下，报社和记者是可以依据"附条件特权"作为防卫抗辩的。而原告张三，不但不可以获得名誉损失的经济赔偿，连让报社发文更正的权利也没有。

这公平吗？当然不公平！

法律委员会说既然上诉法院的判例在先，那就听之任之吧[1]。但是法律委员会建议，这一抗辩理由可以成立，但必须符合以下两大前提：

第一，被告在"合理基础上"相信报导所说属实；

第二，媒体依原告要求登出更正和纠错声明。

这个建议实际上是通过纳入"合理要素"的前提，使新西兰判例与其他先例一致。"合理要素"包含了对记者和编辑的一些具体要求（如求证、调查等等）。无论如何，未经核查只图报导独家而闯祸，想凭"附条件特权"来抗辩这是不可能的。条件不符则构不成媒体特权。不要小看这简短的两行字，第一个前提是在法律上对报社记者提出要求，听到传言必须求证，否则别想脱开干系。这是防止出错。第二个前提则是出错后如何纠错和挽回局面。

虽然这只是一份特别报告而非法院判决，但别忘了法律委员会作为独立机构，其主要职能是追踪修订新西兰的法律。法律委员会通过立法设立，向国会负责。这份报告虽没有法庭判决意义上的约束力，但具有极大的判例法意义上的参考作用。法官断案时除沿用先例，也常常参考和引用最具权威性的教科书和学术观点，从某种意义上看，在上诉法院和最高法院没有机会对这一先例重新考量的时候[2]，法律委员会的这份特别报告能起到某种程度的定向作用。当然，在法院不告不理而法律委员会的专门报告（实际上有两份）又未曾受到重视的情况下如何推动呢？[3]

---

[1] 因为只有同级和高一级的法院才能修正或推翻该先例。

[2] 因为法院"不告不理"，只能等受理同样性质的大案时才能审理。

[3] 请看本书最后一部分：国会议员的个人立法。

那么"雷诺兹案"又是如何判的呢？

4.2.4 老三篇之三：雷诺兹案[1]

爱尔伯特·雷诺兹（Albert Reynolds），1992年2月到1994年12月期间担任爱尔兰总理[2]。

《泰晤士报》（The Times）是英国一份对全球政治、经济和文化发挥巨大影响力的综合性报纸[3]。

雷诺兹告《泰晤士报》是因为两篇报导。第一篇发表在爱尔兰，第二篇在英国。内容相仿，称雷诺兹向爱尔兰国会"故意撒谎"并对当时的政治事件"颇多失察"。所不同的是，英国版本的报导又删除了原文中雷诺兹本人对这件事情的解释。

授予性特权

被告律师自然是绞尽脑汁地寻找抗辩理由。鉴于报导内容，引用常见的"有理可据"（Justification）、"诚实观点"（Honest Opinion）或"公允评论"（Fair comment）自然不成立。因此"Qualified Privilege"（授予性特权）成为抗辩理由。"特权"有"绝对"（absolute）和"附条件"（qualified）两种，指行为人履行其法律或道德义务时正确地行使其特权，则可免于被提起诉讼。法官断案、国会议员在众议院辩论，这些都是"绝对特权"，是免于起诉的。而被告在特定条件下如证明其言论并非出于恶意（malice）亦可免于起诉。

上诉法院（Court of Appeal）驳回了《泰晤士报》授予性特权的抗辩。此案便到了终审法院上议院（The House of Lords），上议院要解决的问题是：大众传媒受附条件的授予性特权保护吗？

英国上诉法院参考了澳大利亚和新西兰的两宗判例。但上诉法院的结论与"澳大利亚朗宜案"稍近而与"新西兰朗宜案"甚远。"澳大利亚朗宜案"将言

---

[1] Reynolds v. Times Newspaper Ltd［2001］2 AC 127.

[2] "总理"在这里指的是"The Taoiseach"，是依爱尔兰宪法确定的政府首脑。

[3] 见 Wikipedia. org（wiki）"The Times"直译为"时报"，《泰晤士报》应该是世界上第一张以"Times"命名的报纸。但因世界各地有许多以"时报"命名的报纸——知名的如《纽约时报》——因而将这份在伦敦发行的老本家称作《泰晤士报》。这只是就其读音而已，和流经伦敦的泰晤士河应该没有关系。

论自由与名誉保护的平衡点，从宪法高度拉回判例法高度。对授予性特权进行了判例法上的确认，但同时又设立了"合理性"测试标准。而"新西兰朗宜案"却在这个命题上走得很远。反观英国上诉法院的结论，可圈可点之处是其认定附条件的"授予性特权"适用于传媒，但取决于"当下环境测试"，包括法庭对媒体出版物进行"适当性"审核。

这样的结论对原、被告双方而言均"隔靴搔痒"，于是双方移师终审法院上议院。

终审法院上议院

但指望上议院一锤定音、解决判例问题的期望值，也随着上议院公布结论而大打折扣。顺便说一句，那个时候"新西兰朗宜案"刚在新西兰上诉法院结案，而原告又将此案上诉至当时新西兰的终审法院英国枢密院，而主审大法官们恰巧又是主审"雷诺兹案"的这五位大法官。

"雷诺兹案"的这五位大法官，三位赞成维持上诉法院原判，即此案中的特权抗辩不成立。而两位大法官则主张将此案发回重审。

尽管如此，终审法院大法官多数派意见为在维持上诉法院判决同时，加列"十大标准"，以此明朗了附条件授予性特权的司法界定，这便是著名的"雷诺兹抗辩"（The Reynolds Defence）。

"十大标准"

这十大标准为：

（1）报导内容的严重性。如果媒体报导不是真实的，那么越严重，公众受误导的程度越大、原告受到的伤害越大。

（2）报导内容的性质以及该内容涉及的公共利益和大众关注的程度。

（3）消息来源。有些曝料人未必对事件有直接认知。有的是笃信谣言并希望别人也相信。有些则是拿人钱财，造谣之后再利用公众进行扩散。

（4）发布者（出版方等）采取何种措施核实消息的准确性。

（5）该消息之状态。如果报导内容涉及正在调查的有关事态，则不能随便报导而需要维护调查的严肃性[1]。

（6）事态的急切程度。新闻作为"产品"具有稍纵即逝的特性。

（7）有没有向原告寻求评述。原告往往有别人没有掌握或没有披露的情况。当然寻求原告评述并非时时必要。

（8）文章有没有包括原告一方的说法。

（9）文章语气。新闻报道的语气中可以看出是媒体在探询一件事还是以"公器"的名义敦促调查一件事。文章不必将"声称"或"未经证实的指控"（allegation）当做事实（statement of fact）来陈述。

（10）文章发表的时间、场合。

法官强调以上十大标准不是穷尽的完整清单（当然这里的中文翻译并非逐字直译），但"十大标准"给媒体提供了一个行为准则，也在言论自由和名誉保护之间设立了一个平衡点。"雷诺兹案"，连同这"十大标准"成为一个重要的跨时代的判例，不少学术文章直接称其为 20 世纪最重要的诽谤法判例和 21 世纪最重要的民法判例。

4.3 新三篇之首："加密案"，进一步确认了"雷诺兹案"确定的判例

既然有"老三篇"在先，定会有"新三篇"在后。"加密案"[2]可谓"新三篇"之首。如果说"雷诺兹案"奠定了一个判例，"加密案"则是这个判例的具体应用[3]。

本案原告是沙特阿拉伯亿万富翁加密，被告是《华尔街日报（欧洲版）》。起因是《华尔街日报（欧洲版）》发表的一篇文章，称沙特当局应美国政府要求对一些银行账号进行跟踪调查，以确定是否和支持恐怖组织有关，加密的集团公司被点名。于是加密将《华尔街日报（欧洲版）》告上法庭并在高等法院和上诉法院连胜两局。但是在终审法院上议院，五位大法官一致作出决定，推

---

[1] 传媒法和诽谤法对媒体都有具体规范。这里可以顺带介绍一个概念：Sub Judice，这个拉丁短语的原意是"under the law"，指的是某一案件正在审判中，法庭正在受理和考虑中，尚未作出裁决。正在审理中的案子是不能在新闻媒体中报导的，因为这有可能影响法庭审理，使法庭的公正性受到影响，媒体如果执意报导可能致"藐视法庭罪"（Contempt of Court）。

[2] Jameel v. Wall Street Journal Europe Sprl（2006）UKHL44.

[3] 这是大法官 Lord Bingham 的原话，见判决书第 32 页。

翻了高等法院和上诉法院的判决。

在这份长长的判决书中，五位大法官表达了如下要点：（1）如果对新闻报导公众高度关注且涉及重大公共利益，恐怖主义和反恐体裁自然涉及"公共利益"；（2）报导内容事后发现并不属实；（3）但新闻从业人员负责任地采编——则不应承担诽谤诉讼之后果；（4）在判定新闻从业人员对待该报导是否尽职尽责时，此时此刻的法官不能以后知后觉的认知来揣测彼时彼刻忙着赶截稿期的新闻采编人员所能作出的判断和决定。

《华尔街日报（欧洲版）》的代理律师[1]说，"加密案"无疑为严肃媒体从事深度新闻挖掘在法律上提供了保障，这和哗众取宠、胡编乱造或"标题党"有本质的区别。

"加密案"进一步确认了"雷诺兹案"确定的判例。也就是说，只要符合"公共利益"和"严肃媒体负责任采编"的要求，即使报道的内容事后发现没有证据，被告也可据此判例抗辩。"加密案"对"十大标准"又做出了进一步诠释。强调这不是给新闻从业人员一个实际范例，而是像跨栏比赛一样，媒体需要跨过十个障碍（hurdles）。

严肃的媒体如果依"十大标准"审时度势、认真采编，无论是跨过还是踩过这十个障碍，很难想象如此一来还会留下多大的漏洞。这也是"雷诺兹抗辩"的科学之处。

严肃的媒体是永远为人敬重的，许多新闻从业人员上前线或"潜伏"，冒极大风险去揭黑幕、曝真相。从反恐到食品安全、反贪腐、反偷税漏税……这些都是民众关注的"公共利益"。

"雷诺兹抗辩"包含"公共利益"和"严肃媒体"两大主体，因"加密案"，"雷诺兹抗辩"判例几近完善。

4.4 2013 年《英国诽谤法》

但是令人瞠目结舌的是，几近完善的"雷诺兹抗辩"被取代了！

2013 年《英国诽谤法》设立了一个新的"公共利益"抗辩，以第 4 条第 6

---

[1] 是 Geoffrey Robertson QC，也是传媒法教科书 Media Law 的作者。

款取代了"雷诺兹抗辩"。谈到这里，许多人可能不明白了。既如此，那么前面有必要铺垫那么多吗？直接说结果不就可以了吗？

这正是判例法的精妙之处！既像训诂，要无一字无来历；又要像解数学题，答案正确的前提是要给出求导公式和求导步骤。而"雷诺兹案"就是这样一个重要的求导公式。这正是英国法官在"七字千金"的本案中的断案依据。

顺便说一下，"雷诺兹抗辩"作为判例法被纳入制定法（成文法）之后，学术界也有不少声音希望将2013年《英国诽谤法》进行小范围的修订，使得对媒体的严肃、认真和合理性之规范得到进一步体现。因为目前的第4条"公共利益"抗辩尚不能完整体现"雷诺兹抗辩"中"十大标准"之精髓[1]。

4.5 1992年《新西兰诽谤法》

无独有偶，新西兰早在20年前就有类似的声音，希望对1992年《新西兰诽谤法》相关条款进行修订。新西兰法律委员会在1998年9月公布的第33号

---

[1] 这种观点的代表人物是 Dan Tench。他建议将第4条（1）中（a）（b）修改，并加（c）条，以成文法方式进一步明确"合理"和"责任"的定义。对严肃媒体而言，这是有章可循的规范，否则在言论自由和名誉保护之间，天平容易向前者倾斜。他希望将2013年《英国诽谤法》做如下修改：

Alternative Proposed Text 4 Publication on matter of public interest

(1) It is a defence to an action for defamation for the defendant to show that—

(a) the statement complained of was, or formed part of, a statement on a matter of public interest; and

(b) the defendant reasonably believed that publishing the statement complained of was in the public interest; and

(c) in investigating and publishing the statement, the defendant acted reasonably and responsibly.

(2) Subject to subsections (3) and (4), in determining whether the defendant has shown the matters mentioned in subsection (1), the court must have regard to all the circumstances of the case.

(3) If the statement complained of was, or formed part of, an accurate and impartial account of a dispute to which the claimant was a party, the court must in determining whether it was reasonable for the defendant to believe that publishing the statement was in the public interest disregard any omission of the defendant to take steps to verify the truth of the imputation conveyed by it.

(4) In determining whether it was reasonable for the defendant to believe that publishing the statement complained of was in the public interest, the court must make such allowance for editorial judgement as it considers appropriate.

(5) For the avoidance of doubt, the defence under this section may be relied upon irrespective of whether the statement complained of is a statement of fact or a statement of opinion.

(6) The common law defence known as the Reynolds defence is abolished.

Dan Tench is a partner in the Litigation Department at Olswang LLP.

报告中，要求增补新的 19A 条款[1]。两年后，在第 64 号报告中，对"雷诺兹案"和"朗宜案"[2]又进行了详细回应。而写作此章节的同时，笔者正以自己的名义起草了一份"个人立法"[3]，希望通过对 1992 年《新西兰诽谤法》的修订，能够将"雷诺兹案""加密案"确定的判例以及 2013 年《英国诽谤法》的法律原则以制定法/单行法的方式引入新西兰诽谤法。

4.6 判例法和成文法

至此，从以上各法案形成的判例到各国立法层面的进展，大致勾勒出了英美法系先例与成文法发展的轮廓。

这也是本书的主要意图之一：既介绍判例法的应用，又展现判例与成文法之间的相辅相承。当然，英国、澳大利亚、加拿大和新西兰在这一体系中具备许多共同性。其中，国会议员就一个法案（Bill）变成一部法律（Act）过程中的一读、二读、专业委员会和三读的四阶段辩论，都有一字不漏的记录[4]。这些汇编成册、精装的"国会辩论大全"，往往成为律师和法官核查某一条文真正意愿的依据。有些成文法经历了上百年，法律和语义都有所不同。找回当年的辩论记录能有效还原当时的立法意图和语言环境。这也是为什么说，国会开会绝非空谈，而是有实际意义的。当然媒体找出某些国会议员当年——譬如说 10 年前——的说法并质问如今为何坚持或改变某一观点，也是常有并让国会议员头疼的事。

对于此案的铺垫可以告一段落。我们不妨回顾一下多国判例的大致发展状况。

[1] 19A Restrictions on qualified privilege where general publication.
[2] 上诉到当时新西兰的终审法院英国枢密院，枢密院又将其发回重审，新西兰上诉法院于是又有了第二号判决。
[3] 新西兰国会立法大致上有：（1）（中央）政府立法。（2）（地方）政府立法——注意，是以地方政府所在地的国会议会名义立法，与地方法规（bylaw）性质的立法不同。（3）国会议员"个人立法"（member's Bill）——个人立法起草完毕，置系统里依规则每周抽签，抽到了便在国会进行一读。一读通过后交专业委员会审核，交国会二读等。
[4] The official record，叫"Hansard".

4.7 判例法共同法

首先看加拿大。加拿大最高法院对被告的抗辩归纳为"负责任传播"（responsible communication），基本涵括了"雷诺兹案"的所有抗辩因素[1]。

澳大利亚"朗宜案"确定了两个要件：第一，被告必须采取适当且合理的步骤来核实报导内容的准确性。第二，被告"必须不能认定报导所暗含的内容是不真实的"[2]。也就是说不能将蒙混过关、连自己也不相信的传闻当作新闻报道出去。

相比而言，新西兰"朗宜案"对被告抗辩没有设定"合理"要素，尽管原告可以在法庭引证说明被告因"不负责任"而滥用了授予性特权抗辩[3]。

有趣的是，新西兰"朗宜案"在新西兰上诉法院上诉到当时的终审法院英国枢密院，英国枢密院将此案发回新西兰上诉法院。因枢密院刚刚判下"雷诺兹案"，五位大法官中有一位就是来自新西兰并且担任过上诉法院首席大法官[4]的 The Lord Cooke of Thorndon。由此也可以看出，英美法系就"共同法"而言是没有国界性的。在大法官的任用上也算不拘一格。尤其是英国、加拿大、澳大利亚、新西兰这几个国家的法学院，课程设置、内容和系统也大致相仿。法学院的老师也都相互走动，律师执业也相对对口。

而美国的"萨利文诉《纽约时报》案"判例，则使新闻自由与名誉保护的平衡得到前所未有的调整。诚如《纽约时报》2014年为纪念"萨利文判例"50周年发表的社论所说，尽管互联网和自媒体改变了媒体格局，但围绕美国宪法第一修正案对言论自由和出版自由的原则认定是没有改变的。但需要强调的是，尽管同一法系，不同国家情况不同（这也是规则不同的前提）。例如，在英国（连同澳大利亚、新西兰）很少强迫媒体披露新闻来源。而美国，原告有权进行开庭前调查，包括新闻来源和编辑部就发表作出的决定。这是美国判例偏向

---

〔1〕　Grant v. Torstar Corp 2009 SCC 61，［2009］3.

〔2〕　见 Lange v. Australian Broadcasting Corp［1997］189 CLR 520，第118页。原话是："must not believe the imputation to be untrue."

〔3〕　Lange v. Atkinson［1997］NZLR 22，［1998］3 NZLR 424（HC and CA）；PC 71/98, 28 October 1999.

〔4〕　President of the Court of Appeal.

"言论自由"的原因，因为有平衡因素。详见本书最后一部分"个人法案问答"。

仿佛作诗，功夫在诗外。几个相关和重要的先例介绍完毕，且看"麦考潘勋爵诉萨丽·白扣案"的法官如何审判。

五、文字意义和判断标准

5.1 文字之意义

行文至此，前面的都是铺垫，交待了背景和法理。有了法律依据，将法律依据应用在具体情形中，方可得到结论。法官首先解决被告在推特中这七个字的含义。

法官首先简括了原、被告各自的立场。

原告认为要解读这七个字的含义，无非有两个途径：（1）原本含义（natural and ordinary）；（2）曲笔、影射或暗讽（innuendo）。也就是说，这七个字的效果是指原告是一个犯有性侵罪的恋童癖。

被告否认她这七个字表达这层含义，她认为她这条推特发文无非是问一个简单的问题而已。当然，这个问题有可能暗指原告"热门"，本身是中性的，并不能从中引申别的更多含义。

何为诽谤？

诽谤法究竟如何界定诽谤言论呢？

法官说，就诽谤法而言这很清楚：（1）诽谤言论针对原告；（2）诋毁原告。本案确凿无误，言论针对原告——因为直接点名道姓。

如果这七个字的意义是原告性侵儿童，无疑这是极严重的诽谤。如何认定这七个字究竟是否构成诽谤，法官列举了以下几个步骤：

第一，轻重之分。言论如果构成诽谤也有轻重之别。传统的如1964年判例[1]，报纸发表两篇报导，标题分别为"［原告］公司被警察调查"，"诈欺

---

〔1〕 Rubber Improvements Ltd and Lewis v. Daily Telegraph Ltd〔1964〕AC 234.

专案组调查该公司"。原告认为这两篇报导成立诽谤且指该公司诈欺。被告则承认诽谤但并没有到指责原告诈欺的程度。因此，法官在 1964 年这宗判例中指出，"警察调查" 和 "原告有罪" 是两个概念，如果从报上读到警察在调查某某便意味着某某罪名成立——那也就没法做任何方式的报导了。

而近几年的判例则将诽谤言论列为三个不同等级，例如就谋杀嫌疑而言，这些字词的含义是 "原告有严重犯罪的行为（如谋杀）"；但读起来也有可能是指 "有合理理由怀疑原告有谋杀之嫌"；或 "有理由相信应该进行涉嫌谋杀调查"[1]。

第二，中性报导。顾名思义，指的是不添油加醋的中性报导。媒体对声称的内容不加肯定或否定，只是就这件事进行报导而已[2]。但这个法律概念要和 "重复发表"（repetition）区分开来。重复发表指重复别人的诽谤言论。重复别人的诽谤言论，在法律上视同自己发表的诽谤言论。且重复一次便构成一次新的诉因（原告可以选择被告）。

第三，字词含义。无非两种：一是原本含义；二是影射和暗讽。

何为 "原本含义"？1963 年的 "琼斯案" 判例[3]作出了两个界定：（1）字面含义；（2）推断含义。任何含义不需要超过普通认知的外部事实而能察觉出来的皆可成为原本含义的一部分[4]。所以 "原本含义" 不单指字面含义，也包括那些可以推断出来的含义，但区别在于一个普通读者只需要一般的（而非特别的）认知即可。

听起来很拗口，实际上很简单。也就是说，不需要借助 "圈内人那些事儿" 的额外消息，单凭普通认知就可以推断的，便可构成法律上的 "原本含义"。

与之相对的是 "影射和暗讽"。这不是仅从一段字词中就能推断出来的，而需要借助外部事实。经典的例子是指某某行为不轨，因为他刚从 "那栋房子里出来"，而那栋房子是一所地下妓院。这便是 "外部事实"，不是一般或所有

---

〔1〕 Chase v. Newsgroup Newspapers Ltd〔2003〕EMLR 218,〔2002〕EWCA Civ 1772 at 45.

〔2〕 Flood v. Times Newspapers Ltd〔2012〕UKSC 11；〔2012〕2 AC 273.

〔3〕 Jones v. Skelton〔1963〕1 WLR 1362.

〔4〕 见 Jones 判例第 1370-1 页。

读者都知道的。

因此，要证明"影射"成立，法律上原告需证明：（1）言语之含义；（2）外部之事实；（3）读者知道这些外部事实并据此理解字词含义；（4）在这些读者中[（3）所指读者]造成对原告的诽谤，但在普通读者中（即不知道那栋房子是干什么的）不会造成对原告的诽谤。

第四，本案毋庸置疑的一个基本点在于，原告为撒切尔夫人时代的一个显赫的政治人物。因此，本案关注的问题是，阅读了那则推特的读者是否知道原告是谁。对那些不知道原告是谁，以及在推特发送前没有收看、阅读那些电视或其他媒体报导的人来说，这则推特起不到任何作用。顺着这个思路，法官要解决的问题是：（1）对2012年11月4日阅读了这则推特的人（被告"朋友圈"那些人）来说，那条电视新闻和其他媒体报导是否应该被当做"一般认知"；（2）还是"外部事实"，即一小部分人才知道的认知？如果（2）成立，原告必须证明那一部分人就是"读者"以及这部分人的数量有多大。

如果外部事实是模糊而含混不清的，原告可以从证人或证词中引证，证明本案中的读者知道这些外部事实。但如果是其他情形，原告亦可借推断来证明这些读者具备必要的外部事实。

可能是觉得用词比较晦涩，法官引用了1977年的一则判例[1]。原告诉当地一家报纸诽谤他有一个非婚生子。了解了这个案例，对"一般认知"和"外部事实"两个概念就容易理解了。报导中没有透露细节，例如他和太太是什么时候结婚以及孩子何时出生，但本地人是否知道以及可否推断和取证，就可以判断这则新闻是否构成诽谤，以及造成诽谤的范围和程度。

同样，顺着这个思路，法官认为本案中原告作为一位政治人物，电视新闻以及其他媒体的报导，其综合效果是推特"朋友圈"那些读者对这些基本事实是了解的，对这份了解应视作一般认知。当然，如果原告此说不成立，如原告律师所陈述的，法庭应依 Fullam 判例推断，得到有些读者知道来龙去脉的结论。

第五，合理性测试（the test of reasonableness）。对字词含义的认定确定后，

---

[1] Fullam v. Newestle Chronicle & Journal Ltd［1977］1 WLR.

下一步要解决的问题是读者接触这些字词时的主观状态。2008 年的一则判例[1]将字词含义的法律原则归纳为六要点：

（1）主导原则是合理性。

（2）假想中的一位具备合理性的读者，既不天真又不会太过多疑。他能够读出字里行间的含义。但是需要将这样一位读者视作"具备合理性"的读者，也就是说在那些明明有非诽谤含义的字词当中，他不会只挑出或解读出坏的含义。

（3）分析时不能走极端。

（4）文字发表者的意图无关联。

（5）对一篇报导要结合上下文综合判断。[2]

（6）假想中的读者视作阅读了该出版物的代表。

法官强调对第（6）点的认知。因为推特作为社交媒体并非面向大众和世界的公共传媒，因此"朋友圈"中关注被告的读者应该被认定为一个普通且具有合理性的读者。也就是说，不是所有人都习惯以小人之心度君子之腹。这是"合理性测试"的科学性、公平性所在。以平常心度之，测试出来的结果才有客观性。

5.2 表情符号

以上是关于文字意义的大致总结，涉及表情符号，推文七字以一个"一脸无辜"的表情符号收尾。

原告律师认为，推文中的七个字无论怎么解读，给读者的印象都是原告做了什么错事，而表情符号又加重了这层含义。因为"一脸无辜"在这里是讽刺和反语（irony），与"一脸无辜"的字面意义是相反的，同时引导读者相信原

---

[1] Jeynes v. News Magazines Limited [2008] EWCA Civ 130.

[2] 有些报导，对照上下文才知道报导中有"纠错"内容，典型的案例如 Charleston v. News Group Newspapers Ltd [1995] 2 A. C. 65。报纸恶作剧，将名人的脸通过电脑合成装在三级成人片演员身上且动作夸张。在终审法院，法官虽然谴责了报道中的小报做法下流，但还是判定诽谤罪名不成立，因为原本构成诽谤的标题和图片，被文中的内容纠错，证明图片是电脑合成的，身首不属于同一个人，因此纠错的"解药"稀释或化解了诽谤的毒性。这一概念有一个专有说法："The bane and antidote must be taken together."

告行为不轨（反正是没干什么好事儿）。

如此，到11月4日星期天，在相关报导背景下，被告"朋友圈"中为数众多的那些关注被告的人已经在阅读该推文后，将原告和那位有恋童性侵罪的高官对号入座。

当然，也有许多年轻人未必知道撒切尔夫人任首相时期的事情，但被告的推文对这部分人恰好起到一个引导作用。因此，一个具备合理性的读者，会从推文中得到被告发推文之时自己是知道答案的，推文无非是自问自答而已。

原告律师还认为，如果推文不能够按原意构成诽谤，那么依曲笔和暗讽也应该构成。

被告律师逐条反驳。涉及表情符号，被告律师强调应该以自然和本意来理解。就被告而言，她发现原告在社交媒体上受关注度骤升，于是发一个推文、加了一个表情符号，问问大家为什么。仅此而已。

5.3 法官结论

关于法理、判例以及推导过程已经交待完毕，在考量原、被告双方抗辩陈述之后，法官作出判决，简括如下：

第一，被告"朋友圈"那些关注她的人可能对她所关心的政治和时事同样感兴趣。两大电视网11月4日黄金时段的新闻披露了20多年前的性侵儿童丑闻，受害人指认施虐者为那一时期一名保守党资深政客。BBC没有指名道姓是基于公众争议和关注度。被告"朋友圈"中关注她的人达56 000人之众——比英国一般报纸的发行量还大——尽管这并不代表所有的"推友"都读到了这则推文，但可以认定，有些"推友"对原告的身份是有所了解。有的或记得他是做什么的，或因为留意政治事务而从别的渠道读到关于他的介绍。但推文的读者，不需要这些先期认知也可将他与电视新闻报导事件联系起来。被告推文不仅指名道姓，并且加上"Lord"（勋爵）这个头衔，因此不言自喻。被告推文问这位勋爵为何热门？很显然，基于当时的媒体环境，有两层含义需要注意：(1) 否则原告在2012年11月4日不会出现在公共视线——除非……；(2) 关于20多年前资深政客的身份认定有诸多传言和猜测。一个正常且具合理性的读者可以看出，"一脸无辜"的表情符号只是讥讽绝非本意。

第二，一个20多年前的资深政客怎么到了2012年11月4日突然备受关注了？被告不用给出另一番解释，因为从推文表达的意思，可以推断被告如此反问是因为她知道个中究竟：那就是原告符合电视新闻报导中没有被点名的那位资深政客的身份特点[1]。

这样一来就引发了下一个问题：身份如此，那么传闻所指的严重程度呢？

第三，电视新闻既不是就警察（或别的部门）的调查进行报导，也不是就某一事件进行报导。报导的是针对恋童和性侵的指责与指控。被告推文起到的作用，是通过指名道姓将所有这些新闻报导串联起来。如此，此处适用诽谤法中的"重复原则"。电视新闻连同其他媒体关于原告（在被告推特之外没有被点名）"媒体审判定罪"之诽谤言论，应视作被告的诽谤言论。

第四，法官注意到被告没有在法庭提出公共利益抗辩（如"雷诺兹抗辩"或"中性报导"），因此不予考量。鉴于以上理由，法官判定被告推文构成对原告的诽谤[2]。

5.4 赔偿

法院判决公布后，被告萨丽·白扣向原告麦考潘勋爵正式道歉，并赔偿经济损失。关于赔偿额，双方没有寻求法官裁定，而是通过庭外和解的方式进行。目前没有赔偿额的法庭记录，但原告提出诉讼时要求赔偿50 000英镑。

此前，BBC向麦考潘勋爵道歉、赔偿185 000英镑。ITV道歉、赔偿125 000英镑。麦考潘勋爵将赔偿款捐给儿童慈善机构。在起诉萨丽·白扣之前，麦考潘勋爵对重复相关报导的推特用户进行分而诉之：凡关注人数在500人以下的，可以通过向儿童慈善机构捐款25英镑而庭外和解。这样，其他涉嫌重复、转发诽谤内容的用户也都纷纷公开道歉。至此，这一轰动一时的性侵诽谤案终于划上了句号。

---

〔1〕 这里笔者稍微发挥一下。"政客"（Politician）在英文里已趋向中性化，表达的是"从政""政治人物"之类的意思。实际上英文里有许多词都是中性词汇，不像中文那么旗帜鲜明。"政客"在中文语汇中并没有中性化。

〔2〕 法官判定推文字面（原本）意义指原告恋童、性侵，因此构成诽谤。如果"字面意义说"不成立，法官认为"曲笔和嘲讽说"亦成立，理由见前文解释。

六、结论

麦考潘诉萨丽·白扣"洋微博"诽谤案，为我们提供一个很好的系统了解诽谤法近些年发展的平台。鉴于本书的特点，笔者也不惜笔墨，比较全面地介绍了普通法在判例法和成文法并用的前提下是如何相得益彰的。

澳大利亚的"朗宜案"引入了"合理性测试"。加拿大则提出"负责任传播"，将"雷诺兹抗辩"要素纳入其中。在英国，"雷诺兹抗辩"在随后的"加密案"中得以确定和完善，但2013年《英国诽谤法》以制定法的方式纳入成文法，形成统一的"公共利益"抗辩。

新西兰"朗宜案"先是在上诉法院审理，然后上诉到当时的新西兰终审法院英国枢密院。主审"雷诺兹案"的五位大法官又将"朗宜案"发回新西兰上诉法院重审。因此，新西兰"朗宜案"在新西兰上诉法院实际上有两份裁决。

20年过去了，新西兰法律委员会为回应"朗宜案"作出的第33号和第64号报告依旧，而新西兰法院体制随英国发展而发展，也有了自己的终审法院新西兰最高法院。

在这本书完稿之时，笔者又以国会议员的身份起草了一份个人立法：《新西兰诽谤法（授予性特权抗辩）修正案》。该法案是笔者在国会议员"博文楼"的办公室起草的，办公室恰巧可俯瞰新西兰最高法院。不能不说这是冥冥之中的一种巧合。

2014年是纽约"萨利文案"50周年纪念，《纽约时报》为此发表社论，表示美国对言论自由的认定基本上源自于这份联邦最高法院的判例。50年弹指一挥间，但传统媒体和现代媒体有了很大的不同。诚如社论所云，互联网时代，对政治（或公众）人物的监督，动动鼠标就可以发表图文。当然，动动鼠标也有可能瞬间让一个人名誉扫地。

自媒体时代应该如何应对呢？

在自媒体时代，动动手（发微博、微信）、动动口（语音信息），甚至发表表情符号（如本案中"一脸无辜"的表情符号），其效果与传统媒体发表文章和新闻报导一样。

从本案的背景介绍，到普通法几个代表性国家近 20 年的判例中可以看出，言论自由和名誉保护永远是相辅相承的，之间永远有一个平衡点。

本案无疑为自媒体时代诽谤法的理解和适用提供和明确了司法界定。

有趣的是，本案开庭当天，不少人模仿被告口吻也发了一条推文："为什么莎丽·白扣热门？一脸诽谤。"[1]此话似乎也应了那句老话："水可载舟，亦可覆舟。"坐拥众多关注者自然是件暖心和得意的事，但更需要时时提醒自己，切不可被这种表象所蒙蔽，以为关注者众多自己便有"代表民意"之势。这种表象是靠不住的，靠得住的是法律准则和常识。

规范这一领域的法律前文已做了详细介绍，判断文字含义无非两个方面：一是原本含义；二是暗讽，弦外之音。

判断的前提（或测试标准）为"合理性"（reasonableness），本案中法官认定一个普通、正常和合理的读者，看到这则推文自然会联想到电视新闻里报导的"那位高官"。而推文中用了"Lord"这个头衔自然也表明目标所指为社会地位显赫人士。即使读者不知道弦外之音的事情（法律上称为"外部认知"），一般读者也能猜出推文所指何人。而"热门"则是因为恋童、性侵，等等。如此，也适用诽谤法的"重复发表"原则。别人的诽谤言论你拿来重复，法律视同你自己的诽谤言论，可单独构成一个新的诉因。

本案中被告"朋友圈"关注者数量众多，法官对此有不少评述。但不代表关注者数量少就没事。2012 年英国上诉法院的判例[2]中被告被判赔偿 90 000 英镑，而被告推特关注者数量只有 65 人。

本案判决公布后，萨丽·白扣在发表的书面声明中强调：

这份判决对所有社交媒体使用者而言都是一份警示。尽管你没有诽谤别人的意愿，也没有明确的意思表示，但是说出来的话有可能带来极严重的诽谤法后果。

用被告此番话作为"判例四"结语，似乎很恰当。

---

〔1〕 Why is Sally Bercow trending? * Libel Face * .
〔2〕 Cairns v. Modi〔2012〕EWCA Civ 1382.

附 针对"语言暴力"的两部立法：1992 年《新西兰诽谤法》和 2015 年《新西兰有害数字通讯法》

1992 年《新西兰诽谤法》（Defamation Act 1992）
简介

英国法中，诽谤分为两种：文字诽谤（libel）和言语诽谤（slander）。1954 年《新西兰诽谤法》实施以后，不再有这种法律上的区分。

诽谤法有三大要素：（1）诽谤言论；（2）诽谤言论针对原告；（3）针对原告的诽谤言论已经发表。

诽谤言论

何为诽谤言论？大致说来，那些旨在诽谤、中伤、损害名誉、降低人格的言论，都有诽谤言论之嫌。诽谤法中还有一个概念颇似中国文化中的"春秋笔法"。Innuendo 的原意是讽刺、讥讽、曲笔，即表面上一层含义，但弦外有音，知情人能看出另外一层含义。

诽谤言论针对原告

测试标准是：一个正常、合理的人是否正常、合理地认为这些言论针对原告。

假定诽谤言论是针对某一组或某一类人，如果其中一人能确定这些言论是针对他个人的，则可成为原告。例如，"所有政客全是骗子"，自然谁是原告很难确定。但是如果说"那个区的国会议员全是骗子"，而那个区住了三个国会议员，则这三个国会议员可以分别成为原告。

言论已经发表

如果在日记里写了"诽谤言论"，但是日记是写给自己看的而不是被传阅，便不构成发表。

1891 年英国 Pullman v. Hill & Co. 案确定，一个老板向自己的秘书口述一封信，便构成将该信内容对那位秘书的发表。如果诽谤言论是写在电报、传真或明信片上，不管是寄/发给谁，自然构成发表。

重复发表

对诽谤言论的每一次重复，便构成新的一次诉因。最典型的例子是时下流行的电台脱口秀 "talk show"（包括那些有话慢慢说或快快说的打电话节目）。1976 年新西兰 Russell v. Radio i Ltd 案说明，如果听众电话打进电台说了一通诽谤言论，电台也要负法律责任。

同理，英国在 1964 年 Dingle v. Associated Newspapers Ltd 案中确定，报纸如果重复发表同行已经发表的诽谤言论，并不代表后发表的报纸就没有责任或责任较轻。既然已经重复发表，自然因此构成新的一重诉因（重要的是原告可以选择被告）。

互联网

互联网因为实时性以及"地球村"式的无国界特点，许多人认为应该比传统媒体空间享有更多的宽松和优待。但是新西兰判例已经驳回了这种观点。O'Brien v. Brown [1] 案确定，法庭不接受互联网有特定文化氛围、较之其他空间诽谤比较容易的说法。

澳大利亚 Dow Jones Ltd v. Gutnick [2] 案对司法管辖权有了明确的界定。澳大利亚高等法院裁定，维多利亚州的原告可以在维多利亚州法院就美国一家报纸在其网站所发表的诽谤言论提出诉讼。该裁决的依据是，该网站所刊言论在澳洲下载、阅读，构成在澳大利亚的发表，因此在当地对原告名誉构成损害。

因为无国界性，不排除原告"择优而告"的可能。也就是说，原告可以依据各国立法程度及原告在某一国的影响和受挫程度，选择不同国家和司法管辖区进行诉讼。

文章链接（Hyperlinks）

假如文章中没有诽谤言论，但是提供了有诽谤言论之嫌的链接，加拿大 2011

---

[1]　O'Brien v. Brown (2001) DCR 1065.

[2]　Dow Jones Ltd v. Gutnick (2002) 194 ALR 433.

年的一则案例将链接视作"注脚"而判定不构成发表（Crookes v. Newton[1]），但是随后新西兰高等法院判定新西兰不必遵循加拿大的这则判例（Karam v. Fairfax NZ Ltd HC Auckland）。而澳大利亚则更加明朗，2015 年 Duffy v. GoogleInc 案[2]判谷歌搜索因为提供直接将读者导向原文的链接而承担法律责任。

诽谤后果

法律上的补救（赔偿）措施大致有五种：

（1）根据《诽谤法》第 25 条庭外和解。

（2）被告更正。

（3）法庭禁止令。

（4）法庭宣告。

（5）损害赔偿（damages）。

抗辩

比较常见的有三种：

（1）诚实观点。

（2）真实报道。

（3）特权。特权分两种，绝对性特权（absolute privilege）和限制性（合格性）特权（qualified privilege）。国会讨论的所有言论皆受绝对特权保护。

需要注意的是，以上抗辩理由，有成文法和判例法的明确界定。也就是说诚实观点和故意诽谤实际上是有质的区别的。

2015 年《新西兰有害数字通讯法》
（Harmful Digital Communications Act 2015）简介

需要重点提醒的是，1992 年《新西兰诽谤法》实施以后，取消了"刑事诽谤"，因此新西兰的诽谤法在这个层面只属于民法（torts）范围。但是在 2015

---

〔1〕 Crookes v. Newton（2011）SCC 47.

〔2〕 Duffy v. GoogleInc（2015）SASC 170.

年颁布的《新西兰有害数字通讯法》重新将刑事处罚纳入立法体系。或许是从过去的经验来看，对于诽谤一类的案件，单纯民事诉讼不足以起到威慑作用。

2015 年《新西兰有害数字通讯法》至少会影响到两大人群：

（1）自媒体时代使用脸书或微信、微博等的人群；（2）为自媒体提供平台，经营网站（甚至包括网络运营商）、微信、微博等。

"数字通讯"有一个广义的定义，指的是使用数字传输方法发表、传输文字、图片、音像作品等。听起来挺拗口，实际上在微信上发一个朋友圈，这就是数字通讯的方式了。

"有害"——顾名思义指的就是通过数字通讯的方式，造谣、中伤、诋毁受害者（原告）。

发布朋友圈的这些人在这部法里面被定义为"作者"。作者们需要注意的是，哪怕传输的内容是真实的也不一定能给被告百分百的抗辩。原因在于传播内容真实与否以及对受害人造成的伤害，要视受害人的年龄、传播的语言语境以及大环境等相对因素来综合考量。

刑事责任（第 19 条）

根据该法第 19 条，符合以下三个条件的被告须承担刑事责任：

（1）通过数字通讯发布有意伤害受害者的内容（发布的内容包括公开的发帖和私下的短信——是否构成"发表"参见诽谤法的解释）。

（2）把受害者放到一个普通正常人的位置，该受害者看到这些内容会受到伤害。

（3）发表这些内容对受害者造成伤害。

如果成立，法院可判被告长达两年的有期徒刑或个人罚款可达 50 000 美元（公司、法人等罚款达 200 000 美元）。

"安全港湾"

为那些自媒体和网站提供平台的公司和个人，法律提供一个"安全港湾"式的保护。也就是当他们收到针对某一具体内容的投诉，而依据一定程序在一定时间将这些涉嫌诽谤的内容删除，则免予刑事和民事处罚。

"48 小时删帖"（第 20 条）

第 20 条引入一个美国 DMCA 式"48 小时删帖"机制。大致说来，如果收到投诉，网管必须在 48 小时以内通知作者该投诉的性质，如果联络不上作者，需要采取措施删帖。如果联络上作者，但是作者反对删帖，可能有以下几种情形：（1）作者同意公布自己的身份和联络方式，网管将这些交给原告；（2）作者不同意公布自己的身份和联络方式同时又反对删帖，网管可以根据自己网站的规定删帖。

换句话说，这是法律给那些无辜的网站平台提供一个网开一面的机会，也就是说如果网站采取了措施则可有效规避责任。

也需要注意一个现象，许多网站和自媒体看到受害者被涉嫌诽谤，往往是睁一只眼闭一只眼不愿意及时删帖的，因为这些涉嫌诽谤的画面和字句，能够帮助网站和自媒体提高点击率。所以受害者往往需要托人情、找渠道寻求各种方式让网站删帖。

有了这部立法之后就不一样了，只要受害者将投诉交给网管，网站和自媒体必须在规定的时间内采取行动，否则难免刑事、民事责任。因为"知情与否"是法庭测试的一个标准，投诉信发出之后，这些网站便不能假装无辜。

也有一种可能，就是一些想借受害人（尤其是影星、名人等）的痛苦提高点击率的网站会用足 48 个小时，但是这种做法会有一定的惯性，当惯性累积到一定程度，也可以证明网站的动机（犯意）。

总之，言论自由与名誉保护是相辅相成的，1992 年《新西兰诽谤法》和 2015 年《新西兰有害数字通讯法》从不同领域涵括和规范了传统的媒体和新环境下的现代媒体。

（本文写于 2017 年 2 月）

第二部
和华人贴近的四则案例

　　本部分收集了判例四则，所涉事务均跟华人贴近，涉及海外投资法、公司法、民商法、未成年人监护权法、选举法以及司法审核等。

　　与第一部分不厌其烦力求说透相反，第二部分点到为止，决不多说。每一则案例分"导读"和"判决书"两大部分，导读足以说清判例，而判决书均以英文原文登出，供研究者延伸阅读。这也是本书的特别之处。需要注意的是，限于篇幅，判决书中与本案判例要点关系不大的段落有大幅度删减。删减部分在判决书原文中标明。

　　许多人对英美法系判决书很好奇，选登的这一部分涵盖了高等法院、上诉法院和最高法院的判决，因涉及的人和事与华人贴近，判决书行文规范、流畅且篇幅很长，自成一体，也不失为英语学习的一个原汁原味的范本和不可多得的素材。

　　本书第一部分和第二部分前后呼应，不同读者可各取所需。

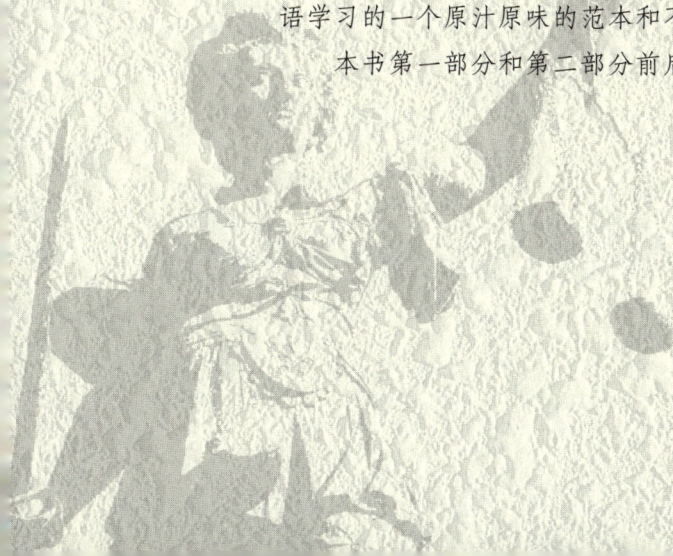

案例一　上海鹏欣新西兰农场收购案

案　名

新西兰高等法院：Tiroa E and Te Hape B Trusts v. Chief Executive of Land Information NZ［2012］NZHC 147

新西兰上诉法院：Tiroa E and Te Hape B Trusts v. Chief Executive of Land Information NZ［2012］NZCA 355

新西兰最高法院：Tiroa E and Te Hape B Trusts［2012］NZSC 85

导 读

一、博弈双方

这是一桩在新西兰政界、商界、投资界和畜牧业界引起轰动的收购案，涉及商法、行政法（司法审核）和海外投资法，从高等法院、上诉法院一直打到最高法院。介绍案情之前，先看看博弈双方：在高等法院的原告是一个由公司、银行财团和毛利部落组成的企业联盟——因此在高院的原告以及在上诉法院和最高法院两院的上诉方为 Tiroa E and Te Hape B Trusts，其关键人物是迈克尔·菲（Sir Michael Fay），新西兰十大富豪之一、银行家，因对美洲杯帆船赛作出贡献，于 1990 年封爵。被告有四位：第一被告是主管审批海外投资的新西兰国土部首席行政官[1]；第二被告是财政部部长；第三被告是新西兰国土部部长；第四被告才是鹏欣公司在新西兰收购农场的公司——新西兰牛奶股份有限公司（Milk New Zealand Holdings Limited）。为表述方便，以下统称为"上海鹏欣"。财政部部长被告，是因为依《海外投资法》，是由财政部部长授权财政部副部长和国土部部长负责海外投资的最终决定。步骤有二：（1）海外投资办公室（OIO）对投资申请进行审核（程序很复杂），如果符合法律规定的要件则建议批准并报上述两位部长。（2）上述两位部长依海外投资办公室的建议作出最终决定（批准或不予批准）。

---

〔1〕 Land Information New Zealand 勉强译成"新西兰国土部或土地局"，由一位部长负责，首席行政官负责日常业务，包括海外投资办公室，简称 OIO。部长负责制定政府相关政策，首席行政官所领导的团队负责政策的执行。新西兰循英制，政府部长在国会议员中产生，由总理任命，首席行政官则依其他法规产生。这样的首席行政官在不同部委有不同的称谓，在国防部叫"Secretary"。以英国为例，"the Home Secretary"是内政部长；"a Secretary of State"为国务大臣。因此要注意，不是所有的"secretary"都是"秘书"的意思。新西兰、澳大利亚等国沿袭了这些用词。在确定不同身份、不同翻译的时候，要特别注意。

本案中上海鹏欣拟收购的是新西兰北岛 16 个农场约 8000 公顷的土地。这 16 个农场是由克莱法（Crafar）兄弟拥有和经营，兄弟俩将农场（主要是奶牛业）从小到大做到今天的规模，也是畜牧业中的一个传奇。但上海鹏欣收购前，这些农场处于"破产在管"的状态（receivership）。这里作为卖方的克莱法兄弟也觉得冤，一边被银行追债，一边有人出高价买但法律（政府）却不让卖！

原告也有意购买，据说出价比上海鹏欣低很多。但法律规定本地人有优先权。当两位部长依海外投资办公室建议批准上海鹏欣的收购后，原告提起诉讼，认为上海鹏欣"不具备应有的商业经验"，要求高等法院对部长的决定进行审核，并宣告批准无效。

二、《新西兰海外投资法》

在介绍高等法院判决之前，请大家将视线从这里暂时移开，跳读导读后面附上的一篇文章："想到新西兰买农场、酒庄、豪宅或并购？绕不开的一步：《新西兰海外投资法》"，这篇文章是依据笔者的一次讲座改写，用词比较轻松随意。《新西兰海外投资法》是 2005 年生效的，这篇文章是 2016 年 6 月写的。截至本书这个章节完成之时（2018 年 7 月），该法修正案在国会通过二读，因此《新西兰海外投资法》要进行修订是肯定的。但通过这篇文章，可以了解该法的要件和注意要点。

总体来说，海外人士要购买新西兰"敏感资产"，必须向海外投资办公室提出申请，申请批准后合同才能生效。敏感资产包括"敏感土地"（面积超过 5 公顷的非城市土地），重大商业资产（超过 1 亿新西兰元）以及捕鱼配额等。

需要注意的是，《新西兰移民法》对"海外人士"（外国人）的法律定义和《新西兰海外投资法》的定义不同。也就是说哪怕移民局批准了你的移民申请，拿到"绿卡"，并不代表你就不是"海外人士"。

其他要点，这篇文章均做了介绍。

三、高院"虚拟测试"

上海鹏欣通过合同提出要约收购克莱法兄弟的 16 个农场，要约（offer）——

对价（consideration）——接受（acceptance）是合同成立的三要素，但依《新西兰海外投资法》的规定，OIO 批准为合同成立之条件。

2012 年，海外投资办公室对上海鹏欣收购案审核完毕，上报部长并建议批准。财政部副部长和国土部部长据此批准。原告起诉，要求法院宣告批准无效。

长话短说，高等法院对此案进行了两大类审核，对原告提出的第一类审核不予支持；对第二类审核予以支持，宣布部长批准无效并要求部长重新审核上海鹏欣的申请。

高等法院判决要点

高等法院的司法审核裁定有四大要点：

第一，原告认为上海鹏欣不具备畜牧业和农场管理的经验和技能（第一类审核），高院不予支持。换句话讲，上海鹏欣的规模和实力以及现代化管理的水平和载体，这是不言而喻的。在此也不用展开。

第二，本案具备判例价值的要点所在，是高等法院认为海外投资办公室适用本法时将"测试标准"（test）错误地局限在过去的"before and after"测试标准层面，片面地考量了海外人士"投资前和投资后"带来的效果。

这里需要说明一下，在应用法律条文时，常借助一种虚拟（反事实条件）测试，即"counterfactual test"。这种虚拟，类似于自然语言中的"如果……那么……"陈述。与实质条件陈述不同，虚拟条件可以为假，即使它的前件为假。

本案中，高等法院认为部长（以及部长所依据的海外投资办公室的建议）使用的"测试标准"有误，错误地将上海鹏欣承诺投资新西兰币 1400 万以"恢复农场运营原状"（注意该农场彼时处于破产在管的状态）当作给新西兰带来经济效益，而给新西兰带来经济效益则是批准海外人士投资新西兰的要件之一。投资以及农场恢复运营原状这是类似收购案的可预见效果——不管谁最终拥有这些农场。

因此高等法院认为"投资前后"（"before and after"）的测试标准不妥，应取而代之一个新的测试标准为"投资有无"（"with and without"）——有这项投资和没有这项投资是否给新西兰带来经济效益，也就是"如果有这项投资那么会如何"，才是批准与否所依照的一个标准。

虽然高等法院给出了一个新的测试标准，但高等法院并没有推翻"现状"（"status quo"）虚拟测试，即若能证明维持收购前基本现状也可证明经济效益，尽管高等法院强调本案中部长错误地强调了"现状"测试，但没有完全推翻这一测试标准，也就是说高等法院并没有以偏概全，而是注重具体问题具体分析。

注意，虽然这只是高等法院的判定，但随后原告上诉、被告应诉并不涉及这一决定，并且被告确定不就"测试标准"事宜进行上诉，表明高等法院关于"测试标准"的决定是《新西兰海外投资法》这方面的权威判例（除非将来在更高一级的法院被推翻）。

第三，高等法院宣告部长批准无效并发回重新审批。海外投资办公室根据高等法院最新判例对上海鹏欣收购申请重新评估，虽标准不同但得到的结论一样，建议部长批准。部长于 2002 年 4 月 20 日再次批准。

第四，原告上诉到上诉法院，然后是最高法院，均未获支持。至此，"上海鹏欣收购案"完美收官。一个"海外人士"收购案，居然惊动高等法院、上诉法院直到终审最高法院，实属难得！本书将三级法院判决书同时登出，供专业人士延展研读。这无疑为英美法系司法审核提供了一个最贴近、最现实、最完整的例证。这也是如何完善英美法系判例法的具体说明。上海鹏欣收购克莱法兄弟农场虽一波三折，但在商业实践中却留下了一个高等法院判例。判例所确定的虚拟测试标准是大家现在共同遵守的一个标准。

三项注意

海外人士购买"敏感资产"，在尽职调查、签订合同时至少要尤其注意几个要点：

（1）有这项投资和没有这项投资对效益要求有何关联（即所谓"投资有无"测试标准），是评估的着眼点。"效益要求"指经济、环保、社会和文化等要写进申请报告的指标性要点。

（2）高等法院虽未推翻"现状"虚拟测试，但维持现状不足以证明投资必须。而高等法院确定的新的虚拟测试，需要以实际证据和商业实效作为依托。"不接地气"的远景和宏图不具备说服力。

（3）投标和准备相关合同时，要综合考虑价格、执行力度以及有无本地人士为竞争对手等因素。

总之，从"上海鹏欣收购案"也可以看出，作为行政手段的"部长批准"在实际运用中被放置在一个"法律适用"的角度，这样可以在不用大幅度修改法律的前提下，通过调节法律适用达到调节市场（或政治）需要的效果。

四、罗肯坞

仿佛给这句话做注解，随后的 2015 年，上海鹏欣欲收购一个更大的农场，但申请遭拒。

罗肯坞（Lochinver Station）约 13 800 公顷，在新西兰北岛美丽的陶波湖（Taupo）附近，估计市值新西兰币 7600 万左右，上海鹏欣出价新西兰币 8800 万[1]，海外投资办公室审核批准并报部长建议批准，但被部长驳回。这是 2015 年 9 月的事情。10 月份，上海鹏欣在高等法院提起诉讼要求司法审核政府部长这一决定[2]。2016 年 4 月上海鹏欣撤回诉讼[3]。

罗肯坞这个号称比新西兰一般农场要大 30 多倍的一个放养牛羊的大农场，最终还是卖给了一家本地企业，售价未曾公开。

附　想在新西兰买农场、酒庄、豪宅或并购？绕不开的一步：《新西兰海外投资法》[4]

规范海外投资的是 2005 年《新西兰海外投资法》（The Overseas Investment Act 2005）和 2005 年《新西兰海外投资规章》（The Overseas Investment Regulations 2005）以及高等法院及其以上级别法院的判例。[5]

海外投资办公室即习惯简称的"OIO"负责投资法律、法规的实施和管理。

---

〔1〕　Shanghai Pengxin purchase of NZ's Lochinver Station rejected by Government. Stuff, September 17, 2015.

〔2〕　Shanghai Pengxin going to High Court over Lochinver decision. Stuff, October 15, 2015.

〔3〕　Shanghai Pengxin withdraws judicial review of Lochinver rejection. Stuff, April 1, 2016.

〔4〕　本文写于 2016 年 6 月。

〔5〕　新西兰属于英美法系，上一级法院的判例对下一级法院有拘束力。

但凡涉及"海外人士"的交易均需事先得到 OIO 的批准。

"海外人士"

本法所称"海外人士"指：

非新西兰公民或居民的自然人；

合伙公司、法人团体或信托（如果其中一位或多位海外人士控股 25%）；

在新西兰境外注册的公司，其中有一位或多位海外人士控股 25%。非新西兰公民或居民的自然人或公司/法人/信托中有一位或多位海外人士控股 25%，都属于《新西兰海外投资法》定义的"海外人士"。

需要注意的是，《新西兰移民法》对"海外人士"（外国人）的定义和《新西兰海外投资法》的定义是不一样的，也就是说，移民局批准了你的移民申请，拿到了所谓"绿卡"，并不代表你就不是"海外人士"了。这一点要小心，否则哪怕你合同成立，执行完毕，OIO 照样可以宣告你的合同无效。

但凡涉及海外人士购买"敏感资产"的，均需事先报批。"敏感资产"包括四大部分：

重大商业资产；

"敏感"和"特殊"土地，这部分土地的定义适用于对土地拥有"永久产权"（Freehold）以及三年或以上的土地租赁（Lease）；

农地；

捕鱼配额。

重大商业资产

重大商业资产包括三大类：

成立新企业涉及总开支超过 1 亿新西兰币；

并购现有企业（不管是一笔交易还是系列相关交易）总开支超过 1 亿新西兰币；

购买现有公司股份支付额超过 1 亿新西兰币或股份被收购的公司净资产毛值超过 1 亿新西兰币。需要注意的是，1 亿新西兰币之标的仅指澳大利亚之外的"海外人士"。针对澳大利亚"非政府投资"，标的额放宽到 4.77 亿新西兰币。

敏感土地

大致来说，如果土地属于以下几种性质的，则为"敏感土地"（Sensitive-Land）：

面积超过 5 公顷的非城市土地。1 公顷 = 10 000m²，超过 50 000m² 的非城市土地是"敏感土地"的第一个门槛。

某些已被命名的岛屿上面积超过 0.4 公顷（4000 m²）的土地。

不包括新西兰南北大岛的任何其他岛屿上的土地（无论面积多大）。

海滩或海床。

任何超过 4000 m² 并属于以下情形的土地：（1）属于湖床；（2）依 1987 年《新西兰环保法》出于环保目的而持有的土地；（3）依地区计划及《新西兰资源管理法》《新西兰历史遗址法》等规划为保留地、公共娱乐或"毛利圣地"或历史遗迹等。

超过 2000 m² 并与海滩毗邻的任何土地。

超过 4000 m² 并毗邻以下部分，则该土地也属于敏感土地：（1）湖床；（2）依《新西兰环保法》出于环保目的而持有的土地，如果该环保土地本身超过 4000m²；（3）依《新西兰保留地法》属于任何科学、观光、历史或自然保留地，而该土地本身超过 4000m²；（4）任何地方性区域公园；（5）任何被 OIO 列为保留地或公园的土地；等等。

"敏感土地"定义之内涵、外延很详尽，以上名单只是几个典型例子。具体问题需要专业人士依实际情况分析，必要时还需要借助 OIO 的权威意见。

除此以外，另有两个原因会使"敏感土地"的界定扑朔迷离。一是"相毗邻"（adjoin），如果土地与任何以上列明的土地相毗邻，这块土地或许也变成"敏感土地"。另外一个则是"相关联"（associated with），如果某一块土地与已经由海外人士控制的土地相关联，这种关联性也可能使其成为"敏感土地"。

特殊土地

特殊土地（Special Land）在 2005 年《新西兰海外投资规章》中被定义为

海滩、海床、河床和湖床。如果投资者想要购买海外投资法律法规定义中的"敏感土地",而该"敏感土地"包含了任何特殊土地,业主(拥有者)首先必须向政府提供这部分土地,由政府购买。政府只有在海外人士实际上已经完成对"敏感土地"的收购之后才可以收购该部分土地。

政府判断的依据是"公众利益"(public interest),标准也是多重的,例如公众对这块土地的认知,该土地与周围地区的相互关系,除政府拥有之外有没有更加节约成本的做法,收益是否超过成本,政府购买对海外人士的投资是否造成负面影响,等等。

农地

在海外投资法律法规定义中,但凡"专门"(exclusively,即具备排他性)或"主要"(principally)用作以下用途的,则视作农场用地:

农业;

园艺;

牧业;

养蜂;

养禽;

养畜。

只要是农场地,卖方需要在公开市场上广而告之,由本国人(非海外人士)首先购买。只有在本国人士行使了优先购买权而决定不买之后,海外人士才能购买。从上海鹏欣收购农场的案例中可以看出,在价格和其他因素上,许多内国人(本地人)是竞争不过外国人(海外投资人)的。

此项规定也有例外,在特殊情况下并经政府相关部长批准,卖方可获特许,免除这一要件。何种情况构成"特殊情况"以及在何种情况下可以申请这种豁免,需要具体问题具体分析,由专业人士向主管部门申请。

当然,以上所说都是书本上的,实际运作远比这些复杂得多。每一个案子都有自己的独特性,个中故事千奇百怪。而且相关部门特别敬业,动不动要和你的律师交流,而律师再忙,也得放下手头其他工作耐心解答。还要提醒的是,写申请报告时切忌随口说大话,比如,"只要能买下那片农场地,就给周围修路、植树——只要能批就行！"结果发现人家有跟踪制，你要说了大话不兑现，他们的处罚机制甚至会让你的合同无效。

"童叟无欺"在新西兰是制度，是法律规范。美德和愿望靠自觉，而制度和规范却成为法律/合同关系——"该死"的合同不比"该活"的美德，那是可以强制的！

高等法院判决书（一折）

Tiroa E and Te Hape B Trusts v. Chief Executive of LandInformation

[2012] NZHC 147

High Court, Wellington (CIV-2012-485-101) 3 February;

Judge Miller 15 February 2012

Administrative law — Judicial review — Grounds — Illegality — Error of law — Overseas Investment Office and relevant Ministers approved sale of large areas of farm land to overseas person — Whether purchaser possessed relevant business experience and acumen — Whether acquisition would benefit New Zealand — Whether Ministers misdirected themselves in law by adopting "before and after" approach to economic factors in s 17 (2)(a) of the Overseas Investment Act 2005 — Overseas Investment Act 2005, s 17 (2); Overseas Investment Regulations 2005, reg 28.

Commercial law — Investment — Overseas investment — Overseas Investment Office and relevant Ministers approved sale of large areas of farm land to overseas person — Whether purchaser possessed relevant business experience and acumen — Whether acquisition would benefit New Zealand — Whether Ministers misdirected themselves in law by adopting "before and after" approach to economic factors in s 17 (2) (a) of the Overseas Investment Act 2005 — Overseas Investment Act 2005, s 17 (2); Overseas Investment Regulations 2005, reg 28.

Property — Real — Sale and purchase agreements — Overseas Investment Office and relevant Ministers approved sale of large areas of farm land to overseas person — Whether purchaser possessed relevant business experience and acumen — Whether acquisition would benefit New Zealand — Whether Ministers misdirected themselves in law by adopting "before and after" approach to economic factors in s 17 (2) (a) of the Overseas Investment Act 2005 — Overseas Investment Act 2005, s 17 (2); Overseas Investment Regulations 2005, reg 28.

The first and second plaintiffs were members of a consortium known as the Crafar Farms Independent Purchaser Group ("CFIPG"). CFIPG wished to buy 16 North Island farms which were to be sold due to receivership and distribute them among its members.

The fourth defendant, Milk New Zealand Holdings Ltd ("Milk NZ"), was a subsidiary of a Chinese company owned by a highly successful Chinese businessman, Zhaobai Jiang. Milk New Zealand Holdings Ltd had conditionally agreed to buy the farms from the receivers. The agreement for sale and purchase of the farms remained conditional on Milk NZ getting ministerial consent on terms satisfactory to it.

Under the Overseas Investment Act 2005, any overseas person wanting to buy a farm was required first to get ministerial consent. Consent would be withheld unless, among other things, the overseas person possessed relevant business experience and acumen and the transaction will be likely to bring substantial and identifiable benefit to New Zealand. Milk NZ had engaged New Zealand agribusiness Landcorp Farming Ltd to manage the farms. The Overseas Investment Office accepted that those who controlled Milk NZ possessed relevant business experience and acumen, and that the acquisition would benefit New Zealand. It recommended the acquisition to the responsible Ministers, who approved it.

On a judicial review, the plaintiffs wanted the Court to quash the Ministers' consent, submitting that the people who controlled Milk NZ lacked the necessary skills. They further submitted that the Ministers' decision was flawed because it had attributed to the transaction benefits which any buyer, including a domestic buyer such as themselves, would bring, notably the $14 million (approximately) needed to bring the farms into full production.

The Ministers and the Overseas Investment Office denied the allegations. All of the defendants contended that the plaintiffs should be denied standing because they had no interest, or none that the law should dignify, in the Ministers' decision.

The issues were: (i) whether those controlling Milk NZ possessed the relevant business experience and acumen and whether the acquisition would benefit New Zealand in terms of the factors set out in s 17 (2) of the Overseas Investment Act 2005, specifically whether the defendant's experience and acumen must be directly related to dairy farming, or whether generic business experience and acumen may suffice; and (ii) whether the economic counterfactual was the state of affairs before overseas investment or the likely state of affairs if investment did not proceed.

Held, (1) the business skills criterion required that the defendants possess acumen and experience relevant to the particular investment for the benefit of the New Zealand economy. Relevant experience and acumen included any skill or attribute that may ensure the investment's success. It did not follow that the Ministers must require narrowly-focused business skills. A wide range of business skills may be relevant, depending on the nature and scale of the particular investment. The language of the Act is broad and flexible and allowed the Ministers to require different or more or less specific expertise in a given case. The first ground of review failed. (paras 22, 25, 28) (2) In terms of the s 17 (2)(a) economic factors, the real issue was whether the economic counterfactual was the state of affairs before the overseas investment or the likely state of affairs if the investment did not proceed. Such economic factors may be accounted benefits only if they will not or might not happen absent the overseas investment, for three reasons: (i) it is expressly stated in s 17 (2)(a)(i), by inquiring whether the overseas investment is likely to result in the retention of existing jobs that would or might otherwise be lost; (ii) the statute's perspective is forward-looking and the counterfactual must similarly be forward-looking, requiring that the Overseas Investment Office ask what will happen if the investment is not made; and (iii) causation occupies a central place in the statutory scheme. The benefits of overseas investment must be identifiable and substantial, and if a given benefit will happen anyway, it cannot be described as a substantial consequence of the overseas investment. Consequently, a "with and without" counterfactual was not unworkable. The Ministers had misdirected themselves in law by adopting the Overseas Investment Office's "before and after" approach to the economic factors in s 17 (2)(a). The statute required that they assess those factors by assessing what would happen "with and without" the overseas investment that they were being asked to approve. The second ground of review was made out. (paras 33, 35, 37, 44)

Talleys Fisheries Ltd v. Cullen HC Wellington CP287/00, 31 January 2002, considered

(3) The plaintiffs enjoy standing to bring the application. There was undoubted public interest in overseas investment generally and the administration of the legislation. Public interest was shared by the plaintiffs despite their private interest as purchasers which also distinguished them from other members of the public. (para 51)

Jeffries v. Attorney−General HC Wellington CP287/00, 31 January 2002, distinguished

(4) The error was not a mere technicality. The economic benefits caused by the overseas investment were materially overstated in the Overseas Investment Office's recommendation. The error mattered enough to justify a risk to the transaction with the fourth defendant. The Ministers are directed to reconsider the fourth defendant's application. (para 57)

Cases referred to

Air Nelson Ltd v. Minister of Transport [2008] NZCA 26, [2008] NZAR 139

Jeffries v. Attorney−General HC Wellington CIV−2006−485−2161, 20 May 2008

Moxon v. The Casino Control Authority HC Hamilton M324/99, 24 May 2000

Riverside Casino v. Moxon [2001] 2 NZLR 78 (CA)

Society for the Protection of Auckland City & Waterfront Inc v. Auckland City Council [2001] NZRMA 209 (HC)

Talleys Fisheries Ltd v. Cullen HC Wellington CP287/00, 31 January 2002

Talley's Fisheries Ltd v. Minister of Immigration HC Wellington CP201/93, 10 October 1995

Application

This was a successful application for a judicial review of decisions made by the Ministers of Finance and Land Information approving sale of a group of New Zealand dairy farms to Milk New Zealand Holdings Ltd, an overseas person registered in Hong Kong.

A R Galbraith QC and *D Cooper* for plaintiffs

H S Hancock and *P G W Morgan* for first, second and third defendants

R B Stewart QC and *R J Gordon* for intervenors

Cur adv. vult

MILLER J

Introduction

[1] Parliament has declared it a privilege for overseas persons to own sensitive New Zealand assets, including farms. Any overseas person wanting to buy a farm must first get ministerial consent, which will be withheld unless, among other things, the overseas person possesses relevant business experience and acumen and the transaction will likely bring substantial and identifiable benefit to New Zealand.

[2] Milk New Zealand Holdings Ltd ("Milk NZ"), an overseas person, has agreed to buy a group of dairy farms which are known, indeed notorious, as the Crafar farms. The Overseas Investment Office accepted that those who control Milk NZ possess relevant business experience and acumen and the acquisition would benefit New Zealand, so it recommended the acquisition to the responsible Ministers, who approved it.

[3] The plaintiffs want the Court to quash the Ministers' consent on judicial review. They complain that the people who control Milk NZ lack the necessary skills, and that the Ministers' decision was flawed because it attributed to the transaction benefits

which any buyer, including a domestic buyer such as themselves, would bring, notably the $14 million (approximately) needed to bring the farms into full production. The Ministers and the Overseas Investment Office [1] deny those allegations, and all defendants say that the plaintiffs should be denied standing because they have no interest, or none that the law should dignify, in the Ministers' decision.

[4] I am told that the agreement for sale and purchase of the farms remains conditional on Milk NZ getting ministerial consent on terms satisfactory to it. [2] Milk NZ and the receivers have responsibly agreed that the agreement will remain conditional for a short time to facilitate this proceeding, which has been brought and heard urgently. I am grateful to all counsel for their co-operation.

Background

[5] By dint of energy and debt the Crafar family created one of New Zealand's largest dairy farming businesses, comprising 7,892 hectares in 16 North Island farms. [3]

Thirteen of them are working dairy farms and the rest drystock units. Their notoriety results in part from poor compliance with environmental obligations, and in part from the Crafars' well-publicised efforts to hold their creditors at bay. In October 2009 the Crafars succumbed to their indebtedness and their farm-owning companies went into receivership. Since then the receivers, who appear here as intervenors, have been trying to sell the farms, which are in poor condition. Their productivity is unsatisfactory because they have been starved of investment.

[6] The first plaintiffs are Maori trusts which own and operate farms in the central North Island, and the second plaintiff is a company directed by Sir Michael Fay and David Richwhite. All plaintiffs are members of a consortium known as the Crafar Farms Independent Purchaser Group ("CFIPG"). CFIPG wants to buy the farms and dis-

---

[1] Which the first defendant administers.

[2] The consent included a number of conditions which Milk NZ must meet.

[3] The material before me also gives the area affected by the application as 5,990 hectares, but that appears to be the area given over to dairying. I have relied on the affidavit of Annalies McClure of the OIO.

tribute them among its members. The receivers have instructed Mr Stewart that CFIPG came late to the sale process and has still to commit itself to a formal offer, but he conceded that it has nominated a price, albeit one that the receivers claim to find unworthy of acknowledgement.

[7] Milk NZ is a Hong Kong-registered company and a subsidiary of Shanghai Pengxin Group Co Ltd, a Chinese company which in turn is a subsidiary of Nantong Yingxin Investment Co Ltd, the ultimate parent company. Nantong Yingxin Investment Co is owned as to 99 per cent by Zhaobai Jiang, a most successful businessman. His brother owns the remaining shares. Neither Mr Jiang nor anyone else who may be said to share control of Milk NZ, namely his fellow directors of Shanghai Pengxin Group Co, is a New Zealand citizen, or ordinarily resident here, or intending to reside here indefinitely.

[8] The transaction involves a large area of farm land, which is deemed sensitive when more than five hectares is involved, and it exceeds $100m in value. For these reasons Milk NZ may not acquire the farms without first obtaining official consent under the Overseas Investment Act 2005. [1] The Overseas Investment Office ("OIO") decides some applications under delegated powers, but this decision lay with the Ministers of Finance [2] and Land Information.

[9] Milk NZ and the receivers entered an agreement for sale and purchase on 19 November 2010, and Milk NZ sought consent under the Act in April 2011.

On 19 January 2012 the OIO submitted a comprehensive recommendation to the Ministers, and on 26 January the Ministers adopted the recommendation by signing it.

The legislative scheme and the issues

[10] The Act's stated purpose is that of acknowledging that it is a privilege for overseas persons to own or control sensitive New Zealand assets by requiring that overseas investment meet criteria for consent and imposing conditions on such invest-

---

[1] There are separate but overlapping criteria for the acquisition of business assets and sensitive land. It is common ground that I need only concern myself with those affecting land.

[2] The Associate Minister of Finance actually made the decision.

ment. [1] The Act sets no limit on overseas investment. Rather, it relevantly insists that farm land first be offered for sale in New Zealand, that overseas owners possess relevant business experience and acumen, and that the acquisition must benefit New Zealand, or some part of it or group of New Zealanders, in certain ways.

[11] Under s 10, an overseas investment in sensitive land requires consent. An overseas person's acquisition of an interest in such land is an overseas investment. Consent must be secured before effect is given to such investment by acquiring the land. [2] It is an offence to acquire sensitive land without consent, [3] although the Act allows a retrospective application. [4]

[12] As regulator under the Act, the OIO enforces the legislation and advises the Ministers how applications should be determined. [5] Its duty to advise Ministers is a statutory power, [6] but I accept Mr Hancock's invitation to focus on the Ministers' decision, since they adopted the OIO's recommendation and reasoning. The Ministers' decision is judicially reviewable, although the defendants urge restraint.

[13] Under s 14, the Ministers, in considering whether to grant consent, must have regard to "only the criteria and factors that apply to the relevant category of overseas investment". The Ministers must grant consent if satisfied that all of the relevant criteria in s 16 are met and must otherwise decline it. They may also determine which overseas person is making the overseas investment and which individuals control such overseas person. [7] It is not suggested that the Ministers have failed to identify the relevant people here.

[14] Section 16 contains the criteria for overseas investment in sensitive land. All of them must be satisfied. They begin with what are known as the investor criteria,

---

[1] Section 3.

[2] Section 11 and associated defined terms.

[3] Section 42.

[4] Section 25 (1)(f).

[5] Section 31.

[6] McGechan on Procedure (*Brookers, Wellington*) at JA3. 05. 09.

[7] Section 15.

which include good character and demonstrated financial commitment to the investment. For present purposes the important investor criterion is that the relevant overseas person or, if it is not an individual, the individuals who control it, "collectively" have "business experience and acumen relevant to that overseas investment" . [1] I will call this the business skills criterion. It addresses personal attributes of the individuals who are or control the overseas person. The first issue for decision here is whether their experience and acumen must be directly related to dairy farming, as the plaintiffs claim, or whether generic business experience and acumen may suffice, as the defendants respond. I examine that issue at [22] below.

[15] Section 16 also requires that farm land to be acquired by an overseas person must first have been offered for acquisition on the open market to persons who are not overseas persons. [2]

[16] Where the relevant overseas person and all of those individuals who control it are not New Zealand citizens or residents or intending to reside indefinitely in New Zealand, the Ministers must also be satisfied, using factors in s 17, that the overseas investment "will, or is likely to, benefit New Zealand (or any part of it or group of New Zealanders) " . [3] Where the acquisition involves non-urban land exceeding five hectares, the Ministers must further be satisfied that the benefit will be, or is likely to be, "substantial and identifiable. " [4] The second issue for decision is whether the Ministers must assess benefits by reference to a counterfactual (an alternative state of affairs) and, if so, whether that counterfactual is the status quo (a before and after approach) or what will happen if the transaction does not proceed (a with and without approach). I examine that issue at [30] below.

[17] The factors for assessing benefit to New Zealand in this case are found in s

---

[1] Section 16 (1)(a).

[2] The Overseas Investment Regulations 2005 require that the land was available for acquisition on the open market for at least 20 working days after public notice of the sale was given.

[3] Sections 14 (1)(c) and (d), and 16 (1)(e)(ii).

[4] Section 16 (1)(e)(iii).

17 (2). No other factors may be considered. [1] The Ministers must consider all of them to decide which are relevant to the particular overseas investment and how important they are relative to one another. [2] Subsection 17 (2) must be set out in full:

17. Factors for assessing benefit of overseas investments in sensitive land

...

(2) The factors are the following:

(a) whether the overseas investment will, or is likely to, result in—

(i) the creation of new job opportunities in New Zealand or the retention of existing jobs in New Zealand that would or might otherwise be lost; or

(ii) the introduction into New Zealand of new technology or business skills; or

(iii) increased export receipts for New Zealand exporters; or

(iv) added market competition, greater efficiency or productivity, or enhanced domestic services, in New Zealand; or

(v) the introduction into New Zealand of additional investment for development purposes; or

(vi) increased processing in New Zealand of New Zealand's primary products;

(b) whether there are or will be adequate mechanisms in place for protecting or enhancing existing areas of significant indigenous vegetation and significant habitats of indigenous fauna, for example, any one or more of the following:

(i) conditions as to pest control, fencing, fire control, erosion control, or riparian planting;

(ii) covenants over the land;

(c) whether there are or will be adequate mechanisms in place for—

(i) protecting or enhancing existing areas of significant habitats of trout, salmon, wildlife protected under section 3 of the Wildlife Act 1953, and game as defined in sections 2 (1) of that Act (for example, any 1 or more of the mechanisms referred to in paragraph (b) (i) and (ii)); and

---

[1] Section 14 (1)(a).

[2] Section 17 (1).

(ⅱ) providing, protecting, or improving walking access to those habitats by the public or any section of the public;

(d) whether there are or will be adequate mechanisms in place for protecting or enhancing historic heritage within the relevant land, for example, any 1 or more of the following:

(ⅰ) conditions for conservation (including maintenance and restoration) and access;

(ⅱ) agreement to support registration of any historic place, historic area, wahi tapu, or wahi tapu area under the Historic Places Act 1993;

(ⅲ) agreement to execute a heritage covenant;

(ⅳ) compliance with existing covenants;

(e) whether there are or will be adequate mechanisms in place for providing, protecting, or improving walking access over the relevant land or a relevant part of that land by the public or any section of the public;

(f) if the relevant land is or includes foreshore, seabed, or a bed of a river or lake, whether that foreshore, seabed, riverbed, or lakebed has been offered to the Crown in accordance with regulations;

(g) any other factors set out in regulations.

[18] Additional factors have been specified in reg 28:

28. Other factors for assessing benefit of overseas investment in sensitive land

The other factors that are referred to in section 17 (2)(g) of the Act for assessing whether an overseas investment in sensitive land will, or is likely to, benefit New Zealand are as follows:

(a) whether the overseas investment will, or is likely to, result in other consequential benefits to New Zealand (whether tangible or intangible benefits (such as, for example, additional investments in New Zealand or sponsorship of community projects));

(b) whether the relevant overseas person is a key person in a key industry of a country with which New Zealand will, or is likely to, benefit from having improved relations;

(c) whether refusing the application for consent will, or is likely to, —

(i) adversely affect New Zealand's image overseas or its trade or international relations;

(ii) result in New Zealand breaching any of its international obligations;

(d) whether granting the application for consent will, or is likely to, result in the owner of the relevant land undertaking other significant investment in New Zealand;

(e) whether the relevant overseas person has previously undertaken investments that have been, or are, of benefit to New Zealand;

(f) whether the overseas investment will, or is likely to, give effect to or advance a significant Government policy or strategy;

(g) whether the overseas investment will, or is likely to, enhance the ongoing viability of other overseas investments undertaken by the relevant overseas person;

(h) whether the overseas investment will, or is likely to, assist New Zealand to maintain New Zealand control of strategically important infrastructure on sensitive land;

(i) whether New Zealand's economic interests will be adequately promoted by the overseas investment, including, for example, matters such as all or any of the following;

(i) whether New Zealand will become a more reliable supplier of primary products in the future;

(ii) whether New Zealand's ability to supply the global economy with a product that forms an important part of New Zealand's export earnings will be less likely to be controlled by a single overseas person or its associates;

(iii) whether New Zealand's strategic and security interests are or will be enhanced;

(iv) whether New Zealand's key economic capacity is or will be improved;

(j) the extent to which persons who are not overseas persons (New Zealanders) will be, or are likely to be, able to oversee, or participate in, the overseas investment and any relevant overseas person, including, for example, matters such as all or any of the following:

(i) whether there is or will be any requirement that 1 or more New Zealanders must be part of a relevant overseas person's governing body;

(ii) whether a relevant overseas person is or will be incorporated in New Zealand;

(iii) whether a relevant overseas person has or will have its head office or principal place of business in New Zealand;

(iv) whether a relevant overseas person is or will be a party to a listing agreement with NZX Limited or any other registered exchange that operates a securities market in New Zealand;

(v) the extent to which New Zealanders have or will have any partial ownership or controlling stake in the overseas investment or in a relevant overseas person;

(vi) the extent to which ownership or control of the overseas investment or of a relevant overseas person is or will be dispersed amongst a number of non-associated overseas persons.

[19] The Minister of Finance has also exercised his power under s 34 of the Act to direct the OIO about, inter alia, the Government's general policy approach to overseas investment in sensitive assets and the relative importance of criteria or factors. By letter of 8 December 2010 the Minister notified the OIO of two specific concerns about overseas investment in the land-based primary sector: investment in vertically integrated firms which produce and distribute products on a large scale, and undue aggregation of farm land by overseas investors. Where overseas investment involves large areas of farm land, criteria in s 17 (2)(a)(i) – (vi) (economic benefits), reg 28 (i) (economic interests) and reg 28 (j) (mitigating factor) are of "high relative importance". The OIO evidently saw this transaction as a large one under the ministerial directive; in its recommendation it flagged some of the factors as having high relative importance.

[20] Although the Act allows the Ministers to rely on benefits to a subset of New

Zealanders, the s 17 factors do not include economic benefits to the vendor. Presumably for this reason, the OIO made no mention of such benefit in its recommendation. From an economic perspective, the price paid to a domestic vendor benefits the New Zealand economy by releasing capital for investment. Mr Stewart accordingly invited me to treat the price as an added benefit, assuring me that Milk NZ's price is much higher than any other offer. In my opinion the OIO correctly ignored financial benefit to the vendors. The Act finds New Zealand ownership of sensitive assets desirable, and it advances that preference in several ways; for example, by requiring that sensitive land first be offered for sale to non-overseas persons. By excluding financial benefits to the vendor, s 17 ensures that an overseas investor cannot pass the benefit test merely by outbidding others.

[21] I have already noted that an offence is committed when effect is given to an overseas investment that has not received consent. A party may also cancel a transaction where the other party needed consent but did not get it, and the OIO may ask the Court to cancel such transaction. [1] However, a transaction completed without consent is not void for want of consent, nor is it illegal under the Illegal Contracts Act 1970. The Court may also impose civil penalties, again on the OIO's application, for contravening the Act. [2] The Act does not authorise anyone else to intervene in civil proceedings, a point to which I must return when addressing the third issue, the plaintiffs' standing. I now turn to the first issue.

Relevant business experience and acumen

以下 [22] – [28] 略

[29] The first ground of review fails.

Measuring the benefits of an overseas investment

[30] The Act requires that the Ministers be satisfied, using the s 17 factors, that the overseas investment will benefit New Zealand, or is likely to do so.

以下 [31] – [43] 略

----

[1] Section 29.
[2] Section 48.

[44] For these reasons I conclude that the Ministers misdirected themselves in law by adopting the OIO's "before and after" approach to the economic factors in s 17 (2)(a). The statute requires that they assess those factors by assessing what would happen "with and without" the overseas investment that they are being asked to approve.

[45] The second ground of review is made out.

Standing

以下 [46] – [53] 略

[54] I find that the plaintiffs enjoy standing to bring this application.

Relief

以下 [55] – [60] 略

Decision

[61] The application for review is granted. The Ministers' consent to the overseas investment to be made by Milk NZ in the Crafar farms is set aside. I direct that the Ministers reconsider Milk NZ's application.

[62] The plaintiffs will have one set of costs on a 3B basis with provision for two counsel and disbursements as fixed by the Registrar. Memoranda may be filed if counsel cannot reach agreement.

Application granted

Reported by Philippa Breaden

高等法院判决书（二折）

IN THE COURT OF APPEAL
OF NEW ZEALAND

CA88/2012

CA284/2012 [2012] NZCA 355

BETWEEN   TIROA E AND TE HAPE B TRUSTS

First Appellant/Applicant

AND   BAYTOWN INVESTMENTS LIMITED

Second Appellant/Applicant

AND   CHIEF EXECUTIVE OF LAND INFORMATION NEW ZEAL-
AND

First Respondent

AND   MINISTER OF FINANCE

Second Respondent

AND   MINISTER FOR LAND INFORMATION

Third Respondent

AND   MILK NEW ZEALAND HOLDINGS LIMITED

Fourth Respondent

Hearing：   2 July 2012

Court：   O'Regan P, Arnold and White JJ

Counsel: A R Galbraith QC and D J Cooper for Appellants/Applicants D J Goddard QC and H S Hancock for First, Second and Third Respondents B D Gray QC and R A Rose for Fourth Respondent

Judgment: 7 August 2012 at 10 am

JUDGMENT OF THE COURT

TIROA E & TE HAPE B TRUSTS v. CE LAND INFORMATION NEW ZEALAND COA CA88/2012 [7 August 2012]

A The appeal in CA88/2012 is dismissed.

B The application for judicial review in CA284/2012 is dismissed.

C The appellants/applicants are jointly and severally liable

to pay costs for one standard appeal on a band B basis to:

(i) the first, second and third respondents (collectively); and

(ii) the fourth respondent.

We certify for two counsel in each instance.

REASONS OF THE COURT

(Given by Arnold J)

Table of Contents

Introduction

[1] These appeals [1] raise a short but important point concerning the regime applicable to overseas persons who wish to invest in New Zealand. The regime is contained in the Overseas Investment Act 2005 (the Act) and requires that overseas persons have the consent of the responsible Minister (s) to acquire certain assets in New Zealand, including significant tracts of farm land. If the overseas persons meet certain statutory criteria, the responsible Minister (s) must give consent. In effect, then, overseas persons have a right to acquire the assets if they meet the statutory criteria.

[2] One of the statutory criteria is that the overseas person or, in this case, the persons who control the relevant overseas person, must have "business experience and acumen relevant to" the investment in New Zealand. [2] The essential question raised by the appeals concerns the meaning of this criterion in the context of an application by the fourth respondent, Milk New Zealand Holdings Ltd (Milk NZ), to acquire some farms for dairying, an application to which the second and third respondents, as the responsible Ministers in this instance, [3] have consented.

Factual background

以下 [3] – [12] 略

---

[1] Technically, CA88/2012 is an appeal whereas CA284/2012 is not: it relates to a judicial review proceeding that has been transferred directly to this Court. However, for ease of reference we will refer to both as appeals in the body of the judgment.

[2] Overseas Investment Act 2005, s 16 (1)(a).

[3] Section 24 (1).

The statutory background

[13] We do not propose to give a comprehensive overview of the overseas investment regime, but rather will focus on those aspects that are relevant for the purposes of these appeals.

[14] The purpose of the Act is set out in s 3, which provides:

Purpose

The purpose of this Act is to acknowledge that it is a privilege for overseas persons to own or control sensitive New Zealand assets by—

(a) requiring overseas investments in those assets, before being made, to meet criteria for consent; and

(b) imposing conditions on those overseas investments.

[15] A notable feature of this provision is the use of the word "privilege". In this context, Mr Gray QC for Milk NZ drew attention to s 23 (1) of the Citizenship Act 1977, which provides that people who are not New Zealand citizens have the same right to own land as New Zealand citizens. By contrast to the position set out in that Act, s 10 (1) of the Act provides that a transaction requires consent if it is an overseas investment in sensitive land or an overseas investment in significant business assets. Under s 11 (1), consent must be obtained before the transaction is given effect.

[16] Section 14 deals with the approach to be taken by the responsible Minister (s) to the question whether consent should be granted. It provides:

Approach to criteria for consent

(1) The relevant Minister or Ministers, in considering whether or not to grant consent to an overseas investment transaction, —

(a) must have regard to only the criteria and factors that apply to the relevant category of overseas investment under this subpart (subject to this section); and

(b) may consult with any other person or persons, as the Minister or Ministers think appropriate; and

(c) must grant consent if satisfied that all of the criteria in section 16 or section

18 (as the case may be) are met; and

(d) must decline to grant consent if not satisfied that all of the criteria in section 16 or section 18 are met.

(2) For a transaction that is in more than 1 category of overseas investment, the relevant Ministers must have regard to the criteria that apply to all of the relevant categories.

...

A noteworthy feature of this provision is that the Ministers*must* grant consent if they are satisfied that all of the relevant criteria are met. Accordingly, overseas persons who can satisfy the Minister (s) that they meet the criteria have a right to invest in New Zealand.

[17] The relevant criteria for consent are set out in s 16. It provides:

Criteria for consent for overseas investments in sensitive land

(1) The criteria for an overseas investment in sensitive land are all of the following:

(a) the relevant overseas person has, or (if that person is not an individual) the individuals with control of the relevant overseas person collectively have, business experience and acumen relevant to that overseas investment;

(b) the relevant overseas person has demonstrated financial commitment to the overseas investment;

(c) the relevant overseas person is, or (if that person is not an individual) all the individuals with control of the relevant overseas person are, of good character;

(d) the relevant overseas person is not, or (if that person is not an individual) each individual with control of the relevant overseas person is not, an individual of a kind referred to in section 15 or 16 of the Immigration Act 2009 (which sections list certain persons not eligible for visas or entry permits under that Act);

(e) either subparagraph (i) is met or subparagraph (ii) and (if applicable) subparagraph (iii) are met;

(i) the relevant overseas person is, or (if that person is not an individual) all the individuals with control of the relevant overseas person are, New Zealand citizens, ordinarily resident in New Zealand, or intending to reside in New Zealand indefinitely;

(ii) the overseas investment will, or is likely to, benefit

New Zealand (or any part of it or group of

New Zealanders), as determined by the relevant

Ministers under section 17;

(iii) if the relevant land includes non-urban land that, in area (either alone or together with any associated land) exceeds 5 hectares, the relevant Ministers determine that that benefit will be, or is likely to be, substantial and identifiable;

(f) if the relevant land is or includes farm land, either that farm land or the securities to which the overseas investment relates have been offered for acquisition on the open market to persons who are not overseas persons in accordance with the procedure set out in regulations (unless the overseas investment is exempt from this criterion under section 20).

...

[18] Two aspects of the s 16 (1) requirements came under scrutiny in CFIPG's judicial review proceeding:

(a) The requirement in s 16 (1)(a) that the individuals in control of Milk NZ (the controlling individuals) have "business experience and acumen relevant to [the proposed] investment";

(b) The requirement in s 16 (1)(e)(ii) and (iii) that the responsible Ministers reach the view that there will be benefit to New Zealand from the proposed investment that "will be, or is likely to be, substantial and identifiable". (The factors for assessing that benefit are set out in s 17 and in reg 28 of the Overseas Investment Regulations 2005.)

[19] There are other provisions of the Act to which we will refer in passing below, but those identified above are the most important for the present purposes.

The High Court proceeding and subsequent events

以下 [20] – [27] 略

Basis of appeals

[28] Mr Galbraith QC submitted on behalf of the appellants that there were four overlapping errors in the approach adopted by the OIO and the Ministers in relation to the "business experience and acumen" requirement in s 16 (1)(a). Mr Galbraith submitted that they were wrong to rely on:

(a) the generic investment experience of the controlling individuals, as that experience is unrelated to dairy farming or the dairy industry;

(b) the experience and acumen of Landcorp under its contractual arrangements with Milk NZ; and

(c) the experience of companies related to Milk NZ in other forms of agriculture.

In addition, he submitted that the OIO and the Ministers wrongly concluded that the individuals had relevant business experience and acumen without obtaining sufficient information to support that conclusion.

[29] We will deal with the arguments raised in support of these points as we address the points in the discussion that follows.

Discussion

以下 [30] – [48] 略

Adequacy of information available to OIO and Ministers

(i) *Appellants' arguments*

[49] The appellants allege that the OIO and the Ministers failed to obtain reasonably adequate information to enable them to conclude that s 16 (1)(a) was satisfied. Accordingly, they did not have sufficient information to make an informed decision. They cited the following passage from Dr Taylor's book, *Judicial Review: A New Zealand Perspective*:[21]

If a factor is to be considered there is a duty on the authority doing so to be sufficiently informed on it so far as it appears to be necessary in terms of the enactment. ⋯

What is reasonable depends on the circumstances, such as time available, resources at hand, existing knowledge and expertise, reliability or apparent reliability of sources, and the like. One relevant consideration in deciding this is how readily available the missing information might be. ⋯

[50] In the extract quoted above at [21], Mr Williamson says that he relied particularly on the experience that Mr Jiang "will have obtained" through Shanghai Pengxin's investments in agribusiness in Bolivia and in China. The Minister described this experience as "particularly relevant" to the proposed investment in the Crafar farms, although he did not explain what it was about that experience that made it particularly relevant. Mr Williamson also said that he relied on Mr Jiang's extensive general business experience and acumen, as reflected in his substantial property developments in China.

[51] The appellants say that the information in the material available to the OIO and Ministers concerning Mr Jiang's investments in agribusiness was minimal: it was insufficient for decision-making purposes. It would have been a straightforward matter for the OIO and the Ministers to have obtained more detailed information.

(ii) *Our evaluation*

[52] The appellants' argument that the Ministers gave weight to a consideration (the agribusiness experience of Mr Jiang) [1] when they did not have sufficient information to justify doing so is, in effect, an argument that the Ministers proceeded on the basis of a state of facts that was not supported by appropriate evidence.

[53] Before addressing this, we reiterate that, on the material before the Ministers, it is clear that Mr Jiang has, from modest beginnings, become a highly successful commercial property developer in China and that his business interests have grown to encompass significant enterprises in countries other than China. It is clear, also, that he is a person of some stature in the Chinese commercial world. In our view, the information provided to the Ministers was sufficient to enable them to determine that he and the other controlling individuals had generic business skills and acumen relevant to the Crafar farms investment.

[54] Turning to the experience in agribusiness, we do not, as we have said, re-

---

[1] Mr Williamson's affidavit refers simply to Mr Jiang's experience in agribusiness. It does not mention the business experience and acumen of the other controlling individuals of Milk NZ.

gard the agribusiness involvement as necessary to a determination that the controlling individuals had relevant business experience and acumen: their general business experience and acumen was sufficient. However, Mr Jiang's agribusiness involvement was clearly important to Mr Williamson's decision to grant consent. In light of that we would have expected to see in the supporting materials, in addition to the brief description of the investments given, some detail of the nature of those investments and the involvement of Mr Jiang (and the other controlling individuals) in them. The material before the Ministers showed that the investments had been made, but little more. Mr Williamson seems to have proceeded on the assumption that the investments were successful, there being nothing in the OIO's reports to indicate that they were unsuccessful. But that is an aspect that could easily have been checked. If it was regarded as important, additional detail should, in our view, have been obtained.

[55] However, we do not see this oversight as undermining the validity of the Ministers' decision to grant consent. The Ministers had sufficient material relating to the general business experience and acumen of Mr Jiang and his fellow controlling individuals to justify their conclusion that the requirements of s 16 (1)(a) had been met. The agribusiness experience was only one of the factors relied on by the Ministers in concluding that the controlling individuals had the necessary business skills and acumen; while apparently important, it did not lead to a conclusion that was insupportable or unreasonable in the absence of that experience. [1]

[56] Moreover, even if we had found that the Ministers' decision was defective in this respect, it is unlikely that we would have exercised our discretion to grant a remedy. There are three reasons for this. First, Ministers have determined that the proposed investment will have a substantial and identifiable benefit for New Zealand. There has been no challenge to that assessment. Accordingly, if a form of relief involving a referral back to the Ministers was granted, the Ministers would undoubtedly decide again to grant consent in the public interest and would be entitled to do so without rel-

---

[1] Bryson v. Three Foot Six Ltd [2005] *NZSC* 34, [2005] 3 *NZLR* 721 *at* [28]; Lewis v. Wilson & Horton Ltd [2000] 3 *NZLR* 546 (*CA*) *at* [92].

ying on the challenged material. There would therefore be little or no practical value in granting such a remedy. [1] Second, we understand that the transaction has not yet settled. Accordingly, there are other interests at stake, in particular those of the creditors of the Crafars' farming companies, who have been seeking to recover substantial sums of money for some time. These would be prejudiced by further delay. Third, the farms are being operated in the meantime by the receivers, presumably on a basis that involves minimal further investment. This state of affairs is obviously undesirable and should not be prolonged unnecessarily.

Decision

[57] The appeals are dismissed. The appellants/applicants are jointly and severally liable to pay costs for one standard appeal on a band B basis to:

(a) the first, second and third respondents (collectively); and

(b) the fourth respondent.

We certify for two counsel in each instance.

Solicitors

Bell Gully, Auckland for Appellants/Applicants

Crown Law Office, Wellington for First, Second and Third Respondents Chapman Tripp, Auckland for Fourth Respondent

---

[1] We acknowledge that courts should be cautious to decline relief on the basis of the inevitability of the same outcome: see *Chiu v. Minister of Immigration* [1994] 2 NZLR 541 (CA) at 552-553. See also *Air Nelson Ltd v. Minister of Transport* [2008] NZCA 26, [2008] NZAR 139 at [59] – [60]; *GXL Royalties Ltd v. Minister of Energy* [2010] NZCA 185, [2010] NZAR 518 at [63] – [75].

高等法院判决书（三折）

IN THE SUPREME COURT
OF NEW ZEALAND

SC 58/2012

[2012] NZSC 85

BETWEEN   TIROA E AND TE HAPE B TRUSTS

                Applicants

AND   CHIEF EXECUTIVE OF LAND INFORMATION

                First Respondent

AND   MINISTER OF FINANCE

                Second Respondent

AND   MINISTER OF LAND INFORMATION

                Third Respondent

AND   MILK NEW ZEALAND HOLDINGS LIMITED

                Fourth Respondent

Court: McGrath, William Young and Glazebrook JJ

Counsel: D J Cooper and T B Fitzgerald for Applicants

            D J Goddard QC and H S Hancock for First, Second and Third respondents

            B D Gray QC and R A Rose for Fourth Respondent

Judgment: 17 October 2012

JUDGMENT OF THE COURT

A The application for leave to appeal is dismissed.

B The applicants must pay costs of $2, 500 to both Milk
New Zealand Holdings Ltd and the Crown respondents.

REASONS

TIROA E AND TE HAPE B TRUSTS v. CHIEF EXECUTIVE OF LAND INFOR-MATION SC 58/2012 [17 October 2012]

[1] This application for leave to appeal concerns the exercise of powers under legislation which regulates the acquisition by overseas persons of "sensitive New Zealand assets". These include interests in rural land exceeding five hectares in area. Under the Overseas Investment Act 2005, such acquisitions require Ministerial consent, which will be granted if, and only if, certain criteria in the Act are satisfied. The issue in the proposed appeal is whether it was open to Ministers to conclude that a particular criterion was satisfied when giving their consent to an application under the Act.

[2] Milk New Zealand Holdings Ltd is an overseas person which has agreed to buy a group of dairy farm properties known as the Crafar Farms. The agreement is subject to consent being given under the Act. The mandatory criterion for consent that is in issue is the requirement under s 16 (1)(a) that the individuals "with control of the relevant overseas person collectively have, business experience and acumen relevant to that overseas investment".

[3] The applicants for leave to appeal are members of a consortium who collectively wish to acquire the Crafar farms. They have brought two proceedings for judicial review of the successive Ministerial decisions consenting to the investment. The first respondent is the Chief Executive of the government department which has responsibility for the Overseas Investment Office. That office advised the responsible Ministers that it

was open to them to conclude the s 16 (1)(a) criterion was satisfied. The Ministers, who adopted that advice and consented to the investment, are the second and third respondents. Milk New Zealand Holdings Ltd is the fourth respondent.

[4] The issues the applicants wish to address in the proposed appeal are whether the s 16 (1)(a) criterion can lawfully be satisfied, first, by generic investment experience of individuals controlling the applicant and, secondly, by business experience and acumen of other corporate entities which are related to the applicant. The third issue is whether the business experience and acumen requirement can be satisfied by the overseas person contracting with outside parties, with those attributes, to manage and operate the dairy farms. Milk Holdings Ltd proposes to engage Landcorp Farming Ltd, a State-Owned enterprise, which undertakes dairy and other farming operations, for this purpose. The fourth proposed ground of appeal concerns the nature of the information Ministers were required to have to justify a lawful decision that an applicant had the required business experience and acumen.

[5] The High Court accepted that those in control of Milk New Zealand Holdings were astute and experienced managers and investors. [1] Miller J decided it was open to Ministers to conclude that their skills, while not specific to dairy farming or agriculture, would help ensure the business delivered promised benefits. The requirement of possession of the relevant business experience and acumen did not require skills of a narrow or specific kind. The Judge held that the aim of the criterion was to ensure delivery of benefits to New Zealand; therefore a wide range of such skills was covered by the statutory language. The s 16 (1)(a) requirement was accordingly satisfied.

[6] The Court of Appeal agreed with the High Court that a range of business experience and acumen could contribute to the success of a particular investment and properly be treated as relevant in terms of satisfying s 16 (1)(a). [2] It also agreed that the use by an overseas investor of the experience and acumen of others, as a supplementary means of ensuring the business would succeed, fitted within the broad and

---

[1] *Tiroa E and Te Hape B Trusts v. Chief Executive of Land Information* [2012] NZHC 147.

[2] *Tiroa E and Te Hape B Trusts v. Chief Executive of Land Information* [2012] NZCA 355 at [42].

flexible language expressing this criterion. Furthermore, the Court held that the Ministers had sufficient material relating to the business acumen and experience of those in control of Milk New Zealand Holdings to justify their conclusion that the requirements of s 16 (1)(a) had been met.

[7] For these largely common reasons, both Courts decided it was open to Ministers to decide in this case that those individuals controlling the fourth respondent had been entitled to conclude that s 16 (1)(a) was satisfied.

[8] The applicants contend that a further appeal to this Court against the Court of Appeal judgment would address the correct interpretation of s 16 (1)(a). We accept that an issue concerning the true meaning of that provision would raise a matter of general or public importance, and also of general commercial significance, so that it would become necessary in the interests of justice for the Court to hear the appeal. But we do not see the present case as being of that nature. The conclusions that the controlling individuals had the requisite business experience and acumen, and that the information before the responsible Ministers was sufficient for them to so conclude, were essentially assessments which turned on the particular circumstances of the applicant and application. As such, they involved matters of fact and degree rather than the true meaning of the statute. The points which the proposed appeal would raise are accordingly too dependent on the specific facts to raise questions qualifying for an appeal to this Court. We also see no obvious error in the careful and common factual assessments made by the High Court and Court of Appeal. Overall, we do not see that it is necessary in the interests of justice for the Court to give leave to the applicants for a further appeal.

[9] The application is dismissed. The applicants must pay costs of $2, 500 to both Milk New Zealand Holdings Ltd and the Crown respondents.

Solicitors

Bell Gully, Auckland for Applicants

Crown Law Office, Wellington for First, Second and Third Respondents

Chapman Tripp, Auckland for Fourth Respondent

案例二　公司法先例：上市母公司为
倒闭子公司偿债

案　名

新西兰高等法院：Lewis Holdings Ltd v. Steel & Tube Holdings Ltd［2014］

NZHC 3311

新西兰上诉法院：Steel & Tube Holdings Limited v. Lewis Holdings Limited

［2016］NZCA366

导　读

一、高等法院[1]

L公司为商业建筑及仓库之业主（房东）。承租人为Stube（子公司），母公司为Steel & Tube。租约到期后，子公司依母公司常年法律顾问的意见，续租21年。后发现续租是错误的商业决定。但长期租约已经生效，子公司随即倒闭。

房东将母公司告上法庭要求替子公司偿债，母公司以有限责任公司独立法人这一传统公司法的概念抗辩。

二、《新西兰公司法》第271（1）（a）条款

《新西兰公司法》第271（1）（a）条款为"罕见条款"，不曾被引用过，且只有新西兰、爱尔兰等国在制定法/单行法中有类似的体现。

有限责任公司以及公司"法人面纱"等都是大家熟知的公司法概念。第271条实际上以成文法的方式设立了一个例外，即允许法庭在特定情形下，判母公司为倒闭的子公司偿还部分或全部债务。

在高等法院，L公司的代理律师成功地证明了以下几大要素：

（1）子公司为承租人，但租约主体和租金账单承付人均为母公司。

（2）续租法律意见由母公司法律顾问提供。

（3）母公司首席行政管理及总会计师担任子公司董事。

（4）子公司无独立雇员，母、子公司实质上为"一套班子、两块招牌"。

（5）母公司视长期租约为其法律上的权利及义务。

---

[1]　Lewis Holdings Ltd v. Steel & Tube Holdings Ltd［2014］NZHC 3311.

高等法院支持原告的主张，依第 271 条"经济同一体"的概念判母公司为倒闭的子公司清偿债务。

三、上诉法院[1]

2016 年 8 月 1 日上诉法院驳回母公司的上诉请求，除维持高等法院的原判以外，上诉法院还强调了以下两点：

（1）母、子公司之间缺乏法律上的因果关系（causation），以及子公司对母公司的"危害性依赖"（detrimental reliance）对高等法院作出的判决起不到决定性作用。

（2）第 271 条并没有要求证明"行为之行使不能"，而焦点则在"经济同一体"上，也就是说关注的是母公司董事没有能够划清两个公司职能上的界限。不同的公司——尤其是集团公司——往往有共同或交叉行使的管理职能。但董事和职员需要厘清不同公司之间独立法人之界限。如高等法院所言，本案中子公司倒闭可追溯到母公司，因母公司知悉子公司长期租约在先，而撤资不承担其租约在后，任其走上清偿（liquidation）之路。

四、新的公司法判例

公司法这则判例可概况为简单一句话：如果子公司成为母公司经济共同体中之一单元，母公司可能因此为子公司的债务承担连带责任。

（1）中国公司法中的母公司、子公司、分公司概念与英美法系概念不同，不可生搬硬套。

（2）公司的有限责任和独立法人资格这一概念是明确的，但是"一套班子几块牌子"有可能会削弱法人资格的独立性。

（3）华人喜欢成立"group"集团公司，个中利弊需仔细考量。

---

[1] Steel &Tube Holdings Limited v. Lewis Holdings Limited [2016] NZCA366.

高等法院判决书

IN THE HIGH COURT OF NEW ZEALAND
WELLINGTON REGISTRY

CIV-2013-485-6104

[2014] NZHC 3311

UNDER	Part 18 of the High Court Rules
IN THE MATTER	of ss 271 (1)(a) and 272 (1) of the Companies Act 1993
BETWEEN	LEWIS HOLDINGS LIMITED
	First plaintiff
	BORIS VAN DELDEN and PERI MICAELA FINNIGAN
	Second plaintiffs
AND	STEEL & TUBE HOLDINGS LIMITED Defendant
Hearing:	20-24 October and 4-7 November 2014
Counsel:	K J Crossland and J S Langston for Plaintiffs
	S A Barker and P J Niven for Defendant
Judgment:	18 December 2014

INTERIM JUDGMENT OF MACKENZIE J

I direct that the delivery time of this judgment is

233

11. 30 *am on the* 18*th day of December* 2014.

Solicitors: Shieff Angland, Auckland, for Plaintiffs.

Buddle Findlay, Wellington, for Defendant

LEWIS HOLDINGS LTD v. STEEL & TUBE HOLDINGS LTD [2014] NZHC 3311 [18 November 2014]

Table of Contents

Introduction

[1] The plaintiff, Lewis Holdings Ltd (Lewis), is the owner of a property at 15 Fisher Crescent, Mt Wellington, Auckland. Lewis purchased the property in about

1996 from Ports of Auckland Ltd. The property was subject to a perpetually renewable ground lease which had originally been granted under the Public Bodies Leases Act 1969. At the time of purchase, the lessee was Stube Industries Ltd (Stube), a wholly owned subsidiary of the defendant Steel & Tube Holdings Ltd (STH). The then current 21 year term of the lease expired in 2009. The lease was renewed in 2009. Stube was put into liquidation by a shareholders' resolution on 4 June 2013. On 10 June 2013 the liquidators appointed by the shareholders disclaimed the lease as onerous property, under s 269 of the Companies Act 1993 (the Act). Lewis filed a proof of debt with the liquidators who were subsequently replaced by the second plaintiffs (the liquidators). Lewis and the liquidators claimagainst STH, under s 271 (1)(a) of the Act, that STH pay to the liquidator the whole of Lewis' claim in the liquidation. By an amendment to the statement of claim which I allowed during the hearing, the plaintiffs also seek a decision from the Court under s 307 of the Act on the amount of Lewis' claim.

The s 271 claim

History

[2] Stube, previously called Healing Industries Ltd (Healing), acquired its interest in the property in September 1979. By the mid-1980s, Healing had become a wholly owned subsidiary of EMCO Group Ltd (EMCO). EMCO was acquired by STH in 1985. Healing operated a metallisation plant on buildings erected on the land. The plant prepared the surface of fabricated steel products by blasting with grit or sand, then painting the steel to improve its resistance to corrosion. In 1988 STH decided to dispose of non-strategic assets, poorly performing businesses and non-mainstream businesses. That included the metallisation business. The metallisation plant was transferred in around 1990 to Robt Stone & Co Ltd, which amalgamated with STH and became a division of STH. STH occupied the property under an informal sublease from Stube. On that transfer of its metallisation business, the Healing brand and business ended and the only ongoing assets and liabilities of the company were the ground lease

and associated informal sublease, and a superannuation scheme. Healing changed its name to Stube to reflect this change. From that time, Stube had no employees and management was effectively shifted to the property manager at STH.

[3] The situation when Lewis purchased the property in early 1996 was that Stube had the ground lease, which had been renewed for a 21 year term from 1 December 1988, while the buildings and plant on the land were operated by Robt Stone, a division of STH. [1]

[4] In 1998, STH sold the metallisation plant under a management buy-out. A new company, Mt Wellington Metalisation (1998) Ltd was formed. Stube and that company entered into a deed of lease in relation to the plant and a deed of sublease in relation to the land in April 1998. The new company did not prosper, and the metallisation plant was shut down. The sublease was terminated in 2003.

[5] The metallisation process caused contamination of the land over the years in which it was operating. STH undertook decontamination work in 1996 and 1997, at a cost of approximately $900,000. That remediation work did not extend to the building itself, or the soil beneath the building. On the termination of the sublease in 2003, it was clear that considerable contamination still existed. STH carried out further remediation work at a cost of some $418,000 after that time. In that process, the buildings and plant were removed and the site was reduced to predominantly bare land.

[6] After the closure of the metallisation plant and the remedial work, STH investigated options for the land. The possibilities it considered included using the land for a division of STH, or selling the lessee's interest in the land.

Renewal of the ground lease

以下 [7] – [12] 略

The application of the legislation

[13] It is convenient to discuss the application of the legislation to the facts of this case by addressing each of the four matters listed in s 272 (1). Before doing so,

---

[1] It seems that the buildings and plant Robt Stone acquired as part of the transfer of the business were owned by STH, so that Stube's interest in the land was limited to the lessee's interest in the land itself.

some broader comments on the approach to pooling orders under the legislation are appropriate.

[14] Our company law is firmly grounded in the principle that a company is a legal entity in its own right separate from its shareholders. That principle is expressly stated in s 15 of the Act. It continues the well-established common law principle first established in *Salomon v. A Salomon & Co Ltd*, [1] and confirmed in New Zealand in *Lee v. Lee's Air Farming Limited*. [2] It is a corollary of that principle that the shareholders are not generally liable to meet the obligations incurred by the company beyond the extent of their liability to the company for payment of the share capital. [3]

[15] Section 271 creates an exception to that general principle. It had its origin in a recommendation in the 1973 Macarthur Committee *Final Report of the Special Committee to Review the Companies Act*, responding to a submission that in at least two recent cases well-known public companies had abandoned subsidiaries. [4]

[16] Section 271 has not been frequently invoked. It is, apart from a similar provision in Ireland, unique to New Zealand in the common law world, so no assistance is available from other similar jurisdictions. All but one of the authorities to which I was referred are cases under s 271 (1)(b), not s 271 (1)(a).

[17] The most comprehensive discussion of the approach to be adopted in applying s 271 is the decision of Baragwanath J in *Mountfort v. Tasman Pacific Airlines of NZ Ltd*. [5] He noted the reluctance, in common law jurisdictions without a pooling provision, to extend the narrow range of exceptions in s 15. He noted the tension between:

(a) the separate legal identity of companies, and the right of commercial enterprises to run their businesses through subsidiary and related companies as they see fit; and

---

[1] *Salomon v. A Salomon & Co Ltd* [1897] AC 22 (HL).

[2] *Lee v. Lee's Air Farming Limited* [1961] *NZLR* 325 (*PC*).

[3] Companies Act 1993, s 97.

[4] Macarthur Committee *Final Report of the Special Committee to Review the Companies Act* (Ministry of Justice, March 1973).

[5] *Mountfort v. Tasman Pacific Airlines of NZ Ltd* [2006] 1 *NZLR* 104 (*HC*).

(b) the mischief that can result from an unyielding application of separate corporate identity.

[18] He held that to carry an unyielding application of separate corporate identity across into the construction of ss 271 and 272 would defy the legislative policy. [1]

[19] I do not propose to embark on a detailed analysis of the competing principles involved. In the end, what is required is an application of the statutory criteria in s 272 (1) to the facts of this case as I determine them to be. In applying the criteria I must balance two policy considerations inherent in the legislation which weigh on different sides of the scales. The first is that the separate corporate identity of the company in liquidation is to be respected. The second is that s 271 is directed to the mischief that an overly strict application of that separate corporate identity may cause.

[20] In applying the first policy consideration, that the separate corporate identity of the company in liquidation is to be respected, I must bear in mind the rationale for the provision in our law that a company is a legal entity separate from its shareholders. That rationale is to enable a business to be carried on by a separate legal entity, so as not to expose the shareholders (be they one or many) to the liabilities which the business may incur. It is inherent in that rationale that the company will be not only a separate legal entity, but also a separate commercial entity. Its business will be conducted in such a way that the company is not a mere "front" for a business actually carried on by others. The "corporate veil" shields the substance of the company and its business from the shareholders who own the company. It does not, if the company is a mere facade, shield that facade from the operators of the business which is carried on in its name.

[21] A particular aspect of the separate corporate identity of a company which must be taken into account in the balancing exercise is the common business practice of using the principle of separate corporate identity in the creation of group structures. The evidence shows, if indeed evidence was necessary, that it is common practice in com-

---

[1] See especially [63] to [74].

pany groups that a range of services are undertaken centrally, group staff are used to manage subsidiaries, and senior officers of the parent act as directors of the subsidiary. STH places considerable reliance on such matters. Those propositions are largely uncontroversial as statements of general practice. What is required is a factual assessment of the practices adopted in this case, to determine whether there is some conduct or other circumstance falling within the s 272 guidelines that disentitles STH from relying on the separate legal existence of Stube.

[22] Because the policy considerations which I must bear in mind require application to the circumstances of this case, I do not consider it helpful to elaborate on those policy considerations in a general way at this stage. It is preferable that I address relevant points as they arise in my discussion of the matters I must take into account under s 272. To those matters I now turn.

The matters in s 272 (1)

(a) The extent to which STH took part in the management of Stube

[23] The positions of the parties on this issue are diametrically opposed, as the following summary of their submissions shows. Mr Crossland says:

[Stube] was always managed by its parent STHL. The facts referred to shortly of themselves alone may not be determinative. However, it is their cumulative effect and in some instances their duration that lead to the inescapable conclusion in that a contribution order is just [.]

[24] Mr Barker submits:

Although employees of STHL took part in the management of [Stube], [Stube] was at all times managed as a separate company.

[25] I must examine the point in some detail. That requires a consideration of the evidence about the management of the company which goes beneath the formal legal structure and looks at what actually happened.

[26] I begin with the directors. As STH submits, the appointment of senior employees of a holding company as directors of a subsidiary is common practice and does not of itself amount to participation by the holding company in the management of the

subsidiary. But that does not mean that actions of such directors cannot amount to such participation. What is required is an examination of the acts of the employee directors, to determine whether they were, in the way they operated, acting as directors of the subsidiary, or as senior managers of the parent.

[27] STH called evidence from Mr Dent as to usual practice on the use of subsidiary companies in the structuring of business enterprises. I need not describe and discuss that evidence. It is for the most part uncontroversial. But it is of little assistance to me in deciding the issues I must address. Mr Dent's evidence was expressed only in broad general terms. He had not been instructed to look at what had been done in this case. I am concerned with the application in this case of the business practices which Mr Dent describes.

[28] At all material times up to 2009, the directors were MessrsCalavrias and Candy. Mr Calavrias was the CEO of STH, and Mr Candy the CFO. They were both called as witnesses by the plaintiffs. Mr Candy, in his affidavit evidence in chief, said that at all times he and others in STH management considered that the property (albeit in Stube's name) was a leasehold asset of STH. He said that during his tenure they treated the property both as to its benefits and liabilities as something that lay with STH. His recollection is that any expense and revenue related to the property was treated for taxation purposes at the STH parent level. He was asked in cross-examination about his understanding of the basic concepts that underpin the operation of companies in New Zealand, and the concept of separate corporate personality of different companies. He was questioned about the provision in Stube's constitution which, in accordance with s 131 (2) of the Act, permitted its directors to act in the best interests of the parent. He was asked whether he was aware that when he was a director of Stube he was entitled to take into account or to act in the best interests of STH in making decisions as a director. He said:

I can't say it was top of my thought processes, however, having said that, the superannuation fund which was attached to Stube at the time was being used by Steel & Tube Holdings Limited in the interests of Steel & Tube Holdings Limited, so I think I,

I would have had some cognisance without actually being totally aware of it.

以下［29］-［36］略

［37］Under s 136 of the Act, a director of a company must not agree to the company incurring an obligation unless the director believes at the time on reasonable grounds that the company will be able to perform the obligation when it is required to do so. The way the group operated meant that this issue was not separately addressed for Stube. Any obligation was, for MessrsCalavrias and Candy, an obligation of the group, not a separate obligation of Stube. That point emerged clearly in cross-examination of Mr Candy about the following statement in his reply affidavit in evidence in chief:

2. 4 4. 14/6. 3: I do not remember the costs being accredited to ［Stube］.

Nick Calvarias ［sic］, my fellow ［Stube］director and STHL CEO, took the view that STHL, to be a good corporate citizen, would need to clean up the site. I also recall that Ceramco had walked away from a lease it had through a subsidiary. We had discussed how that did not seem to be appropriate for a publicly listed company to be seen to do. This came up between Nick and I because for a period of time a Ceramco executive (Charles Bidwill) sat on the STHL board.

以下［38］略

［39］From the perspective of the extent to which STH took part in the management of Stube, I find that MessrsCalavrias and Candy, in their involvement in the management of Stube, did so in their capacity as the CEO and CFO of STH, and that their status as directors of Stube did not isolate STH from the management of Stube. In making those findings, I intend no criticism of Mr Calavrias or Mr Candy. The formal distinction between Stube and STH was not a distinction which they needed to make, in the way the group operated under their stewardship. But, while it was not necessary for Mr Calavrias and Mr Candy to consider Stube's separate position, in the light of the way the Steel and Tube group then operated, the matter must now be viewed through a different lens. The liabilities of Stube and STH must be considered separately. When that is done, it is clear that Stube did not have the financial capacity to continue to trade without the support of STH. If they were treated as separate legal entities, legal arrangements were required to ensure support. There were none.

[40] In reaching that conclusion, I have taken into account and given full weight to the well established practice of appointing senior managers of a holding company as directors of subsidiaries, to which I have referred at [26] . Nothing which I have said is intended to suggest that practice is inappropriate. But, as I have observed, when that practice is adopted, the directors must approach their duties as directors in a way which recognises the separate legal personality of the two entities. They must conduct the affairs of the subsidiary as a separate board. They must ensure that there are appropriate legal and commercial arrangements in place to recognise and give effect to the separate legal status of the subsidiary. The ability of the directors to act in the best interests of the parent does not obviate the need to have regard to the separate legal status of the subsidiary.

[41] STH also took part in the management of Stube in other ways. Stube had no employees of its own, and all matters which needed to be attended to for Stube were carried out by employees of STH. This too is common practice within groups and does not of itself mean that when employees of the parent carry out actions on behalf of the subsidiary, the parent is taking part in the management of the subsidiary. But again, what is necessary is a close examination of the employees' actions, to determine whether those are in reality actions taken on behalf of the subsidiary, or on behalf of the parent or the wider group.

[42] Many of the steps undertaken by group employees were effected on STH letterhead, without the employee concerned stating that he or she was acting for Stube rather than STH. Also, there were no recorded arrangements for STH to provide management services to Stube, and no inter – company charge for the provision of services. Again, neither of those factors is of itself of particular significance in indicating the extent to which STH was involved in the management of Stube. Of more importance is the extent to which, when the issues are examined in detail, the steps taken fell within the purview of STH, not Stube. I examine some examples.

[43] The first is the action which was taken with regard to the administration of the lease, and attempts to find an alternative use for the property, or a buyer for the leasehold interest. Mr Anastasiadis, who was the company solicitor for STH until July 2003, managed the lease and issues to do with the property. In evidence, he said he did so on behalf of Stube. That needs to be tested against the contemporary record. Once the metallisation plant closed, and the sublease terminated, there was no income from the land. Considerable efforts were made to find an alternative use for the site within the STH group, or to sell the leasehold interest. In April 2003, Mr Anastasiadis arranged a sole agency agreement for the sale of the property with C B Richard Ellis (Agency) Ltd. The formal agency agreement was between STH and the agent. On 14 April 2003 the agent submitted an offer which it had obtained for a transfer of the leasehold interest in the property. The vendor was described in the offer document as Stube. Mr Anastasiadis wrote to the solicitors for the offeror on 1 May 2003. He said that the form of agreement was inappropriate for the transaction being contemplated by STH, and proposed instead a sale of the shares in Stube to the proposed purchaser, rather than a transfer of the leasehold interest. On 13 June 2003, Mr Calavrias sent a memorandum to the directors of STH in which he said that management at STH had been in negotiation for some time to formulate an exit strategy from the lease. He said STH had negotiated a sale and purchase agreement for the sale of the shares. One of the conditions of the agreement was a unanimous resolution from the board of STH accepting the appointment of the purchaser as a director of Stube. He submitted a draft resolution for consideration by the board.

[44] That proposed transaction did not eventuate. But it demonstrates very clearly that Mr Anastasiadis was acting for STH, not Stube. The proposal he put forward could only have been implemented by STH, not Stube. Stube's separate legal existence was relevant to the form of transfer proposed, but Stube had no control over it.

以下 [45] – [48] 略

[49] Mr Crossland places some emphasis on Mr Joubert's description of the leasehold rights as being vested in STH. The letter was carefully worded. It is clear that Mr

Joubert was aware of, and had in mind, the separate existence of Stube. In my assessment, when he described the rights as vested in STH, he accurately described the commercial reality as it was understood and administered within STH.

[50] In 2008, an arrangement was reached for Carr & Haslam Ltd to take a licence of the site, for $1, 000 per month. The documentation of that arrangement was in the hands of Mr Joubert's successor as company solicitor, Mr Jenkins. He prepared a licence agreement in the name of STH as licensor. The agreement was signed on behalf of STH by Mr Calavrias and Mr Candy. Mr Jenkins was cross-examined as to why he had prepared that licence in the name of STH rather than Stube. His answer was that he thought he originally drafted it for Stube, but changed the name of the licensor to STH after a discussion with Mr Candy or possibly someone in the finance section. The deliberate change in the identity of the licensor in the licence agreement indicates clearly that the company with the real financial interest in the transaction was STH, not Stube.

[51] The evidence about STH's accounting arrangements supports the proposition that Stube was treated as a division of STH, for financial purposes. Stube had no separate bank account. All receipts and payments on its behalf had to be made through STH's bank account. The use of the parent's bank account would not of itself indicate involvement by the parent in the management of the subsidiary, at least so long as a clear record of the transactions was kept within the internal records of the group. However, the evidence shows that the financial intermingling of the affairs of Stube and STH went well beyond the use of a common bank account. Receipts and payment were not only transacted through STH's bank account, they were accounted for as STH's transactions.

[52] This is illustrated by the arrangements for payment of the rent and rates, payable by Stube under the lease. Lewis sent quarterly invoices for the ground rent. Those invoices were, at the request of STH, addressed to STH, not Stube. They were paid by STH. The rates on the property, payable by the lessee, were also invoiced to STH by Auckland City Council. It was important to STH that the rent and rates be invoiced in this way. That is demonstrated by an exchange of emails involving the STH

accounts department, following registration of the renewal of the lease in late 2009. That exchange indicates that the property had been recorded by the Auckland City Council as being in the name of STH, and rate demands had been addressed to STH. When the renewal of the lease was registered in late 2009, in the name of Stube, Auckland City Council altered the name. Ms Wong from STH sent an email to Mr Beecroft on 24 August 2010 which said:

We have contacted the Auckland City Council and found out that it is them that changed the address details. No-one at Steel & Tube contacted them at all. Auckland City Council saw the notice of sale in December 2009 and they think that Stube Industries own the property now, which is incorrect. The new owners have to contact the Council to get it changed to the correct name and address. Steel & Tube cannot pay the rates directly because it is not addressed to the right party, that is, Steel & Tube Holdings Limited.

Steel & Tube Holdings Limited would like to keep the previous arrangement where we get an invoice from whoever owns 15 Fisher Crescent. The invoice is to be addressed to Steel & Tube Holdings Limited, Finance Department, Private Box 30-543, Lower Hutt 5040

[53] In a further email following Mr Beecroft's reply, Ms Wong said:

For tax purposes we need ALL invoices to be addressed to Steel & Tube Holdings Limited and not Stube Industries. If Steel & Tube are to pay the rates directly, they (Auckland City Council & ARC) will have to reissue the 2 invoices changing the name to Steel & Tube Holdings Limited and NOT Stube Industries.

Sorry to be particular on this. Because IRD is particular about this, we will have to be as well.

[54] That exchange indicates a deliberate intention to treat STH as the owner, not a mistaken view on the part of an STH employee about the ownership of the lease.

[55] A particularly important stage, in considering the extent of participation of STH in the management of Stube, is the renewal of the lease in 2009. Until late 2008, STH had been investigating options for the redevelopment of the property or the sale of

the leasehold interest. I have described some of those initiatives. It is not necessary to describe them all. By late 2008, STH had been unable to come up with a plan which would extract value from the lease. Mr Jenkins reported regularly to Messrs Calavrias and Candy, as CEO and CFO of STH, on all STH's property holdings, including 15 Fisher Crescent. In his monthly report of October 2008, Mr Jenkins recorded the position in this way:

- Ground lease review date is 30 November 2009.

- Barry Wither wrote to us on 5.09.08 advising that Quadrant are willing to continue discussion with an open mind but with the lease terms certain only 15 months to run the options are limited.

- Tse advise that despite the uncertainty in the market they do not entirely discount the possibility of there being a highly motivated owner/occupier developer in the market.

- Recommend marketing the Lessee's interest in the land for sale by calling for expressions of interest on the basis that any offer will be seriously considered.

[56] In the next monthly report which is in evidence, for January 2009, the position is recorded:

Ground lease review date is 30 November 2009.

Will not renew

[57] In answer to questions from me as to what had happened in that intervening three month period to change the situation, Mr Jenkins answered that he could not recall exactly what occurred. He said they would have investigated as many options as possible to do something with the lease and explored any and every viable option, but probably came to a blind end. He must have gone to Mr Calavrias and said that we do not see any viable options. He said that he then got a firm instruction from Mr Calavrias in late November or early December that the lease would not be renewed. He could not recall anything in writing but did remember Mr Calavrias telling him verbally "no we are not going to renew".

[58] Later events do not support the proposition that a firm decision not to renew

had been made by then. STH continued to investigate whether it could obtain value for the lessee's interest by a sale. Mr Jenkins had been taking advice from an external valuer. The valuer suggested that Mr Jenkins respond to Mr Beecroft's letter of 12 March 2009 advising the proposed new rent by asking him for the detail of the assessed land value and the market yield which had been used in fixing the proposed rental. The valuer said: "By requesting this information it will demonstrate to the lessor you are seriously researching and considering taking up the new term." Asked why they should give an indication that they might renew, Mr Jenkins said that STH wanted to keep its options open as long as it could, in the hope that Lewis or Quadrant might offer some sort of deal, or a sweetener, to STH to not renew the lease. Quadrant had made a proposal to a client of Colliers for a redevelopment proposal on the land, conditional on Stube's lease not being renewed.

[59] Also, when the new ground rent valuation of \$ 195, 000 was received, it was less than the approximately \$ 250, 000 estimated earlier. Mr Calavrias said to Mr Jenkins:

As you know it was our view that we should exit (abandon) the lease at the appropriate time before the renewal date. Does the lower ground lease rental increase the value of this site now and should we be pursuing a buyer for the lease?

[60] Mr Barker submits that a firm decision had been made by the directors of Stube not to renew the lease, and its renewal was the result entirely of a mistake by Mr Jenkins in failing to give the required notice. I do not accept that submission. The evidence which I have described indicates that STH was endeavouring to keep its options open as long as possible in the hope that it could extract some value from the lease. In adopting that stance, those involved, particularly Mr Jenkins and Mr Calavrias, were not acting in their capacity as employees and/or directors of Stube. Mr Jenkins, in answer to a question from me, accepted my description of his efforts to show Lewis and Quadrant that it might be renewing the lease as brinkmanship. That form of brinkmanship was not, and could not properly have been, undertaken on behalf of Stube. Rental under the lease was a significant liability to Stube. It had no income to meet that liabil-

ity. It had no realistic means of extracting, from its own resources, any value from the right to renew the lease.

[61] Mr Jenkins made a mistake in not appreciating that notice not to renew was required. But he made that mistake in the context of the background of STH's actions in keeping its options open as long as possible, and so not advising Lewis that it did not intend to renew. The mistake was not one which an employee acting on Stube's behalf was likely to have made.

[62] The steps taken after the mistake was discovered give an insight into the extent to which the lease had become ingrained in the corporate culture as belonging to STH. As I have recorded at [8], STH claimed legal professional privilege for the external legal advice obtained following the deemed renewal of the lease. That advice must therefore have been obtained by STH, not Stube. If it had been obtained by Stube the privilege would be that of Stube, claimable by the liquidators. That indicates that even when an issue serious enough to require external legal advice arose, STH did not have any regard to the separate legal existence of Stube. If it had, it would have ensured that it was Stube that obtained advice.

[63] STH submits that Lewis was aware that the failure to give notice not to renew was a mistake, and that this weighs against a s 271 order. I do not accept that submission. As Mr Jenkins's evidence makes clear, STH was involved in "brinkmanship", and took steps to suggest to Lewis that it might renew. The letter proposing the new rent had drawn Mr Jenkins's attention to sch 1 of the Public Bodies Leases Act. There was no reason for Lewis to think that Mr Jenkins might have overlooked or misread the relevant clause. The evidence does not support the proposition that Lewis was aware that STH intended not to renew, and that the failure to give notice was a mistake.

以下 [64] – [65] 略

(b) *The conduct of STH towards Lewis as a creditor of Stube*

[66] It is not in dispute that Lewis, and its agent Quadrant, knew that the legal entity Stube was the lessee. The plaintiffs do not put their case on the basis that the ac-

tions of STH caused any confusion for Lewis as to the legal entity with which it contracted. Rather, the case is that STH conducted itself towards Lewis as if the property was STH's and that STH stood behind its subsidiary. The plaintiffs assert that STH's conduct demonstrated its commitment by continuing to fund Stube. It says that all negotiations were conducted on this basis and that in none of the many negotiations over many issues was there any suggestion that STH would not continue to support Stube.

[67] Mr Crossland submits that STH's conduct once it had decided to abandon Stube was in sharp contrast to how the company had behaved until then. He submits that its conduct was contrived and specifically designed to create a post facto veneer of separate legal personality between Stube and STH. Mr Crossland submits that the pains taken by STH at that stage to draw a distinction between Stube and STH are in stark contrast to its earlier behaviour, and throw into sharp relief the conduct over the previous two decades **where Stube was treated as part and parcel of one economic unit, namely STH.** [1]

以下 [68] – [77] 略

[78] STH's conduct towards Lewis in relation to the renewal of the lease is relevant, under s 272 (1)(b), in deciding whether it is just and equitable to make an order under s 271. I have discussed that conduct in considering s 272 (1)(a). The issue under s 272 (1) (b) is whether that conduct makes it just and equitable that STH should pay part or all of Lewis' claim against Stube. I consider that the fact that, if events had transpired differently, there would have been no claim against Stube is also not relevant to this question. The conduct of STH towards Lewis in relation to the lease is a factor weighing in favour of an order, under s 272 (1)(b).

[79] Mr Baker submits that s 271 is directed at circumstances where the related company deprives the company in liquidation of assets to the detriment of creditors in disentitling circumstances, such as the sweep of cash when the related company is insolvent, or causes the company in liquidation to enter into a liability to the detriment of

---

〔1〕 黑体字部分为编者添加。

creditors in disentitling circumstances, for example causing the company in liquidation to do so when insolvent. As to the first example of disentitling circumstances, a sweep of cash, Mr Barker submits that STH has not deprived Stube of assets to the detriment of creditors in disentitling circumstances. Instead, it has made significant contributions to Stube by paying the rent and meeting the remediation costs.

[80] I do not intend to examine whether STH's meeting the remediation costs can be regarded as a contribution to Stube. That would require an examination of the legal responsibility for the remediation of the site, which it is not appropriate to undertake here. It is sufficient to observe that the evidence does not establish that STH had no legal liability to meet the cost of remediation necessary to meet regulatory requirements.

[81] STH has been a substantial contributor to Stube by payment of rent over the period which I have considered it appropriate to examine, namely from about 2003. Over a longer time period, STH has not necessarily been a net contributor to Stube. When Stube, as Healing, was acquired by STH, it had a business which was presumably a viable one. The income from the business was presumably sufficient to pay the rent. STH restructured that business. The financial details of the restructuring are not in evidence. The outcome of the restructuring was that Stube was left with no business. It was left with the lease, and no source of income to pay the rent. There is no evidence from which I can assess whether the value taken by STH from Stube was more or less than its later payment of rent.

[82] To the extent that s 271 is directed at circumstances where the related company deprives the company in liquidation of assets to the detriment of creditors in disentitling circumstances, the consideration of the Court should not be confined to actions in the period just prior to the liquidation. Over the long run, the evidence does not establish that STH has been a net contributor to Stube.

[83] In any event, s 271 is not limited to situations where there has been a deprivation of assets from the company in liquidation. There may be other disentitling circumstances. I consider that STH's actions in relation to the lease fall within that description.

[84] Stube had for many years been unable to pay the rent without STH's support. It had no legally enforceable arrangements for support. If the directors of Stube had consciously entered into a contract to renew the lease, they would have been incurring an obligation, which the directors could not have had reasonable grounds to believe Stube would be able to perform from its own resources or by recourse to legally enforceable financial arrangements, as required by s 136 of the Act. Furthermore, the renewal of the lease was a major transaction which should not have been entered into unless approved by a special resolution, under s 129 of the Act. STH, as shareholder, did not pass a resolution authorising the transaction. Nor did it take any steps to put in place legally enforceable funding arrangements to enable Stube to meet its obligations. Sections 129 and 136 apply to a transaction deliberately entered into. They do not cease to apply, even if I was to accept the proposition that the renewal was the result of a mistake by Stube.

[85] STH and the directors of Stube did not comply with those provisions, and STH continued to pay the rent. Its conduct towards Lewis in relation to the renewal was such as would reasonably lead Lewis to believe that Stube was not treated as a legal entity distinct from STH. That conduct is directly relevant to s 271 (1)(b). It weighs in favour of an order.

(c) The extent to which the circumstances that gave rise to the liquidation of Stube are attributable to the actions of STH

[86] Mr Crossland submits that Stube was not a real company actually trading that had faced a fiscal calamity caused by some extraneous event. He submits that STH made a decision sometime in 2012 or 2013 through its new CEO, and its CFO who was then the sole director of Stube, to withdraw funding from Stube, knowing that the renewal creating a 21 year obligation had been signed in 2009. STH deliberately ceased funding and then passed a shareholders' resolution to appoint a liquidator. He accordingly submits that Stube's liquidation is directly and solely attributable to the actions of STH.

[87] Mr Barker submits that the circumstances that gave rise to the liquidation

are not attributable to STH, and are largely attributable to the actions of Lewis and Quadrant. He submits that the main cause of Stube's liquidation was the onerous lease and that had it not been for the unreasonableness of the lessor in not allowing Stube to assign the lease, and imposing unreasonable demands on Stube, Stube would not have had this burden. Mr Barker relies upon this asserted unreasonableness both under this heading, as the extent to which the actions of STH have contributed to the liquidation, as well as under the next heading, "such other matters as the Court thinks fit". He submits that the Court should consider Lewis's "contribution to the loss, including breaches of the lease and unreasonableness". I deal with his submissions on this aspect under s 272 (1)(d).

[88] So far as s 272 (1)(c) is concerned, I find that the circumstances that gave rise to the liquidation of Stube are attributable entirely to the actions of STH, in deciding to withdraw the support which it had previously provided to Stube.

(d) *Such other matters as the Court thinks fit*

[89] Under this heading, counsel for the plaintiffs submit that there are a number of matters which are relevant and support an order under s 271:

(a) Section 136 of the Act requires directors of a company not to agree to the company incurring an obligation unless the directors believed at the time on reasonable grounds that the company would be able to perform the obligation when it was required to do so.

(b) The treatment of the lease liability in the group accounts demonstrates that STH regarded it as its own liability.

(c) There is an absence of documents that one would expect to find, such as a resolution approving entry into a major transaction for the 21 year lease by Stube. Mr Crossland submits that this was a major transaction for Stube, but was treated as being within the delegated authority of the CEO of STH to enter into renewals of leases. He submits that this indicates that the renewal, while signed by the Stube directors, was comprehended by them as an act carried out by them on behalf of STH.

(d) There is no evidence that STH's own creditors or its employees would be prejudiced if the s 271 order were made.

(e) STH, as a publicly listed company with a company solicitor to attend to the legal requirements of itself and its subsidiaries, cannot properly complain to the Court that an order is not just and equitable, by relying on separate legal personality, when for years it has treated itself as a single economic enterprise.

(f) The constitution of Stube, which enabled the directors to take account of the interests of the holding company STH, does not operate as what Mr Crossland describes as "a prophylactic against a pooling order".

(g) STH is seeking sympathy from the Court on a number of grounds.

This is not a factor weighing against the making of an order.

[90] Mr Barker submits that the Court should consider, under s 272 (1)(d):

(a) Lewis's contribution to the loss, including breach of the lease and unreasonableness;

(b) Lewis's failure to mitigate loss; and

(c) whether in fact Lewis suffered loss.

[91] I have addressed Mr Crossland's first three points in discussing the earlier paragraphs of s 272 (1). His fourth point is that there is no evidence of prejudice to the creditors or employees of STH. That is so. However, I must address Mr Barker's submission that under s 272 (2), the extent to which the businesses of the relevant companies have been combined is an express matter to be taken into account, whereas under s 272 (1) it is not.

[92] Sections 272 (1) and (2) address different situations under s 271. Section 272 (1) applies to a s 271 (1)(a) case; s 272 (2) applies to a s 271 (1)(b) case. Section 271 (1)(a), which is relied upon here, applies where the related company is not itself in liquidation. Subsection (b) applies where both or all of the related companies are in liquidation. The reference in s 272 (2) to the extent to which the businesses of the companies have been combined is explicable by the need, in cases under s 271 (1)(b), to have regard to the position of the creditors of all the companies in liquidation. The extent to which the businesses have beencombined is a relevant

consideration in determining what is just and equitable as between the separate creditors of each of those insolvent companies.

[93] Similar considerations do not arise under s 271 (1)(a). So, the absence of a similar provision in s 272 (1) does not mean that the extent to which the business of Stube and STH have been combined is not relevant. It may be relevant under any of paragraphs (a) to (d). I have taken into account, in considering paragraph (a), the extent to which the business of Stube has been subsumed into that of STH, and have upheld Mr Crossland's submission that it has been treated as a division of STH.

[94] I attach some weight to Mr Crossland's fifth point that STH as a publicly listed company ought to have known better. The separate legal existence of Stube, on which STH relies, carries with it a responsibility to ensure that the legal requirements which apply to that separate legal entity are observed. A failure to observe those requirements cannot readily be ignored or excused where the company concerned is the subsidiary of a publicly listed company.

[95] Mr Crossland's sixth point is that s 131 (2) does not operate as "a prophylactic against a pooling order". I have addressed s 131 (2) in considering s 271 (1) (a). For the reasons given there, I find that the existence of the provision in the constitution of Stube enabling it to act in the best interests of STH does not preclude an order under s 271, because the directors of Stube did not act as s 131 (2) requires.

以下 [96] - [104] 略

[105] The matters which I have considered under s 272 (1) (d) weigh in favour of a s 271 order.

[106] In what he describes as a "cross check" for the proposition that Stube has been the "slave" of STH, Mr Crossland submits that the circumstances are such as to make STH a shadow director of Stube, in terms of s 126 of the Act. That includes within the meaning of director, for the purpose of those sections dealing with director's duties, any person in accordance with whose directions or instructions the actual directors or the board are required or accustomed to act.

[107] In *Re Hydrodam (Corby) Ltd* 180 Millet J described the nature of a

shadow director under the equivalent English provision in these terms: [1]

A de facto director, I repeat, is one who claims to act and purports to act as a director, although not validly appointed as such. A shadow director, by contrast, does not claim or purport to act as a director. On the contrary, he claims not to be a director. He lurks in the shadows, sheltering behind others who, he claims, are the only directors of the company to the exclusion of himself. He is not held out as a director by the company. To establish that a defendant is a shadow director of a company it is necessary to allege and prove: (1) who are the directors of the company, whether de facto or de jure; (2), that the defendant directed those directors how to act in relation to the company or that he was one of the persons who did so; (3) that those directors acted in accordance with such directions; and (4) that they were accustomed so to act. What is needed is first, a board of directors claiming and purporting to act as such; and secondly, a pattern of behaviour in which the board did not exercise any discretion or judgment of its own, but acted in accordance with the directions of others.

[108] As I have held, it is perfectly proper and usual commercial practice to appoint employees of the holding company as directors of a subsidiary. It is also permissible for those employee directors to act in accordance with the best interests of the holding company, even although that may not be in the best interests of the subsidiary, provided the constitution so provides, as it does here. What is not permitted is that those employee directors have regard only to the interests of the holding company, without giving separate consideration to the separate legal existence of the subsidiary, or the separate best interests of the subsidiary. A director who acts in that way, having regard only to the interests of the holding company or the wider group, without separate consideration of the position of the subsidiary, may potentially bring the holding company within the scope of that description by Millet J. However, as I have reached the conclusions which I have as to the roles which the directors played by considering the matters in s 272 (1), it is unnecessary to say more about this aspect.

---

[1] Re Hydrodam (Corby) Lte [1994] 2BCLC 180 (Ch) at 183.

The outcome of the s 271 application

[109] The matters which I have considered under s 272 have led me to the conclusion that it is just and equitable to make an order under s 271 (1)(a). The order which can be made is that STH pays to the liquidators "the whole or part of any or all of the claims made in the liquidation".

[110] There is only one claim in the liquidation, that of Lewis. I have had regard only to that claim in considering whether it is just and equitable to make an order. Mr Barker suggested that STH may itself be able to make a claim in the liquidation. It would be inappropriate that any amount which STH was ordered to pay should be returned in part to STH as a creditor. For this reason, the order should not be in respect of all of the claims, but should be limited to the claim by Lewis.

[111] I do not consider that it is necessary, in making an order under s 271 (1) (a), that the relevant claims have been quantified. I addressed that point in an interlocutory judgment. [1] I do not repeat what I said there. I make some additional comments. The section may have to be applied in a liquidation in which there are many creditor claims. It would be potentially inconvenient if all claims had to be quantified before an order could be made. The wording of s 271 does not suggest that this is required. The words "the whole or part of any or all of the claims" indicate that the order may be expressed in general terms, and that quantification of the amount to be paid is not a prerequisite of the order.

[112] That conclusion is supported by the purpose of the section. That is to require a contribution by a related company to a liquidator when the actions of the related company make it just and equitable to lift the corporate veil to some extent. The extent to which the veil is tobe lifted is determined principally by a consideration of the actions of the related company, rather than by a consideration of the nature and quantum of the claims made in the liquidation.

[113] For these reasons, I conclude that quantification of Lewis's claim under the

---

[1] *Lewis Holdings Lte v. Steel & Holdings Lte* [2014] NZHC 2650.

s 307 application is not necessary before an order can be made.

［114］I consider that it is appropriate to make the order now. For the reasons I later give, the s 307 application cannot be finally determined now, but this judgment should give the parties the greatest level of finality that is possible. The essential issue is whether the matters which I have considered should result in an order that STH pay all, or only part, of the claim, whatever the amount of that claim may ultimately be. I do not consider that the quantum must be fixed before that issue can be decided. The section does not provide any guidance on the circumstances in which it may be just and equitable to make an order, having regard to the s 272 factors, but to limit that to part of the claims only. That lack of specific guidance is, I infer, deliberate. The circumstances must be considered, and the order which is made must be one which achieves justice and equity for both the related company and the creditors of the company in liquidation.

［115］When the extent of involvement of the related company has been limited, the extent of the contribution may also be limited to only part of the claims. STH took part in the management of Stube to an extent which was, in essence, total. That justifies a total contribution under s 271. There is nothing in the other circumstances, which I have held also support an order, which justifies any proportionate reduction. I have determined that it is just and equitable that STH make a contribution to Lewis' claim. The circumstances as I have described them lead me to the conclusion that the contribution should be total, not partial.

［116］For these reasons I find it just and equitable that STH should pay the whole of Lewis's claim.

Determination of the amount of Lewis's claim under s 307

［117］To quantify the extent to which STH is required to contribute, it is necessary to determine the amount of Lewis's claim against Stube in the liquidation. Section 307 of the Act provides:

(1) If a claim is subject to a contingency, or is for damages, or, if for some other

reason, the amount of the claim is not certain, the liquidator may—

(a) make an estimate of the amount of the claim; or

(b) refer the matter to the court for a decision on the amount of the claim.

(2) On the application of the liquidator, or of a claimant who is aggrieved by an estimate made by the liquidator, the court shall determine the amount of the claim as it sees fit.

[118] Stube's leasehold interest under the lease was disclaimed by the liquidators under s 269. The effect of a disclaimer is prescribed in s 269 (3) and (5) which provide:

(3) A disclaimer under this section—

(a) brings to an end on and from the date of the disclaimer the rights, interests, and liabilities of the company in relation to the property disclaimed:

(b) does not, except so far as necessary to release the company from a liability, affect the rights or liabilities of any other person.

...

(5) A person suffering loss or damage as a result of a disclaimer under this section may—

(a) claim as a creditor of the company for the amount of the loss or damage, taking account of the effect of an order made by the court under paragraph (b):

(b) apply to the Court for an order that the disclaimed property be delivered to or vested in that person.

以下 [119] – [123] 略

[124] In discussing the normal measure of damages arising from a disclaimer of the lease, Lord Hobhouse said: [1]

After the disclaimer the right to rent is lost. There is only a right to compensation. That involves a comparison between the pre–disclaimer and post–disclaimer positions. For material purposes this difference is the aggregate of the differences between

---

[1] *At* 181.

the contractual rent and the market rent over the period of the remainder of the lease discounted to allow for advancement. …

[125] To similar effect, Lord Millett said: [1]

This gives the landlord an immediate right to prove for the loss or damage which he has sustained in consequence of the operation of the disclaimer, that is to say in consequence of the determination of the lease and the acceleration of the reversion. This is normally measured by reference to the difference between the rents and other payments which the landlord would have received in future but for the disclaimer and the rents and other sums which the disclaimer will enable him to receive by reletting. But the subject matter of the landlord's proof is compensation for loss of his right, inter alia, to future rent, not the rent itself, to which he no longer has any claim. The amount of this loss has to be assessed. This involves giving credit for the receipts which the disclaimer will enable him to obtain by reletting. …

[126] In calculating damages, allowance must be made for the fact that the damages will be payable earlier than the rental would have been payable under the lease. As Lord Hobhouse said: [2]

Any award of damages involves arriving at a single monetary figure which in present terms quantifies that loss. Where the loss will be suffered over a period in the future, the computation will have to make allowance for any advancement that has occurred (e. g. *Overstone Ltd. v. Shipway* [1962] 1 W. L. R. 117). To fail to take into account the element of advancement leads to an over-compensation of the claimant.

…

… Making an adjustment for the element of advancement is an essential ingredient in the quantification of the compensation.

[127] On this point Lord Millett said: [3]

There is no justification for employing a different approach in the assessment of

---

[1] At 183~184.

[2] At 180 and 181.

[3] At 184.

compensation for such damage than would be employed if the claimant were claiming damages for breach of a contract which had been wrongfully terminated. In assessing damages in such a case, however, allowance would have to be made for accelerated receipt of any sums which had not fallen due at the date of breach (and which the contract did not make immediately due and payable in the event of breach). An award of compensation which failed to take this into account would over-compensate the claimant.

[128] The starting point is therefore that the prima facie measure of Lewis's loss is the difference between the present value of the rent until 2030, less the amount which Lewis could have obtained, in June 2013, if it had let the property on similar terms, that is, a perpetually renewable ground lease.

以下 [129] – [138] 略

[139] A future cash flow might be derived from the land in one or other of three broad ways:

(a) by leasing the land;

(b) by developing the land and earning a return on the development; or

(c) by selling the land and investing the proceeds in some other income earning asset.

以下 [140] – [144] 略

[145] My comments about the appropriate means of calculating the quantum of Lewis's claim in the liquidation, under s 307 of the Act, are intended as guidance to the parties on the issues which require further consideration. They are not firm views, and are not intended to limit or define the scope of the further inquiry which is needed.

Result

[146] I order under s 271, that STH pay to the liquidator the whole of Lewis's claim in the liquidation of Stube. The quantum of that claim is to be determined following a further hearing.

[147] Costs on both applications are reserved for determination after the further hearing.

"A D MacKenzie J"

上诉法院判决书

IN THE COURT OF APPEAL
OF NEW ZEALAND

CA49/2015

[2016] NZCA 366

BETWEEN	STEEL & TUBE HOLDINGS LIMITED
	Appellant
AND	LEWIS HOLDINGS LIMITED
	First Respondent
	BORIS VAN DELDEN AND PERI MICAELA FINNIGAN (AS LIQUIDATORS OF STUBE INDUSTRIES LIMITED)
	Second Respondents

Hearing:	20 April 2016
Court:	Harrison, Wild and Kós JJ
Counsel:	D Chisholm QC and P Niven for Apppellant
	K Crossland and J S Langston for Respondents
Judgment:	1 August 2016 at 3 pm

JUDGMENT OF THE COURT

A   The appeal is dismissed.

B The appellant must pay the respondents' costs for a standard appeal on a band A basis, together with usual disbursements.

REASONS OF THE COURT
(Given by Kós J)

STEEL & TUBE HOLDINGS LIMITED v. LEWIS HOLDINGS LIMITED [2016] NZCA 366 [1 August 2016]

[1] When should a parent company that has put its subsidiary into liquidation nonetheless be liable to the subsidiary's creditors?

[2] The appellant Steel & Tube Holdings Ltd (STH) is parent to a group of companies. One wholly owned subsidiary is Stube Industries Ltd (Stube).

[3] Stube is the lessee of industrial land at Mount Wellington from the first respondent lessor, Lewis Holdings Ltd (Lewis).

[4] In 2013 STH put Stube into liquidation by shareholder's resolution. The liquidators disclaimed the lease as an onerous property.

[5] Lewis then claimed from the liquidators damages consequent on disclaimer of the lease and sought an order under s 271 (1) (a) of the Companies Act 1993 (the Act) that STH pay those damages as a company related to Stube.

[6] In the High Court, MacKenzie J made such an order, finding it just and equitable that STH pay the whole amount of Lewis's claim. [1]

[7] STH appeals against the order that it is liable to pay Lewis's claim.

Factual background

以下 [8] – [19] 略

[20] Lewis then claimed from the liquidators for the loss of the right to future rent under the lease, and sought orders under s 271.

---

[1] *Lewis Holdings Ltd v. Steel & Tube Holdings Lte* [2014] NZHC 331, [2015] 2 NILR 831 [High Court decision].

Section 271 of the Act

［21］It is convenient at this point to explain the role of s 271. Section 271 creates an exception to the general principle that a subsidiary company is a legal entity separate from its parent. ［1］ It allows the High Court to order the parent company to pay claims made against the subsidiary in liquidation.

［22］The predecessor to s 271 was introduced by the Companies Amendment Act 1980, following a recommendation of the 1973 Report of the Special Committee to Review the Companies Act (the Macarthur Report). ［2］The Committee was concerned that at least two well-known public companies had recently abandoned subsidiaries. It considered it was inequitable for a holding company to be able to benefit from losses of a subsidiary in structuring its tax affairs but then be able to walk away from the subsidiary and leave creditors with unpaid debts. It considered this inequity could be remedied by giving the High Court power to order the holding company to meet claims by the subsidiary's creditors. ［3］

［23］Section 271 provides:

271 Pooling of assets of related companies

(1) On the application of the liquidator, or a creditor or shareholder, the court, if satisfied that it is just and equitable to do so, may order that—

(a) a company that is, or has been, related to the company in liquidation must pay to the liquidator the whole or part of any or all of the claims made in the liquidation;

(b) where two or more related companies are in liquidation, the liquidations in respect of each company must proceed together as if they were one company to the extent that the court so orders and subject to such terms and conditions as the court may impose.

---

［1］　*Salomon v. A Salomon & Co Ltd* ［1987］AC 22 (HL); *Lee v. Lee's Air Farming Ltd* ［1961］NZLR 325 (PC); Companies Act 1993, s 15.

［2］　*Final Report of the Special Committee to Review the Companies Act* (March 1973).

［3］　At 159-160.

(2) The court may make such other order or give such directions to facilitate giving effect to an order under subsection (1) as it thinks fit.

(3) This section is subject to section 139 (4) of the Reserve Bank of New Zealand Act 1989.

[24] The order in this case was made under s 271 (1)(a). Section 271 (1) (b) addresses the different situation where related companies are both in liquidation.

[25] STH is a company "related to" Stube because it owns all the shares in Stube. [1]

[26] The issue for the High Court was whether it was just and equitable to order STH to pay Lewis's claim against Stube. Section 272 provides guidance on that issue:

272 Guidelines for orders

(1) In deciding whether it is just and equitable to make an order under section 271 (1)(a), the court must have regard to the following matters:

(a) the extent to which the related company took part in the management of the company in liquidation;

(b) the conduct of the related company towards the creditors of the company in liquidation;

(c) the extent to which the circumstances that gave rise to the liquidation of the company are attributable to the actions of the related company;

(d) such other matters as the court thinks fit.

(2) In deciding whether it is just and equitable to make an order under section 271 (1)(b), the court must have regard to the following matters:

(a) the extent to which any of the companies took part in the management of any of the other companies;

(b) the conduct of any of the companies towards the creditors of any of the other companies;

(c) the extent to which the circumstances that gave rise to the liquidation of any

---

[1] Companies Act, s 2 (3)(b).

of the companies are attributable to the actions of any of the other companies;

(d) the extent to which the businesses of the companies have been combined;

(e) such other matters as the court thinks fit.

(3) The fact that creditors of a company in liquidation relied on the fact that another company is, or was, related to it is not a ground for making an order under section 271.

[27] We agree with MacKenzie J's observation that s 271 requires the Court to balance two policy considerations. First, respect for the separate corporate identity of the company in liquidation. Second, avoiding the mischief that can result from an overly strict application of separate corporate identity. [1] We also agree with the Judge that it is inherent in the rationale of separate legal identity that the subsidiary company will be a separate commercial entity. As MacKenzie J put it: [2]

Its business will be conducted in such a way that the company is not a mere "front" for a business actually carried on by others. The "corporate veil" shields the substance of the company and its business from the shareholders who own the company. It does not, if the company is a mere façade, shield that façade from the operators of the business which is carried on in its name.

High Court decision

[28] The Judge undertook a detailed factual assessment of the case before him in terms of the four guidelines in s 272 (1), namely:

(a) the extent to which STH took part in the management of Stube;

(b) the conduct of STH towards Lewis as creditor of Stube;

(c) the extent to which the liquidation of Stube is attributable to STH; and

(d) other matters as the Court thinks fit.

The extent to which STH took part in the management of Stube

以下 [29] – [32] 略

[33] Overall, the Judge considered there to be no evidence of the independent

---

[1] High Court decision, above n 1, at [19].

[2] At [20].

exercise of management of Stube. Stube was a puppet of STH's, devoid of capacity to conduct its own affairs. [1]

Conduct of STH towards Lewis as creditor of Stube

[34] The Judge found STH's conduct was such to indicate to Lewis that STH stood behind Stube and was taking responsibility for the leased property. [2] [黑体字由编者加]

以下 [35] – [39] 略

Other factors as the Court thinks fit

[40] The Judge considered a number of other factors in his overall assessment. Two are relevant to this appeal.

[41] First, the Judge said that STH as a publicly listed company ought to have known better. Its failure to ensure the legal requirements applying to Stube's separate legal identity could not readily be ignored or excused. [3]

[42] Secondly, he rejected a suggestion that the absence of a guarantee by STH to Lewis was a factor weighing against making an order. An order under s 271 is not a-nalogous to a parent guarantee because Lewis will only obtain damages for disclaimer of the lease, not necessarily full rental for the remainder of the 21 – year term of the lease. [4]

Result

[43] In light of the matters under s 272 (1), the Judge said it was just and equitable to make an order under s 271 (1)(a). The order was for the total amount of Lewis's claim for damages against Stube. STH's role in the management of Stube was total; accordingly the Judge refused to make any proportionate reduction. [5]

---

[1] At [65].

[2] At [71].

[3] At [94].

[4] At [103].

[5] At [115].

[44] The Judge was unable to reach a view as to the quantum of the claim at the time of assessment of liability. In a subsequent judgment he quantified damages at $750 000 based on the period of time Lewis was likely to be deprived of rental income. [1]

Issues on appeal

[45] For STH Mr Chisholm QC raised the following issues in oral and written submissions:

(a) Did STH's conduct cause any loss to Lewis, and if so, should the absence of causation or detrimental reliance by Lewis tell against an order?

(b) Was STH's conduct disentitling?

(c) Was STH a net contributor to Stube prior to liquidation and, if so, should that weigh in its favour?

(d) Should responsibility for actions taken by Stube's directors be attributed to STH?

(e) Did the Judge err in considering the extent to which the businesses were combined?

(f) Did the Judge err in considering STH's status as a publicly listed company?

(g) In determining that STH was to pay 100 per cent of Lewis's claim, did the Judge ignore relevant factors?

[46] We will address these issues in turn.

Did STH's conduct cause any loss to Lewis, and if so, should the absence of causation or detrimental reliance by Lewis tell against an order?

[47] Mr Chisholm focussed on this issue in his oral submissions. He submitted that STH did not cause Lewis loss in any relevant sense. In the "but for" scenario where STH meticulously ensured Stube was treated as a separate legal entity, the mistaken renewal would still have occurred and Lewis would be in the same position of having a lessee without any income. If the renewal had not occurred, then Lewis would

---

[1] *Lewis Holdings Ltd v. Steel & Tube Holdings Ltd* [2015] NZHC 2189 at [101].

have been worse off, not better off, because the still contaminated land would have been difficult to market to a new lessee. So Lewis did not suffer any loss caused by STH.

[48] As a separate but related submission, Mr Chisholm submitted Lewis had not detrimentally relied on STH's conduct. He suggested the Judge did not complete the estoppel-type analysis we have referred to at [34] above. Lewis did not detrimentally rely on STH's conduct because the nature of a perpetual lease is such that Lewis could not have taken any action to alter its position.

[49] When pressed by the Court where in the Act the concepts of causation and detrimental reliance come from, Mr Chisholm pointed to the reference in s 272 (1)(c) to whether the circumstances giving rise to the liquidation are attributable to the parent company's actions. [1] He also suggested it could not be just and equitable to make an order in the absence of causation given legal and equitable causes of action are generally premised on some wrongful or disentitling conduct causing loss.

[50] We accept it is difficult to say Lewis detrimentally relied on STH's conduct. STH represented by ongoing conduct that it stood behind Stube and would pay the rental. But if it had not, Lewis would likely have been in the same position of having to hope that someone (STH or Stube) paid the rent as it fell due. The risk that the lessor takes in a perpetual lease is that the creditworthiness and solvency of the lessee may vary over time. The fact a lessee is in financial difficulty is not grounds justifying cancellation of the lease in the absence of persisting non-payment. [2] In short, Lewis could not have altered its position in reliance on STH's conduct — it was stuck with the perpetual lease.

[51] The question whether STH's breaches of the Act in failing to distinguish between itself and Stube caused loss to Lewis is more complex. It is speculative whether Stube would also have renewed by mistake if STH had been meticulous in differentiating itself from Stube. It is also difficult to assess whether Lewis would have

---

[1] Reference was also made to s 301 of the Act, but we do not see it offering any assistance on this issue.

[2] Property Law Act 2007, s 245 (1).

been worse off had Stube given notice that it did not wish to renew the lease in 2009. Regardless of when the lease ended, Lewis would have been left with a non-income producing block of land, requiring considerable development to become income producing. In the absence of a finding by MacKenzie J as to whether Lewis suffered loss, [1] we are not ourselves prepared to reach a conclusion on causation. That is because it is unnecessary in any event to do so.

[52] Even if we assume that causation and detrimental reliance are absent here, we do not consider that to be determinative of whether a s 271 (1)(a) order should be made.

[53] First, the Macarthur Report contemplated exactly this sort of situation of a parent abandoning its subsidiary when recommending the Court be given the power contained in s 271. STH has abandoned its subsidiary after, it seems, extracting some benefit from Stube's retained tax losses. Mr Candy gave evidence that Stube's revenue and expenses were treated as STH's for tax purposes. There is nothing in the legislative history to suggest the causation and detrimental reliance are necessary ingredients in making an order.

[54] Secondly, the language of "attributable" in s 272 (1)(c) does not import a wide-reaching causation inquiry. The section requires inquiry into whether the liquidation is attributable to STH's actions. That is a narrower and more neutral question than whether there is disentitling conduct causing damage. The Judge made a realistic finding that the liquidation was due entirely to STH's actions in withdrawing its financial support of Stube. [2] The section did not require him to go further and assess whether STH acted wrongfully in withdrawing support. Causation of loss may be a relevant aspect of conduct addressed under s 272 (1)(b), but is by no means a prerequisite for relief under s 271 (1)(a).

[55] Thirdly, we consider the Judge correctly focussed on the extent to which there was "amalgamation by conduct", under s 272 (1)(a). That was the dominant

---

[1] See High Court decision, above n 1, at [77].
[2] At [88].

factor here. The evidence analysed by the Judge shows STH was extensively involved in the management of Stube to such an extent Stube was treated no differently from any division of STH. It appears the only reason Stube was not amalgamated with STH like most of STH's other subsidiaries is that would have triggered winding up of the Healing superannuation scheme. In reality, however, Stube was treated no differently to the other subsidiaries that were amalgamated with STH. In particular, STH treated the land and lease as its own. That overwhelms the absence of causation or detrimental reliance.

Was STH's conduct disentitling?

[56] Mr Chisholm submitted the Judge erred in considering as disentitling conduct that Stube's directors had breached their duties by:

(a) agreeing to renew the lease when the directors did not believe on reasonable grounds Stube would be able to perform that obligation (s 136); and

(b) entering into a major transaction, namely renewal of the lease, without securing a shareholder's resolution (s 129).

He said the directors did not breach these duties because the lease was renewed by deeming provision, not by agreement of the directors. The directors had instructed the relevant company officer that the lease was not to be renewed. Further, the directors did not breach their duty in s 136 because they could rely on the reasonable expectation of ongoing shareholder support from STH.

[57] It is important to consider the Judge's finding of breaches of ss 129 and 136 in context. In assessing STH's conduct towards Lewis as a creditor of Stube, the Judge said:[1]

>[83] … *s 271 is not limited to situations where there has been a deprivation of assets from the company in liquidation. There may be other disentitling circumstances. I consider that STH's actions in relation to the lease fall within that description.*

>[84] *Stube had for many years been unable to pay the rent without STH's support. It had no legally enforceable arrangements for support. If the directors of Stube*

---

[1] 以下 [83] ~ [85] 引用的是一审高等法院的判决。

*had consciously entered into a contract to renew the lease, they would have been in-
curring an obligation, which the directors could not have had reasonable grounds to
believe Stube would be able to perform from its own resources or by recourse to
legally enforceable financial arrangements, as required by s 136 of the
Act. Furthermore, the renewal of the lease was a major transaction which should not
have been entered into unless approved by a special resolution, under s 129 of the
Act. STH, as shareholder, did not pass a resolution authorising the transaction. Nor
did it take any steps to put in place legally enforceable funding arrangements to enable Stube to meet its obligations. Sections 129 and 136 apply to a transaction deliberately entered into. They do not cease to apply, even if I was to accept the proposition that the renewal was the result of a mistake by Stube.*

[85] *STH and the directors of Stube did not comply with those provisions, and
STH continued to pay the rent. Its conduct towards Lewis in relation to the renewal
was such as would reasonably lead Lewis to believe that Stube was not treated as a
legal entity distinct from STH. That conduct is directly relevant to s 271 (1)(b).
It weighs in favour of an order.*

[58] On our reading of this passage, whether there was a breach of ss 129 or 136
was neither here nor there. The essential reasoning is captured in the final three sen-
tences of [85]. STH's actions in relation to the renewal of the lease indicated to Lewis
that Stube was not treated as a separate legal entity. That conclusion does not depend
on there being a breach of ss 129 and 136. Section 271 does not refer to pejorative concepts such as "disentitling conduct". The presence of such elements may weigh in favour of an order, but their absence does not positively point in the other direction. That
would be an unjustified gloss on the criterion of "just and equitable".

**Was STH a net contributor to Stube prior to liquidation and, if so, should
that weigh in its favour?**

[59] In written submissions, Mr Chisholm said STH was a net contributor to
Stube prior to liquidation by paying rent to Lewis and for the remediation. He said the
Judge erred in finding those contributions may have been offset by STH's earlier deci-

sion to remove Stube's sources of income when it ended the Healing brand.

[60] We do not consider that the payment of remediation costs or rent should weigh in STH's favour.

[61] Mr Joubert, one of STH's company solicitors, gave evidence that STH paid the remediation for its own reasons, not solely out of charity to Stube. STH was concerned that it may be found liable to pay the remediation as the polluter. It was concerned also about the negative publicity that might follow if it left a contaminated site.

[62] As to the rent paid, we accept the Judge's finding that STH made these payments to keep alive the lease and the option of developing the land for its own commercial benefit. [1] It cannot be said there was no benefit to STH when retaining the lease may have been in its favour had it found a method for extracting value.

[63] Accordingly these financial contributions do not weigh in STH's favour. Rather, the payment of rent supports the Judge's conclusion that STH was extensively involved in the management of Stube and undertook a de facto amalgamation. STH sought to extract value by treating Stube's asset as its own.

Should responsibility for actions taken by Stube's directors be attributed to STH?

[64] Mr Chisholm submitted the conduct of Messrs Calavrias and Candy should not be attributed to STH. STH owed no duty to take reasonable care that Stube's directors discharged their duties to Stube and so cannot be liable for the directors failing to adequately distinguish between Stube and STH.

[65] We consider this requires an artificial approach to the attribution of responsibility in light of the policy of s 271. As we have indicated, it is not necessary to focus on disentitling conduct or breaches of director's duties. The language, for example, of s 272 (1) (a) requires consideration of the extent to which STH has taken part in the management of Stube. That mandates a detailed consideration of in what capacity the relevant persons were acting, rather than a focus on whether those persons were acting

---

[1] At [58] – [60].

in a disentitling manner. The Judge's assessment correctly focussed on the failure by Messrs Calavrias and Candy to distinguish between their role as directors of Stube and as chief executive officer and chief financial officer of STH. [1]

Did the Judge err in considering the extent to which the businesses were combined?

[66] Mr Chisholm submitted the extent to which the businesses were combined was not relevant to whether an order should be made under s 271 (1)(a). That factor is expressly stated as relevant to an order under s 271 (1)(b), so by implication must be excluded from consideration in s 271 (1)(a) cases.

[67] We reject this submission. The Judge's consideration of the extent to which the businesses were combined was entwined with his analysis of STH's involvement in the management of Stube. It would be artificial to separate those inquiries. In cases where a parent is involved in the management of a subsidiary, there will inevitably be some combination of businesses.

Did the Judge err in considering STH's status as a publicly listed company?

[68] Mr Chisholm submitted the Judge erred in relying on STH's status as a publicly listed company in concluding its ignorance of the requirements of separate legal personal cannot be readily excused. The listing rules for the New Zealand Stock Exchange do not impose any relevant obligations on STH in terms of maintaining separate corporate personality.

[69] We do not consider the Judge attached undue significance to STH's status as a publicly listed company. His point simply was that a company economically significant enough to be listed on the stock exchange ought to be aware of the obligation on all groups of companies (listed or otherwise) to structure their affairs in accordance with the principle of separate corporate personality. That must affect whether it is just and equitable to make orders under s 271.

In determining that STH was to pay 100 per cent of Lewis's claim, did the Judge

---

[1] At [58] – [60].

ignore relevant factors?

[70] Mr Chisholm submitted the Judge's analysis of the proportion of Lewis's claim STH was to pay was not thoroughly considered. The Judge should have rebated the proportion to a nominal level because:

(a) STH did not cause Lewis's loss by disentitling conduct;

(b) STH had a low level of culpability for the position Lewis is in;

(c) Lewis did not seek a parent guarantee from STH; and

(d) STH contributed to Stube by paying rent and for the remediation.

[71] This aspect of the appeal is an appeal against the exercise of discretion. Once the Judge was satisfied that it was "just and equitable" to make an order, he had a discretion to order STH to pay "the whole or part of" Lewis's claim. Accordingly, our focus is on whether the Judge has proceeded on an error of principle, has failed to consider a relevancy, has considered an irrelevancy, or is plainly wrong. [1]

[72] We do not consider the Judge erred in not considering the matters to which Mr Chisholm referred.

[73] First, the absence of causation or detrimental reliance by Lewis is not a significant factor in this case. The decisive factors here are the total extent to which Stube was absorbed into STH without consideration given to its separate corporate personality, and the ongoing representations by STH to Lewis that it stood behind and supported Stube.

[74] Secondly, as we have already explained, s 271 is not focussed on disentitling conduct. [2] It is about what is just and equitable as between the parent company and the subsidiary's creditors. An absence of culpability by STH does not necessarily justify a rebated position. But here STH's consistent failure to comply with the requirements of the Act to treat Stube as a separate legal and corporate entity justified the Judge's adverse culpability assessment.

[75] Thirdly, in terms of culpability it may have been appropriate to reduce the proportion if there were evidence Lewis had some responsibility for its loss. This is not

---

[1] *May v. May* (1982) 1 NZFLR 165 (CA) at 170.

[2] See above at [54].

such a case, however. Lewis did not fail to take any step that would have diminished its loss. And the Judge found Lewis did not act unreasonably as lessor. [1]

No attempt has been made to challenge that finding.

[76] Fourthly, the failure by Lewis to seek a parent guarantee is not relevant. Patently s 271 orders are likely to be sought and made in the absence of such guarantee. Mr Chisholm's submission would lead in effect to an automatic discount in the absence of a parent guarantee. That cannot have been the legislature's intention.

[77] Finally, as we have indicated above, STH's contributions in paying the rent and for the remediation were for its own benefit and are neutral in the assessment of what is just and equitable. [2] They must equally be neutral in considering what proportion an order should be for.

[78] We therefore agree with MacKenzie J's order that STH pay the full amount of Lewis's claim. The Judge's analysis was entirely appropriate given the total extent of STH's involvement in the management of Stube, and the de facto amalgamation that had occurred.

Result

[79] None of the grounds of appeal has persuaded us that it was not just and equitable to make an order under s 271 (1)(a) and for the full amount of Lewis's claim.

[80] Accordingly, the appeal is dismissed.

[81] The appellant must pay the respondents' costs for a standard appeal on a band A basis, together with usual disbursements.

Solicitors

Buddle Findlay, Wellington for Appellant

Shieff Angland, Auckland for Respondents

---

[1] High Court decision, above n 1, at [98].

[2] See above at [60]~[63].

案例三　诗人顾城之子监护权案

案　名

新西兰高等法院：Powell v. Duncan，1996 年 8 月 8 日

导 读

"黑夜给了我黑色的眼睛，我却用它寻找光明。"诗人顾城 1979 年写下的这行诗，为一代人传颂。诸多对顾城的介绍大抵从诗的角度，也都离不开这行诗。1999 年 10 月 9 日《新西兰先驱报》发表纪念文章，也围绕"黑色"展开，但是从完全相反的角度，标题为"Dark night, dark mind"[1]。不知怎么翻译才确切，比较客气的译法是"黑夜、黑心境"。大多不客气的英文文章则充满"谋杀""自杀""三角恋""精神折磨"等字眼。

这里介绍的是鲜见的一则关于顾城之子监护权的新西兰高等法院判决。顾城之子监护权案不但渐渐为人所忘，甚至原本就不太为人所知。

顾城、谢烨夫妇 1987 年来到新西兰，一开始在奥克兰大学教中文，他们的儿子"S"[2] 1988 年出生。他们住在离奥克兰市中心 20 多公里的一个叫做 Waiheke Island 的岛上。一般人称这个美如梦境的岛为"激流岛"，但它的英文原文为"cascading waters"——因此很多人将其译作"细流岛"。但据"野史"，这名字也算阴差阳错。岛的名字应该是"Te Motu Arai Roa"，一个毛利名字，因为毛利部落在这里居住逾千年。19 世纪中叶一群欧裔白人到岛上核对地图上的地名，问溪边一位垂钓的毛利人这个岛叫什么，答曰"细流"。于是地图上就将这个岛标为"细流岛"。其实"细流"者溪流也，正是那位毛利老兄钓鱼的地方，而不是全岛的名字。当然，"激流岛"是不是"细流岛"的口误，不得而知。只是近些年有一些华人将"激流岛"称作"顾城岛"，这是很难为本地人所接受的。当然，许多来自中国的游客常把这个岛当做一个游览项目，也有不少人专门去寻找顾城生前住过的小屋，在此凭吊一番。

回到本案，这是从初审"家庭婚姻"法庭上诉到高等法院的一个上诉案

---

〔1〕 "Dark night, dark mind" by Helene Wong, Weekend Herald, October 9~10, 1999 J3.
〔2〕 沿用新西兰家庭婚姻法案件汇编的习惯只用简称。主要是考虑到这类案件的敏感程度和个人隐私，尤其涉及未成年人。

例。按理说接受上诉的高等法院只就法律问题作出裁决。但是因为当事人各方各执一词，高等法院法官决定从头审起，于是调出所有的原始档案。

因为只是导读，在此不赘述。要注意的要点如下：

第一，法官对本案涉及的人物和背景做了陈述，并表示顾城是一位知名诗人，顾城的妻子谢烨[1]也是一位为人知晓的作家。他们育有一子，简称"S"。S的福祉（即生存保障、生活质量、文化传承及幸福指数等）为本案考量的唯一要件。

第二，本案中的当事人为（1）孩子的最初抚养人（领养人）Powell（音译为"鲍维尔"）和（2）孩子父母出事后暂时获得领养权的 Duncan（音译为"当肯"）夫妇。这两位都是"洋人"，目前判决书有两个版本，一个是 Powell v. Duncan，另一个简称为 P v. D。当肯是顾城姐姐顾乡的丈夫，也就是顾城的姐夫、孩子的洋姑父。顾城夫妇均为中国国籍，孩子出生后一年左右，顾城夫妇将孩子寄养在鲍维尔家，顾城夫妇双双离去时，孩子才5岁，也就是孩子5岁之前有4年左右的时间是在鲍维尔家度过的，和鲍维尔家建立了很深的情感纽带。在当肯申请监护权时，孩子的舅舅（即谢烨的弟弟），也申请监护权，但不在本案考量之列。

第三，初审庭（家庭婚姻法庭）将监护权判给孩子的姑姑和姑父（即本案中的"当肯"），家庭氛围和文化传承是主要依据，但依法庭程序而出具的孩子心理报告显示，根据判令而改变的监护权，使孩子从一个熟悉的环境来到一个虽有一定血缘关系却无感情纽带的相对陌生的家庭（姑姑家），使孩子的身心倍受打击——这是高等法院受理此案并对初审法庭判决提出质疑的主要原因。

第四，高等法院法官一改常态，不是就上诉案件的法律（理）层面进行考量，而是"to determine the matter de novo"——就基本事实和提供给初审庭的证据重新开始、从头来过。高等法院指出初审法庭两个程序性的问题：（1）改变孩子监护权有争议性，鲍维尔上诉前申请将新的监护权暂缓执行未获法庭支持——这一点违背同类案件的判例，是错误的。（2）根据《新西兰监护人法》有一项针对孩子心理状况由心理学专业人士出具的报告（即俗称的"第29条心

---

[1]　判决里按她的姓名依英文顺序简称为"Y"。

理报告"），初审法庭在处理该报告时程序失当。

第五，高等法院法官强调孩子的福祉为考量监护权第一要件。1995 年的 D
v. W 判例[1]提供了考核孩子福祉的一份清单和基本要点，主要包括：与领养
家庭之间现有和未来的情感纽带；领养父母的态度和能力；和孩子相处的能动
性与质量；家庭环境及稳定性、安全性；领养父母行为榜样程度；（与监护家庭
相关的亲、友）大家庭环境对孩子的正面或负面影响；对孩子提供的教育机会；
孩子的主观意愿，等等。法官又依据另两则判例[2]综合得出结论，即物质生
活虽然重要，但还是第二位。第一位则是孩子的精神因素以及与领养父母之间
的亲情纽带。

高等法院判定："将孩子还给鲍维尔。"

这里需要补充几点：

第一，法官将顾城描述为"革命诗人、性情不定"（a revolutionary poet of
unstable temperament），尽管孩子的母亲性情稳定，但父母关系不睦是显然的，
并且父亲时而会对孩子"动粗"——法官表示接受这类证据[3]。相比而言，
鲍维尔夫妇对孩子体贴有加。鲍维尔先生是英裔，从事海员职业，出海一段时
间但在家也待很长时间。鲍维尔太太则有萨摩亚和华人血统，法官称其为"具
备所有太平洋岛裔母亲的坚韧"。两人膝下有一孙女（比 S 大），与 S 相处甚
好。从 S 在学校拍的照片看，他很适应养父母给他提供的生活和教育环境。

第二，选择鲍维尔来照顾孩子是顾城夫妇做的决定（最初的出发点可能是
顾城夫妇出国讲学、写作时，希望给孩子找一个稳定的生活环境），并且由律师
起草了正式的协议。

第三，顾城的姐姐向法庭表示希望以"华人方式"来抚养 S。她的丈夫当
肯是一位渔业专家、环保人士；她自己自然是中文流利并通英文。他们的孩子
比 S 年长，可充当兄长角色。但法官也注意到谢烨的弟弟也有意申请监护权。
他在中国获得财经方面的大学学位，夫妇皆为华人。虽然有意申请监护权，但
经过法庭取证和讨论，谢烨的弟弟认为维持鲍维尔夫妇现有的监护权对孩子的

---

[1]　D v. W（1995）13 FRNZ 336.

[2]　Walker v. Walker 9/4/81，Hardie Boys J, HC Christchurch D 326/80 和 C v. C [1995] NZFLR 562.

[3]　参见判决书 The merits 部分第 5 段。

身心最有利，并表示可以在中文（语言、文化、社区）方面尽自己的一份力量。

因为是导读，尽量不展开，而由读者自己通过阅读高等法院的判决来体会——这也是附录部分将判决书全文登出的主要功能。华人传统理念中的"血浓于水"，在西方法律上是有不同层面考量的。

高等法院判决书

P v. D

High Court, Auckland (HC35/96)   8-12, 17, 18
July; HammondJ   8 August 1996

Custody—Cultural concerns—Child of Chinese nationals living with foster family—Foster parents highly suited and child had bonded with them—Family Court awarded father's sister and her husband custody of child after parents'death as providing more "culturally appropriate" care—Child traumatised by custody change—Child's uncle supportedfoster parents' claim and prepared to provide cultural heritage—Culturalfactors important—Psychological welfare of child overrides any more abstract concerns—Guardianship Act 1968, ss 23 (2), 29A.

S was the son of G and Y, Chinese nationals who had settled in New Zealand. For 4 years until the age of 5, S's parents entrusted the Ps with his upbringing. He was very happy living with the Ps, and bonded very deeply with them. When S was 5 years old both his parents died in violent circumstances. He continued to live with the Ps until X, his aunt, and her husband, D, applied for custody. S's uncle, Z, his mother's brother, had also sought custody. The Family Court granted custody to the Ds on the basis that, while there was nothing wrong with the care offered by the Ps, S's best interests lay in a home environment where his heritage and cultural background would receive greater support. Accordingly S was removed from the Ps' home.

The Court-appointed psychologist had substantial reservations about S's removal. Her evidence was that S suffered from psychological disablement and was at significant psychological risk. Between the time of the Family Court decision and the hearing of the appeal, Z had altered his earlier views. He now supported the Ps in their custody application and offered to provide assistance from himself and the Chinese community for S on cultural matters.

Held, ordering S's return to the Ps' custody:

(1) The first and paramount consideration must be the welfare of the child. In reaching its decision, the Court must have regard to all appropriate factors relating to a child's welfare. Foremost among those factors are the particular psychological needs of the particular child, with cultural factors also featuring significantly. Material considerations are of secondary importance. As cultural factors are viewed within the general welfare context, psychological health will take precedence over more abstract cultural concerns. Without diminishing the breadth of the inquiry undertaken, there must also be very real caution in upsetting settled, quality care. (p 474, line 38; p 475, line 43; p 476, line 7; p 476, line 27; p 478, line 30)

Brown v. *Brown* (1987) 2 FRNZ 355 (HC)

C v. *C* [1995] NZFLR 562 (HC)

D v. *W* (1995) 13 FRNZ 336

Walker v. *Walker* unreported, Hardie Boys J, 8 April 1981, HC Christchurch D326/80, noted [1981] NZ Recent Law 257 considered.

(2) Applying these principles to the present case, S must return to the care of the Ps. Distinct separation from the Ds was necessary for a respectable period of time. A mediated approach was not realistic given S's psychological problems. The need for a distinct separation required a consideration of the comparative merits of the respective domestic arrangements. On a psychological level it was clear that S's needs would be better met in the P household. Further, his cultural needs could also be met in that household with the assistance of his uncle Z, while the Ps provided a materially better home life, although this was of less importance. (p 479, line 44; p 480, line 9; p

482, line 6; p 482, line 32)

Obiter, (1) it was difficult to understand why the Family Court Judge refused to grant a stay of execution of the judgment pending the appeal, especially when no reasons were given. The normal approach for the Court is that it is inappropriate to disturb the status quo pending an appeal. A decision to remove the child from quality care, for essentially cultural reasons, to where that removal had significant risks, was highly controversial. Refusing the stay was pre-emptive and caused psychological difficulties for the child. (p 473, line 22)

(2) Common sense suggests that when a custody appeal is lodged the parties should obtain clear directions as to the manner in which (if at all) they are to procure reports on the child and how (if at all) interviews are to be conducted. In this case, the usual restrictive direction was given, but was not followed. The tense situation that resulted had disturbed S to the point where it was inappropriate for the Court to consider seeing the child, notwithstanding the statutory injunction that the Court "shall ascertain the wishes of the child" in s 23 (2) Guardianship Act 1968. (p 473, line 34)

Statutes and regulations referred to

Guardianship Act 1968, ss 23 (2), 29A

Cases referred to

Brown v. *Brown* (1987) 2 FRNZ 355 (HC)

C v. *C* [1995] NZFLR 562 (HC)

C v. *R* (1994) 12 FRNZ 291; [1994] NZFLR 778 (HC)

D v. *W* (1995) 13 FRNZ 336

Walker v. *Walker* unreported, 8 April 1981, Hardie Boys J, HC Christchurch D326/80, noted [1981] NZ Recent Law 257

Texts referred to

Caldwell, J "The Limits of Section 29A Reports in Custody Hearings" (1995) *Butterworths Family Law Journal* 188

Seymour, F and McDowell, H "The Realistic Role of Psychological Reports in Custody/Access Disputes" (1996) *Butterworths Family Law Journal* 35

Appeal

This was an appeal against a change of custody decision in the Family Court.

T Wood for appellants

M Rawnsley for first respondents

R von Keissenberg for second respondents

K Willoughby for child

HAMMOND J (reserved):

Introduction

This is an appeal from the Family Court in a difficult custody case.

G was a respected–though tormented–Chinese poet. Born in China, he spent some years during the cultural revolution in a labour camp. Ultimately, he was allowed to leave China. He moved to New Zealand with his wife Y, who was also a recognised writer. They had an infant son, ["S"] . It is his welfare that is the only issue in these proceedings.

The parties resided on .... G wrote and lectured in New Zealand and elsewhere. Relations between G and his wife were unhappy. For that, and other reasons, from an early age S (then aged about 18 months) was placed in the care of the appellants ("the Ps"), He continued to reside with, and was cared for, by them.

In September 1993 G, then clearly unstable, violently attacked his wife at the home ofthe first respondents ("the Ds"). She died in hospital. G killed himself.

The question then arose: who was to care for S? A three–way contest for custody developed between the Ps, who by then had been the caregivers for S for about four years; X (G's sister), who is married to [Mr] D; and the dead woman's brother, the second respondent, Z, at various times also contemplated or sought custody.

Without opposition, in December 1993 the Ps were given interim custody by the

Family Court. That order was made fmal in April of 1995. The Ds were given access to S. In June 1995, the Ds lodged a fresh application for custody of S, alleging that access arrangements had not been properly adhered to. That application proceeded to a defended hearing (over 4 days) in February of 1996 before a Family Court Judge. The Judge delivered a judgment on 16 February 1996. He removed S from the Ps' care, and enforced—that very day—custody in favour of the Ds. The result was that S was taken from the caregivers he had lived with for several years, and transferred to live in the very home in which his mother had been murdered.

Counsel all confirmed from the Bar that counsel for the appellants, immediately the Family Court judgment was delivered, made an oral application for a stay of execution of that judgment pending an appeal. Such was declined without reasons being given —or even, so far as I can see—a note being made. The appellants sensibly decided to press on with the merit appeal rather than contesting the refusal of a stay on appeal.

The Family Court Judge had concluded that whilst there was nothing amiss with the Ps' care, S's best interests lay in his being removed to a home where his heritage and cultural background would be better supported.

The (then) Court – appointed psychologist clearly had substantial reservations about such a removal, and told the Judge so. The (now) Court—appointed psychologist maintains that, in the result, that caution was amply justified. In her view, the transfer of custody has created such controversy amongst the adults, and has had such an impact on S, that he is suffering from present psychological disablement. The child psychologist sees S as now being even more "at risk", in psychological terms.

To further complicate what has been, in the result, a bitter and unhappy experience for all concerned—and in S's case possibly a disabling one—Z has now thrown his hand in with the Ps. He now says the original Family Court decision was wrong; and that custody should be with the Ps, with assistance from himself and the Chinese community for S on cultural matters. So both the appellants and the second respondent seek to overturn the Family Court decision.

Process

This is an appeal. But I am required to determine the matter de novo. Hence, an the affidavits in the Family Court have been brought forward; as has the record of the viva voce evidence in that Court; voluminous further affidavits have been filed; and there was extensive cross−examination on them. Despite the endeavours of this Court to keep matters to essentials, a 3−day fixture inexorably marched to a 7−day conclusion. On several occasions the Court had to intervene to try and keep the hearing to the more focused and forward−looking inquiry which is the central issue in the case: what is to be done now, and for the foreseeable future, with respect to S's wellbeing?

There are two procedural points which have occasioned this Court a good deal. of concern. The first is that the Court cannot understand why a stay was not granted in this case. Some of the authorities on a stay were considered in C v. R (1994) 12 FRNZ 291, 295−296; [1994] NZFLR 778, 781−782. It was there noted that a Court will normally start from the proposition that disturbing the status quo pending an appeal is an inappropriate course, although that proposition is not cast in stone, and is itself an application of the central and overriding principle that it is the welfare of the child which is paramount. The Family Court decision was clearly highly controversial in re-moving (essentially for cultural reasons) a child from care which it was agreed on all sides was quality care; and which transfer had some distinct downside risks which were specifically drawn to the attention of the Family Court. The refusal of the stay was pre−emptive, and has itself created very significant difficulties.

The second point of concern is as to the handling of the report under s 29A of the Guardianship Act 1969 by the D's counsel; and the interviewing of S since the Family Court decision. Careful consideration has been given to how s 29A reports should be obtained, prepared and utilised by the Principal Family Court Judge. He was assisted by outside experts. Guidelines were then issued to operate "universally from 1 October 1995" (see (1995) Butterworths Family Law Journal 236). In passing, it would be a useful thing if those guidelines could also be reproduced in the specialist series of Family Law Reports, for ease of reference. The purpose, preparation and use of such reports have also been helpfully canvassed in Caldwell, "The Limits of Section 29A Reports in Custody Hearings" (1995) Butterworths Family Law Journal 188, and Seymour and McDowell, "The Realistic Role of Psychological Reports in Custody/Access Disputes" (1996) Butterworths Family Law Journal 35.

In this case, consequent on the appeal, Barker J made an order for a further s 29A Report. Such was procured. On 27 June 1996 Tompkins J minuted the file (HC35/96) that that Report "may be released to counsel and the parties". That minute was distributed – in those explicit terms – by a Deputy Registrar on 28 June 1996. But it is clear that the report has been distributed beyond the terms of the Court's Minute. That is quite wrong.

As 29A Report is one made to the Court. The consultant psychologist is the Court's expert. It is the Court who decides what shall happen with respect to the evidence of the consultant. Under s 29A (8) it is the Court's discretion as to whether that psychologist will even be called as a witness. It is true that the parties can tender evidence on a s 29A Report—and Mr Rawnsley rightly said that must include expert evidence—but the point here is that the prior leave of this Court must be obtained to go beyond the usual (statutory) distribution.

This last point is inevitably coupled with a concern that has arisen in this case that S is literally "interviewed out". Because of the unbearably tense situation in which he has found himself he has "closed down". So much so that the experts called before me indicated to me that it wouldbe inappropriate for the Court to even consider seeing the child itself, notwithstanding that s 23 (2) of the Act states that the Court "*shall* ascertain the wishes of the child".

I am well aware that there is a division of opinion amongst some Judges on the mandatory "shall". There are Judges who take the view that it means nothing less than seeing the child themselves. Others think such to be a statutory direction to see that the wishes of the child are ascertained in some appropriate way. I express no view on which is the correct interpretation; it is unnecessary for me to decide that point here. But what has happened in this case, and it is of the greatest concern, is that the overpursuit of S has made it imprudent for the Court to pursue what might well be a statutory imperative. Some of the parties have pre-empted the situation in a way which, with respect, is quite undesirable.

Common sense, if nothing else, suggests that it is important when a custody appeal is lodged for the parties to obtain clear and explicit directions as to the manner in which (if at all) the obtaining of reports on the child are to be procured, and how, if at all, interviews will be conducted. This is a situation in which the usual restrictive direction was given; it was not followed; and I have no doubt that the continuing uncertainty as to his position has exacerbated S's position. The point about custody decisions and appeals is that the whole exercise-process and all-has to be subordinated to the best interests of the child.

The principles to be applied

The first and paramount consideration is the welfare of the child. In reaching a decision the Court must identify and have regard to all appropriate factors going to a child's welfare. A "checklist" of "possible considerations" was suggested by Fisher J in *D* v. *W* (1995) 13 FRNZ 336. These include such things as the strength of existing and future bonding; parenting attitudes and ability; availability for, and commitment to, quality time with a child; support for continued relationships [with other parties]; security and stability of the home environment; availability and suitability of role models; positive or negative effects of a wider family group; provision for physical care and help; material welfare; stimulation and new experiences; educational opportunities; and the wishes of the child. his Honour clearly did not intend that list to be exhaustive.

This Court has consistently stressed that, generally speaking, material considerations, are secondary matters. In*Walker* v. *Walker* unreported, 9 April 1981, HC Christchurch *D*326/80, noted in [1981] NZ Recent Law 257 Hardie Boys J said;

"while material considerations have their place, they are secondary matters. More important are the stability and the security, the loving and understanding care and guidance, warm and compassionate relationships that are essential for the full develop-ment of the child's own character, personality and talents. "

And in *C* v. *C* [1995] NZFLR 562 I suggested at pp 571, 572:

"Once the straightforward matters are disposed of—particularly the social and ma-terial environments, which are easier to assess—the really critical and long-lasting is-sues in my view must surely go to the child's own psychic status and development and the likely quality of the parenting to support that development. And in assessing such the Court is inevitably—as a process—engaged in the difficult exercise of prediction.

"As to the child's own psychic status and development, the concerns here are surely as to the child's own self-perception; that child's perception of the world; and his or her ability to make effective adjustments to his or her lifestyle. This is no easy matter, and interacts closely with the social environment. This is not restricted to such obvious things as material needs but includes adequate social stimulation and ongoing relationships with other children; progressively more complex social experiences which facilitate individual maturation and development; learning to interact socially on a day to day basis with other children and adults; appreciating male and female roles, and so on. In the context of this case I think it important to remember that by and large a 'ge-netic' concept of personality development is still a foundation stone of contemporary psychological theories. That is, an individual mind to some extent always reflects past experiences. The individual mind is reflective of a feedback system, and there is a re-sponse which modifies the individual's reactions to subsequent stimuli. Pope probably caught it concisely as well as anybody with his famous line 'just as the twig is bent, the tree is inclined'.

"As to parenting, leaving aside again the more measurable things such as distinct day to day skills—attending to meals, clothing, transport, assistance with homework and the like—truly effective parents surely have the capacity to become deeply involved with their children as they provide for these daily needs? They derive deep satisfaction from vicariously living through—with their children—the various stages of development and maturation of those children as individuals in their own right. And it is surely a commonplace observation of life that effective parents must enjoy the role of parents; and what they see.

"The important point here is that it is less the external environment and tangible benefits which should be emphasised in child custody cases; rather much greater (even overwhelming) emphasis should be placed on the particular psychological needs of a given child. "

Cultural factors are obviously also a significant factor to be considered. And it is to be borne in mind that there is now a considerable body of learning on interracial and cross-cultural foster care, adoption and custody. That said, again as I had occasion to observe in *C* v. *C* at p 572:

"To a Judge struggling for a humane and workable solution to a terrible human dilemma, the social science authorities are a compelling reminder that there are many different schools of thought on child rearing and psychology and the best approach to custody cases. But these works are also a testament to the danger of committing blindly to any particular school of thought. Then too there is the obvious indeterminacy and impermanence of custody decisions. Inthe end, each case has its own problems and parameters. No formulae can be applied. Finally, the case for candour seems even more than usually compelling in custody judgments, however painful that may be for the parents. "

Further, under the head of general principle, and without in any way seeking to diminish the necessary breadth of the inquiry, there must surely be very real caution (particularly in a case such as this where several traumas of a huge order had affected the young child's life) in upsetting settled, quality, care. As Tipping J said in *Brown* v. *Brown* (1987) 2 FRNZ 355, 367:

"it seems to me that the Court must take into account the undesirability of uplifting a child from a known settled and satisfactory environment, if found to be such, unless sufficient advantage can be seen from taking that course to outweigh the disruption and uncertainty implicit in making such a change. "

The merits

After perusing the volume of affidavits in both the Court below, and this Court; and reviewing the oral evidence, I have come to the very clear conclusion that the Judge's placement decision for S was wrong. But that does not of course end the matter. Some months have now passed; the sands of events have now shifted under the feet of S and those about him. It could be quite rational to arrive at the conclusion that an initial placement was wrong, but that more harm than good would be done in attempting to reverse that situation. The critical question never varies in a child custody case: what is in the child's best interests? But all things considered I am of the view that, with appropriate safeguards, S must return to the Ps.

I remind myself, as doubtless does every Judge who has to struggle with custody cases, that there are few presumptions in human relations more dangerous than the idea that one knows what another human being needs better than they do themselves, or those closest to them. But with those ever-present concerns firmly in mind I have come to the conclusion that S's psychological state was then, and is now even more, at risk from the decision to transfer custody. I would have thought that a very prudent approach was required for a clearly traumatised child. Instead, abstracted, cause-driven cultural considerations were given primacy. And when those things are mixed into two distinctly contending camps (as there now are) of persons who even then, but certainly now, are profoundly distrustful of each other and have been unable to come to a sensible solution, then the mix is highly volatile and enormously damaging to a child.

I do not propose to traverse my factual findings in extensive detail. The general picture is quite clear to me. And overly extensive canvassing of some of the factual dispute would do even more harm to whatever can be salvaged in adult relationships in the future. At the same time however, I do have to give a sufficient indication of how I have reached my factual conclusions.

I begin with the large school photograph of S produced in evidence. In its own way it is very revealing. It shows a dark-eyed, dark-haired and rather shrewdlooking little individual.

That person's life has been difficult, to say the least. His father was a revolutionary poet of unstable temperament and worldwide renown; his mother a more stable individual. But the relationship between the father and the mother was clearly difficult. I accept the evidence that S was physically abused on occasion by his father. And his father's volatile temperament did not lend itself easily to child rearing.

It was partly on that account, and partly for practical reasons such as his parents' travel and academic activities, that S was quite literally entrusted to the care of the Ps at a very young age. I use the formal "entrusted" quite deliberately. Mrs P was selected by S's mother and father. An agreement for S's care while his parents were overseas for many months was drawn up by a solicitor and executed.

In many ways the Ps were an obvious choice. [Mrs] P is of mixed Chinese/Samoan descent; her husband [Mr] P is a British merchant seaman, though he has lived in New Zealand for many years. He is engaged in the coastal service. He is away at sea for a number of days and then at home for like periods. The couple have their own home on …. And they have a granddaughter, E, (who is older than S) who lives with them.

[Mrs] P has all the strengths of a Polynesian mother. Looking after other children in a more extended kind of family way came quite naturally to her as part ofher culture. And her attitude is that "care" is not a possessive thing; it lasts until a child is of a sufficient age and ability to fend for himself or herself and make elections as to where that child wishes to go in the future, and live his or her life.

Over a period of about four years until he was 5, S lived very happily with, and was well cared for, by the Ps. And very clearly S became deeply bonded to the Ps. In everyday terms, [Mr] P became a father figure; and [Mrs] P was a mother to him. And within that general context there was the trauma of a deliberate, negotiated, change from his natural parents to a foster parent environment.

The second great trauma in S's life was the massive family tragedy of his parents' death when he was 5 years old. He remained with the Ps thereafter, and it appeared that that would continue. But then there was the sudden removal from his psychological family at the age of 7 years as a result of the Family Court decision, to a family whose reason for wishing to remove him from the Ps was (as it necessarily had to be, given the good care he was getting there) based on "cultural factors".

The Ds (and in fairness, some of the experts called on their behalf) see it as being critically important not just to S's general knowledge of the world, but to his very identity, to bring him up in a "Chinese" way. [Mr] D is a university, trained environmentalist and fisheries expert. He does not speak Mandarin, although I accept that in a general way he would like to learn such. His wife, X, is fluent in Mandarin and speaks English to a reasonable degree, although notably she required an interpreter in Court. They have a child (M) who speaks English and who the Ds have always conceived would (and who has in fact assumed) a role of something of an "older brother" to S. I accept that in Chinese culture this role is a particularly important one in the absence of a father, and that its fundamental importance transcends even the importance of such a relationship on a European understanding.

It is convenient to add here some brief observations about the position of Z, the second respondent. He was born in China. He has a Chinese University degree in finance. He worked for a Chinese bank, but then moved to New Zealand. He is married to a Chinese woman. They have a small child. He is of course fluent in Chinese; his English is making steady progress. At one point in time after S's parents' death he became convinced that he should seek custody of S himself. But ultimately he came to the view that the correct solution to S's welfare required that S be with the Ps. Uncle Z however was, and is, fully prepared to do everything he can to expose his nephew to Chinese culture; he says with the assistance of the Chinese community.

Children are, by and large, enormously resilient. And I agree with all the experts who were called before me that S was in many ways lucky to have three sets of adults who were prepared to "contend" for his upbringing. It could perhaps have been expected that once a Family Court Judge had struggled with all that is involved in a case of this kind that an three contending "parties" would then have composed themselves for

S's present and long-term benefit. But they did not. There has been a great deal of perhaps over-refined examination of what precisely went wrong here before me. The Ds blame the Ps for what they say was an attempt to cut S off from them completely; the Ps have said that the Ds care was less than adequate; there was some scheming and furtive dealings between Uncle Z and the Ds as to whether a deal might be struck between them as to who would look after S in the future. But, however these things were triggered, things just did not mesh well together. And there were a variety of incidents which sparked controversy and recriminations. In the midst of all of this was S.

Evidence was presented in this case, particularly for the Ds, as to the vital necessity for a person's very identity, of truly knowing one's own culture from being immersed in it right from the outset. In particular, Dr Prasad, now the national Race Relations Conciliator (then a Professor of Social Work) gave evidence for the Ds, as did Miss Van Hees, whose qualifications span a number of areas. Both were impressive witnesses in their own way. I had no difficulty in accepting the critical importance of what they had to tell the Court in relation to the cultural development of a child. Significantly however, both accepted that if there was evidence which the Court accepted of underlying psychological problems—what Dr Prasad termed a "safety" issue —then they agreed that would have to take priority.

The reasons for this are obvious: a psychologically disturbed individual is just that. The deep-seated difficulties that can then arise are what health professionals term "prepotent" issues. This does not mean that cultural considerations are displaced entirely. But the fundamental psychological problems necessarily have to be resolved. I did not understand there to be, in all the expert evidence that was called before me, any difference of opinion on the primacy of psychological needs— "safety issues" —if such exist in fact.

But there *was* a distinct difference of opinion as to whether S is now psychologically disturbed, and if so to what extent. Dr Prasad thought that S's presenting behaviour indicates *some* disturbance; but he did not think it amounted to gross emotional disturbance. He thought that S's present behaviours are merely reactive to the adult conflict around him. He did not see there to be any emotional bonding issue—he categorised both the Ds and the Ps as occupying special status for S. And he thought that there was a growing acceptance and bond with the Ds.

Although it is an oversimplification, Miss Van Hees' conclusion was along the same lines.

The Court-appointed psychologist, Miss Adamiak, who is a registered clinical psychologist, and who had carried out a (with respect) very careful and thorough analysis is however of the very definite view that S is presently distinctly psychologically disturbed and in a "risk" category. This arises in part from his abrupt removal from the Ps and his own grieving on that account. In fact there may be a predisposition to depression in his familial history of disorder. But the most alarming phenomenon is a clinical one: she found S to be internalising and fragmented in his behaviour. Principally she attributed this to his stress at being suspended, as it were, between two contending factions.

She found his internalisation to be evident in two separate but related areas. His thoughts present an extraordinary degree of contradiction and confusion. And he is extremely adept at complying with the expectations of whichever adults he was with at a given moment. She thought his process had gone so far as to present two quite different personas, depending on who he was with. And she found the degree of placation to be neither age-appropriate nor psychologically healthy for an 8-year-old child.

S is too presenting regressively at times (that is, to child-like behaviour), excessive clinging, and anxiety behaviours.

And in one of the more moving and instructive passages, she was asked if she had talked about "death" with S. She said she had, and:

"He did actually talk about death, talked about his parents death and he talked something very disturbing. S said to me whilst talking about his mother, I was asking about his memories of his parents and he had talked about how his mother was chopped with a knife and bled everywhere until she was dead. And I asked him how he knew that and he said gugu M (which means 'older brother M') had told him and S said sometimes he gets scared when we go up and down the path [at the Ds house where his parents were killed] I get scared, I have bad dreams, my heart bleeds like her head sometimes. Whose head? My mother's head. I asked him if he told anybody and he said only gugu. And I said when did this bleeding of your heart happen. He said *when that Judge said/or me to leave, I forgot I don't want to talk any more.* I said it bleeding more or less the same? He said now and then bleeding. I asked what makes it stop and he says you can't bandage it you know and he didn't want to talk any more so I left it."

(Italics added.)

Miss Adamiak, as indeed did all the other experts called before me, maintained that the absolute and compelling present need is to reduce the adult conflict in S's life. She agreed that this would introduce other traumas, but thought a continuation of the present conflict to be disastrous. Her own view was that if S should return to the Ps he would "act out" his behavioural concerns to some extent, but that in many ways that would be better than his continuing to internalise those matters. Her assessment was that should S remain with the Ds his presenting behaviours would be likely to continue.

I have come to the view that a distinct separation from one family or the other is necessary, at least for a fairly respectable period of time, and that a clear cut decision must now be made one way or the other. That is, for S to be with the Ds or with the Ps, A good deal was said before me as to the desirability of some sort of mediated approach between the Ds and the Ps for S's ongoing benefit. I think such an approach is neither immediate enough, nor is it frankly realistic. S's problems are sufficiently pressing that I think they have to be addressed now. His present world is one in which, although on the surface he is happy enough at the Ds, there are these very deep-seated and particularly troublesome psychological problems. He is doing well enough at school: average or slightly above average in all of his subjects; very high marks in mathematics. But Miss Adamiak found that to be for the reason that school represents a "safe haven" for him. It is one place that he is out of the adult conflict.

Inevitably, once the conclusion is reached that there must be a distinct separation, such necessarily invites a reconsideration of the comparative merits of the Ds arrangements versus the Ps.

The Ds' circumstances, as to material matters, are much less secure than the Ps'. Mr D is still embroiled in resolving "matrimonial property" matters with a former de facto partner. He was inclined to downplay the difficulties there. But clearly buying out his partner's interest in the home occupied by the Ds is going to raise some difficulties. And, he has only limited present employment prospects. He has been unemployed, and a short-term contract soon runs out. The Ps are well settled in life. I do not accord the material factor all that much weight. But taken in isolation, it would favour the Ps.

On the question of physical care, there was some dispute. The Ps suggested that S had not been as well cared for as he should have been by the Ds. He has suffered from some things such as eczema. But really this is not a case of misuse or abuse of a child or anything like it. I think this factor should be put to one side, or is neutral in the central problem in this case.

At the psychological level I have no doubt at all that S was deeply bonded to the Ps, and that he was torn away from them. He then suffered a distinct grieving process there. He has been removed from them now for several months. I think Miss Adamiak is correct to say that some problems could be expected on a resumption of the relationship. But the Ps impressed me as mature people, with their feet firmly on the ground who were deeply and genuinely committed to S's care. There is no question in my mind but that they will do well by him.

The Ds on the other hand, partly because of the structure of the household, present a much more complex situation. On the evidence the Ds are more indulgent towards S, and he may well be getting some mileage out of that. I also consider, on the evidence, that the strength in the relationship with the D household for S may well lie in the relationship between S and M, although there were distinct indicators that there may be an unhealthy reliance by S on M. S said things like "where M goes I go".

I was left troubled, and I am afraid I must say this in all candour, by the motivation for the Ds' pursuit of S. Mr D's views and expressions had a curious abstractness to them. He struck me as being in any event somewhat cause-oriented. And he is one of those persons who, when he takes on a cause, reads everything that he can find about it and rationalises the matter to a high degree. "Finding out more" is entirely commendable, but simple love for an injured child may in the long run do a great deal more than an enforced diet of Mandarin. The point cannot be pushed too far: I do not suggest that Mr D does not deeply care for S and have his best interests at heart. But S's case has become something of a cause.

X's situation is much more complex. I think she clearly feels a need to fulfil Chinese expectations of the son of a famous poet; and I think there are fair inferences that can be taken as to the complexity of her emotions in trying to assuage, to some extent, the shocking death of Y at the hands of her brother, and other like "deep" factors. Significantly, I thought that what was missing in her evidence was a deep sense of a human feeling for S as a little person. Again, I am conscious of a European perception with respect to a Chinese woman. Any culture or person that would judge the perceptions of another, particularly one outside its own traditions, should proceed extremely cautiously. But in the end, difficult though it is, I am driven to the conclusion that S's psychological needs as a person would be significantly better met in the P household than the Ds.

Then there is the cultural factor, of which so much was made in this case. Dr Prasad's views (as indeed are those of Miss Van Hees) on cultural development are entitled to the greatest respect. I accept that if S is to be "fully" Chinese that the kind of approach they endorse would be preferable. The object of that approach is to make S "truly Chinese". Dr Prasad defends such on the basis that S "is Chinese". He advocated the concept of "banking". This would involve accumulating learning in the Chinese language which would then be "expendable", should S later elect to recognise his "Chineseness". This, I suppose, could be contrasted with a system of acculturation at a later point of time, on a more deferred basis. On Dr Prasad's thesis this could never be the real thing.

I am bound to accept the views of a distinguished expert on these matters and no contradictory evidence was called—that the Ds could present a model of the kind argued by Dr Prasad. At the same time, his approach presupposes that S will be truly immersed in things Chinese at the Ds. But on the facts it is clear that that has not worked out all that well to this date. X admitted that endeavouring to teach her husband, M and S Mandarin at the same time has been a daunting, and not entirely successful exercise. I do rather fear that Dr Prasad's insight—whilst doubtless valid in its terms—has come up against some hard practice obstacles in this particular case.

Moreover, it is not at all the case that S would be pushed into a monocultural environment at the Ps. [Mrs] P is clearly well attuned to different cultural perspectives, and welcomes them. [Mr] P has an English sort of pragmatism on the subject. His most compelling reason for S learning Mandarin is that it will be useful in the future because (as he put it) "there are a lot of them out there".

Any account of the cultural advantages and disadvantages to S cannot leave out the significant place of Uncle Z and his family, who are fluent in Chinese. Uncle Z has a Chinese tertiary qualification, good connections in the Chinese community, and he has made a successful and committed transition into New Zealand society. He clearly has a very good relationship with S, and is committed to doing all that he can for him. That relationship I find, turns on a genuine fondness; commitment to S's Chinese background; and of course a real sense of loyalty to his murdered sister to do all that he can properly do by her offspring. It may well be that more progress can be made on S's "Chineseness" in a settled and happy home environment than could be made with the Ds in any event.

But the fundamental point here is that, even taking on board Dr Prasad's concerns, I do not see the dichotomy between the Ds and the Ps as being as sharp—or indeed anything like it—in cultural terms as was suggested.

In my view S's best interests lie in his return, by a careful process, to the Ps.

The orders of the Court

(1) The appeal is allowed.

（2）The Ps are henceforth to have custody of S, until the further order of the Court, from a date to be determined in accordance with point 3.

（3）The appointment of Miss Adamiak is continued under s 29A of the Guardianship Act 1968. She and counsel for the child are to settle the most appropriate date for a changeover of custody. S will have to be advised of what is going to happen, and suitable arrangements then made with the Ds and the Ps. Some counselling of the Ds and the Ps may well be appropriate in this respect. If it is necessary, an order of the Court can be obtained in the event of disagreement. Counsel for the Child, whose appointment is continued, should take the initiative in this respect, if such further orders are necessary. I make it plain that this change over in custody is not to be long deferred—certainly not a matter of weeks. But an appropriate process will have to be put in place. Leave generally is reserved to apply on this question.

（4）From the date of the change–over in custody there will be no access to the first respondents（the Ds）for a period of 12 months from that date.

（5）It is important for S to continue to see M. That will occur to some extent at school. But M should be enabled to visit S at the Ps（or elsewhere, as might be a-greed）. But not at the Ds. The parties should settle this access by M prior to the custody changeover so that both S and M know where they stand. Again leave is reserved to apply.

（6）No order for access is needed by Uncle Z. I would urge the Ps to allow the fullest access that can be arranged between S and Uncle Z and his family. Leave is reserved to Uncle Z to apply if necessary.

（7）The file is remitted to the Family Court. The references to further orders of the Court or leave reserved will of course enable recourse by the parties to that Court.

（8）Given the difficulties that this case has raised, Mr Willoughby's appointment as counsel for the child is continued. His fees should be met from the fund set aside for that purpose by the legislation.

（9）After the expiration of the 12 months' "separation" period I would hope that the adult parties could come to a sensible arrangement regarding access for the Ds. I contemplate that such will be on a regular, but limited, footing so that there are no misapprehensions in S's mind as to who his permanent family is. The resources of the State are not infinite in disputes of this kind, and I hesitate to confirm an open-ended expenditure on this one case. I therefore make no order for the continuation of Miss Adamiak's services beyond the change-over date. But I do reserve leave for any party to these proceedings to apply to the Family Court after the expiration of the 12-month period if the parties are unable to agree on access for the Ds. That Court might then wish to obtain an updated report from Miss Adamiak.

(10) As to costs, all parties are legally aided. Counsel have apparently had to struggle to date with the burden of limited grants of legal aid. This was clearly always going to be a difficult and demanding custody case, and one raising matters going considerably beyond the norm. I would urge the legal aid authorities to respond with appropriate grants.

Appeal allowed

Appeal allowed; arrangements to be put into place for transfer of custody
Reported by S Condie

第四章　关于温斯顿·彼得斯和行动党华人候选人的一则选举法判例

案　名

新西兰高等法院：Winston Peters v. The Electoral Commission［2015］NZHC 394

导　读

背景

新西兰 2014 年大选于 2014 年 9 月 20 日举行。

竞选期间，行动党（Act Party）的副党魁王小选（Kenneth Wang）用中文录制了一段录像，就新西兰优先党党魁温斯顿·彼得斯（NZ First Leader Winston Peters）的一段讲话发表评论，认为彼得斯"反对华人"。

这段录像何时上传于网络不详，但与本案有关的记录是，该录像于 2014 年 9 月 7 日起在 Youtube 上以及 8 日起在行动党官网上均能播放，至 9 月 18 日、19 日该视频在两个网站上继续保留。

9 月 18 日，彼得斯的律师致函选举委员会，认为王小选先生曲解彼得斯的观点，该录像（作为竞选广告）违背了《新西兰选举法》第 199A 条，要求选举委员会审核该录像并交警方处理。

依《新西兰选举法》第 199A 条，如果有人明知内容有误，却在大选当日或大选前两日将该内容发表则构成违法。但选举委员会在回复彼得斯律师的信函中表示，虽然王小选的录像内容有误，但却在选举法规定的禁播期之前就已经上传发表，因此不构成违法。

彼得斯起诉至高等法院要求进行"司法审查"（Judicial Review）撤销选举委员会的决定。但选举委员会则认为，法院支持司法审查的前提必须是针对某项涉及某人之权利和义务的司法意义上的"决定"，而选举委员会给彼得斯的回函不属于判定王小选录像是否违背《新西兰选举法》第 199A 条的具备司法约束力的裁定，况且没有任何力量可以阻止彼得斯先生自己将此事直接移交警方处理，因此彼得斯此案不符合司法审查的要求，法庭应予驳回。

高等法院要解决的两个问题

高等法院需要解决以下两个问题：

第一，选举委员会的回函符合司法审核意义上的"裁定"吗？

第二，如果是，那么选举委员会判定王小选的录像不违法是对法律的错误解读吗？

相关立法

1993 年《新西兰选举法》第六部分规定了选举程序以及大选过程中的相关限制，包括在大选当日严格禁止"干扰或影响选民"的行为。这些行为包括以民调名义来误导选民或发表言论影响选民。第六部分相关条款亦包括涉及本案的违法行为，即在大选日或前两日发表错误的和虚假的言论。

回函是法律意义上的"决定"吗？

高等法院认为，选举委员会是依 1993 年《新西兰选举法》设立的，行使重要的涉及选举程序及其他具体立法意义上的职能。因此，选举委员会的意见极大可能被警方采纳以判定某行为是否违背第 199A 条款。正因如此，选举委员会给彼得斯的回函履行的是选举法意义上对 199A 条款进行司法解释的权力，因此该信函构成"裁定"，属于司法审查的范围。那么，该"裁定"对法律的解读是否有误呢？

何为发表？

彼得斯认为，任何言论，哪怕是在限制期限之外发表（注：限制期指大选日当天或前两日），但是在限制期内仍然存在，便构成选举法意义上的发表。

选举委员会则认为，构成发表需要有一个在限制期内实施的动作。如果"第一个动作"发生在限制期之外，则属于限制期之外的发表，不构成违法。哪怕在限制期内仍能接触这些言论，因为这些言论只是在被动状态下存留在某一媒介上而已，因此不构成违法。

高等法院对"发表"的认定

高等法院对"发表"做了以下几个认定：

第一，"文字+意图"是解读司法条款时的两大参照。而基本原则是要从立法意图中推断出文字意义[1]。

第二，1993年《新西兰选举法》中"发表"这个词用的是一般现在时态"publishes"。在限制期内发表构成发表，限制期外发表但是限制期内没有删除，凭借互联网或其他电子媒介继续保留的，则构成限制期内的发表。即使引用选举委员会的推断方法，认为在限制期内虽不具备发表动作，但是被动保留的，也构成继续发表。

因此，高等法院的结论是，只要那些虚假言论在限制期内仍然继续发表的，便有可能继续错误地影响选民。而第199A条立法意图是防止误导选民，因此选举委员会对该条款的解读有误，该言论违背第199A条。

此判例意味着什么？

1993年《新西兰选举法》实施时，互联网尚未兴起，新闻传播还是以传统纸媒以及电台、电视为主。大选日的前一个晚上，大街小巷的竞选广告和大小招牌也都有序地瞬间消失。

随着互联网和电子媒介的兴盛，对"大选日或前两日"限制期的规范越来越困难。高等法院这则判例无疑对1993年《新西兰选举法》的相应条款起到补充和更新作用。

民主选举是"言论自由"和"法律限制"相辅相成的体现。涉及种族角度的言论容易在少数族裔选民中引起共鸣。但是，随着"主流"与"少数族裔"社区之间的互动加深，因语言和文化形成的传统意义上的边界越来越不明显，华人社区和其他任何社区的一举一动也都及时地出现在彼此的视线中。因此，煽情的狠话好说，而可能引起的后患却不易躲。

---

[1] 参见判例 Commerce commission v. Fonterra Co-operative Group Ltd [2007] NZSC 36 at [22]。

  高等法院对"发表"的司法解释外延很宽，因此，在互联网时代，对1993年《新西兰选举法》第199A条的解读和遵守，使用录音、录像以及微信、微博等社交媒体应该加倍小心。

高等法院判决书

IN THE HIGH COURT OF NEW ZEALAND
WELLINGTON REGISTRY

CIV 2015−485−222

［2016］NZHC 394

UNDER   the Judicature Amendment Act 1972

IN THE MATTER OF an application for judicial review

BETWEEN   WINSTON PETERS

                 Applicant

AND   THE ELECTORAL COMMISSION

                 Respondent

Hearing：   12 October 2015

Appearances：   B P Hemy and AM Dunlop for the Applicant

            P J Gunn and M J McKillop for the Respondent

Judgment：   9 March 2016

JUDGMENT OF MALLON J

Table of Contents

PETERS v. THE ELECTORAL COMMISSION [2016] NZHC 394 [9 March 2016].

Introduction

[1] The issue before me is the meaning of "publishes" in s 199A of the Electoral Act 1993 (the Act). Under that section a person who "publishes" a statement of fact that he or she knows is false, with the intention of influencing the vote of any elector, commits an offence if they do so at any time on polling day or the two days immediately preceding polling day.

[2] The issue arises in the context of the 2014 general election which was held on 20 September 2014. It concerns two political party advertisements which were available

on the internet on 18 and 19 September 2014 and earlier. The particular issue is whether "publishes" means first published in the prohibited period (that is, on polling day or the two preceding days), or whether it includes advertisements which were first published earlier than the prohibited period but which continue to be published during that period.

[3] The issue comes to this court on an application for judicial review brought by the Right Honourable Winston Peters, the Leader of New Zealand First, a party contesting the 2014 election. He made a complaint to the Electoral Commission about the two advertisements, contending that they breached s 199A and that the Commission should refer the matter to the police. The Electoral Commission responded advising that it considered the advertisements did not breach s 199 A and it gave reasons for this view.

[4] The Electoral Commission considers that its response to the complaint is not a reviewable decision. [1] If I accept that submission, the parties are content for the Court to consider the issue as though it was before me as an application under the Declaratory Judgments Act 1908.

Background

[5] One of the advertisements that gave rise to this proceeding was a video recorded in Mandarin for Kenneth Wang, the Deputy Leader of the ACT Party, a party also contesting the 2014 election. The video commented on a speech which Mr Peters had made about the opening of a brothel in Auckland owned by the Chow brothers. The commentary in the video was to the effect that Mr Peters was "anti Chinese" and believed that Chinese people had turned Auckland "evil" and into "the Capital of Sin". The video was available on the internet on YouTube from 7 September 2014, and also on the ACT Party website from 8 September 2014. It remained on those two sites on 18 and 19 September 2014.

[6] By letter dated 18 September 2014, Mr Henry, counsel for Mr Peters, aler-

---

[1] The Electoral Commission has, as it has in other cases, participated in order to assist the Court in the absence of another named contradictor.

ted the Electoral Commission to this advertisement. He provided a signed translation of the video. He set out the relevant paiis of Mr Peters' speech and the statements in the video which Mr Peters considered had falsely represented what he had said in that speech. He contended that these statements breached s 199 A of the Act. He asked the Electoral Commission to review the material and to refer the advertisement to the Police.

[7] The second advertisement was a pamphlet for the Conservative Party, a party also contesting the 2014 election. This pamphlet compared the policies of the Conservative Party with those of New Zealand First. It was posted to New Zealand households on about 12 September 2014. It was also hosted on the Conservative Party's website from 14 September 2014 and remained there on 18 and 19 September 2014.

[8] A complaint was made to the Advertising Standards Authority (ASA) about the pamphlet. On 18 September 2014, the ASA determined that the pamphlet "contained a substantive e1rnr of fact". This related to a statement that the Conservative Party "would implement the 5 key recommendations of the Law Commission Report" on alcohol reform and the corresponding statement that Mr Peters would not implement them. The ASA noted the correct position was that there were four paiis to the Law Commission's repmi and a substantial number of recommendations. The ASA considered the enor was likely to mislead the consumer and breached the Code of Ethics. The complaint was therefore upheld in this respect.

[9] By letter dated 19 September 2014, Mr Remy, on behalf of Mr Peters, wrote to the Electoral Commission about this advertisement. He set out the statement at issue and the ASA's decision about that. He noted that, although the ASA had directed that the advertisement be amended, the pamphlet remained unaltered on the Conservative Party's website as at 19 September 2014. He asked the Electoral Commission to review the advertisement and to refer it to the Police.

[10] The Electoral Commission replied to both letters on 5 November 2014. It said:

In the Electoral Commission's view, putting aside whether or not the other elements of the offence were made out, section 199A of the Act does not apply to the items at issue because they were not first published within the required time period.

[11] In reaching that view the Electoral Commission stated that s 199A was enacted to address a specific concern about parties or candidates publishing false statements on the eve of an election which meant that other candidates and parties had insufficient time to correct Tect the statement. It also said that throughout the Act a distinction was drawn between the act of publication or distribution in the first instance and a continuing publication. Because the Electoral Commission considered the items did not breach s 199A it would not be refeffing these matters to the police. The letter was signed by the Chief Electoral Officer (Mr Peden).

[12] Mr Henry wrote a further letter to the Electoral Commission dated 14 November 2014 setting out reasons why the Commission's view was not accepted. The Electoral Commission responded by email on 16 December 2014 advising that, if Mr Peters disagreed with the Commission's view, he could refer the matter to the police. He could also make a submission to the Justice and Electoral Select Committee Inquiry into the 2014 general election.

[13] On 16 March 2015, Mr Peters filed this proceeding seeking judicial review. It pleaded that the Electoral Commission's letter of 5 November 2014 was a decision that there was no breach of s 199A. It pleaded that this decision was wrong in law. An order quashing the decision was sought.

The legislation

[14] The Electoral Act 1993 was enacted in anticipation of the introduction of the mixed member propmtional system of representation (MMP) if carried at the referendum to be held alongside the 1993 general election. The Act provided for the reform of the electoral system if that were to occur (as it duly did) and established the Electoral Commission. [1]

[15] The Electoral Commission is a crown entity. [2] Its three members, ap-

---

[1]   Electoral Act 1993, long title.

[2]   Section 4B (2).

pointed by the Governor-General on the recommendation of the House of Representatives, are the Chief Electoral Officer, the chairperson and the deputy chairperson. [1] Its objectives are as follows:

4C Objective

The objective of the Electoral Commission is to administer the electoral system impatiially, efficiently, effectively, and in a way that

(a) facilitates patiicipation in parliamentary democracy; and

(b) promotes understanding of the electoral system and associated matters; and

(c) maintains confidence in the administration of the electoral system.

[16] Its functions are as follows:

5 Functions

The functions of the Electoral Commission are to—

(a) carry the provisions of this Act into effect;

(b) carry out duties in relation to parliamentmy election programmes that are prescribed by Part 6 of the Broadcasting Act 1989;

(c) promote public awareness of electoral matters by means of the conduct of education and imformation programmes or by other means;

(d) consider and report to the Minister or to the House of Representatives on electoral matters referred to the Electoral Commission by the Minister or the House of Representatives;

(e) make available information to assist parties, candidates, and others to meet their statutory obligations in respect of electoral matters administered by the Electoral Commission;

(f) cany out any other functions or duties conferred on the Electoral Commission by or under any other enactment.

[17] Part 6 of the Act is concerned with the election process from the issue of the writ, to nominations for electoral districts, the voting process, the counting of votes, the

---

[1] Section 4D (1).

endorsement and return of the writ and determining the list seats. It also provides a number of election offences. These include a number of prohibitions on what can be done on polling day, which come under the heading "interfering with or influencing voters" . [1] These prohibitions include, for example, conducting a public opinion poll. They also include a prohibition on statements made on polling day intended to influence a voter. [2] Part 6 of the Act also includes the offence at issue here, namely publishing false statements on polling day or the two days preceding polling day. [3]

[18] Under the Act there are also restrictions on election advertising (Part 6AA) and election expenses and donations (Part 6A) in the three month period before the election polling day. Amongst other things, these provide who may authorise election advertisements and cap the amount that may be spent on election advertising during the regulated period. [4] Editorial content in a periodical, radio or television programme or in a publication on the internet is not restricted. [5] Nor is there a restriction on the expression of personal views on the internet, for which no payment is received. [6] It is an offence to avoid the limits that are prescribed and to fail to comply with procedures related to these limits. [7]

[19] Part 7 of the Act provides other offences collectively described as "conupt and illegal practices" . These include voting as some other person (personation) [8] and bribing a voter. [9] There is also an offence for publishing any advertisement relating to an election, that is not an "election advertisement", [10] without stating the

---

[1]　Section 197.

[2]　Section 197 (1)(g).

[3]　Section 199A.

[4]　See, for example, s 204B.

[5]　Section 3A (2)(c).

[6]　Section 3A (2)(e).

[7]　Sections 204D, 204E, 204F, 204G, 204H, 205B, 205F, 205N, 2050, 206B, 206D, 206E, 206N, 2060, 206U, 206X, 206Y, 206ZE, 206ZF, 207D, 207F, 207H, 207J, 2071, 207LA, 209B and 209C.

[8]　Section 215.

[9]　Section 216.

[10]　As defined in s 3A.

name of the person at whose direction it is published. [1] This Part of the Act also provides the punishment for a conupt practice. [2] The offence in s 199A is categorised as a cormpt practice. The penalty is a term of imprisonment not exceeding two years or a fine not exceeding $40, 000. [3]

Industry regulation of advertisements

[20] There are other restrictions in place which bear upon what may be said about candidates or parties contesting an election. For present purposes the relevant restrictions are provided by the Broadcasting Act 1989 and by the Advertising Standards Authority (the ASA).

[21] Broadcasters (television and radio) are subject to the Broadcasting Act. This requires broadcasters to adhere to codes of practice issued by the Broadcasting Standards Authority (the BSA). Under the current provisions a viewer who considers that a broadcaster has breached the code in relation to an election programme is able to complain directly to the BSA. [4] No timeframe is provided within which the BSA will make its decision. Prior to 19 December 2007 the complaint had to first go to the broadcaster who was required to respond within 48 hours. If the viewer was dissatisfied with the response they could then lodge a formal complaint with the BSA which endeavoured to provide a response within 48 hours. Under the present provisions, and under the procedures prior to 19 December 2007, if the BSA upholds the complaint it can make an order, amongst other things, directing the broadcaster to refrain from broadcasting or from broadcasting advertising programmes for specified periods. [5]

[22] The ASA was established by the advertising industry to provide selfregulation. The ASA has issued codes of practice intended to maintain acceptable standards of advertising and to ensure that advertisements are not misleading or deceptive. The

---

[1] Section 22 1A.

[2] Sections 3 and 224.

[3] Section 224 (1).

[4] Broadcasting Act 1989, s 8.

[5] Section 13.

codes are intended to complement the law. Anyone can complain about any advertisement in any media (traditional and digital media) that they consider to breach of the codes. An advertisement is to be taken in its broadest sense and includes advertising that promotes a political viewpoint. It also includes pamphlets delivered directly to individual voters. [1] The Advertising Complaints Board considers the complaint and if it concludes the advertisement breaches the codes it issues a decision upholding the complaint. Such a finding does not carry any particular legal consequences.

Is the decision reviewable?

[23] The Electoral Commission says that its letter of 5 November 2014, expressing its view that the two advertisements did not breach s 199A, was given pursuant to its function to make available information to assist parties and candidates to meet their statutory obligations. [2] It says that in providing this view it was not exercising a statutory power of decision under the Judicature Amendment Act 1972.

[24] An application for review may be made under that Act in respect of the exercise of a "statutory power". [3] That is defined as including the "exercise of a statutory power of decision". That in turn is defined as "a power or right conferred by or under any Act …to make a decision deciding or prescribing or affecting …the rights … or liabilities of any person". [4] The exercise of a statutory power is also defined as including a power "to make any investigation or inquiry into the rights, powers, privileges, immunities, duties, or liabilities of any person". [5]

[25] The Electoral Commission's letter of 5 November 2014 set out its opinion on the meaning of s 199A. It was not a legally binding determination of whether the advertisements breached s 199A and it did not prevent any person from referring the adver-

---

[1] Advertising Standards Authority, *Advertising Codes of Practice* 2014 (ASA, Wellington, 2014) at 11, also found at Advertising Standards Authority "advertising Code of Practise 2014" <www. asa. govt. nz> at 11.

[2] Electoral Act 1993, s 5 (e).

[3] Judicature Amendment Act 1972, s 4.

[4] Section 3.

[5] Section 3.

tisements to the police. In that sense it was not a decision.

[26] However it arguably was an investigation into the rights or liabilities of a person. The advertisements were considered and an opinion was provided pursuant to the Electoral Commission's statutory function to assist parties and candidates to meet their statutory functions. The Electoral Commission does not have a statutory duty to refer a suspected breach of s 199A to the police (in contrast with some other offences).[1] But it does have an important role in the electoral process. In light of the Electoral Commission's objectives and functions, the police would likely take into account the Commission's considered view on s 199A in deciding whether to proceed on a complaint that someone had breached that section. The Electoral Commission's view therefore has potentially important public consequences.[2]

[27] I therefore consider that when the Electoral Commission provides its considered view on the interpretation of s 199A it is exercising a reviewable statutory power. The fact that its view is not a decision which legally determines rights or liabilities is relevant to the appropriate relief if the Commission makes an error of law. The relief sought here was an order quashing the "decision". Such relief would not in my view be appropriate. However a declaration that the view was an error of law may be appropriate if that is the conclusion I reach.

[28] The alternative is to bring an application under the Declaratory Judgments Act 1908. That has been the procedural avenue taken in other cases.[3] While that route is available, it my view it does not preclude the procedural avenue chosen in this case. The possibility of either procedural route was recognised in one of the cases brought as an application under the Declaratory Judgments Act where the Judge said:[4]

---

[1] See ss 120, 204J, 2041, 205P, 206P, 206ZG, 2070 and 215 which set out a large number of offences in respect of which the Electoral Committee has a repelling duty.

[2] Royal Australasian College of Surgeons v. Phipps [1999] 3 NZLR 1 (CA) at 11 to 12.

[3] Greenpeace of New Zealand Inc v. Electoral Commission [2014] NZHC 2135; and Watson v. Electoral Commission [2015] NZHC 666.

[4] Watson, above n 27, at [238].

[238] … the challenge here is, in reality, to the correctness of the Commission's advisory opinion. The issue of that advisory opinion reflects the exercise of a statutory power. Although brought in the form of an application for a declaratory judgment, these proceedings can be seen as raising the judicial review question as to whether or not the exercise of that power reflected a proper application and interpretation of laws. …

The meaning of "publishes"

Approach

[29] The meaning of an enactment is ascertained from its text in the light of its purpose.[1] As explained in *Commerce Commission v. Fonterra Co-operative Group Ltd*, this makes "text and purpose the key drivers" in interpreting a statutory provision. To give effect to these dual requirements, "even if the meaning of the text may appear plain in isolation of purpose, that meaning should always be cross-checked against purpose". In determining purpose the court has regard to both the immediate and the general legislative context. The social, commercial and other objective of the enactment may also be relevant.[2]

Section 199A

[30] Section 199A is in the following terms:

199A Publishing false statements to influence voters

Every person is guilty of a corrupt practice who, with the intention of influencing the vote of any elector, at any time on polling day before the close of the poll, or at any time on any of the 2 days immediately preceding polling day, publishes, distributes, broadcasts, or exhibits, or causes to be published, distributed, broadcast, or exhibited, in or in view of any public place a statement of fact that the person knows is false in a material particular.

"publishes"

---

[1] Interpretation Act 1999, s 5.

[2] Commerce Commission v. Fonterra Co-operative Group Ltd [2007] NZSC 36 at [22].

[31] Counsel for Mr Peters submits that the words of s 199A are clear and unambiguous. A statement that is on the internet during the prohibited period (polling day and the two preceding days) is published and will breach s 199A if the other requirements of that section are met. He submits that the Electoral Commission's interpretation requires the word "first" to be inserted in the section, so that it would read "first publishes". He says there is no basis on which that should be done.

[32] The Electoral Commission refers to the dictionary definition of "publish", namely "to make public or generally known; to declare openly; to announce." [1] It submits that the prohibited period adds a temporal qualification to this. Publication must occur on polling day or on the preceding two days. It says a natural reading of s 199A indicates the section only applies to publications first occurring within the prohibited period. The verbs constituting the *actus reus* require some positive action to be taken on the relevant days before an offence can be committed. The Commission says that simply leaving material on display in whatever medium—the passive continuation of a prior publication—could not be said to constitute publication on the relevant days.

[33] I start with the definition of "publish" provided in the Act itself. That definition is as follows:

3D Meaning of publish

In this Act, unless the context otherwise requires, publish, in relation to an election advertisement, means to bring to the notice of a person in any manner—

(a) including—

(i) displaying on any medium;

(ii) distributing by any means;

(iii) delivering to an address;

(iv) leaving at a place;

(v) sending by post or otherwise;

(vi) printing in a newspaper or other periodical;

---

[1] Oxford University Press "publish v." (December 2015) Oxford English Dictionary <www. oed. com> at [I, 2. a].

(vii) broadcasting by any means;

(viii) disseminating by means of the Internet or any other electronic medium;

(ix) storing electronically in a way that is accessible to the public;

(x) incorporating in a device for use with a computer;

(xi) inserting in a film or video; but

(b) excluding addressing one or more persons face to face.

[34] The definition refers to "election advertisement", which is also defined in the Act, whereas s 199A refers to "a statement of fact" which is intended to influence a voter. There is likely to be considerable overlap. The statements at issue here, for example, were electoral advertisements.

[35] In s 199A the present tense "publishes" is used. The offence is committed by a person who "publishes" the statement in the prohibited period. Applying the s 3D definition, in the case of a statement on the internet it is the act of:

> bring [ing] to the notice of a person in any manner...including ...displaying on any medium; ...disseminating by means of the Internet or any other electronic medium; storing electronically in a way that is accessible to the public.

[36] Applying that definition the question is whether a person is disseminating a statement by means of the internet on 18 and 19 September 2014 if they have placed the statement on the internet on an earlier date, and have left it there so that it remains on the internet on 18 and 19 September 2014? In my view it is the natural meaning of those words to answer that question "yes". Similarly, is a person storing a statement electronically in a way that is accessible to the internet on 18 and 19 September 2014 if they put the statement on the internet on an earlier date and have not removed it by 18 and 19 September 2014? In my view it is the natural meaning of those words to answer that question "yes".

[37] On the other hand it is also possible to read those words in the way the Electoral Commission contends. That is, a person is not disseminating a statement by means of the internet or storing the statement electronically on polling day, because the

disseminating or storing occurred earlier. However that reading seems to me to be the less natural and ordinary one. When something is put on the internet it is accessible to the public each moment that someone is accessing the internet. It is a continuing dissemination or storing of the statement until it is removed.

[38] The definition in s 3D is consistent with the dictionary definition of "publish". In addition to the dictionary definition referred to by the Electoral Commission above, [1] other dictionary definitions include:

1 v. t. Make generally known; declare or report openly; announce; disseminate (a creed or system); …6. b v. t. Make (a work, information, etc.) generally accessible or available; place before the public; [2]

3 (tr) to announce formally or in public; [3]

vt to issue to the public; …to put into circulation. [4]

[39] Applying the dictionary definition, where a statement is on the internet on 18 and 19 September 2014, having been put there on an earlier date and not removed by 18 September 2014, the statement is generally accessible or available, and is placed before the public. It is a natural and ordinary meaning of "publishes" to say that when a person accesses the internet and reads the statement, the statement is brought to their notice at that time. On the other hand, I accept that it is possible to read "publishes" as meaning the time at which thestatement is put on the internet (that is, a single publication). [5] Which meaning is to be preferred must be determined in light of the purpose ofthe section, as may be derived from its immediate and

---

[1] At [I, 2. a] .

[2] Lesly Brown (ed) The New Shorter Oxford English Dictionary-Volume 2 N-2 (4th ed, Claredon Press, Oxford, 1993) at 2405.

[3] Duncan Black (ed) Collins English Dictionary (10th ed, Harper Collins Publishers, Glasgow, 2010) at 1329.

[4] Vivian Man (ed) The Chambers Dictionary (11th ed, Chambers Harrap Publishers Ltd, Edinburgh, 2008) at 1258.

[5] I note that this is a current issue also in the context of a defamatory statement on the internet; see the discussion in Stephen Todd (ed) The Law of Torts in New Zealand (6th ed, Brookers, Wellington, 2013) at 840-842 and fn 224.

general legislative context and objectives.

"publishes" in context of s 199A

［40］The word "publishes" appears in s 199A with "distributes, broadcasts, or exhibits". Its meaning should be considered in that context:

(a) "Distributes": is the act of distributing (giving out) a statement in a public place. That would apply naturally to the delivery of pamphlets to households. A statement is distributed each time a pamphlet is delivered to a household. This would mean that pamphlets delivered on 17 September 2014 would not be caught by s 199A, but pamphlets delivered on 18 September 2014 would be (if the other requirements of the section were met). In the case of an overnight delivery those before midnight would not be caught and those delivered after midnight would be.

(b) "Broadcasts": a broadcast is something transmitted in some way for reception by a person or persons. Most naturally a broadcast refers to something that can be seen or heard on the radio or television although there may be other forms of communication that also qualify as broadcasts. A statement broadcast on the radio or television before midnight on 17 September 2014 would not be caught by s 199A. But if the broadcast continued into the early hours of 18 September 2014 it would then be caught by s 199A (if the other requirements of the section were met). It would be the same position with any other forms of broadcasting.

(c) "Exhibits": to exhibit something is to show or display something. A statement is being exhibited while it is on show or displayed. A statement might be exhibited by being placed on a billboard for example. A person who exhibits a statement on 17 September 2014 by placing a billboard in a public place, will still be exhibiting the statement if the billboard remains in place on 18 September 2014.

［41］It is therefore possible to conceive of situations caught by s 199A when the person has brought the statement to the notice of the public before the prohibited period, and continues to do so during the prohibited period unless the person takes action to bring the publishing, distributing, broadcasting or exhibiting to an end. No exclusion for such situations is provided. This suggests that Parliament intended such statements to be covered. To adopt what I consider the ordinary and natural meaning of "publishes" in the context of a statement disseminated or stored on the internet is consistent with that apparent intention.

"publishes" in the context of s 197

[42] Section 199A overlaps with s 197 because that section also provides an offence in relation to statements made on polling day. Section 197 covers a wider range of prohibited activities on polling day than that but, insofar as is covers statements, it provides:

197 Interfering with or influencing voters

(1) Every person commits an offence and shall be liable on conviction to a fine not exceeding $20, 000 who at an election—

...

(g) at any time on polling day before the close of the poll exhibits in or in view of any public place, or publishes, or distributes, or broadcasts, —

(i) any statement advising or intended or likely to influence any elector as to the candidate or party for whom the elector should or should not vote; or

(ii) any statement advising or intended or likely to influence any elector to abstain from voting; or

(iii) any party name, emblem, slogan, or logo; or

(iv) any ribbons, streamers, rosettes, or items of a similar nature in party colours:

...

[43] The scope of s 197 (g) is limited by a number of provisos. Relevantly they include:

provided that this paragraph shall not apply to any statement, name, emblem, slogan, or logo in a newspaper published before 6 pm on the day before polling day;

provided also that where any statement, name, emblem, slogan, or logo which does not relate specifically to the election campaign and which is so exhibited before polling day in afixed position and in relation to the New Zealand or regional or campaign headquarters (not being mobile headquarters) of a political party, it shall not be an offence to leave the statement, name, emblem, slogan, or logo so exhibited on polling day;

...

[44] The scope of this offence is further limited through two defences. The first, which is provided by s 197 (2), is as follows:

(2) It shall be a defence to a prosecution for an offence against subsection (1) (g) that relates to the exhibition in or in view of a public place of a statement, name, emblem, slogan, or logo, if the defendant proves that—

(a) the exhibition was inadvertent; and

(b) the defendant caused the exhibition to cease as soon as the defendant was notified by a Returning Officer or a manager of the polling place that the exhibition was taking place.

[45] The second defence is provided by s 197 (2A), which is as follows:

(2A) It is a defence to a prosecution for an offence against paragraph (g) of subsection (1) that relates to the publication on an Internet web site of a statement or other material specified in that paragraph, if the defendant proves that

(a) the statement or material was placed on the web site before polling day; and

(b) the defendant did not operate or permit the operation of systems that cause the statement or material on the web site to be made available, on polling day, to persons other than persons who voluntarily access the web site; and

(c) the defendant did not, on polling day, distribute, broadcast, or exhibit in or in view of a public place, or publish, or at any time cause to be published, in an issue of a newspaper or magazine that is first issued on polling day any material promoting or advertising the web site.

[46] Section 199A is not subject to these exceptions. The overlap between ss 199A and 197 is that both may apply to a knowingly false statement made on polling day which is intended to influence voters. If the statement is charged as an offence un-

der s 197 it will not be necessary to prove that it was knowingly false but the provisos and defences may arise and a lower maximum penalty will apply.

[47] The provisos and defences in s 197 contemplate the possibility that statements may be published before polling day and may continue to be seen by the public on polling day. The exceptions that are made for such statements are limited. Newspapers published before 6 pm on polling day are not captured even though it may be presumed that members of the public may read them on polling day. Statements which do not relate specifically to the election campaign, which are exhibited in a fixed position at the paiiy's headquarters, do not need to be removed on polling day. Statements exhibited in a public place before polling day are to be removed by polling day, but inadvertence is a defence. A statement placed on the internet before polling day is able to remain there on polling day, but operating a system that causes the statement to be available other than via voluntary access of the website and promoting the website are prohibited.

[48] Section 197 (2A), which provides the exception for statements remaining on the internet, was inserted into the Act at the same time as s 199A. [1] This indicates that at the time s 199A was enacted Parliament contemplated the possibility of statements being placed on the internet before the prohibited period and remaining there during the prohibited period. Parliament expressly stated what was and was not covered by s 197 in this respect. It would not be an offence under s 197 to merely leave it on the internet. Something more was required under this section.

[49] As Parliament did not include a similar defence in relation to s 199A it appears that the of fence of publishing knowingly false statements was intended to be wider. An inference can be drawn that, in contrast with s 197, leaving a knowingly false statement on the internet where it could be voluntarily accessed by the public was intended to be caught (as would access of the kind not covered by the defence provided by s 197 (2A)). The wider reach of s 199A is explicable by the potentially greater

---

[1] Pursuant to the Electoral Amendment Act 2002.

culpability and hatm to a free and fair election associated with a knowingly false statement left on the internet, than a statement that remains on the internet which is not knowingly false.

[50] The alternative inference is that Parliament did not intend either section to capture statements placed on the internet before the prohibited period, which remain there during the prohibited period if that was all that a defendant was responsible for. Section 197 (2) makes it clear what additional circumstances are required before there can be liability for online publications on polling day. If those circumstances exist, there is liability under s 197 but not under s 199A.

[51] I consider the first inference to be the more likely one. If simply leaving a statement on the internet was not caught by ss 199A and 197 (g), I would expect the wording to have been clearer. I consider it to be implicit in the wording of s 197 (2A) (a) that leaving material on a website on polling day was potentially covered by the words of s 197 (g). Section 197 provided that it was not caught by s 197 (g) unless the requirements of s 197 (2) (b) were met. No such additional circumstances were stipulated for liability under s 199A. I therefore consider that, in so far as Parliament's intent can be gauged from s 197 in relation to statements on the internet, that intent is consistent with what I consider to be the natural and ordinary meaning of" publishes" in s 199A.

Distinction between first publication and continuing publications elsewhere in the Act

[52] The Electoral Commission refers to the distinction that is drawn between first and continuing publications in relation to the regulation of election advertisements and expenses under Parts 6AA and 6A of the Act. It submits that this is consistent with its interpretation of s 199A in that where the Act intends to provide for continuing publications it does so expressly, and it has not expressly provided in s 199 A for continuing publication.

[53] By way of example the Electoral Commission refers to s 204C. Section 204C appears in Part 6AA, under Subpart 1 which concerns the general rules governing election advertising. Under s 204B a party secretary, a candidate or a registered promoter is

entitled to promote an election advertisement. An unregistered promoter is entitled to promote an election advertisement if they do not incur advertising expenses beyond a maximum amount, currently $12, 600, "during the regulated period" (which is the three month period before polling day).[1] It is an offence to exceed the maximum amount.[2] Section 204C is concerned with determining how advertising expenses are calculated during the regulated period. It provides:

204C Apportionment of advertising expenses for publication of election advertisement promoted by unregistered promoter both before and during regulated period

(1) This section applies if an election advertisement that is promoted by an unregistered promoter—

(a) is published both before the commencement of the regulated period and during the regulated period; or

(b) is published before the commencement of the regulated period and continues to be published during the regulated period.

(2) If this section applies, —

(a) the election advertisement is deemed to have been published during the regulated period; but

(b) the advertising expenses for the publication of the election advetisement must be app01iioned so that only a fair proportion of the expenses is attributed to being incurred during the regulated period.

(3) Only the advertising expenses attributed to being incurred during the regulated period determined in accordance with subsection (2) are advertising expenses for the purposes of section 204B (1)(d).

[54] I do not agree with the Electoral Commission that this section distinguishes between when something is first published and a continuing publication. Rather the section recognises two situations in which there might be confusion about how to calculate

---

[1] Section 204B (1)(d).

[2] Section 204D.

expenses to determine if they exceed the maximum amount. Each situation relates to an advertisement that is published both before and during the regulated period. One situation is where an advertisement is published before the commencement of the regulated period and then republished during the regulated period. [1] The other situation is where an advertisement is published before the commencement of the regulated period and continues to be published during the regulated period. [2] In both situations the advertising is covered by the restriction that applies to an unregistered promoter who promotes an election advertisement [3] and it is only the amount incuned during the regulated period that is relevant in determining whether the expenses fall within the maximum amount. [4] The relevant amount is the fair proportion of the expenses of the advertisement for the regulated period. [5]

[55] The section therefore has quite a different purpose than ss 197 and 199A. It is not concerned with determining when something was first published in order to attract liability. It is concerned with ensuring that advertisements during the regulated period are covered by the restriction on advertising expenses and determining how they are to be calculated. I consider that this section does not provide support for the Electoral Commission's view on the advertisements which led to Mr Peters's complaint in the present case. If anything, it is another example of Parliament recognising the possibility both of republications and continuing publications during the prohibited or restricted periods, and despite that recognition not providing any exception for either in relation to s 199A. [6]

[56] I take the same view of the other examples provided by the Electoral Commission. One of those is s 205. That section is under Part 6A, Subpart 1 which concerns

---

[1] Section 204C (1)(a).

[2] Section 204C (1)(b).

[3] Section 204C (2).

[4] Section 204B (3).

[5] Section 204C (2)(b).

[6] Although not too much can be taken from this example given the different time the provisions were enacted.

election expenses of candidates. Section 205C sets a maximum amount of election expenses a candidate may incur during the regulated period. Section 205F provides that it is an offence to exceed the maximum amount. For the purposes of these sections s 205 defines election expenses as meaning advertising expense in relation to a candidate advertisement that "is published, or continues to be published, during the regulated period". Section 205D relates to apportioning advertisement expenses for candidate advertisements published before and after the regulated period and is in similar terms to s 204C. To similar effect are ss 206, 206C, and 206CA (which contain similar provisions in relation to expenses for party advertisements) and ss 206S, 206V, and 206W (which contain similar provisions in relation to expenses of registered promoters).

Parliamentary materials

[57] The Electoral Commission contends that the legislative history of s 199A assists in determining the mischief that it was intended to address. It submits that the purpose of s 199A was to limit the ability to propagate falsehoods with the intention of influencing voters close to the election when there was no sufficient opportunity to correct or respond to the false statements. It refers to the Justice and Electoral Committee's report on the inquiry into the 1999 general election in support of this submission. [1]

[58] The Justice and Electoral Committee is a parliamentary select committee which undertakes a post-election review of the practices and procedures involved in each election. It also examines proposed legislative amendments in relation to elections and makes suggestions in relation to them. Section 199A was inserted following the inquiry into the 1999 general election. One of the issues considered in that inquiry was statements containing errors of fact made in the last days of the electoral campaign.

[59] Alongside that inquiry, the Electoral Amendment Bill (No 2) 2001, a bill to improve and modernise election procedures and simplify enrolment and voting procedures, was introduced. At this time the Committee had not completed its report on the

---

[1] Justice and Electoral Committee Inquil) ' into the 1999 General Election (December 2001) at 8. 4.

1999 general election inquiry. When introduced, the Bill did not contain a clause dealing with the issue of false statements made in the last days of the election campaign. The Bill did contain a clause that would prohibit publication of public opinion polls on polling day and the 28 day period prior to polling day. [1] On the recommendation of the Justice and Electoral Committee, this clause was removed and a new clause, which became s 199A, was inserted. The Bill also included the clause which became s 197 (2A).

[60] In respect of these provisions the Committee's report on the Bill said: [2]

If information is being published that is false or misleading, it would be more appropriate to seek a remedy to solve that particular problem rather than aiming generally at opinion polls. We have therefore proposed an amendment to the Act that would make it an offence to make any false or misleading statement of fact intended to influence voters. That proposal will be discussed in more detail in our report on the inquiry into the 1999 general election.

...

It will be a corrupt practice for a candidate knowingly to make a statement containing untruths in the two days before an election, for the purpose of influencing the vote. This will provide an incentive against any candidate attempting to sway voters by spreading false information so late in the election that the media, other candidates or parties are unable to test it in time to respond.

...

Websites of parties and candidates will be allowed to operate on election day as long as they are accessed voluntarily by web-surfers and do not appear in automatic pop-up windows. Electors should always be able to access information about political parties if they wish to do so, but that information should not be sprung upon them on e-

---

[1] Clause 54. This provision originated from a member's bill in the name of the Rt Hon Winston Peters. The Attorney-General tabled a paper in the House reporting her view that s 54 of the Bill was inconsistent with s 14 of the New Zealand Bill of Rights Act 1990.

[2] Justice and Electoral Committee Electoral Amendment Bill (No 2) Commentary (29 September 2001) at 9, 14 and 15.

lection day without their request.

[61] Subsequently the Committee reported on its inquiry. [1] In that report the Committee said: [2]

We have considered the situation where people, in particular, candidates make an inaccurate or misleading statement on the eve of an election and where the statement attracts a lot of attention and may sway the minds of voters....

The current regime requires that advertisements and broadcasts containing false or misleading statements be withdrawn after complaints against them have been upheld. In the case of complaints made under the Broadcasting Act 1989, the process of complaint and decision may take four days or more, which is no remedy when the misleading statement has been broadcast on the eve of the election.

...

Statements containing errors of fact in the last days of the election campaign present a particular problem. It is difficult for other candidates or parties to respond to such statements in time to correct the error of fact, and there may be insufficient time for electors to evaluate the statements and ascertain the truth. This means that there is a real danger in such situations that electors will base their electoral choices on erroneous information. There is also a temptation for unscrupulous candidates to exploit media and voters over the last few days of the campaign by issuing misleading statements.

[62] In deciding what was the appropriate response to that mischief the Committee said: [3]

We do not wish to see people's right to freedom of expression unduly limited, especially during election campaigns, but we consider that there is a very narrow class of expressions that should be limited in order to protect the integrity of the electoral decision. The expressions that should be limited are deliberately false statements of fact

---

[1] This committee undertakes a post-election review of the practices and procedures involved in each election. It examines proposed legislative amendments and makes suggestions in relation to them.

[2] Justice and Electoral Committee Report, above n 46, at [8.4.1].

[3] At [8.4.1].

made on election day and the two preceding days with the intention of influencing the vote of any elector. We have recommended an amendment to the Electoral Amendment Bill (No. 2) to this effect.

[63] In relation to whether this was consistent with the right to freedom of expression, the Committee said: [1]

We have considered the interests involved in this issue: on one hand the right to freedom of expression, as set out in section 14 of the New Zealand Bill of Rights Act 1990, and on the other hand the importance of preventing any deliberate deception of voters by candidates and other people at a general election. We recommend some changes to the law, as set out in the following discussion.

[64] In relation to what became s 197 (2A), the Committee's report said: [2]

The Chief Electoral Office received seven complaints about political party websites being active on polling day, but was unsure if websites were covered by the ban on advertising under section 197 (1) (g). Laws governing electronic media will have to be developed in the near future. Until there is a comprehensive review of the laws governing electronic media, we have recommended amendments to the Electoral Amendment Bill (No. 2) to exempt websites from the ban on election advertising on polling day. It takes a positive action the part of a computer user to access a website, so we see no harm in allowing websites to remain active on election day as long as they are not activated by pop-up windows or e-mail spam. Pop-up windows and e-mail spam are methods of distributing information over the Internet to unsuspecting Internet users who have not actively sought out that information. In the context of electoral law, we regard these methods as forms of advertising.

[65] The Committee also recommended that the Government consult with broadcasters and the BSA about whether a better process might be developed for consideration of false and misleading statements broadcast as part of election programmes. The ASA complaint procedures were considered to be adequate and no

---

[1] At [8.4.1].
[2] At [5.12.1].

similar recommendation was therefore made with respect to non – broadcast advertisements.

[66] The Committee considered but decided against recommending a defamation offence. [1] It considered such an offence would be inconsistent with the right to freedom of expression under the New Zealand Bill of Rights 1990. [2] It considered that the proposed new clause 199A provided "adequate interim disincentive to false and misleading statements". [3]

[67] When the Bill was reported back the responsible Minister tabled a Supplementary Order Paper which proposed a new provision reintroducing the offence of defaming a candidate at election time. The offence would apply to untrue statements about a candidate made in the month before an election. This amendment was not passed. Clause 199 A was retained.

[68] There were speeches in Parliament during the passage of the legislation that commented on s 199A. Following the second reading Richard Worth (National) questioned its workability. [4] He said: [5]

It is an unusual provision in many respects, and I question its workability …. I would like the Minister …to explain the justification for that 2 – day period. I suggest that particularly in rural electorates throughout New Zealand, if such defamatory material was published to influence voters, then 2 days would be nowhere near sufficient time to correct what might be highly objectionable, highly offensive, and possibly criminally libellous material.

…

In the context of the Defamation Act, for example, 2 days will not permit resort to the range of remedies available in the legislation.

---

[1] Until 1992 there had been a defamation provision. It was removed at that time on the basis that criminal liability for slander could not be justified.

[2] Justice and Electoral Committee Report, above n 46, at 95.

[3] At 96.

[4] The responsible Minister's response did not address this query.

[5] (15 November 2001) 596 NZPD 13167.

[69] Richard Worth was also concerned that s 197 had not been reviewed. He considered the wording was old fashioned and there were significant gaps in the way the provision was drafted. Warren Kyd (National) was concerned about what would qualify as a "false" statement. Alec Neill (National) asked if s 199A was introduced because of statements made by Mr Peters two days out from the last election about Work and Income expenditure which Mr Neill said were never proved.

[70] Warren Kyd (National) also said National was pleased to see the defamation provision go and s 199A stay because they deal with very different matters. He said s 199A deals with: [1]

...false statements being made within 2 days of an election, when no one has the oppmiunity to rebut them. [The defamation provision] would have damped down the whole election campaign period.

[71] Stephen Franks (ACT) said that the tactic of: [2]

...deliberately raising contentious or unsubstantiated issues immediately before an election was a pernicious practice, and I believe I can correctly claim the initiative that will result in section 199A appearing in the Electoral Act.

[72] Having reviewed these materials I accept that the intention was to capture false statements made shortly before an election. The reason for the provision was to address the problem of statements which could influence a voter when there would not be a sufficient opportunity to correct them. This was seen as a justified limit on freedom of expression in contrast with the defamation provision which was viewed as an unjustified limit and excluded from the Act.

[73] The materials do not particularly assist with why the two day time frame was selected. The Committee noted the four day time frame which, at that time, applied to complaints under the Broadcasting Act. [3] There would therefore be insufficient time for a false statement made three days before polling day to be dealt with under the

---

[1] (19 February 2002) 598 NZPD 14458.

[2] (26 February 2002) 598 NZPD 14622.

[3] Refer to [61] above.

Broadcasting Act procedures.

[74] The conclusion I draw is that the two day time frame was selected to ensure the offence was not too widely cast. If it was too widely cast it could have a chilling effect on legitimate campaigning and thereby potentially impinge on the right to freedom of expression beyond that which was justified. False statements three days out would not be criminal because a candidate or party would at least have three days before polling day to respond in some way (not necessarily through the BSA processes). Two days out from polling day was regarded as insufficient time to respond.

[75] This appears to provide some support for the Electoral Commission's view that only statements that are first published during the two days before or on polling day are intended to be caught by s 199A. If a statement is first published earlier than that, the candidate or party who takes objection to the statement is able to respond in some way to the false statement so that voters are not misled.

[76] However, on this rationale, a statement that is first published before the prohibited period (for example, via an article in a printed daily newspaper) which is republished during the prohibited period (for example, via a second article in a subsequent edition of the newspaper) would not be caught by s 199A. A candidate or a party who took objection to the statement would have had the oppmiunity to respond to the statement when it was first made (in the earlier edition in this example). Yet it is clear that on the words of s 199A the republication would be caught. The Electoral Commission acknowledges the possibility that republications are caught by s 199A.

[77] The mischief of a republication in the prohibited period is that it brings the false statement to the notice of members of the public for a second time. It may not be the same members of the public that see or hear the republished false statement as those who saw or heard the false statement the first time. Nor may they be the same members of the public who heard any response to the first publication of the false statement from the candidate or party which was the subject of the false statement. Each time a false statement is brought the notice of a member of the public the harm to a fair election, which s 199A is intended to address, arises. This is the same with a continu-

ing publication. The harm continues to arise for so long as the false statement continues to be brought to the notice of the public.

［78］I therefore conclude that the legislative history does not support the Electoral Commission's view that s 199A applies only to statements that are first published in the prohibited period.

Public place

［79］The Electoral Commission submits that it is not clear that online publications were intended to be captured by s 199A. It says it is doubtful that a political party's website or YouTube could be considered a "public place". It says that "public place" is defined with a particular focus on physical locations and does not appear to contemplate digital environments.

［80］I do not agree with this submission. Section 3 defines "public place" as having the same meaning as in section 2 of the Summary Offences Act 1981. That meaning is as follows:

public place means a place that, at any material time, is open to or is being used by the public, whether free or on payment of a charge, and whether any owner or occupier of the place is lawfully entitled to exclude or eject any person from that place; and includes any aircraft, hovercraft, ship or ferry or other vessel, train, or vehicle carrying or available to carry passengers for reward.

［81］The definition is a wide one. It begins with "a place that, at any material time, is open to or is being used by the public". It expands upon that by saying it is a public place "whether free or on payment of a charge" and "whether any owner or occupier of the place is lawfully entitled to exclude or eject any person from that place". It goes on to provide that various modes of transport are included within the definition.

［82］The internet is a place open to the public and used by the public. It is often free of charge although a fee is payable for access to some sites. As already discussed Parliament must have had the internet in mind at the time s 199A was enacted, given s 197 (2A). If Parliament did not intend to capture false statements published on the internet then it could be expected to have made this clear, as it did when deciding upon the appropriate limits to the defence under s 197 in respect of websites.

[83] I note that the Justice and Electoral Committee's discussion about websites on election day suggests a view that websites are not "advertisements". [1] However this discussion was in the context of not wishing to prevent a person from voluntarily accessing information on a website on election day. It saw no harm in allowing websites to remain active on election day. The Committee did not discuss this issue specifically in relation to s 199A. While there may be no harm in a person accessing a website on election day, potential harm arises if that website contains knowingly false statements intended to influence a voter. I therefore consider that the Committee's limited discussion of this issue does not particularly assist in deciding whether s 199A was intended to apply to publications on the internet.

[84] Additionally, as set out above, "publish" in relation to "election advertisements" is defined as bringing something to the notice of the public in various ways, including via the internet. This definition was inserted on 1 January 2011. No amendment was made to s 199 A at that time, as it might have been if the section was not intended to cover internet publication of election advertisements.

Interpretation consistent with New Zealand Bill of Rights Act 1990

[85] The Electoral Commission submits there is an ambiguity as to the application of s 199A. It submits that rights under the NZBORA are engaged: the right to vote in genuine periodic elections (s 12) and the right to freedom of expression (s 14). It submits that its view of s 199A is consistent with NZBORA in that the right to freedom of speech is minimally infringed and the limit is connected and proportionate to the objective. It submits that it is also consistent with the right to vote in genuine periodic elections because a genuine election is one which reflects the will of the people and is free from intimidation or fraud.

[86] The same, however, can be said about the interpretation of s 199A which I consider is the correct one. It impinges slightly more on the right to freedom of expres-

---

[1] Refer to [64] above.

sion in that it is wider in scope (covering continuing publications and republications as well as those first published during the prohibited period). However it remains a minimal infringement in that it applies for a short time frame and only limits statements known to be false. The limit is proportionate to the objective in the same way that the Electoral Commission's interpretation is. The limit was regarded by the Justice and Electoral Committee as consistent with NZBORA in contrast with the proposed defamation provision which was not. Parliament enacted the provision recommended by that Committee.

Is relief appropriate?

[87] The Electoral Commission notes that Mr Peters had asked the Electoral Commission to refer the two advertisements to the police. It says it has no duty to refer suspected offences under s 199A to the police. It says it is unlikely to refer the matter to the police even if its letter of 5 November 2014 is quashed. It submits that the Court might therefore conclude that it is futile to grant the relief sought.

[88] However the relief sought in this proceeding is not an order requiring the Electoral Commission to refer the matter to the police. The order sought is a quashing of the decision. Counsel for Mr Peters made it clear that Mr Peters has no intention now of referring the two advertisements that were at issue here to the police. The concern is only to have the issue clarified going forward. The Electoral Commission agrees it is important to clarify the issue and that a declaratory order would therefore be useful.

[89] The Court is cautious about issuing declarations in respect of criminal matters. However there is now no intention to refer the complaint to the police in this case. Moreover there are other elements that must be proved for a s 199A offence and the Commission's view was that "it is unlikely that the available evidence would be sufficient to establish the other elements of the offence to the criminal standard". The other elements include that the statements about which complaint is made are "statements of fact". It also includes that the statement made be "knowingly false" and that the statement is published with the intention of influencing voters. The *mens rea* compo-

nents of the offence would need to be established at the time the offence is committed. The declaration sought in this case does not touch on these issues at all. In these circumstances I consider the appropriate relief is a declaration.

Result

[90] The application for judicial review is granted. I make an order declaring that the Electoral Commission's view, as conveyed in its letter to counsel for Mr Peters on 5 November 2014, was an incorrect interpretation of the law. It was incorrect because s 199A applies to statements on the internet on polling day or on the two days preceding polling day, whether they were first placed on the internet at that time or were first placed on the internet at an earlier time.

Costs

[91] The statement of claim sought costs. The Electoral Commission submits that an order for costs is not appropriate and it did not seek them even if succeeded. It refers to the view taken by the Court of Appeal in *Alliance Party v. Electoral Commission* [1] that a costs order would risk operating as a disincentive to the Commission's active assistance on appeals from its decisions. Counsel for Mr Peters accepted this point had merit but did not have instructions to forego costs. For the reason observed by the Court of Appeal I agree that an order for costs is not appropriate. Costs are to lie where they fall.

Mallon J

---

[1] *Alliance Party v. Electoral Commission* [2010] NZCA 4 at [46].

新西兰国会议员霍建强个人立法

《新西兰诽谤法（附条件特权抗辩限制）法案》

新西兰国会沿用的是英国西敏制（Westminster system，也译作威斯敏斯特制），立法大致有三种：中央政府立法、地方政府立法和个人立法。这里的"地方政府立法"和地方政府主导的"By-law"不同。也就是说在国会层面，主要部分还是以中央政府为主的"政府立法"。

而"个人立法"（Member's Bill）比较有趣，是国会议员针对自己的立法意愿起草法案，递交国会系统，然后定期（通常是每周四）抽签，抽中的交国会大会一读，如获通过，则交相关的专业委员会进行审核，报国会二读。如此，如获通过，则进行三读，等等。

新西兰国会许多非政府立法范围的法律，例如"同性恋合法结婚法"（已通过三读成为法律）和"临终生命选择法"即"'安乐死'法"（目前已通过一读，正在由法制委员会审订），都是通过个人立法实现的。在一定程度上，个人立法是政府立法的一个有效弥补。

这里附上的是笔者一份最新的个人立法。相关立法意图和方式，请参阅第一部分案例四。

这里的个人立法分为两个部分：第一部分是法案的具体条款。第二部分是问答，解释立法缘由和其他类似司法管辖区（英、美、澳、加）的法律（制定法和判例法）发展状况。

需要注意的是，这只是个人立法的第一稿，还很粗糙。作为附录登出，第一，可以为不同立法提供一个实例。第二，可以让大家看到，法律条文就是这么写出来的。

Raymond Huo's Members Bill Q&A

1. What is the purpose of the Bill?

"Let us imagine a parliamentary candidate named Artemus Jones. Let us imagine further that on the Sunday preceding the election at which he is standing there appears on the front page of a nationally circulated newspaper, under a suitably lurid headline, the statement, "Would-be MP Artemus Jones has nine convictions for sexual offences with boys aged between 7 and 11 years".

"Let us suppose further that what appears in the newspaper is wrong and that the man with the regrettable criminal history is not the parliamentary candidate but his second cousin who has the same name. The newspaper has not acted maliciously. The situation has come about because a reporter, over-eager to use what appears to be a scoop, has failed to carry out the appropriate checking.

"In New Zealand, the unfortunate parliamentary candidate has no redress against the newspaper whatsoever. [1]

The intent of the Bill is to strike a balance between freedom of expression and protection of reputation.

2. How does the Bill achieve that purpose?

The Billadopts the Law Commission's suggestion by inserting a new s 19A to align New Zealand law with the best practice of comparable jurisdictions.

3. Where does New Zealand sit compared with similar jurisdictions?

In Australia, *Lange v. Australian Broadcasting Corp* introduced a reasonableness test. [2]

---

[1] Law Commission, Preliminary Paper 33, Defaming Politicians: A Response to Lange v. Atkinson.

[2] *Lange v. Australian Broadcasting Corp* [1997] HCA 25, (1997) 189 CLR 520.

In Canada, in *Grant v. Torstar Corp*, the Supreme Court laid out its defence of "responsible communication". [1]

In the United Kingdom, *Reynolds v. Times Newspapers Ltd*, [2] which was affirmed in 2006 by the House of Lords in *Jameel and others v. Wall Street Journal Europe Sprl*, [3] sets out a public interest defence to an action for defamation, and responsibility requirements.

Section 4 of the Defamation Act 2013 now largely captures the *Reynolds* defence and requires the defendant to have "reasonably believed" that publishing the statement complained of was in the public interest. [4]

In the United States, *New York Times Co. v. Sullivan* [5] sets out their strong reliance on freedom of the press. But as Lord Steyn said "a plaintiff in the United States is entitled to a pre-trial enquiry into the sources of the story and editorial decision-making." [6]

4. Really? What did Lord Steyn say?

Lord Steyn in Reynolds stated "the rule and practice in English is not to compel a newspaper to reveal its sources [···] By contrast a plaintiff in the United States is entitled to a pre-trial enquiry into the sources of the story and editorial decision-making. Without such information a plaintiff suing for defamation in England will be substantially handicapped." [7]

5. Why is it important that a defendant to a defamation case be held to a reasonableness standard?

See Point 4 of what Lord Steyn said. This Bill fixes that disparity.

---

[1] *Grant v. Torstar Corp* 2009 SCC 61, [2009] 3 SCR 640.

[2] [2001] 2 AC 127 (HL).

[3] [2006] UKHL 44.

[4] The New Zealand High Court has also suggested that if *Lange* is extended further, "there is a risk that it would unduly weigh freedom of expression over protection of reputation unless there was a responsibility or reasonableness element incorporated as part of that test": *Durie v. Gardiner* [2017] NZHC 377.

[5] *New York Times Co v. Sullivan*, 376 U. S. 254 (1964).

[6] *Reynolds v. Times Newspapers Ltd* [2001] 2 AC 127 (HL) at 1032.

[7] *Reynolds v. Times Newspapers Ltd* [2001] 2 AC 127 (HL) at 1032.

A plaintiff in New Zealand currently has the burden of rebutting the defence of qualified privilege by establishing the defendant was predominantly motivated by ill will or had otherwise taken improper advantage of the occasion of publication. [1] This places the plaintiff in an unfair situation where they have to establish facts not within their knowledge.

Bear in mind that "carelessness, impulsiveness or irrationality in arriving at a positive belief" do not constitute malice. [2]

6. How does this Bill take into account the nature of new media?

A New York Times article has noted that "the Internet has turned everyone into a worldwide publisher — capable of calling public officials instantly to account for their actions, and also of ruining reputations with the click of a mouse. " [3] This Bill encourages responsible publication in an increasing number circumstances. New s 19A encourages steps to be taken to inform the truthfulness behind the making of general statements no matter what the medium.

7. Is the Bill going against freedom of expression?

This Bill will not have a chilling effect on freedom of speech. Rather, it provides certainty in relation to the defence of qualified privilege. It strikes a better balance between freedom of speech and protection of reputation. More importantly, the Bill seeks to align New Zealand law with the best practice of comparable jurisdictions. This Bill fixes that disparity.

8. Will the media hate this Bill?

No, they won't. Interestingly, most of the recent high-profile defamation cases in New Zealand did not involve media as a defendant. Responsible media will like this bill as it provides a tool to draw a clear line. In that regard, the bill puts all media on an equal footing in terms of competition, especially in a digital era.

---

[1] Defamation Act 1992, s 19.

[2] *Horrocks v. Lowe* [1975] AC 135, 150.

[3] New York Times editorial dated March 8, 2014 in celebration of the 50 years anniversary of the Sullivan case "The Uninhibited Press, 50 Years Later".

9. Does this case have anything to do with recent proceedings involving politicians?

No, this Bill is introduced by RaymondHuo MP who is also an Honorary Professor of Law. The Bill is a result of his years of work in the area of torts for which subject he has been working on a new book in his capacity as a law partner, prior to his return to Parliament in March 2017.

DRAFT FOR CONSULTATION

Defamation (Restriction on Qualified Privilege) Amendment Bill

Member's Bill

Explanatory note

General policy statement

The law of defamation is intended to achieve a balanced approach between protection of reputation and freedom of speech.

This Bill amends the Defamation Act 1992 (the principal Act) to insert a new section (section 19A) specifying restrictions on qualified privilege that apply when publication is to a general audience. The intent of this Bill is to provide a balanced approach and certainty in relation to the availability of the defence of qualified privilege.

Qualified privilege is available in situations where the maker of a statement has a duty to make it and the recipient of the information has a duty or interest (which requires more than mere curiosity) in receiving it. Section 19 of the principal Act already contains a restriction on the defence, providing that it is not available in situations where the publisher is predominantly motivated by ill will or has otherwise taken improper advantage of the occasion of publication.

The common law defence of qualified privilege was famously extended by the Court of Appeal in *Lange v. Atkinson* [1] to cover political discussion published generally to a wide audience. Some believed the 1998 landmark judgment gave publishers too

---

[1] [1998] 3 NZLR 424 (CA); [2000] 1 NZLR 257 (PC); [2000] 3 NZLR 385 (CA).

much freedom, particularly because the majority declined to impose a requirement of reasonableness as an element of the availability of the defence.

In almost two decades since the Court of Appeal delivered its decisions in *Lange v. Atkinson*, judicial developments in this area of the law have been limited. In a similar vein, the issues addressed, and concerns raised, in the Law Commission's Preliminary Paper 33 and Report 64, Defaming Politicians—a Response to Lange v. Atkinson, have remained outstanding.

This Bill adopts the legislative solution proposed in the Law Commission reports by inserting a requirement that a defendant relying on the defence of qualified privilege in respect of a statement of fact published generally, must have believed on reasonable grounds that their statement of fact was true. This will ensure the defence of qualified privilege is not abused.

The legislative changes are necessary for many reasons. First, the changes address a procedurally unfair situation for plaintiffs, when a defendant seeks to rely on qualified privilege. In certain situations, it should be the responsibility of the defendant to show that he or she acted reasonably in publishing information.

Second, "as the Internet has turned everyone into a worldwide publisher" [1], this Bill encourages responsible publication in an increasing number circumstances. New section 19A encourages steps to be taken to inform the truthfulness behind the making of general statements no matter what the medium.

Third, the development of the qualified privilege defence in New Zealand law seems to suggest a tilting of the balance in favour of freedom of expression, without appropriate safeguards in favour of protection of reputation. [2] The right balance needs to be struck.

Finally, we are out of step with comparable jurisdictions. Over the last two dec-

---

[1] New York Times editorial dated March 8, 2014 in celebration of the 50 years anniversary of the Sullivan case "The Uninhibited Press, 50 Years Later".

[2] See a comprehensive discussion of the developments in the law of qualified privilege in Durie v. Gardiner [2017] NZHC 377, [2017] 3 NZLR 72 and in particular, at [97]. See also Williams v. Craig [2017] NZHC 724, [2017] 3 NZLR 215; Williams v. Craig [2018] NZCA 31.

ades, both case law and statutory law in comparable jurisdictions have provided much more stability and certainty in terms of a requirement of reasonableness when relying on the defence of qualified privilege. [1]

The "wait and see" approach over the last two decades is no longer desirable. It is not helped by the relatively slight volume of litigation in this jurisdiction. Nor is it fair for future litigants to fund expensive cases to progress the judicial developments.

Clause by clause analysis

Clause 1 is the Title clause.

Clause 2 is the commencement clause and provides for the Bill to come into force on the day after it receives the Royal assent.

Clause 3 states that the Bill amends the Defamation Act 1992 (the **principal Act**). Clause 4 inserts new section 2A into the principal Act, providing for transitional, savings, or related provisions relating to the Bill or to further bills that may amend the principal Act.

Clause 5 inserts new section 19A into the principal Act, which provides for restrictions on qualified privilege where publication is made generally, rather than to a specific audience.

Clause 6 inserts new Schedule 1AA into the principal Act to contain transitional, savings, or related provisions required by this Bill or other Bills that may amend the principal Act.

---

[1] For example, in Australia, Lange v. Australian Broadcasting Corp [1997] HCA 25, (1997) 189 CLR 520 introduced a reasonableness test. In Canada, in Grant v. Torstar Corp 2009 SCC 61, [2009] 3 SCR 640, the Supreme Court laid out its defence of "responsible communication". In the United Kingdom, section 4 of the Defamation Act 2013 requires the defendant to have "reasonably believed" that publishing the statement complained of was in the public interest.

RaymondHuo

Defamation（Restriction on Qualified Privilege）Amendment Bill

Member's Bill

Contents

The Parliament of New Zealand enacts as follows:

1 Title

This Act is the Defamation（Restriction on Qualified Privilege）Amendment Act 2018.

2 Commencement

This Act comes into force on the day after the date on which it receives the Royal assent.

3　Principal Act

This Act amends the Defamation Act 1992 (the principal Act) .

4　New section 2A inserted (Transitional, savings, and related provisions) After section 2, insert:

2A　Transitional, savings, and related provisions.

The transitional, saving, and related provisions set out in Schedule 1AA have effect according to their terms.

5　New section 19A inserted (Restrictions on qualified privilege where general publication)

After section 19, insert:

9A　Restrictions on qualified privilege where general publication

(1) In any proceedings for defamation in respect of matter that consists of a statement of fact published generally, a defence of qualified privilege shall fail unless the defendant proves that the defendant believed on reasonable grounds that the statement of fact was true.

(2) In any proceedings for defamation in respect of matter that consists of a statement of fact published generally by a news medium, a defence of qualified privilege shall fail if the plaintiff alleges and proves—

(a) that the plaintiff requested the defendant to publish, in the manner in which the original publication was made, a reasonable letter or statement by way of explanation or contradiction; and

(b) that the defendant has refused or failed to comply with that request, or has complied with that request in a manner that, having regard to all the circumstances, is not adequate or not reasonable.

(3) This section does not apply where the publication is protected by qualified privilege conferred by section 16 (1) or section 16 (2) .

6　New Schedule 1AA inserted Insert the Schedule 1AA set out in the Schedule of this Act as the first schedule to appear after the last section of the principal Act.

Schedule
New Schedule 1AA inserted

Schedule 1AA
Transitional, savings, and relatedprovisions

Provisions relating to Defamation（Restriction on Qualified Privilege）Amendment Act 2018

1　Restriction on Qualified Privilege

（1）For the purpose of this clause, commencement date means the date on which the Defamation（Restriction on Qualified Privilege）Amendment Act 2018 comes into force.

（2）Section 19A does not apply where the publication of the matter that is the sub-ject of the proceedings occurred before the commencement date.